James H Campbell
Dec 4, 1871

THE

POETICAL WORKS

OF

ROBERT BURNS.

A. Nasmyth pinxt. J. F. Hunt sc.

ROBERT BURNS.

THE POETICAL WORKS OF ROBERT BURNS.

EDITED BY

THE REV. ROBERT ARIS WILLMOTT.

NEW EDITION,
WITH NUMEROUS ADDITIONS.

BOSTON:
LEE AND SHEPARD, PUBLISHERS,
NEW YORK:
LEE, SHEPARD, & DILLINGHAM.
1872.

UNIV CO
WELCH, BIGELOW
UNIVERSITY PRESS
1839
CAMBRIDGE, MASS.

Dedication of the Second Edition of Poems.

TO THE

NOBLEMEN AND GENTLEMEN

OF THE

CALEDONIAN HUNT.

MY LORDS AND GENTLEMEN,

A Scottish Bard, proud of the name, and whose highest ambition is to sing in his Country's service—where shall he so properly look for patronage as to the illustrious names of his native Land,—those who bear the honours and inherit the virtues of their Ancestors? The Poetic Genius of my Country found me, as the prophetic bard Elijah did Elisha—at the plough; and threw her inspiring mantle over me. She bade me sing the loves, the joys, the rural scenes and rural pleasures of my native soil, in my native tongue; I tuned my wild, artless notes, as she inspired.—She whispered me to come to this ancient Metropolis of Caledonia, and lay my Song under your honoured protection: I now obey her dictates.

Though much indebted to your goodness, I do not approach you, my Lords and Gentlemen, in the usual style of dedication, to thank you for past favours; that path is so hackneyed by prostituted learning, that honest rusticity is ashamed of it. Nor do I present this Address with the venal soul of a servile Author, looking for a continuation of those favours: I was bred to the Plough, and am independent. I come to claim the common Scottish name with you, my illustrious Countrymen; and to tell the world that I glory in the title. I come to congratulate my Country, that the blood of her ancient heroes still runs uncontaminated; and that from your courage, knowledge, and public spirit, she may expect protection, wealth, and liberty. In the last place, I come to proffer my warmest wishes to the Great Fountain of Honour, the Monarch of the Universe, for your welfare and happiness.

When you go forth to awaken the Echoes, in the ancient and favourite amusement of your forefathers, may Pleasure ever be of your party; and may Social Joy await your return. When harassed in courts or camps with the jostlings of bad men and bad measures, may the honest consciousness of injured worth attend your return to your native Seats; and may Domestic Happiness, with a smiling welcome, meet you at your gates! May corruption shrink at your kindling indignant glance, and may tyranny in the Ruler, and licentiousness in the People, equally find you an inexorable foe!

I have the honour to be,

With the sincerest gratitude, and highest respect,

My Lords and Gentlemen,

Your most devoted humble servant,

ROBERT BURNS.

Edinburgh, April 4, 1787.

PREFACE.

The Poems of Burns have been edited, and his Life has been written by eminent countrymen, with a copiousness of illustration and a minuteness of inquiry altogether beyond my abilities and my limits. Perhaps an English reader sometimes thinks the work slightly overdone, and even feels a very languid curiosity about the character of "Poosie Nansie," or the politics of Dumfries. I have not, however, intentionally underrated the interest of my subject. The Text has been carefully examined, and the notes convey the information which was incidentally furnished by the Poet and his Brother, and generally in their own language. With a hope of rendering the Scottish Poems less difficult to the inexperienced eye, the harder words are explained at the foot of the page, and, I trust, with sufficient accuracy.

*** Since the lamented death of Mr. Willmott, another edition has been called for; and the Publishers have taken the opportunity of inserting various Poems and Songs of great merit, which had been omitted in previous editions. Many of them are accompanied by editorial annotations, which will be found useful in giving the dates, and explaining the circumstances under which they were originally written.

To facilitate immediate and ready reference to any of the numerous Poems, Songs, Epigrams, &c., scattered throughout the volume, the Editor has prefixed a comprehensive list of CONTENTS, and also appended at the close of the volume (in addition to the GLOSSARY) two copious INDEXES, alphabetically arranged. In this respect, nearly all the previous editions of the Works of Burns are extremely defective.

P. A. N.

CONTENTS.

POEMS, *continued.* PAGE

POEMS, *continued.* PAGE

POEMS, *continued.* PAGE

SONGS, *continued.* PAGE

SONGS, *continued.* PAGE

SONGS, *continued.* PAGE

SONGS, *continued.* PAGE

SONGS, *continued.*

SONGS, *continued.*

SONGS, *continued.* PAGE

EPIGRAMS, EPITAPHS, &c. :—

EPIGRAMS, EPITAPHS, &c., *continued.* PAGE

LIFE AND WRITINGS

OF

ROBERT BURNS.

UPON a winter day of 1786-7, the boy Jeffrey stopped in the High-street of Edinburgh to stare at a man whose appearance greatly struck him. A shopkeeper, standing at his door and observing the boy's look of wonder, tapped him on the shoulder, saying, "Aye, laddie, ye may weel look at that man—he is Robert Burns." Since that day, admiration has shown itself in every shape, the most touching and the most grotesque, from the panegyric of Wordsworth to the phrensy of Wilson, rolling himself on the spot where "Tam O'Shanter" was composed.

Robert Burns was born January 25th, 1759, the eldest child of William and Agnes Burns, or Burness, as they were accustomed to spell the name. His father, bailiff and gardener of a country gentleman, Mr. Ferguson, rented a few acres of land, on which he had built a small hovel of clay and straw. It stood by the roadside, a Scotch mile and a half from the town of Ayr, and near the famous Alloway Kirk. Robert was sent to school before his sixth year, and soon found a zealous instructor in John Murdoch, who was chosen, a few months afterwards, to replace the former teacher. We are told by Gilbert Burns, that his brother greatly benefited by the lessons in grammar, and became "remarkable for the fluency and correctness of his expressions." He read the few books that came in his way with much pleasure and improvement. Murdoch's library was not rich, but it contained a "Life of Hannibal," which gave to the ideas of Burns such a military turn that he used to strut up and down after the recruiting drum and bagpipe, and wish himself tall enough to be a soldier. The warlike ardour was heightened, when, later in youth, he borrowed the story of Wallace from the blacksmith, and walked half-a-dozen miles, on a summer day, "to pay his respects to Leglen Wood, with as much devout enthusiasm as ever pilgrim did to Loretto." In truth, we might say of him, in poet's words,—

"He had small need of books; for many a tale,
Traditionary, round the mountains hung,
And many a legend, peopling the dark woods,
Nourished Imagination in her growth,
And gave the mind that apprehensive power,
By which she is made quick to recognize
The moral properties and scope of things."

Burns tells us, in his delightful "Confessions"—"In my infant and boyish days, too, I owed much to an old woman who resided in the family, remarkable for her ignorance, credulity, and superstition. She had, I suppose, the largest collection in the country of tales and songs concerning devils, ghosts, fairies, brownies, witches, warlocks, spunkies, kelpies, elf-candles, dead-lights, wraiths, apparitions, cantraips, giants, enchanted towers, dragons, and other trumpery. This cultivated the latent seeds of poetry; but had so strong an effect on my imagination, that to this hour, in my nocturnal rambles, I sometimes keep a sharp look-out in suspicious places; and though nobody can be more sceptical than I am in such matters, yet it often takes an effort of philosophy to shake off these idle terrors. The earliest composition that I recollect taking pleasure in, was 'The Vision of Mirza,' and a hymn of Addison's, beginning, 'How are thy servants blest, O Lord!' I particularly remember one half-stanza which was music to my boyish ears:—

'For though on dreadful whirls we hung
High on the broken wave—.'"

His memory was strong, and, when he was in Edinburgh, he repeated to Mr. Stewart some long ballads in the Scottish dialect which, in childhood, he had learned from his mother. And thus, though he "cost the schoolmaster some thrashings," he grew up an excellent English scholar, and by the time that he was ten or eleven years old, he had obtained a critical acquaintance with substantives, verbs, and participles; nor was he without robuster training, for in the first season that he held the plough, "he made a shift" to unravel "Euclid" by his father's hearth.

When the period drew nigh that the boy, in his own strong words, must have marched off to be one of the little underlings about a farm-house, William Burns ventured upon a speculation, which, he hoped, might enable him to keep his children at home longer. His employer had a farm, Mount Oliphant, comprising eighty or ninety English acres, and he accepted William Burns as the tenant, at a rent for the first six years, of forty pounds; moreover, he assisted him with money

:o provide the necessary stock. The family went to their new abode, Whitsuntide, 1766. William Burns was a well-informed and thoughtful man, and turned the onely life of his children to good account. In the winter evenings he taught ırithmetic and geography to the boys, and procured from a book society in Ayr, the vorks of Derham and Ray upon the Wisdom and Power of God. Better books ıe could scarcely have found; and Gilbert assures us that his brother read them vith eagerness. Stackhouse's "History of the Bible" was also a treasure, for its nformation is large and curious. A fortunate accident increased his wealth: a :elation wanting to purchase a "Complete Letter Writer," the shopman, by nistake, as Gilbert tells us, produced "A small Collection of Letters, by the most eminent Writers, with a few sensible Directions for attaining an easy Epistolary Style." He adds—"This book was to Robert of the greatest consequence."

Between his thirteenth and fourteenth years, the poet's handwriting was much mproved by a few lessons in the parish school of Dalrymple; and about the same :ime "a bookish acquaintance" of their father obtained for the brothers "a reading of two volumes of Richardson's 'Pamela;'" and Murdoch, then the teacher of English in Ayr, sent the works of Pope. Gilbert writes:—"The summer after we had been at Dalrymple school, my father sent Robert to Ayr to revise his English grammar with his former teacher. He had been there only one week, when he was obliged to return, to assist at the harvest. When the harvest was over he went back to school, where he remained two weeks; and this completes :he account of his school education, except one grammar quarter some time afterwards, that he attended the parish school of Kirk Oswald (where he lived with a brother of my mother) to learn surveying." Murdock happened to be learning French, and he generously imparted his knowledge to his pupil, who entered on he study with such zeal, that in the second week he assaulted "Telemachus." 'But now," in the swelling language of the pedagogue, "the plains of Mount Oliphant began to whiten, and Robert was summoned to relinquish the pleasing scenes that surrounded the grotto of Calypso." He took back with him a French grammar, and the beautiful tale of Fénélon; and, in a little time, by the help of hese books, he was able to read and understand any French authors who fell in ıis way. An attack upon Latin was not equally successful; his perseverance seldom outlasting a week, and the study being regarded as a sort of penance, or refuge in ill-humour. He used it for a cold-bath. This, writes the Ettrick Shepherd with pleasant confidence, is exceedingly good, and rates the Latin much as I have always estimated it. English literature, however, retained its full charm, and the love was nurtured by the kindness of a widow lady, Mrs. Paterson, who lent Pope's translation of Homer, and the "Spectator," to the youthful student.

Mount Oliphant wanted every gleam to cheer it. The parish contained no farm so intractable; the soil being almost the poorest to be found under the plough.

On the part of the family, no effort was wanting. Every member of it taxed his strength to the utmost. Robert was the principal labourer, Gilbert driving the plough, and helping him to thrash the corn. The food of the hermit was indoors, as well as the gloom, butcher's meat being quite unknown.

In this dreary weather Burns reached his sixteenth year, toiling and sad-hearted, until in the harvest-field Love found him. He relates his first passion:—"You know our country custom of coupling a man and woman together as partners in the labours of harvest. In my fifteenth autumn my partner was a bewitching creature, a year younger than myself. My scarcity of English denies me the power of doing her justice in that language; but you know the Scottish idiom—she was a *bonnie, sweet, sonsie lass.* In short, she altogether, unwittingly to herself, initiated me in that delicious passion, which, in spite of acid disappointment, gin-horse prudence, and book-worm philosophy, I hold to be the first of human joys, our dearest blessing here below! How she caught the contagion I cannot tell: you medical people talk much of infection from breathing the same air, the touch, &c.; but I never expressly said I loved her. Indeed, I did not know myself why I liked so much to loiter behind with her, when returning in the evening from our labours; why the tones of her voice made my heart-strings thrill like an Æolian harp; and particularly why my pulse beat such a furious rattan when I looked and fingered over her little hand, to pick out the cruel nettle-stings and thistles. Among her other love-inspiring qualities, she sung sweetly; and it was her favourite reel to which I attempted giving an embodied vehicle in rhyme. I was not so presumptuous as to imagine that I could make verses like printed ones composed by men who had Greek and Latin; but my girl sung a song, which was said to be composed by a small country laird's son, on one of his father's maids, with whom he was in love! and I saw no reason why I might not rhyme as well as he; for, excepting that he could smear sheep, and cast peats, his father living in the moor-lands, he had no more scholar-craft than myself."

And here I am reminded of that sweet passage in Virgil, which Mr. Rogers thought so true to nature, that he must have drawn it from early recollections:—"You were little when I first saw you. You were with your mother, gathering fruit in our orchard, and I was your guide. I was entering my thirteenth year, and just able to reach the boughs from the ground."

At the end of six years, William Burns endeavoured to find a farm of happier promise, but he sought it in vain, and, continuing his anxious toils through five years, he removed, Whitsuntide, 1777, to the larger farm of Lochlea, in the parish of Tarbolton. There the first four years passed in comfort, until the want of a written agreement involved the landlord and the tenant in legal disputes; and during the long period of three years, William Burns was "tossing and whirling in the vortex."

The little chapter of Lochlea includes some important passages in the story of Burns; for there his good and bad blossoms began to set with large promise of fruit. Although he confesses himself to have been the most ungainly lad in the parish, his mind was growing into shape. He was familiar with the "Spectator," and he carried a collection of songs in all his field-work, poring over them as he drove his cart. Slowly, too, the outward man improved, and a spreading rumour of his "book-knowledge" made him a welcome guest. But his chief fame was of another kind. Tarbolton was not less amorous than other country places in Scotland, and Robert became the confidant of the parish. He informs us that his curiosity, zeal, and dexterous boldness recommended him for a comrade in every love adventure; and that the secrets of Tarbolton hearts were as gratifying to him as the intrigues of Europe are to the statesman.

In an evil hour Burns turned flaxdresser, in the small town of Irvine, where he rented a room at a shilling a week. His health and his spirits seem to have been much disordered at this time. He speaks of his sleep as a little sounder, although the weakness of his nerves troubled his whole body at the least anxiety and alarm. He despairs of making a figure in the world; "being neither formed for the bustle of the busy, nor the flutter of the gay;" and when he "glimmered" a little into the future, the only prospect was poverty and contempt. In the midst of these doubts and fears, the flax business was brought to a sudden close; for while he was giving a welcome carousal to the new year, the shop took fire, and Burns found himself among the ashes, and, like a true poet, without a sixpence. His moral loss at Ayr had, probably, been larger than his commercial; for in a young man, whom an American privateer had lately stripped and set ashore, he met a companion and a tempter whose practice appears to have kept up with his theory. Meanwhile, blacker shadows gathered round the homestead of Lochlea. For two years the strength of the old man had been going, and just as the horrors of a jail were full in view, a consumption "kindly stepped in" and carried him away, February 13, 1784. Robert and Gilbert had made some preparation for the support of the family, when their father's affairs drew near a crisis, by taking a neighbouring farm, Mossgiel, which was held in tack, of the Earl of Loudon, by that Mr. Gavin Hamilton whose name is lastingly united to the poet's. The farm contained one hundred and eighteen acres, and the rent was fixed at ninety pounds. We learn the particulars from Gilbert:—

"It was stocked by the property and individual savings of the whole family, and was a joint concern among us. Every member of the family was allowed ordinary wages for the labour he performed on the farm. My brother's allowance and mine was seven pounds per annum each. And during the whole time this family concern lasted, which was four years, as well as during the preceding period at Lochlea, his expenses never in any one year exceeded his slender income. His temperance and frugality were everything that could be wished." But darker scenes were coming.

There lived in Mauchline a master stone-mason, James Armour, who had a black-eyed daughter, Jean, ranking high among the six *belles* of the village. It fell out on a certain day, that the poet's dog ran over the clothes which Jean Armour was spreading on the grass, and she flung a stone at the trespasser. The old proverb rose to the tongue of Burns, and the love-story began. It fills a melancholy page in the lives of the man and the woman. They sinned, and they suffered. A meeting of the lovers ended in a gift by Burns to Jean of a written promise, which Scottish law accepts as legal evidence of an "irregular" union. The marriage was not to be disclosed until the last moment, and when it came, the stone-mason showed himself less indulgent than the law. His indignation was great; and overpowered by the anger and the grief of her father, Jean destroyed the document, or permitted him to burn it. Under circumstances so afflicting, she became the mother of twins, for the charge of whose maintenance security was demanded of Burns. James Armour proved to be violent and relentless, with a view, it is conjectured, of driving Burns from the country, and setting his daughter free. If he had the design, it was almost fulfilled. Several Scotchmen were at that time engaged as assistant overseers in the West India Plantations. The salary was small, and the disagreeable nature of the occupation may be imagined. But it offered shelter to Burns, and he obtained an appointment in Jamaica, engaging himself to Dr. Douglas, of Port Antonio, for three years, at a salary of thirty pounds. To pay for his passage, he resolved to publish his "Poems." They had grown up, silently and sweetly, like the wild-flowers in the fields. The Daisy under the Plough—the Mouse driven from her nest—the Winter-dirge—the Cotter's Saturday Night—The Vision—and other pieces, seemed to steal upon his fancy, in its warm spring weather, with the bloom and freshness of opening life. The Muse had walked by his plough, and cheered and illuminated him. Even the coal-cart was sometimes hallowed by song. Lochlea is rich in these poetic remembrances, but Mossgiel excels it. Lately, perhaps now, you might see the "ingle," and the "spence," with its boarded-floor, and the recess-beds so common in Scotland, where he composed some of his most pathetic and humorous pieces. A small deal table was also pointed out. At the beginning of April, 1786, Burns sent his "Proposals" to the press of John Wilson, in Kilmarnock. In the mean time, he underwent a less agreeable form of publication in the parish kirk, by the tongue of Mr. Auld. A certificate of Bachelordom was the reward of the exposure. On June 12th, he communicated to a Glasgow acquaintance the news of his literary progress:—"You will have heard that I am going to commence poet in print; to-morrow my works go to the press. I expect it will be a volume of about two hundred pages. It is just the last foolish action I intend to do, and then turn a wise man as fast as possible." His story of the enterprise is extremely interesting:—

"I weighed my productions as impartially as was in my power: I thought they had merit; and it was a delicious idea that I should be called a clever fellow, even though it should never reach my ears—a poor negro driver, or perhaps a victim to that inhospitable clime, and gone to the world of spirits! I can truly say, that *pauvre inconnu* as I then was, I had pretty nearly as high an idea of myself and of my works as I have at this moment, when the public has decided in their favour. It ever was my opinion, that the mistakes and blunders, both in a rational and religious point of view, of which we see thousands daily guilty, are owing to their ignorance of themselves.—To know myself, had been all along my constant study. I weighed myself alone; I balanced myself with others; I watched every means of information, to see how much ground I occupied as a man and a poet; I studied assiduously Nature's design in my formation—where the lights and shades in my character were intended. I was pretty confident my poems would meet with some applause; but, at the worst, the roar of the Atlantic would deafen the voice of censure, and the novelty of West Indian scenes make me forget neglect. I threw off six hundred copies, of which I had got subscriptions for about three hundred and fifty. My vanity was highly gratified by the reception I met with from the public; and besides, I pocketed, all expenses deducted, nearly twenty pounds. This sum came very seasonably, as I was thinking of indenting myself, for want of money to procure my passage. As soon as I was master of nine guineas, the price of wafting me to the torrid zone, I took a steerage passage in the first ship that was to sail from the Clyde; for

'Hungry ruin had me in the wind.'

"I had been for some days skulking from covert to covert, under all the terrors of a jail; as some ill-advised people had uncoupled the merciless pack of the law at my heels. I had taken the last farewell of my few friends; my chest was on the road to Greenock; I had composed the last song I should ever measure in Caledonia, 'The gloomy Night is gathering fast,' when a letter from Dr. Blacklock, to a friend of mine, overthrew all my schemes, by opening new prospects to my poetic ambition. The doctor belonged to a set of critics, for whose applause I had not dared to hope. His opinion that I would meet with encouragement in Edinburgh for a second edition, fired me so much, that away I posted for that city, without a single acquaintance, or a single letter of introduction. The baneful star, that had so long shed its blasting influence in my zenith, for once made a revolution to the nadir; and a kind Providence placed me under the patronage of one of the noblest of men, the Earl of Glencairn."

The "Poems" appeared in July, 1786, at the price of three shillings; a dignified preface opened the volume :—

"The following trifles are not the production of the poet who, with all the advantages of learned art, and, perhaps, amid the elegancies and idlenesses of upper life, looks down for a rural theme, with an eye to Theocritus or Virgil. To the author of this, these and other celebrated names their countrymen are, at least in their original language, *a fountain shut up, and a book sealed.* Unacquainted with the necessary requisites for commencing poet by rule, he sings the sentiments and manners he felt and saw in himself and his rustic compeers around him, in his and their native language. Though a rhymer from his earliest years, at least from the earliest impulses of the softer passions, it was not till very lately that the applause, perhaps the partiality, of friendship, wakened his vanity so far as to make him think anything of his worth showing; and none of the following works were ever composed with a view to the press. To amuse himself with the little creations of his own fancy, amid the toil and fatigues of a laborious life; to transcribe the various feelings, the loves, the griefs, the hopes, the fears, in his own breast; to find some kind of counterpoise to the struggles of a world, always an alien scene, a task uncouth to the poetical mind;—these were his motives for courting the Muses, and in these he found Poetry to be its own reward.

"Now that he appears in the public character of an author, he does it with fear and trembling. So dear is fame to the rhyming tribe, that even he, an obscure, nameless Bard, shrinks aghast at the thought of being branded as 'an impertinent blockhead, obtruding his nonsense on the world; and, because he can make a shift to jingle a few doggerel Scotch rhymes together, looking upon himself as a poet of no small consequence forsooth!'

"It is an observation of that celebrated poet, Shenstone, whose divine elegies do honour to our language, our nation, and our species, that 'HUMILITY has depressed many a genius to a hermit, but never raised one to fame!' If any critic catches at the word GENIUS, the Author tells him, once for all, that he certainly looks upon himself as possessed of some poetic abilities, otherwise his publishing in the manner he has done would be a manœuvre below the worst character which, he hopes, his worst enemy will ever give him. But to the genius of a Ramsay, or the glorious dawnings of the poor unfortunate Ferguson, he, with equal unaffected sincerity, declares, that even in his highest pulse of vanity, he has not the most distant pretensions. These two justly admired Scotch poets he has often had in his eye in the following pieces; but rather with a view to kindle at their flame, than for servile imitation.

"To his subscribers the Author returns his most sincere thanks; not the mercenary bow over a counter, but the heart-throbbing gratitude of the Bard, conscious how much he is indebted to benevolence and friendship, for gratifying him, if he deserves it, in that dearest wish of every poetic bosom—to be distinguished. He begs his readers, particularly the learned and the polite, who may honour him with a perusal, that they will make every allowance for education and circumstances of life; but if, after a fair, candid, and impartial criticism, he shall stand convicted of dulness and nonsense, let him be done by as he would in that case do by others—let him be condemned, without mercy, to contempt and oblivion."

"The Cotter's Saturday Night" was the gem of the collection, and did for the writer what the "Elegy" had done for Gray—it made him famous. When Gilpin, in 1789, published his "Observations on the Highlands," he described the pleasing simplicity of country life, the small Erse Bible which was the Highlander's usual companion, the mother spinning or knitting, and the children standing round her reading God's Book, or repeating the "Catechism;" and by way of illustrating his description, he quoted the poem of Burns—"a Bard, as he calls himself, from the plough,"—and pronounced "the whole to be equal to any praise." Gilbert gives a touching anecdote of the composition:—

"Robert had frequently remarked to me that he thought there was something peculiarly venerable in the phrase, 'Let us worship God,' used by a decent sober head of a family introducing family worship. To this sentiment of the Author the world is indebted for the 'Cotter's Saturday Night.' The hint of the plan, and title of the poem, were taken from Ferguson's 'Farmer's Ingle.' When Robert had not some pleasure in view in which I was not thought fit to participate, we used frequently to walk together when the weather was favourable on the Sunday afternoons (those precious breathing-times to the labouring part of the community), and enjoyed such Sundays as would make one regret to see their number abridged. It was in one of these walks that I first had the pleasure of hearing the author repeat the 'Cotter's Saturday Night.' I do not recollect to have read or heard anything by which I was more highly *electrified.* The fifth and sixth stanzas, and the eighteenth, thrilled with peculiar ecstasy through my soul. I mention this to you, that you may see what hit the taste of unlettered criticism."

The edition of the "Poems" was exhausted in a month by the subscribers and the public. Wherever the book came, it was admired. Farm-servants spent their wages to get it; and educated readers turned an eye of interest upon the writer. Among these were Dugald Stewart and Mrs. Dunlop, who continued to the end of his life to be true and generous friends. A new issue of his "Poems" was now suggested to him, as likely to increase the comforts of his voyage; but the Kilmarnock printer required the cost of the paper to be advanced, and Burns had no money for the purpose, though friends were not unwilling to provide it.

To this period belongs a romantic incident in the poet's life: his parting with Mary Campbell, the dairymaid of Colonel Montgomery, and the Highland Mary of Poetry. All tradition describes her as a gentle-hearted, loving creature, willing to trust her happiness to an eloquent and daring admirer. I apprehend that, in some particulars, the biographers of Burns have been warmed by his raptures. His own narrative is sufficient for my purpose :—"After a pretty long trial of the most ardent, reciprocal affection, we met, by appointment, on the second Sunday of May, in a sequestered spot on the banks of the Ayr, where we spent a day in taking a farewell before she should embark for the West Highlands, to arrange matters among her friends for our projected change of life. At the close of the autumn following, she crossed the sea to meet me at Greenock, where she had scarce landed when she was seized with a malignant fever, which hurried my dear girl to her grave in a few days, before I could even learn of her illness." The Bible over which the lovers uttered their vows, and a tress of Mary's long, shining hair, are still preserved. Let me not be deemed unkind to Burns, if I remember that while he was thus pledging himself with such solemnity of circumstance to a Mary, a Jean was rueing the day that she met him in the house of her sorrowful parents.

A circumstance, which his letter has already told, rendered pecuniary help unnecessary. Burns was acquainted with Dr. Laurie, minister of Loudoun, and that gentleman sent a copy of the "Poems" to Dr. Blacklock, with a slight outline of the Poet's life. The amiable scholar was delighted by the pathos, the grace, and the humour of the volume, and strongly urged the immediate preparation of an enlarged impression. The pleasure of the Poet was equal to his critic's; and he exchanged the voyage to Jamaica for the road to Edinburgh. He arrived in that city November 28, 1786. Dugald Stewart had already awakened some interest in his behalf by reading his poems, and speaking of his struggles, to several friends, and to Henry Mackenzie among the number. We have the Professor's sketch of the Ayrshire Ploughman, as he appeared in the Scottish metropolis. His dress was plain, but neat. Walter Scott, recalling the vision of his sixteenth year, said that he should have taken the poet for a very sagacious country farmer of the old school—"the douce gudeman who held his own plough!"

Very surprising must have been the change from the playground of Nature to the school of Art. A more striking group of scholars and men of taste might not be found. There was the good and blind son of the bricklayer, whom Johnson hailed at Sir William Forbes's breakfast-table with the tender welcome, "Dear Dr. Blacklock, I am glad to see you." There was Blair, the beau, the novel-reader, the popular preacher, and the vainest man of his time. There was Robertson, neither brilliant nor fruitful in talk, but pleasant and humorous, and praising the generous claret. There was Adam Fergusson, who lived ruddy and vigorous, into his ninety-third year. There was Mackenzie, the gayest of the gay, collecting his rhymes on the edge of the grave, and turning out for a coursing-match with a white hat, green spectacles, and a dog-whistle round his neck. There was Alison, the elegant and the refined. There was Monboddo, enunciating his great axiom that everything was possible, and contemplating the birth of a conversable ourang-outang. But especially eminent and beloved above all the band was "the plain, honest, worthy man, the Professor," Dugald Stewart, exhibiting to the admiration of his rustic friend the blended virtues of "Socrates, Nathanael, and Shakspeare." One distinguished member of Edinburgh society was absent. Adam Smith had just gone to London, when Burns received an introductory letter. We may imagine the delight with which the painter of "The Holy Fair" would have watched the Doctor hovering round the sugar-basin, and continually carrying off a fresh lump from the bewildered spinster who presided. In this brave company of philosophers and critics, the peasant held up his head. He fought them with weapons sharper than their own, and supplied his want of science, or learning, by a various fancy and a glow of language which amazed the scholars, and lifted the beautiful Duchess of Gordon off her feet. Nor was Edinburgh less attractive than its inhabitants. Burns surveyed it with a poet's eye. Arthur's Seat was a favourite haunt, and the cottage smoke, going up into the clear blue sky of morning, awoke in him home-thoughts more tender than poetry. But the great city is not always a safe home for the moralist—never for a poet. We are assured by one, who was darkly stained by its vices, that Burns did not escape the corruption of evil companionship. His Edinburgh life took a downward turn from the period when he exchanged his share of a garret in Baxter's-close and the society of John Richmond, a lawyer's clerk, for the more luxurious dwelling of William Nicol, a teacher in the High School—a clever and noisy admirer, who was at the same time a scoffer and a drunkard. We cannot read this chapter in the story of Burns without remembering the intemperance and the swagger of Savage.

At the beginning of April, 1787, the second edition of his poems issued from the shop of Creech. Lord Glencairn and the Dean of the Faculty had taken him under their wing, and the Caledonian Hunt subscribed in a body. To his learned acquaintances he had recently added Dr. John Moore, formerly a surgeon in Glasgow, afterwards the travelling companion of the Duke of Hamilton, and then settled in London as a physician. The story of "Zeluco" had won a name, and Burns regarded the author with a sort of mysterious reverence. In a letter to Moore, April 23, 1787, he gives his view of a town life on its learned side:—"I leave Edinburgh in the course of ten days or a fortnight. I shall return to my rural shades, in all likelihood never more to quit them. I have formed many intimacies and friendships here; but I am afraid they are all of too tender a construction to bear carriage a hundred and fifty miles."

He had long cherished the desire of making leisurely pilgrimages to the battle-fields, the romantic rivers, and the ruined castles of his country; and his longing was at last in some measure to be gratified in the season most dear to his fancy—

"When rosy May comes in wi' flowers."

On the 6th of that month, having one companion, Mr. Robert Ainslie, he made a hasty excursion into the southern districts, in which Beattie discovered the Arcadia of Scotland, being distinguished by green hills, clear flowing streams, scattered or clustering trees, and especially by its songs, "sweetly expressive of love and tenderness, and the other emotions suited to the tranquillity of pastoral life."

In three weeks, Burns visited the most interesting scenes. At Jedburgh, where orchards and gardens were mingled with the ruins of a stately cathedral, he received the freedom of the borough; the glorious Melrose and the old abbey of Dryburgh affected him greatly, and he carried away in his memory the sound and the colour of

"Ettrick banks now roaring red."

From Arcadia, he passed into Northumberland, and visited the noble castle of the duke, and the hermitage of Warkworth.

Burns returned to Mossgiel in June (8th), 1787, and his biographers have noticed the affecting circumstances under which he revisited his home. Several months were gone since he quitted it, a poor and desperate man; he came back enriched and honoured; and, in the affectionate welcome of his kindred, he might discover a recompense for the glare and the flattery which he had left. He did not, however, long continue under the old roof, but made a fresh expedition into the Highlands, and rejoined his family in July. August found him again in Edinburgh, arranging a third tour with Mr. Adair, of Harrowgate, to whom we owe a slight sketch of the journey:—

"Burns and I left Edinburgh together in August, 1787. We rode by Linlithgow and Carron, to Stirling. We visited the iron-works at Carron, with which the poet was forcibly struck. The resemblance between that place, and its inhabitants, to the cave of Cyclops, which must have occurred to every classical visitor, presented itself to Burns. At Stirling the prospects from the castle strongly interested him; in a former visit to which, his national feelings had been powerfully excited by the ruinous and roofless state of the hall in which the Scottish Parliaments had frequently been held. His indignation had vented itself in some imprudent but not unpoetical lines, which had given much offence, and which he took this opportunity of erasing, by breaking the pane of the window at the inn on which they were written.

"At Stirling we met with a company of travellers from Edinburgh, among whom was a character in many respects congenial with that of Burns. This was Nicol, one of the teachers of the High Grammar School at Edinburgh: the same wit and power of conversation; the same fondness for convivial society, and thoughtlessness of to-morrow, characterized both. Jacobitical principles in politics were common to both of them; and these have been suspected, since the Revolution of France, to have given place in each to opinions apparently opposite. I regret that I have preserved no *memorabilia* of their conversation, either on this or on other occasions, when I happened to meet them together. Many songs were sung; which I mention for the sake of observing, that when Burns was called on in his turn, he was accustomed, instead of singing, to recite one or other of his shorter poems, with a tone and emphasis which, though not correct or harmonious, were impressive and pathetic. This he did on the present occasion.

"From Stirling we went next morning through the romantic and fertile vale of Devon to Harvieston, in Clackmannanshire, then inhabited by Mrs. Hamilton, with the younger part of whose family Burns had been previously acquainted. He introduced me to the family, and there was formed my first acquaintance with Mrs. Hamilton's eldest daughter, to whom I have been married for nine years. Thus was I indebted to Burns for a connection from which I have derived, and expect further to derive, much happiness.

"During a residence of about ten days at Harvieston, we made excursions to visit various parts of the surrounding scenery, inferior to none in Scotland, in beauty, sublimity, and romantic interest; particularly Castle Campbell, the ancient seat of the family of Argyle; and the famous cataract of the Devon, called the "Cauldron Linn;" and the "Rumbling Bridge," a single broad arch, thrown by the Devil, if tradition is to be believed, across the river, at about the height of a hundred feet above its bed. I am surprised that none of these scenes should have called forth an exertion of Burns's muse. But I doubt if he had much taste for the picturesque. I well remember, that the ladies at Harvieston, who accompanied us on this jaunt, expressed their disappointment at his not expressing, in more glowing and fervid language, his impressions of the "Cauldron Linn" scene, certainly highly sublime, and somewhat horrible.

"A visit to Mrs. Bruce of Clackmannan, a lady above ninety, the lineal descendant of that race which gave the Scottish throne its brightest ornament, interested his feelings more powerfully. This venerable dame, with characteristical dignity, informed me, on my observing that I believed she was descended from the family of Robert Bruce, that Robert Bruce was sprung from her family. Though almost deprived of speech by a paralytic affection, she preserved her hospitality and urbanity. She was in possession of the hero's helmet and two-handed sword, with which she conferred on Burns and myself the honour of knighthood, remarking, that she had a better right to confer that title than *some people*. . . . . . You will of course conclude that the old lady's political tenets were as Jacobitical as the poet's,—a conformity which contributed not a little to the cordiality of our reception and entertainment. She gave as her first toast after dinner, *Awa, Uncos*, or, Away with the Strangers.—Who those strangers were you will readily understand. Mrs. A. corrects me by saying it should be *Hooi*, or *Hoohi uncos*, a sound used by shepherds to direct their dogs to drive away the sheep.

"We returned to Edinburgh by Kinross (on the shore of Lochleven) and Queensferry. I am inclined to think Burns knew nothing of poor Michael Bruce, who was then alive at Kinross, or had died there a short while before. A meeting between the bards, or a visit to the deserted cottage and early grave of poor Bruce, would have been highly interesting.

"At Dunfermline we visited the ruined abbey, and the abbey church, new consecrated to Presbyterian worship. Here I mounted the *cutty stool*, or stool of repentance, while Burns from the pulpit addressed to me a ludicrous reproof and exhortation, parodied from that which had been delivered to himself in Ayrshire, where he had, as he assured me, once been one of seven who mounted the *seat of shame* together.

"In the churchyard, two broad flagstones marked the grave of Robert Bruce, for whose memory Burns had more than common veneration. He knelt and kissed the stone with sacred fervour, and heartily (*suus ut mos erat*) execrated the worse than Gothic neglect of the first of Scottish heroes."

He had no sooner ended his third pilgrimage, than he began another, and a more extensive, in the company of his friend Mr. Nicol. The travellers, leaving Edinburgh, August 25, 1787, pursued their way into the heart of the Highlands, and, stretching northward, about ten miles beyond Inverness, took an easterly course over the island, and returned by the shore of the German Sea to Edinburgh. Burns anticipated and found much entertainment in the original humour of his companion. But the ill qualities of Nicol tarnished the good. His manners were coarser than his person, and the "strong in-kneed sort of a soul," which his friend attributed to him, seems to have gained its vigour by the loss of gentleness, for his temper was fierce and ungoverned.

But to Burns the tour brought pleasant fruit. Athole House was a cherished remembrance. The gloom of evening hung over the landscape, when Mr. Walker, whom he had known at Edinburgh, conducted him through the grounds, and witnessed the tender enthusiasm with which he gazed on the scenery. "We rested,"

.he sister of Wordsworth writes, "upon the heather seat which Burns was so loth to quit that moonlight evening when he first went to Blair Castle; and I had a pleasure in thinking that he had been under the same shelter, and viewed the little waterfall opposite with some of the happy and pure feelings of his better mind."

Within-doors, the "fine family piece" was not less charming. To Gilbert he sent a letter from Edinburgh, September 16, 1787.

"I arrived here safe yesterday evening, after a tour of twenty-two days, and travelling near six hundred miles, windings included. My farthest stretch was about ten miles beyond Inverness. I went through the heart of the Highlands, by Crieff, Taymouth, the famous seat of Lord Breadalbane, down the Tay, among cascades and druidical circles of stones, to Dunkeld, a seat of the Duke of Athole; thence cross Tay, and up one of his tributary streams to Blair of Athole, another of the Duke's seats, where I had the honour of spending nearly two days with his Grace and family; thence many miles through a wild country, among cliffs grey with eternal snows, and gloomy savage glens, till I crossed Spey and went down the stream through Strathspey, so famous in Scottish music, Badenoch, &c., till I reached Grant Castle, where I spent half a day with Sir James Grant and family; and then crossed the country for Fort George, but called by the way at Cawdor, the ancient seat of Macbeth; there I saw the identical bed in which, tradition says, King Duncan was murdered: lastly, from Fort George to Inverness.

"I returned by the coast, through Nairn, Forres, and so on, to Aberdeen; thence to Stonehive, where James Burns, from Montrose, met me by appointment. I spent two days among our relations, and found our aunts, Jean and Isabel, still alive, and hale old women. John Caird, though born the same year with our father, walks as vigorously as I can; they have had several letters from his son in New York. William Brand is likewise a stout old fellow: but further particulars I delay till I see you, which will be in two or three weeks. The rest of my stages are not worth rehearsing: warm as I was from Ossian's country, where I had seen his very grave, what cared I for fishing towns or fertile carses? I slept at the famous Brodie of Brodie's one night, and dined at Gordon Castle next day with the Duke, Duchess, and family. I am thinking to cause my old mare to meet me, by means of John Ronald, at Glasgow; but you shall hear further from me before I leave Edinburgh. My duty, and many compliments from the north, to my mother, and my brotherly compliments to the rest. I have been trying for a berth for William, but am not likely to be successful.—Farewell."

Burns was again in Edinburgh during the winter of 1787. He is then supposed to have begun his acquaintance with the lady whom he celebrated under the title of Clarinda. Her real name was M'Lehose, the wife of a gentleman in the West

Indies, and then residing with her children in Edinburgh. The letters which Burns addressed to her, in the pastoral character of Sylvander, are sufficiently amorous and absurd; but a devotee, like Clarinda, required no common homage. She declared that the admiration of fourscore years would not pay her debt of gratitude. Time dealt generously with her in old age; she lived near the Calton Hill, where Mr. Howitt and his wife visited her, and witnessed a most amusing scene. Clarinda invited her guests to drink out of the glasses which Sylvander had presented, and took them from the cupboard, and rang for the servant to bring wine. An aged woman answered the call, and hearing that the strangers "were to drink out of the glasses which stood ready on the table, she gave a look as if sacrilege were going to be committed, took up the glasses without a word, replaced them in the cupboard, locking them up, and brought in three ordinary glasses. It was in vain for Mrs. M'Lehose to remonstrate; the old and self-willed servant went away without deigning a reply, with the key in her pocket."

The settlement of his accounts with Creech, February, 1788, placed more than five hundred pounds in the hands of Burns. He made a noble use of part of the money

His own account to Dr. Moore—January 4, 1789—is simple and pleasing: "I have a younger brother, who supports my aged mother; another still younger brother, and three sisters, in a farm. On my last return from Edinburgh, it cost me about £180 to save them from ruin. Not that I have lost so much—I only interposed between my brother and his impending fate by the loan of so much. I give myself no airs on this, for it was mere selfishness on my part. I was conscious that the wrong scale of the balance was pretty heavily charged, and I thought that throwing a little filial and fraternal affection into the scale in my favour, might help to smooth matters at *the grand reckoning*." With the balance of his profits he entered upon a farm, belonging to Mr Miller, of Dalswinton. Ellisland was pleasantly situated on the banks of the Nith, six miles from Dumfries. The vale of the Nith sweeps just below the house, and from the windows the river is seen flowing with its swift, dark current, broad as the Thames at Hampton Court. Burns began his new life at Whitsuntide, 1788, having previously gone through the ceremony of a justice-of-peace marriage with Jean Armour, in the office of his friend Gavin Hamilton. He considered the head of a wife to be immaterial, in comparison of her heart. He spoke from experience. His Jean had a handsome figure, a sweet temper, and reckoned her husband the finest genius in the world. Her acquaintance with prose and verse was limited to the Bible and the Psalms; but she had studied a certain collection of Scottish songs, and warbled many with a delicious wood-note. In later life, the Ettrick Shepherd frequently saw Mrs. Burns, in the old church of Dumfries, and spoke of her as a brunette, with fine eyes.

A modern poet has said finely,—

> "And there were many strange and sudden lights
> Beckoned him towards them ; they were wrecking lights :
> But he shunned these, and righted when she rose,
> Moon of his life, that ebbed and flowed with her !"

Alas ! that we cannot apply the words to Burns. His wedded life met with difficulties at the beginning. The house of Ellisland was a miserable hovel, open to wind and rain, and giving to the occupant the choice of being drenched or suffocated. Jean could not come under such a roof, and she remained with the poet's family. But forty miles make a wide gap between husband and wife. Burns set himself with all speed to build a better dwelling, and the summer found him busy in the field. His resolutions were excellent. "I have all along, hitherto in the warfare of life, been bred to arms among the light horse—the piquet guards of fancy, a kind of hussars and highlanders of the brain ; but I am firmly resolved to sell out of these giddy battalions, who have no ideas of a battle, but fighting the foe, or of a siege, but storming the town. Cost what it will, I am determined to buy in among the grave squadrons of heavy-armed thought, or the artillery corps of plodding contrivance." In neither of these regiments did he ever get a commission. He brought Jean home in November, and for the first time in his life had the opportunity of realizing his own picture :—

> "To make a happy fire-side clime,
> To weans and wife—
> That's the true pathos, and sublime
> Of human life."

But low spirits dulled his joys. He calls himself such a coward in the world, and so tired of the service, that the desire of his heart was " to lie down in his mother's lap and be at peace." We hear him groaning under the miseries of a diseased nervous system, and of headaches three weeks in duration.

It may be feared that the mirth of the Edinburgh tables often rung in his ears. Dr. Moore had mentioned the friendliness of husbandry to fancy, while he wished for him the prosperous union of the farmer and the poet. But Burns had neither Mæcenas for a landlord, nor Horace for a neighbour. He gives a characteristic sketch of his life at "the very elbow" of existence. "The only things," he told Mr. Bengo, the engraver, " that are to be found in this country in any degree of perfection are stupidity and canting." Prose, he said, they only knew in graces and sermons, which they valued, like plaiding webs, by the ell ; while a poet and a rhinoceros suggested ideas equally distinct and agreeable. It was not always dark in Ellisland. His first winter glided happily by, and golden days of the heart and the fancy often shone, when the father rejoiced in the crown of the poet. In this farm, by the river-side, he composed his noblest lyric, "To Mary in Heaven;" and there, too, the fat and festive Grose came to visit him, and heard of the wonderful jump of Cutty Sark and the magnificent terrors of Tam.

Burns had made a bad choice of a farm; but a momentary sunlight broke over it, and the crops rewarded his industry and care. An agricultural friend once warned him that however situation, soil, and custom might vary, Farmer Attention would be prosperous everywhere. And it is conceivable that even from Ellisland he might have come in joy, bringing sheaves. But Farmer Attention was a stranger under that roof—more familiar to the wedding feast and the harvest dance. The appointment of Burns to the Excise came, to complete the ruin of the husbandman. He owed it to the kindness of a surgeon (Mr. Wood), who got his name placed on the list of candidates. His satisfaction is abundantly shown in his letters. "I thought," he wrote to Mrs. Dunlop, "five-and-thirty pounds a year was no bad *dernier ressort* for a poor poet, if fortune, in her jade tricks, should kick him down from the little eminence to which she had lately helped him up." To Miss Chalmers he placed his new office in the same prudential light. "I do not find my farm that pennyworth I was taught to expect; but I believe in time it may be a saving bargain. To save me from that horrid situation of at any time going down in a losing bargain of a farm to misery, I have taken my Excise instructions, and have my commission in my pocket for any emergency of fortune.' And to another lady he remarked—"The question is not at what door of Fortune's palace shall we enter in? but, What doors does she open to us?" To his friend Ainslie he talked in high spirits:—"I do not know if I have informed you that I am now appointed to an excise division, in the middle of which my house and farm lie. In this I was extremely lucky, without ever having been an expectant, as they call their journeyman exciseman, I was directly planted down, to all intents and purposes, an officer of excise. Fifty pounds a year for life, and a provision for widows and orphans, you will allow, is no bad settlement for a poet."

Before the close of 1791, Burns relinquished his farm, and being placed, with a salary of seventy pounds, in the Dumfries department of Excise, he removed his family to that town. The situation was not promising. The house stood in a narrow street, swarming with tramps; and the worthy sister of a great poet describes its look in the autumn of 1803:—"It has a mean appearance, whitewashed, dirty about the doors, as all Scotch houses are; the parlour walls were washed with blue wash; on one side of the fire was a mahogany desk, opposite the window a clock, and over the desk a print from the "Cotter's Saturday Night." The house was cleanly and neat in the inside; the stairs of stone scoured white, the kitchen on the right hand of the passage, the parlour on the left."

The biographers of Burns concur in putting his Dumfries life into shadow. "I am just risen," are his own sad words--"from a two hours' bout after supper, with silly, or sordid souls, who could relish nothing in common with me but the port." Among companions like these he had long been in the habit—to adopt his striking phrase—of dividing large slices of his constitution; but the biggest slices were given at Dumfries. Many families from the south of Scotland chose that town for their winter residence; and we are told that it abounded in "stately Toryism," which only served to embitter and aggravate the hostility of the Poet. The freedom of his manners was, at least, equalled by that of his tongue, and his epigrams fell thick and fast. One critic is sharp upon the "gentry," because they "cut" Burns. This "cutting" is certain. A friend informed Mr. Lockhart, that upon a fine summer evening he saw the poet walking alone on the shady side of the principal street, while the opposite part was gay with successive groups of gentlemen and ladies, all drawn together for the festivities of the night, not one of whom appeared willing to recognize him. Assuredly he gave ample opportunity to evil-speakers. A single instance will be sufficient. The coasts of Galloway and Ayrshire were the haunts of smugglers, whom it was the especial duty of the revenue officers to watch and intercept. In the February of 1792, an armed brig appearing in the Solway Frith, and getting into shallow water, a party of dragoons was brought down, and, led by Burns, dashed up to the brig and captured her. At the public sale of the vessel, he bought four guns, which he sent with a flattering assurance of his esteem to the French Convention. The gift was stopped at Dover, but the folly of the exciseman reached the ears of the Board, by whom he was naturally regarded as a person disaffected and dangerous. Scared of a sudden by the vision of a helpless wife, and children turned adrift into the world, Burns opened his grief to Mr. Graham, and found the protection which he asked. The displeasure of the Board passed away in a mild and merited censure. Nor is there any reason to suppose that his prospects of promotion were blighted by the imprudence and wilfulness of his conduct. If he became more circumspect in his political walk, the watchfulness did not reach his morals. His most zealous apologists only venture to plead that his errors were occasional; and witnesses are called to speak of his early rising, his punctuality, and his lessons to his children. What is such testimony worth? That life must be utterly reprobate, of which sin is the narrative, not the episode. In general, the phrensy of vice has lucid intervals. Kit Smart was not wheeled home in the barrow on every night. There is enough of the wild beast in sin to make it drowsy when it is fed.

It is the fashion to rebuke any censure of Burns by a reference to passages in which he confesses his guilt, and implores the pity of his brethren. Let the appeal be welcomed. He has left outpourings of a smitten heart, never to be read without sympathy, nor to be remembered except with prayer. But of what avail is sorrow which bears no fruit? Crabbe is believed to have painted Burns in the portrait of Edward Shore:—

> "Griev'd, but not contrite, was his heart; oppress'd,
> Not broken; not converted, but distress'd;
> He wanted will to bend the stubborn knee;
> He wanted light the cause of ill to see;
> To learn how frail is man, how humble then should be."

The picture is a likeness. I do not doubt that in the festival of his riot, or his guilt, the great soul of this wonderful man was shaken by gusts of penitence and fear. A hand on the wall terrified him with the balance; and dreadfully the scales went down before his accusing eyes. Very awful is his confession to a friend:—"Even in the hour of social mirth, my gaiety is the madness of an intoxicated criminal under the hands of the executioner." In such seasons the united Presbytery had no preacher so eloquent, no prayers so pathetic. The Ettrick Shepherd frequently heard one Master Saunders Proudfoot relate a story. There had been a merrymaking at Thornhill Fair, and wine and punch disappeared with more than ordinary swiftness. "By degrees the hale o' the chaps slippit away ane after another. But what I fear was his warst fault—he couldna leave the bowl, and I was determined not to leave him; sae we sat on, an' sat on, till after midnight, and then were shown into a bedroom, an' our bowl an' glasses wi' us. I saw before this time that Burns had gotten rather mair than enough, an' in order to gar him gi' over, I pretended to be drunk, an' lay down on ane o' the beds with my claes on. Burns seemed very ill pleased when I left him, an' looked round and round him as rather disappointed; but he couldna drink by himself, and if he took ae glass after I left him that was a'. I watched him weel, an' he grew exceedingly impatient, an' then throwing himsel' on his knees, with his face leaning on his arms, which were across the chair, he began to pray, and by degrees he got into such a fervent supplication for mercy and forgiveness for all his transgressions, that it was awfu', it was dreadfu' to hear him. It made sic an impression on me, that I crept quietly owre the bed, out o' his kennin, and kneeled down beside him. He confessed himself to be the chief o' sinners, with tears of agony; and siccan fervour o' eloquence I never heard frae the lips o' man. It was awesome to hear him. I was even greetin' mysel', although it's no little that gars auld Sandy cry."

I rejoice in believing the heart of Burns to have been always true. A tender father he surely was. He revered Virtue when he outraged her. The little hands of his children were familiar to his neck in all their "flichterin' noise an' glee;"

and no husband, in his calmer hours, ever felt more deeply the dear associations of the

> "———Wee bit ingle, blinkin bonnily,
> His clean hearth-stane, his thrifty wifie's smile."

The wife of Burns had much to forgive, and she forgave it, in life and in death. Very touching is the anecdote which Hogg tells of Jean Burns the widow. "Na, na, poor fellow, his complaints were a' of himsel'. He never complained either of the bairns or me; he never said a misbehadden word to me a' the days of his life." We have evidence, in the poetry which Burns wrote at Dumfries, that the brighter life within him was continually throwing sunshine into the outward cloud. And a fortunate circumstance cherished the flame. Mr. George Thomson, of Edinburgh, had formed a plan of collecting original Scotch airs for the voice, accompanied by words. He was a man of cultivated taste, fond of painting, and able to bear his part in a violin quartette of Pleyel. The musical assistance he had secured, but he wanted the poetical. His hopes turned to the author of "The Cotter's Saturday Night," and in September, 1792, he stated his wishes to Burns, who on the 16th of the same month answered the application with a frank and cordial enthusiasm. Still further to brighten the prospect, Beattie promised an Essay on the National Music. Burns kept his word, and found his pleasure in his work. He assured Thomson, in the April of the next year, that the business of composing had added to his enjoyments, and that ballad-making was becoming as completely his "hobby-horse as ever fortification was Uncle Toby's." His anticipations of success, too, were largely fulfilled; for in this race he took the right side of the winning-post. By the general verdict of readers, the sixty songs, which he wrote for the collection of Thomson, are pronounced to be the most beautiful and refined of his works. The "Bannockburn" was a blast upon a trumpet which he blew too seldom. But the evening lights begin to melt around us.

The glimpses which the poet gives of himself are in the highest degree mournful: Regret—Remorse—Shame, dog his steps and bay at his heels; he apologizes to a lady for some festive ill-behaviour, by writing a letter "from the dead:" his helpless little folks drive sleep from his pillow; his old friends would not know him. With every month the nervous misery increases; and his feelings, at times, are only to be envied by "a reprobate spirit listening to the sentence that dooms it to perdition." Except in the letters of Cowper, I remember no self-upbraidings more dreadful or pathetic. The storm deepened. He had hardly buried his sweet little girl, when a rheumatic fever of the severest kind bound him to his bed. All these things were against him. To James Johnson he wrote:—"This protracting, slow, consuming illness which hangs over me will, I doubt much, arrest my sun before he has well reached his middle career, and will turn over the poet to far more important concerns than studying the brilliancy of wit or the pathos of sentiment. However, hope is the cordial of the human heart, and I endeavour to cherish it as well as I can." The new year found him making feeble efforts to crawl across his room. But no suffering could teach prudence to Burns The firstfruits of his strength were given to a tavern dinner, prolonged into the late morning. Returning home, he sunk on the snow and slept. The old enemy came in his sleep, and he awoke with the torments of rheumatism, renewed and sharpened. Pale, emaciated, and wanting a hand to help him from his chair, he complained of "spirits fled—fled!" One faint hope remained—it was the shadow of a shade: sea-bathing might restore him. In order to obtain it, he was removed to Brow, a village on the Solway Frith; and there his pains were slightly relieved But the fire was still burning. He returned to Dumfries on the 18th of July, 1796, wasted in body and face, and hardly able to stand. Dr. Maxwell, who attended him, communicated the particulars of his closing hours to Currie:—A tremor pervaded his frame; his tongue was parched, and his mind sunk into delirium when not roused by conversation. On the second and third day the fever increased, and his strength diminished. Upon the fourth day the cord was loosed and the spirit took its flight.

So died Robert Burns, the most remarkable person of that age; alike gifted and wretched; the glory and the shame of literature. Can the tale be more fittingly ended, or moralized, than by the last words of a Scottish minstrel of wider renown, and who did not die in a noisy street, but in the splendid home which his genius had erected. The September afternoon was calm and sunny, and the Tweed, rippling over its pebbles, sounded through the open window, when the expiring poet whispered to a friend by his bed, "I may have but a minute to speak to you,—My dear, be a good man—be virtuous, be religious. Nothing else will give you any comfort when you come to lie here."

Men forgive much to the dead, and round the grave of Burns nothing was remembered but the light that had been quenched. It went down in stormy splendour among clouds and darkness, but the survivors thought only of the full and glowing orb, and the beauty which it had left for ever to illuminate the streams and fields of Scotland. He was buried, July 26th, with military honours, as belonging to the Dumfries Volunteers, and a great multitude followed him. The sun shone brightly all the day, and while the earth "was heaped up, and the green sod was laid over him, the crowd stood gazing for some minutes' space, and then melted silently away."

Few faces are more familiar to poetical readers than the broad, massive, earnest countenance of Burns. A plain-spoken and rough acquaintance said that he was a good-looking, fine fellow, "rather black an' ill-coloured;" and Professor Walker recognized the weather-beaten features of a master of a trading vessel. His black hair, slightly sprinkled with grey, was spread over his forehead, and suited the large dark eye, which really glowed under the impulse of pleasure or anger. "I have seen," wrote Scott, "the most distinguished men of my time; and I never saw such another eye in a human head." His figure was tall—nearly five feet ten inches,—but an ungraceful stoop diminished his height to the observer. Like many poets, he was not captivated by science, or skill, in music. An old strathspey awoke exquisite pleasure, and "Rothemurche's Rant" put him in raptures. In this feeling he resembled Scott, who was melted by the simplest tune, while a complicated harmony seemed to be a babble of sounds. But no ear was wakefuller than that of Burns to every tone of nature: her sigh, her murmur, her breath of love; the rustle of the copse, the wind in the branches, the whistle of the curlew, the cadence of plovers, the moan of the river sedge,—each sound passed over his mind like a cunning finger upon a harp, and left him soothed, inflamed, enamoured, or devout.

His literary taste was instinctively pure and refined. Virgil charmed him by rural pictures and exquisite grace, filling his mind "with a thousand fancies of emulation," and, at the same time, reminding him of a Shetland pony by the side of a racer starting for the plate. His judgment of English poetry was chaste and true. Pope, Dryden, Collins, Gray, Thomson, and Beattie were especially dear. I think that he never read much of Spenser, but Milton he revered. He hailed "the glorious poem, 'The Task,'" and admired the water-colour drawings of Hurdis. In prose he did not show so exact a judgment; for while he loved the sweet serious morals of Addison, he suffered himself to be dazzled and beguiled by the rant of Ossian, and the pantomime of Sterne. Nor may I forget the "Meditations" of Hervey, which have long been among the popular reading of Scotland.

Of his personal character, the key was pride, often manifesting itself in arrogance and injustice. He dines with Lord Glencairn, who has one other guest, a man of rank, to whom he shows becoming attention. The blood of the poet boils against the "blockhead," and he is on the point of "throwing down his gage of contemptuous defiance," for "Dunderpate" to take up. The incident recalls the pleasant story of Selden:—"We measure the excellency of other men by some excellency which we conceive to be in ourselves. Nash, a poet (poor enough, as poets used to be), seeing an alderman with the gold chain upon his great horse, said to one of his companions, "Do you see yon fellow, how goodly, how big he looks? Why, that fellow cannot make a blank verse." "Dunderpate" was probably a usefuller member of society than Burns. Such passages suggest a comparison with the American Cooper, shaking the dust off his feet, because an infirm nobleman entered a drawing-room before him. The temper of Burns occasionally broke into open rudeness and insult. A lady asked him if he had nothing to say of a fine scene before them. "Nothing, madam," was his reply, while his eye glanced to the leader of the party, "for an ass is braying over it."

The politics of Burns took the part of his fancy, his friendship, or his pique. Scott, enclosing a few letters to Mr. Lockhart, remarked—"In one of them (to the singular old curmudgeon, Lady Winifred Constable) he plays high Jacobite, and on that account it is curious; though I imagine his Jacobitism, like my own, belonged to the fancy rather than to the reason." There is no need of conjecture. Burns acknowledges that his "Jacobitism was merely by way of *vive la bagatelle*."

Of his religious opinions, a letter to Mrs. Dunlop (June 21, 1789) gives a full and interesting account:—

"I have just heard —— give a sermon. He is a man famous for his benevolence, and I revere him; but from such ideas of my Creator, good Lord, deliver me! Religion, my honoured friend, is surely a simple business, as it equally concerns the ignorant and the learned, the poor and the rich. That there is an incomprehensibly great Being, to whom I owe my existence, and that he must be intimately acquainted with the operations and progress of the internal machinery, and consequent outward deportment of this creature which he has made,—these are, I think, self-evident propositions. That there is a real and eternal distinction between virtue and vice, and consequently that I am an accountable creature—that from the seeming nature of the human mind, as well as from the evident imperfection, nay, positive injustice, in the administration of affairs, both in the natural and moral worlds, there must be a retributive scene of existence beyond the grave,—must, I think, be allowed by every one who will give himself a moment's reflection. I will go farther, and affirm, that from the sublimity, excellence, and purity of his doctrine and precepts, unparalleled by all the aggregated wisdom and learning of many preceding ages, though, *to appearance*, he himself was the obscurist and most illiterate of our species, therefore, Jesus Christ was from God.

* * * * * * * * * *

"Whatever mitigates to woes or increases the happiness of others, this is my criterion of goodness; and whatever injures society at large, or any individual in it, this is my measure of iniquity."

"I hate," he said, upon another occasion, "the very idea of a controversial divinity; I despise the superstition of a fanatic: but I love the religion of a man." His lines had not fallen in pleasant places. Controversy was rampant; and the truth, if truth it were, was often told with the tongue of a viper. The religion of the heart he seldom found. Born and brought up a Presbyterian, the Gospel came to him in the roar of black Russell and the invectives of Father Auld. In no dress could the creed look fair or engaging. A man of taste, in a kirk, has a feeling of being snowed up in an unfurnished house, without a fire. A chill strikes him from the cold building and the colder worship. In one of the poet's journals, we hear him pouring out his intense disgust:—" What a poor, pimping business is a Presbyterian place of worship: dirty, narrow, squalid, stuck in a corner of old Popish grandeur, such as Linlithgow, and much more, Melrose." His greatest countrymen have shared his dislike: Byron remembered the fiery Calvinism of his boyhood with a sense of personal injury; the heart of Scott yearned for that nobler and purer ritual which has breathed into its prayers the devotion and the language of the Apostles; and the sentiments of Jeffrey are known to have been of the same kind.

Presbyterianism in Burns's time was coarser and fiercer than in ours. Vulgar in attire, wrathful in look, menacing in speech,—it combined in its visage the most repulsive features of the faith. Nor had it always inward virtue to atone for the outward offence. The Elders frequently showed the curiosity of the Inquisition; and in some of the Ministers might be seen the tyranny of the cowl, without the romance.

Wordsworth expressed his regret that, instead of writing poems like "The Holy Fair," in which the religious services of his country are treated with levity and scorn, Burns did not employ his genius in exhibiting religion under the serious and affecting aspect which it so frequently takes. And Jeffrey paints a delightful sketch of a Highland Sacrament, with its Gaelic sermon preached out of tents to picturesque crowds in the open air, grouped on rocks by the glittering sea, in the mountain bays of a long-withdrawing loch. But the vulgar and rabid fanaticism, by which the poet was surrounded, had taken out of Religion the beauty and the love. Her clothing was not " of wrought gold," and she never appeared in raiment of needle-work, nor in the company of beautiful attendants.

Perhaps in no man of his age would the religious life, fitly planted and nurtured, have found a fruitfuller home. The soil was rich and deep. He wrote— " My great constituent elements are pride and passion. The first I have endeavoured to humanize into integrity and honour; the last makes me a devotee, to the warmest degree of enthusiasm, in love, religion, or friendship,—either of them, or all together, as I happen to be inspired." The organ was there, and the anthem slept. How majestic are the thoughts into which his devotional feelings are occasionally breathed;—scattered, but solemn notes of a mind seldom tuned or played upon, but wonderful in its various and swelling music! Read this confession: —"I have been, this morning, taking a peep through, as Young finely says, 'The dark postern of time long elapsed.' 'Twas a rueful prospect! What a tissue of thoughtlessness, weakness, and folly! My life reminded me of a ruined temple. What strength, what proportion in some parts! What unsightly gaps, what prostrate ruins in others! I kneeled down before the Father of Mercies, and said, 'Father, I have sinned against Heaven, and in thy sight, and am no more worthy to be called thy son.' I rose, eased and strengthened."

He approved of "set times and seasons of more than ordinary acts of devotion;" and he had certain Saints'-days in his poetical calendar. These were New Year's Day; the first Sunday of May; "a breezy, blue-skied noon, sometime about the beginning, and a hoary morning and a calm sunny day, about the end of autumn." With these holidays of the mind he associated particular sounds and flowers; and especially in spring, he delighted to look upon "the mountain daisy, the harebell, the foxglove, the wild-brier rose, the budding birch, and the hoary hawthorn." He said—"I have various sources of pleasure and enjoyment, which are, in a manner, *peculiar* to myself, or some here or there such other out-of-the-way person. Such is the peculiar pleasure I take in the season of winter, more than the rest of the year. This, I believe, may be partly owing to my misfortunes giving my mind a melancholy cast; but there is something even in

'The mighty tempest, and the hoary waste
Abrupt and deep, stretch'd o'er the buried earth,'

which raises the mind to a serious sublimity, favourable to everything great and noble. There is scarcely any earthly object gives me more—I do not know if I should call it pleasure—but something which exalts me, something which enraptures me,—than to walk in the sheltered side of a wood, or high plantation, in a cloudy winter day, and hear the stormy wind howling among the trees, and raving over the plain. It is my best season for devotion; my mind is wrapped up in a kind of enthusiasm to Him who, in the pompous language of the Hebrew bard, 'walks on the wings of the wind.'"

A poet seldom keeps his fame with his tongue; but the conversation of Burns was marked by the strong features of his genius: brilliant, sarcastic, tender, and fluent, the roar and the tears of the table were obedient to his summons. An inhabitant of Dumfries gave a lively impression of his manner by saying, that he seemed to be desperately in earnest. He did not always pick his subjects or his words. The schoolmaster of Dumfries, indeed, put in a claim on his behalf for unblemished language and thought; and declared that he had seen Burns dazzling and delighting a party during a long evening by the brightness and rapidity of his flashes, "without even an allusion" that could offend the most delicate hearer. I am unable to reconcile the panegyric with the confession of a biographer, who found the poet's festive sayings quite unrepresentable; but he knew his company and had jests for Nicol, ballads for Stewart, and ribaldry for the bowl.

The accounts of his voice are contradictory. I have seen it called untunable and harsh. Mr. Allan Cunningham once heard Burns read Tam O'Shanter with harmony and skill, following all the undulations of the sense, and expressing the humour and the awfulness of the story. Although he never advanced into England beyond Carlisle and Newcastle, we are told by Currie that he had less of the Scottish dialect than Hume, who was polished by the fashion and literature of London and Paris; or Robertson, whose purity and elegance of composition are his chief characteristics.

Burns came before the world as the "Ayrshire Ploughman;" but a mere farm-servant he never was; and in no sense of the word could he be styled an uneducated poet. We must go to Suffolk, or Northamptonshire, to seek real ploughboys bursting into song. Bloomfield has told his tale; and the painful struggles of Clare are freshly remembered. He paid for such teaching as he got, by extra work in the field or the barn. The toil of eight weeks provided schooling for four. A kind neighbour taught him to write. He was ignorant of grammar, and he had no books; but the appetite was strong.

In his fourteenth year, a boy showed to him the "Seasons;" and Clare, having saved up a shilling, set off to Stamford, in the dawn of a spring morning, to purchase a copy, and reached the town before a shop was open.

Now look at Burns,—over-worked, yet rejoicing in the pleasant scholarship of home; by the time that he was ten or eleven years old, quite a critic in substantives and verbs; improving his handwriting, or giving his manners a brush in the dancing-school; within-doors finding a teacher in his father, a poetic nurse in his mother;—one strengthening his judgment with good books and arithmetic, and the other charming his young fancy with legends and ballads of the country-side. He was probably a better English scholar than most boys of his age who were then at Eton; and his skill and power of composition might hardly be equalled by the lads who had passed into King's.

In the history of every poet we read a new version of the "Faery Queen" found by Cowley in the parlour-window. Ramsay was the Spenser of Burns—"Green be the pillow," Scott said, "of honest Allan, at whose lamp Burns lighted his brilliant torch." Fergusson shared the honour of kindling it, and the later minstrel borrowed from the elder the plan and the measure of several poems; but he justly claimed the name of a disciple, not a copyist, for he repaid his debts with lavish interest. The one flower-seed sprang up a cluster of bloom.

His earliest compositions were satirical; and the first of his poetic offspring, as he informs us, that saw the light, was the ludicrous portraiture of two ministers as "Twa Herds;" "Holy Willie's Prayer" followed it, with "The Ordination," and "The Kirk's Alarm." Probably the "Epistle to Davie" preceded them. Burns was weeding in the kail-yard when he repeated some of the lines to his brother, who thought it equal to Ramsay, and worthy of being printed. Robert was then twenty-five. "Death and Dr. Hornbook" he also recited to Gilbert holding the plough, while the poet was letting the water off the field beside him.

A sweeter tune mingled with these strains; and when turning up the furrow, he composed the verses to the "Mouse," the "Mountain Daisy," and other rural pieces. His poetical growth was quick, and he had only the nightingale's April before the May. Burns has left examples of nearly every shorter form of rhyme; the description, the satire, the epistle, the elegy, the love-song, the war-lay, and the epigram. He considered "Tam O'Shanter" to be his standard performance, and public opinion confirms his own. I must, however, confess that, in my judgment, the story runs down too fast, and the blaze of imagination seems to be unexpectedly and suddenly quenched in a mean catastrophe, which is the mere stick of the rocket. At the same time it is proper to mention the contrary view of those critics—Miss Seward in the number—who regard the jocose moral as admirably in keeping with the general plan, and applaud the poet for laughing at his objectors and retaining the sportive admonition. The story of "The Twa Dogs" is not less admirable in another style.

The Scottish poems of Burns can be thoroughly relished by his countrymen only. Cowper remarked, "Poor Burns loses much of his deserved praise in this country through our ignorance of his language. I despair of meeting with any Englishman, who will take the pains that I have taken to understand him. His candle is bright, but shut up in a dark lantern. I lent him to a very sensible neighbour of mine; but his uncouth dialect spoiled all, and before he had read him through, he was quite *ramfeezled*." Dr. Moore seems to have anticipated this danger, when he warned the poet that all the fine satire and humour of "The Holy Fair" would be lost on the English, and urged him to abandon the Scottish stanza and dialect, and adopt the measure and language of modern English verse. The difficulty of comprehension is specially felt in the poems of humour and common life; where a phrase, or a proverb, to the familiar ear brings with it a train of home recollections and pleasures. In such cases, the dialect is the family accent. Frequently, however, the hindrance is scarcely perceived. In "The Cotter's Saturday Night," nearly every stanza has a different tone. Sometimes he writes pure and simple English; another passage requires a glossary; and occasionally he combines the two languages, and blends, with admirable effect, pathos, sublimity, beauty, and homeliness. Dryden said pleasantly of Theocritus, that even his Doric dialect has an incomparable sweetness in his clownishness—like a fair shepherdess in her country russet, talking in a Yorkshire tone. The Scottish songs of Burns suggest the same agreeable comparison; and a freshness sparkles in every word, like dew on the heather-bell. The "latitudinarianism" of the dialect is very accommodating to the poet, who is able by this Scottish privilege to marry the most opposite and discordant rhymes. Spenser had set the bold example of new spelling a word whenever the exigencies of sound required it; and Burns treated his syllables with the same freedom.

The full harmony of his genius flowed into his songs, of which the remark of Mr. Pitt was pre-eminently true, that he could think of no verse, since Shakspeare, which had so much the appearance of coming sweetly from Nature. Under the fragrant birch trees, in the heathery glens, or among the moonlit sheaves, the gushes of music flowed warm from his heart. The range of it is not large, and one mellow, plaintive, delicious love-note always returns upon the ear in beauty. But the song of Burns was no mere outpouring of rich sounds. He bestowed time and patience. "All my poetry," he said, "is the effect of easy composition, but of laborious correction." Here is the interesting story, from his own pen:—"My way is—I consider the poetic sentiment correspondent to my idea of the musical expression; then choose my theme—begin one stanza: when that is composed, which is generally the most difficult part of the business, I walk out, sit down now and then, look out for objects in nature round me that are in unison or harmony with the cogitations of my fancy and workings of my bosom; humming every now and then the air with the verse I have framed. When I feel my muse beginning to jade, I retire to the solitary fireside of my study, and there commit my effusions to paper; swinging at intervals on the hind legs of my elbow-chair, by way of calling forth my own critical strictures as my pen goes on. Seriously, this, at home, is almost invariably my way." The love-poetry of Burns is, for the most part, desire set to music. The unselfishness, the reverence, and the chivalry of affection he did not appreciate, or felt himself unable to portray. Crabbe's tale, in the second letter of "The Borough," has a sublimity of tenderness and a truthful purity which the Ayrshire Bard never equalled.

Johnson, running down Hammond, denies the reality of all attachment where there is fiction, and despises a lover who courts his mistress with Roman imagery. Burns, too, sweeps away darts, flames, and graces, "as just a Mauchline rabble." I know not why pastoral courtship should be truer than classical, for imagery is only the reflection of feeling. We compare those whom we admire to things which we prize. A woman is not more like a rose on a castle wall, than she is like Diana with her quiver. The rose and the goddess are emblems of beauty, and the poet chooses the one or the other, as the flower or the figure may be most familiar and pleasing to his memory. Taste moulds the lover. Nor is exaggeration incompatible with naturalness. Every poet magnifies a circumstance, and illuminates a heroine; and by so doing, he vanquishes the painter, and wins gratitude for the pen. To Waller, and not to Vandyck, we owe the ideal charms of Saccharisa.

The amatory compositions of Burns are not so pure in spirit as the utterance is melodious. One of his correspondents wished to see the loose sentiments threshed out of a particular song. There is ample room for the flail, and with longer life, and in more thoughtful hours, the author would have handled it himself, with what advantage to the finer wheat and to his own enduring fame, I need not say, for

> "Sweet this man could sing, as morning lark,
> And teach the noblest morals of the heart."

The language of Burns is worthy of the poetry: animated and flexible, it combines symmetry with muscle, and harmony with strength. In the choice of the illustration, the happy daring of the phrase, the delicate turn of the expression, and the tunefulness of the numbers, he is seldom surpassed by the most cultivated of his brethren. Even Pope is not a finer study for distinctness and precision.

Wordsworth expressed surprise that Burns—passing the fruitful season of his poetical life within sight of splendid sea-prospects, bounded by the peaks of Arran—should be quite silent respecting them; and he explains the peculiarity by the fact, that, in the poetry of Burns, natural appearances seldom take the lead. He affects us as a man, rather than as a poet, by common feelings uttered in the poet's voice. Rivers, hills, and woods are blended in his mind with remembrances of place, time, and sentiment. And I am induced to copy here the very elegant observations of a true and a sympathizing critic, a master and a judge of the lyre:[1]—"It is evident, from almost all his pieces, that it was his delight—indeed it was his *forte*—to *localize* the personages of his poetry: whether the offspring of his brain like Coila, supernatural beings—like the dancers in Kirk Alloway, or national heroes—like Wallace and Bruce, with the very woods, and hills, and streams which he frequented in his boyhood. And in his mind, this assimilation was so lively and abiding, that there are few of his descriptions—descriptions in number, diversity, and picturesque features seldom equalled—on which he has not cast such sunshine of reality, that we cannot doubt that they had their prototypes in nature, and not in nature only, but in his native district. It is probable that the mind of every one of us lays the scenes of Scripture-narrative, of history, of romance, of epic poetry, in fact, of all that we hear or read of,—in the places where we spent our childhood and youth: as, for example, the Garden of Eden in our father's orchard, where there were many fruit trees; the battle of Cannæ on the wide Common, intersected with trenches; the enchanted castle of some stupendous giant, upon the hill where the ruins of a Saxon tower rise out of a thick wood. It is of some advantage, then, to the poet, that the features of the landscapes, amidst which he first dwelt, but more especially those of the neighbourhood where he went to school, should afford rich and plastic materials, which imagination can diversify a million-fold, and so accommodate as to make them the perpetual theatre

[1] James Montgomery's "Lectures on Poetry," 1833, pp. 253-5.

of all that he has been taught to remember concerning those who have lived before him, and all that he invents to increase the pleasures of memory to those that shall come after him. For it is not from the real and visible presence of things that the poet copies and displays; wherever he is, his 'heart' is still 'untravelled;' and it is from the cherished recollections of what early affected him, and could never afterwards be forgotten (having grown up into ideal beauty, grandeur, and excellence in his own mind), that he sings, and paints, and sculptures out imperishable forms of fancy, thought, and feeling. In this respect, all the compositions of Burns are homogeneous. He is in every style, in every theme, not only the patriot, the Scotchman, but the Scotchman the patriot of *Ayrshire;* so dear and indissoluble are the ties of locality to minds the most aspiring and independent.

"Burns, according to his own account, was distinguished in childhood by a very retentive memory. In the stores of that memory we discover the hidden treasures of his muse, which enabled her, with a prodigality like that of nature, to pour forth images and objects of every form, and colour, and kind, while, with an economy, like that of the most practised art, she selected and combined the endless characteristics of pleasing or magnificent scenery, with such simplicity and effect, under every aspect of sky or season, that the bard himself seems rather to be a companion pointing out to the eye the loveliness or horror of a prospect within our own horizon, than the enchanter creating a fairy scene visible only to imagination. He appears to invent nothing, while, in truth, he exercises a much higher faculty than what is frequently called invention. The genius of Burns, like his native stream, confined to his native district, reflects the scenery on the 'Banks of Ayr' with as much more truth and transparency than factitious landscapes are painted in the opaque pages of more ostentatious poets, as the reflections of trees, cottages, and animals, are more vivid and diversified in water than the shadows of the same objects are on land."

A word is due to the prose of Burns. The letters of poets include delightful specimens of our language; and the art of Pope, the pictures of Gray, the sunshine of Goldsmith, the heart-scenery of Cowper, and the nature of Scott, afford to some readers a livelier pleasure than their verses. The admirers of Burns add his name to the list. He could and did write noble English, throbbing with life, fashioned in beauty, and moving in grace. But the examples are few. His heart was seldom in the work:—"Except," he assured Mrs. Dunlop, "when prompted by friendship or gratitude, or (which happens extremely rarely) inspired by the Muse that presides over epistolary writing, I sit down, when necessitated to write, as I sit down to beat hemp."

The aversion and the effort are sufficiently conspicuous, and the way to escape them is easily learned. "Just sit down as I do," was the admonition of Goldsmith to a scanty correspondent, "and write forward till you have filled all your paper; it requires no thought; my head has no share in all I write; my heart dictates the whole." In the same temper, Southey assures his wife, after he had seen the young "Roscius,"—"I could tell you how the actor pleased and disappointed me; but the story would take time and thought; and in letter-writing I love to do nothing more than just say what is uppermost." Burns never failed when he let the affections guide his pen, and wrote the uppermost thought as it rose. But Goldsmith was not his model. In youth he had been ensnared by the "wits," and Pope became the object of his imitation. With such an artist who might contend? Burns possessed silver and gold; but only skill the most accomplished, and practice untiring, could raise the rare chasing on the metal. These endowments he wanted, and his celebrated letters are themes. They have a worse fault: his adulation is immense; and no scribbler, bribing Harley for a meal, ever outshamed the reply of Burns to the "Card" of Lord Buchan.

But I will not linger on his faults, of which some did really lean to the side of virtue. And even flattery is occasionally the heart's voice speaking loud. Burns had in him the seeds of a noble character, and the ground was good; but while he slept "his enemy came and sowed tares with the wheat," and the fruit and the weeds grew together. Jeffrey speculated on the healthful influence of pure examples and wise lessons put gently before him. The effort would have been hazardous, for his pride was full of eyes, always wakeful. He boasted of it as a necessity of life, and wished to be stretched to his full length, in the grave, that he might occupy every inch of the ground to which he was entitled. His employment sharpened his tone. A moderate independence, literary leisure, and cultivated friends might have cherished a sweeter temper of charity and meekness in the poet-gauger, weary of a weekly gallop of two hundred miles, and the inspection of yeasty barrels. And what reader of Burns will refuse to echo the voice of Wordsworth, in his sympathy and his prayer?—

"Enough of sorrow, wreck, and blight—
Think rather of those moments bright
When to the consciousness of right
His course was true,—
When Wisdom prospered in his sight,
And Virtue grew.

Yes, freely let our hearts expand,
Freely as in youth's season bland,
When side by side, his Book in hand,
We wont to stray,
Our pleasure varying at command
Of each sweet Lay.

Through busiest street and loneliest glen
Are felt the flashes of his pen;
He rules 'mid winter snows, and when
  Bees fill their hives;
Deep in the general heart of men
  His power survives.

Sweet Mercy! to the gates of Heaven
This Minstrel lead, his sins forgiven;
The rueful conflict, the heart riven
  With vain endeavour,
And memory of Earth's bitter leaven
  Effaced for ever.

But why to him confine the prayer,
When kindred thoughts and yearnings bear
On the frail heart the purest share
  With all that live?—
The best of what we do and are,
  JUST GOD FORGIVE!"

WORKS

OF

ROBERT BURNS.

POEMS.

THE TWA DOGS.[1]

A TALE.

'TWAS in that place o' Scotland's isle,
That bears the name o' Auld King Coil,[2]
Upon a bonnie day in June,
When wearing thro' the afternoon,
Twa dogs, that were na thrang[3] at hame,
Forgather'd ance upon a time.
The first I'll name, they ca'd him Cæsar,
Was keepit for his Honor's pleasure:
His hair, his size, his mouth, his lugs,[4]
Shew'd he was nane o' Scotland's dogs;
But whalpit[1] some place far abroad,
Whare sailors gang to fish for Cod.
His locked, letter'd, braw[2] brass collar,
Shew'd him the gentleman and scholar;
But though he was o' high degree,
The fient[3] a pride, na pride had he;
But wad hae spent an hour caressin,
Ev'n wi' a tinkler-gipsey's messin.[4]
At kirk or market, mill or smiddie,[5]
Nae tawted tyke,[6] tho' e'er sae duddie,
But he wad stan't, as glad to see him,
And stroan't on stanes and hillocks wi' him.
The tither was a ploughman's collie,[7]
A rhyming, ranting, raving billie,[8]
Wha for his friend and comrade had him,
And in his freaks had Luath ca'd him,
After some dog in Highland sang,[9]
Was made lang syne,—Lord knows how lang.
He was a gash[10] an' faithfu' tyke,
As ever lap a sheugh[11] or dike.
His honest, sonsie, baws'nt[12] face,
Ay gat him friends in ilka place;
His breast was white, his towzie[13] back
Weel clad wi' coat o' glossy black;
His gawcie[14] tail, wi' upward curl,

---

[1] "The Tale of Twa Dogs" was composed after the resolution of publishing was nearly taken. Robert had a dog, which he called *Luath*, that was a great favourite. The dog had been killed by the wanton cruelty of some person the night before my father's death. Robert said to me that he should like to confer such immortality as he could bestow on his old friend *Luath*, and that he had a great mind to introduce something into the book under the title of "Stanzas to the Memory of a quadruped Friend;" but this plan was given up for the Tale as it now stands. Cæsar was merely the creature of the poet's imagination, created for the purpose of holding chat with his favourite *Luath*.—G. B.

[2] A Pictish king, said to have given a name to Kyle. [3] Busy. [4] Ears.

---

[1] Whelped. [2] Handsome. [3] Fiend.
[4] A small dog. [5] A smithy.
[6] Dog with matted hair.
[7] A country cur. [8] A brother.
[9] Cuchullin's dog in "Ossian's Fingal."—R. B. [10] Wise.
[11] A ditch. [12] White-striped.
[13] Rough. [14] Large.

Hung owre his hurdies[1] wi' a swirl.
Nae doubt but they were fain o' ither,
An' unco pack an' thick thegither;
Wi' social nose whyles snuff'd and snowkit;[2]
Whyles mice and moudieworts they howkit;[3]
Whyles scour'd awa in lang excursion,
An' worry'd ither in diversion;
Until wi' daffin weary grown,
Upon a knowe they sat them down,
An' there began a lang digression
About the lords o' the creation.

CÆSAR.

I've aften wonder'd, honest Luath,
What sort o' life poor dogs like you have;
An' when the gentry's life I saw,
What way poor bodies liv'd ava.[4]
Our Laird gets in his racked rents,
His coals, his kain, an' a' his stents:[5]
He rises when he likes himsel;
His flunkies answer at the bell;
He ca's his coach; he ca's his horse;
He draws a bonnie, silken purse
As lang's my tail, whare thro' the steeks,[6]
The yellow letter'd Geordie keeks.[7]
Frae morn to e'en it's nought but toiling,
At baking, roasting, frying, boiling;
An' tho' the gentry first are stechin,[8]
Yet ev'n the ha' folk fill their pechan[9]
Wi' sauce, ragouts, and such like trashtrie,
That's little short o' downright wastrie.
Our Whipper-in, wee blastit wonner,[10]
Poor worthless elf, it eats a dinner,
Better than ony tenant man
His Honor has in a' the lan:
An' what poor cot-folk pit their painch[11] in,
I own it's past my comprehension.

LUATH.

Trowth, Cæsar, whyles they're fash't enough.

[1] Loins. [2] Scented.
[3] Digged. [4] At all.
[5] Dues of any kind. [6] Stitches.
[7] Peeps. [8] Cramming. [9] Stomach.
[10] Wonder. [11] Paunch.

A cotter howkin[1] in a sheugh,
Wi' dirty stanes biggin[2] a dyke,
Baring a quarry, and siclike,
Himsel, a wife, he thus sustains,
A smytrie[3] o' wee duddie[4] weans,[5]
An' nought but his han' darg,[6] to keep
Them right an' tight in thack an' rape.[7]
An' when they meet wi' sair disasters,
Like loss o' health, or want o' masters,
Ye maist wad think, a wee touch langer,
An' they maun starve o' cauld and hunger;
But, how it comes, I never kend yet,
They're maistly wonderfu' contented;
An' buirdly[8] chiels, an' clever hizzies,
Are bred in sic a way as this is.

CÆSAR.

But then to see how ye're negleckit,
How huff'd, an' cuff'd, an' disrespeckit!
Lord, man, our gentry care as little
For delvers, ditchers, an' sic cattle,
They gang as saucy by poor folk,
As I wad by a stinking brock.[9]
I've notic'd on our Laird's court-day,
An' mony a time my heart's been wae,
Poor tenant bodies, scant o' cash,
How they maun thole[10] a factor's snash:[11]
He'll stamp an' threaten, curse and swear,[12]
He'll apprehend them, poind[13] their gear;
While they maun stan', wi' aspect humble,
An' hear it a', an' fear and tremble!
I see how folk live that hae riches:
But surely poor folk maun be wretches.

[1] Digging. [2] Building.
[3] A numerous collection. [4] Ragged.
[5] Children. [6] Labour.
[7] Clothing necessaries.
[8] Stout-grown. [9] Badger.
[10] Endure. [11] Abuse.
[12] "My indignation yet boils at the recollection of the scoundrel factor's insolent threatening letters, which used to set us all in tears."—R. B.
[13] Seize their goods.

LUATH.

They're no sae wretched's ane wad think,
Tho' constantly on poortith's[1] brink:
They're sae accustom'd wi' the sight,
The view o't gies them little fright.
Then chance an' fortune are sae guided,
They're ay in less or mair provided;
An' tho' fatigu'd wi' close employment,
A blink o' rest's a sweet enjoyment.
The dearest comfort o' their lives,
Their grushie[2] weans an' faithfu' wives:
The prattling things are just their pride,
That sweetens a' their fire-side.
An' whyles twalpennie worth o' nappy
Can mak the bodies unco happy;
They lay aside their private cares,
To mind the Kirk and State affairs:
They'll talk o' patronage and priests,
Wi' kindling fury i' their breasts,
Or tell what new taxation's comin,
And ferlie[3] at the folk in Lon'on.
As bleak-fac'd Hallowmass[4] returns,
They get the jovial, ranting Kirns,[5]
When rural life, o' ev'ry station,
Unite in common recreation;
Love blinks, Wit slaps, an' social Mirth
Forgets there's Care upo' the earth.
That merry day the year begins,
They bar the door on frosty wins;
The nappy[6] reeks wi' mantling ream,[7]
An' sheds a heart-inspiring steam;
The luntin[8] pipe, an sneeshin mill,[9]
Are handed round wi' right guid will;
The cantie[10] auld folks crackin crouse,[11]
The young anes ranting thro' the house,—
My heart has been sae fain to see them,
That I for joy hae barkit wi' them.
Still it's owre true that ye hae said,
Sic game is now owre aften play'd.
There's monie a creditable stock
O' decent, honest fawsont[12] folk,
Are riven out baith root an' branch,
Some rascal's pridefu' greed to quench,
Wha thinks to knit himsel the faster

[1] Poverty. [2] Thriving. [3] Wonder.
[4] 31st October. [5] Harvest-suppers.
[6] Ale. [7] Cream. [8] Smoking.
[9] Snuff-box. [10] Cheerful.
[11] Conversing merrily. [12] Seemly.

In favour wi' some gentle Master,
Wha, aiblins,[1] thrang a parliamentin,
For Britain's guid his saul indentin—

CÆSAR.

Haith,[2] lad, ye little ken about it;
For Britain's guid! guid faith! I doubt it.
Say, rather, gaun as Premiers lead him,
An' saying aye or no's they bid him:
At operas an' plays parading,
Mortgaging, gambling, masquerading:
Or maybe, in a frolic daft,[3]
To Hague or Calais taks a waft,
To make a tour, an' tak a whirl,
To learn *bon ton* an' see the worl'.
There, at Vienna or Versailles,
He rives his father's auld entails;
Or by Madrid he taks the rout,
To thrum guitars, an' fecht wi' nowt;[4]
Or down Italian vista startles,
W—e-hunting amang groves o' myrtles:
Then bouses drumly[5] German water,
To mak himsel look fair and fatter,
An' clear the consequential sorrows,
Love-gifts of Carnival Signioras.
For Britain's guid! for her destruction!
Wi' dissipation, feud, an' faction!

LUATH.

Hech,[6] man! dear sirs! is that the gate
They waste sae mony a braw estate!
Are we sae foughten an' harass'd
For gear to gang that gate at last?
O would they stay aback frae courts,
An' please themsels wi' countra sports,
It wad for ev'ry ane be better,
The Laird, the Tenant, an' the Cotter!
For thae frank, rantin, ramblin billies,
Fient haet[7] o' them's ill-hearted fellows;
Except for breakin o' their timmer,[8]
Or speakin lightly o' their Limmer,[9]
Or shootin o' a hare or moor-cock,
The ne'er-a-bit they're ill to poor folk.
But will ye tell me, Master Cæsar,
Sure great folk's life's a life o' pleasure?
Nae cauld nor hunger e'er can steer[10] them,
The vera thought o't need na fear them.

[1] Perhaps. [2] A petty oath.
[3] Giddy. [4] Fight with black cattle.
[5] Muddy. [6] Oh—strange.
[7] A petty oath of negation. [8] Timber.
[9] A woman of ill character. [10] Molest.

CÆSAR.

Lord, man, were ye but whyles whare I am,
The gentles ye wad ne'er envy 'em.
It's true, they need na starve or sweat,
Thro' winter's cauld, or simmer's heat;
They've nae sair wark to craze their banes,
An' fill auld age wi' grips an' granes:[1]
But human bodies are sic fools,
For a' their colleges and schools,
That when nae real ills perplex them,
They mak enow themsels to vex them;
An' ay the less they hae to sturt[2] them,
In like proportion, less will hurt them.
A country fellow at the pleugh,
His acres till'd, he's right eneugh;
A country girl at her wheel,
Her dizzens[3] done, she's unco weel:
But Gentlemen, an' Ladies warst,
Wi' ev'n down want o' wark are curst.
They loiter, lounging, lank, an' lazy;
Tho' deil haet ails them, yet uneasy:
Their days insipid, dull, an' restless;
Their nights unquiet, lang, an' tasteless;
An' ev'n their sports, their balls an' races,
Their galloping thro' public places,
There's sic parade, sic pomp, an' art,
The joy can scarcely reach the heart.
The men cast out in party matches,
Then sowther[4] a' in deep debauches.
Ae night, they're mad wi' drink an' w—ring,
Neist day their life is past enduring.
The Ladies arm-in-arm in clusters,
As great an' gracious a' as sisters;
But hear their absent thoughts o' ither,
They're a run deils an jads thegither.[5]
Whyles, owre the wee bit cup an' platie,
They sip the scandal potion pretty;
Or lee-lang nights, wi' crabbit leuks,
Pore owre the devil's pictur'd beuks;
Stake on a chance a farmer's stackyard,
An' cheat like ony unhang'd blackguard.
There's some exception, man an' woman;
But this is Gentry's life in common.

By this, the sun was out of sight,
An' darker gloaming brought the night;
The bum-clock humm'd wi' lazy drone,
The kye[1] stood rowtin[2] i' the loan;
When up they gat, an' shook their lugs,
Rejoic'd they were na *men*, but *dogs*;
An' each took aff his several way,
Resolv'd to meet some ither day.

[1] Groans. [2] Trouble. [3] Dozens.
[4] Cement. [5] Together.

SCOTCH DRINK.

Give him strong drink, until he wink,
That's sinking in despair;
An' liquor guid to fire his bluid,
That's prest wi' grief an' care;
There let him bouse, an' deep carouse.
Wi' bumpers flowing o'er,
Till he forgets his loves or debts,
An' minds his griefs no more.

Solomon's Proverbs, xxxi. 6, 7.

Let other Poets raise a fracas
'Bout vines, an' wines, an' drunken Bacchus,
An' crabbit names an' stories wrack us,
An' grate our lug,[3]
I sing the juice Scots bear can mak us,
In glass or jug.

O thou, my Muse! guid auld Scotch Drink,
Whether thro' wimpling worms thou jink,
Or, richly brown, ream[4] owre the brink,
In glorious faem,
Inspire me, till I lisp an' wink,
To sing thy name!

Let husky Wheat the haught[5] adorn,
An' Aits[6] set up their awnie[7] horn,
An' Pease an' Beans at een or morn,
Perfume the plain,
Leeze me on thee,[8] John Barleycorn,
Thou King o' grain!

On thee aft Scotland chows her cood,[9]
In souple[10] scones,[11] the wale[12] o' food
Or tumbling in the boiling flood
Wi' kail an' beef;

[1] Cows. [2] Lowing. [3] Ear.
[4] Froth. [5] Valleys. [6] Oats
[7] Bearded. [8] An endearing phrase—I am happy in thee.
[9] Chews her cud. [10] Flexible
[11] A kind of bread. [12] The choice

But when thou pours thy strong heart's blood,
There thou shines chief.

Food fills the wame,[1] an' keeps up livin:
Tho' life's a gift no worth receivin,
When heavy-dragg'd wi' pine an' grievin;
But oil'd by thee,
The wheels o' life gae down-hill, scrievin,[2]
Wi' rattlin glee.

Thou clears the head o' doited[3] Lear:
Thou cheers the heart o' drooping Care;
Thou strings the nerves o' Labor sair,
At's weary toil:
Thou even brightens dark Despair
Wi' gloomy smile.

Aft, clad in massy siller weed,
Wi' Gentles thou erects thy head;
Yet humbly kind, in time o' need,
The poor man's wine,
His wee drap parritch, or his bread,
Thou kitchens fine.

Thou art the life o' public haunts;
But thee, what were our fairs and rants?
Ev'n godly meetings o' the saunts,
By thee inspir'd,
When gaping they besiege the tents,
Are doubly fir'd.

That merry night we get the corn in,
O sweetly, then, thou reams the horn in!
Or reekin on a New-year mornin
In cog[4] or bicker,
An' just a wee drap sp'ritual burn in,
An' gusty[5] sucker!

When Vulcan gies his bellows breath,
An' ploughmen gather wi' their graith,[6]
O rare! to see thee fizz an' freath
I' th' lugget caup![7]
Then Burnewin[8] comes on like Death
At ev'ry chaup.[9]

[1] Belly. [2] Swiftly. [3] Stupified.
[4] A wooden dish. [5] Tasteful.
[6] Gear.
[7] A wooden cup with handle.
[8] Burnewin — Burn-the-wind — the Blacksmith. [9] Blow.

Nae mercy, then, for airn[1] or steel;
The brawnie, bainie, ploughman chiel,
Brings hard owrehip,[2] wi' sturdy wheel,
The strong forehammer,
Till block an' studdie[3] ring an' reel
Wi' dinsome clamour.

When skirlin[4] weanies see the light,
Thou maks the gossips clatter bright,
How fumbling cuifs[5] their dearies slight
Wae worth the name.
Nae Howdie[6] gets a social night,
Or plack[7] frae them.

When neebors anger at a plea,
An' just as wud[8] as wud can be,
How easy can the barley-bree[9]
Cement the quarrel!
It's aye the cheapest Lawyer's fee,
To taste the barrel.

Alake! that e'er my Muse has reason
To wyte[10] her countrymen wi' treason!
But monie daily weet their weason[11]
Wi' liquors nice,
An' hardly, in a winter's season,
E'er spier[12] her price.

Wae worth that brandy, burning trash!
Fell source o' monie a pain an' brash!
Twins monie a poor, doylt, druken hash,[13]
O' half his days;
An' sends, beside, auld Scotland's cash
To her warst faes.[14]

Ye Scots, wha wish auld Scotland well,
Ye chief, to you my tale I tell,
Poor plackless devils like mysel,
It sets you ill,
Wi' bitter, dearthfu' wines to mell,
Or foreign gill.

May gravels round his blather wrench,
An' gouts torment him, inch by inch,
Wha twists his gruntle wi' a glunch
O' sour disdain,
Out owre a glass o' Whisky punch
Wi' honest men!

[1] Iron.
[2] A way of striking with their hammer on the arm. [3] Anvil. [4] Crying.
[5] Blockheads. [6] A midwife.
[7] The third part of a Scotch penny.
[8] Mad. [9] Juice. [10] Blame.
[11] Wesand. [12] Ask.
[13] A stupid fellow. [14] Enemies.

O Whisky! soul o' plays an' pranks!
Accept a Bardie's gratefu' thanks!
When wanting thee, what tuneless cranks
Are my poor verses!
Thou comes——they rattle i' their ranks
At ither's a—s!

Thee, Ferintosh![1] O sadly lost!
Scotland, lament fra coast to coast!
Now colic-grips, an' barkin hoast,
May kill us a';
For loyal Forbes' charter'd boast
Is ta'en awa!

Thae curst horse-leeches o' th' Excise,
Wha mak the Whisky stells[2] their prize:
Haud up thy han', Deil! ance, twice, thrice!
There, seize the blinkers!
An' bake them up in brunstane pies
For poor d—d drinkers.

Fortune! if thou'll but gie me still
Hale breeks,[3] a scone, an' Whisky gill,
An' rowth o' rhyme to rave at will,
Tak' a' the rest,
An' deal't about as thy blind skill
Directs the best.

THE AUTHOR'S EARNEST CRY AND PRAYER[4]

TO THE SCOTCH REPRESENTATIVES IN THE HOUSE OF COMMONS.

Dearest of Distillation! last and best—
——How art thou lost!——
Parody on Milton.

YE Irish Lords, ye Knights an' Squires,
Wha represent our brughs an' shires,
An' doucely manage our affairs
In Parliament,
To you a simple Bardie's prayers
Are humbly sent.

Alas! my roupet[1] Muse is hearse!
Your Honor's heart wi' grief 'twad pierce,
To see her sitten on her a—
Low i' the dust,
An' scriechen out prosaic verse,
An' like to brust!

Tell them whae hae the chief direction,
Scotland an' me's in great affliction,
E'er sin' they laid that curst restriction
On Aquavitæ;
An' rouse them up to strong conviction,
An' move their pity.

Stand forth, an' tell yon Premier Youth.
The honest, open, naked truth:
Tell him o' mine an' Scotland's drouth,
His servants humble:
The muckle devil blaw ye south,
If ye dissemble!

Does ony great man glunch and gloom?
Speak out, an' never fash your thoom!
Let posts an' pensions sink or soom
Wi' them wha grant 'em:
If honestly they canna come,
Far better want 'em.

In gath'rin votes you were na slack;
Now stand as tightly by your tack;
Ne'er claw your lug, an' fidge your back,
An' hum an' haw;
But raise your arm, an' tell your crack[2]
Before them a'.

Paint Scotland greetin owre her thrissle;[3]
Her mutchkin stoup as toom's a whissle:[4]
An' d—d Excisemen in a bussle,[5]
Seizin a Stell,
Triumphant crushin't like a mussel,
Or lampit[6] shell.

---

[1] From Ferintosh, in Cromartyshire, where the Forbes family long had the privilege of distilling whisky, duty free.
[2] Stills. [3] Breeches.
[4] This was written before the Act anent the Scotch Distilleries, of Session 1786; for which Scotland and the Author return their most grateful thanks. —R. B.

[1] Hoarse. [2] Story.
[3] Thistle. [4] Whistle.
[5] Bustle. [6] A kind of shell-fish.

Then on the tither hand present her,
A blackguard Smuggler, right behint her,
An' cheek-for-chow,[1] a chuffie[2] Vintner,
Colleaguing join,
Picking her pouch as bare as Winter
Of a' kind coin.

Is there, that bears the name o' Scot,
But feels his heart's bluid rising hot,
To see his poor auld Mither's pot
Thus dung in staves,
An' plunder'd o' her hindmost groat
By gallows knaves?

Alas! I'm but a nameless wight
Trode i' the mire out o' sight!
But could I like Montgomeries fight,
Or gab like Boswell,
There's some sark-necks I wad draw tight,
An' tie some hose well.

God bless your Honors, can ye see't,
The kind, auld, cantie Carlin greet,
An' no get warmly to your feet,
An' gar them hear it!
An' tell them, wi' a patriot-heat,
Ye winna bear it!

Some o' you nicely ken the laws,
To round the period an' pause,
An' with rhetoric clause on clause
To mak harangues;
Then echo thro' Saint Stephen's wa's
Auld Scotland's wrangs.

Dempster,[3] a true blue Scot I'se warran;
Thee, aith[4]-detesting, chaste Kilkerran;[5]
An' that glib-gabbet[6] Highland Baron,
The Laird o' Graham;[7]
An' ane, a chap that's d—d auldfarran,[8]
Dundas his name.

Erskine, a spunkie[9] Norland billie;
True Campbells, Frederick an' Ilay;

[1] Side by side. [2] Fat-faced.
[3] George Dempster, Esq., of Dunnichen, in Forfarshire. [4] Oath.
[5] Sir Adam Ferguson.—R. B.
[6] Quick and smooth-speaking.
[7] The Duke of Montrose.—R. B.
[8] Sagacious. [9] Fiery.

An' Livingstone, the bauld Sir Willie;
An' monie ithers,
Whom auld Demosthenes, or Tully,
Might own for brithers.

Arouse, my boys! exert your mettle,
To get auld Scotland back her kettle;
Or faith! I'll wad my new pleugh-pettle,[1]
Ye'll see't or lang,
She'll teach you, wi' a reekin whittle,
Anither sang.

This while she's been in crankous[2] mood,
Her lost Militia fir'd her bluid;
(Deil na they never mair do guid,
Play'd her that pliskie!)[3]
An' now she's like to rin red-wud[4]
About her Whisky.

An' Lord, if ance they pit her till't,[5]
Her tartan petticoat she'll kilt,
An' durk an' pistol at her belt,
She'll tak the streets,
An' rin her whittle to the hilt,
I' th' first she meets!

For God's sake, Sirs! then speak her fair,
An' straik[6] her cannie wi' the hair,
An' to the muckle house repair,
Wi' instant speed,
An' strive, wi' a' your wit and lear,[7]
To get remead.

Yon ill-tongu'd tinkler, Charlie Fox,
May taunt you wi' his jeers an' mocks;
But gie him't het,[8] my hearty cocks!
E'en cowe the cadie![9]
An' send him to his dicing-box,
An' sportin lady.

Tell yon guid bluid o' auld Boconnock's
I'll be his debt twa mashlum bonnocks,[10]
An' drink his health in auld Nanse Tinnock's[11]
Nine times a-week,

[1] Plough-staff. [2] Fretful.
[3] Trick. [4] Distracted.
[5] To it. [6] Stroke. [7] Learning.
[8] Hot. [9] Terrify the young fellow.
[10] Thick cakes of mixed corn.
[11] A worthy old hostess of the Author's in Mauchline, where he sometimes studies politics over a glass of guid auld Scotch Drink.—R. B.

If he some scheme, like tea an' winnocks,[1]
Wad kindly seek.

Could he some commutation broach,
I'll pledge my aith in guid braid Scotch,
He need na fear their foul reproach
Nor erudition,
Yon mixtie-maxtie[2] queer hotch-potch,
The Coalition.

Auld Scotland has a raucle[3] tongue;
She's just a devil wi' a rung;[4]
An' if she promise auld or young
To tak their part,
Tho' by the neck she should be strung,
She'll no desert.

An' now, ye chosen Five-and-Forty,
May still your Mither's heart support ye;
Then, though a Minister grow dorty,[5]
An' kick your place,
Ye'll snap your fingers, poor an' hearty,
Before his face.

God bless your Honors a' your days,
Wi' sowps o' kail an' brats o' claise,[6]
In spite o' a' the thievish kaes[7]
That haunt St Jamie's!
Your humble Poet sings an' prays
While Rab his name is.

POSTSCRIPT.

Let half-starv'd slaves, in warmer skies
See future vines, rich-clust'ring, rise;
Their lot auld Scotland ne'er envies,
But blyth an' frisky,
She eyes her freeborn, martial boys,
Tak aff their Whisky.

What tho' their Phœbus kinder warms,
While fragrance blooms an' beauty charms!
When wretches range, in famish'd swarms,
The scented groves,
Or, hounded forth, dishonour arms
In hungry droves.

Their gun's a burden on their shouther;
They downa bide the stink o' powther;

[1] Windows. [2] Confusedly mixed. [3] Fearless. [4] Cudgel. [5] Saucy. [6] Clothes. [7] Daws.

Their bauldest thought's a hank'ring swither[1]
To stan' or rin,
Till skelp—a shot—they're aff, a' throw-ther,[2]
To save their skin.

But bring a Scotsman frae his hill,
Clap in his cheek a Highland gill,
Say, such is royal George's will,
An' there's the foe,
He has nae thought but how to kill
Twa at a blow.

Nae cauld, faint-hearted doubtings tease him:
Death comes, wi' fearless eye he sees him;
Wi' bluidy han' a welcome gies him;
An' when he fa's,
His latest draught o' breathin lea'es him
In faint huzzas.

Sages their solemn een may steek,[3]
An' raise a philosophic reek,[4]
An' physically causes seek,
In clime an' season;
But tell me Whisky's name in Greek,
I'll tell the reason.

Scotland, my auld, respected Mither!
Tho' whyles ye moistify your leather,
Till whare ye sit, on craps o' heather,
Ye tine[5] your dam;
Freedom and Whisky gang thegither!
Tak aff your dram!

THE LASSES OF TARBOLTON.

WRITTEN IN 1781, IN THE POET'S 23RD YEAR.

In Tarbolton, ye ken, there are proper young men,
And proper young lasses, and a', man;
But ken ye the Ronalds that live in the Bennals,
They carry the gree[6] frae them a', man.

Their father's a laird, and weel he can spare't,
Braid money to tocher[7] them a', man,

[1] Hesitation. [2] Pell-mell. [3] Shut. [4] Smoke. [5] Lose. [6] Palm. [7] Portion.

To proper young men, he'll clink in the hand
Gowd guineas a hunder or twa, man.

There's ane they ca' Jean, I'll warrant ye've seen
As bonny a lass or as braw, man;
But for sense and guid taste she'll vie wi' the best,
And a conduct that beautifies a', man.

The charms o' the min', the langer they shine,
The mair admiration they draw, man;
While peaches and cherries, and roses and lilies,
They fade and they wither awa, man.

If ye be for Miss Jean, tak this frae a frien',
A hint o' a rival or twa, man,
The Laird o' Blackbyre wad gang through the fire,
If that wad entice her awa, man.

The Laird o' Braehead has been on his speed,
For mair than a towmond or twa, man;
The Laird o' the Ford will straught on a board,
If he canna get her at a', man.

Then Anna comes in, the pride o' her kin,
The boast of our bachelors a', man;
Sae sonsy and sweet, sae fully complete,
She steals our affections awa, man.

If I should detail the pick and the wale
O' lasses that live here awa, man,
The fault wad be mine, if they didna shine,
The sweetest and best o' them a', man.

I lo'e her mysel, but darena weel tell,
My poverty keeps me in awe, man,
For making o' rhymes, and working at times,
Does little or naething at a', man.

Yet I wadna choose to let her refuse,
Nor hae 't in her power to say na, man;
For though I be poor, unnoticed, obscure,
My stomach's as proud as them a', man.

Though I canna ride in weel-booted pride,
And flee o'er the hills like a craw, man,
I can haud up my head with the best o' the breed,
Though fluttering ever so braw, man.

My coat and my vest, they are Scotch o' the best,
O' pairs o' guid breeks I hae twa, man,
And stockings and pumps to put on my stumps,
And ne'er a wrang steek in them a', man.

My sarks they are few, but five o' them new,
Twal' hundred, as white as the snaw, man,
A ten-shilling hat, a Holland cravat;
There are no mony poets sae braw, man.

I never had frien's weel stockit in means,
To leave me a hundred or twa, man;
Nae weel-tocher'd aunts, to wait on their drants,
And wish them in hell for it a', man.

I never was cannie for hoarding o' money,
Or claughlin't[1] together at a', man;
I've little to spend, and naething to lend,
But deevil a shilling I awe, man.

THE HOLY FAIR.[2]

A robe of seeming truth and trust
Hid crafty Observation;
And secret hung, with poison'd crust,
The dirk of Defamation:

---

[1] Gathering.

[2] Holy Fair is a common phrase in the West of Scotland for a sacramental occasion.—R. B.

Fergusson, in his "Hallow Fair" of

A mask that like the gorget show'd,
Dye-varying on the pigeon;
And for a mantle large and broad,
He wrapt him in Religion.
Hypocrisy à-la-mode.

UPON a simmer Sunday morn,
When Nature's face is fair,
I walked forth to view the corn,
An' snuff the caller[1] air.
The risin sun, owre Galston[2] muirs,
Wi' glorious light was glintin;
The hares were hirplin[3] down the furs,
The lav'rocks[4] they were chantin
Fu' sweet that day.

As lightsomely I glowr'd abroad,
To see a scene sae gay,
Three Hizzies, early at the road,
Cam skelpin[5] up the way.
Twa had manteeles o' dolefu' black,
But ane wi' lyart[6] linin;
The third, that gaed a wee a-back,
Was in the fashion shinin,
Fu' gay that day.

The twa appear'd like sisters twin,
In feature, form, an' claes;
Their visage wither'd, lang, an' thin,
An' sour as ony slaes:[7]
The third cam up, hap-step-an'-lowp,
As light as ony lambie,[8]
An' wi' a curchie low did stoop,
As soon as e'er she saw me,
Fu' kind that day.

Wi' bonnet aff, quoth I, "Sweet lass,
I think ye seem to ken me;
I'm sure I've seen that bonnie face,
But yet I canna name ye."
Quo' she, an' laughing as she spak,
An' taks me by the hands,

Edinburgh, I believe, furnished a hint and title of the plan of the "Holy Fair." The farcical scene the poet there describes was often a favourite field of his observation, and the most of the incidents he mentions had actually passed before his eyes.—G. B.

[1] Fresh.
[2] The adjoining parish to Mauchline.
[3] Creeping. [4] Larks.
[5] Tripping. [6] Gray.
[7] Sloes. [8] Lamb.

"Ye, for my sake, hae gi'en the feck
Of a' the ten commands
A screed[1] some day.

"My name is Fun—your cronie dear,
The nearest friend ye hae;
An' this is Superstition here,
An' that's Hypocrisy.
I'm gaun to Mauchline Holy Fair,
To spend an hour in daffin:[2]
Gin ye'll go there, yon runkl'd[3] pair,
We will get famous laughin
At them this day."

Quoth I, "With a' my heart, I'll do't;
I'll get my Sunday sark[4] on,
An meet you on the holy spot;
Faith, we'se hae fine remarkin!"
Then I gaed hame at crowdie-time,[5]
An' soon I made me ready;
For roads were clad, frae side to side,
Wi' monie a wearie bodie,
In droves that day.

Here farmers gash,[6] in ridin graith
Gaed hoddin[7] by their cotters;
There, swankies[8] young, in braw braid-claith,
Are springin owre the gutters.
The lasses, skelpin barefit, thrang,
In silks an' scarlets glitter;
Wi' sweet-milk cheese, in monie a whang,[9]
An' farls,[10] bak'd wi' butter,
Fu' crump that day.

When by the plate we set our nose,
Weel heaped up wi' ha'pence,
A greedy glowr Black Bonnet[11] throws,
An' we maun draw our tippence.
Then in we go to see the show,
On ev'ry side they're gath'rin,
Some carryin dales, some chairs an stools,
An' some are busy bleth'rin[12]
Right loud that day.

---

[1] A rent. [2] Merriment.
[3] Wrinkled. [4] Shirt.
[5] Breakfast-time. [6] Wise.
[7] The motion of a countryman riding on a cart-horse.
[8] Strapping young fellows.
[9] String. [10] Cakes of bread.
[11] The Elder who holds the alms-dish. [12] Talking idly.

Here stands a shed to fend the show'rs,
  An' screen our countra gentry,
There, racer Jess, an' twa-three w——s,
  Are blinkin at the entry.
Here sits a raw o' tittlin jades,[1]
  Wi' heaving breast an' bare neck,
An' there a batch o' wabster[2] lads,
  Blackguarding fra Kilmarnock
      For fun this day.

Here, some are thinkin on their sins,
  An' some upo' their claes;
Ane curses feet that fyl'd[3] his shins,
  Anither sighs an' prays:
On this hand sits a chosen swatch,[4]
  Wi' screw'd up, grace-proud faces;
On that a set o' chaps, at watch,
  Thrang winkin on the lasses
      To chairs that day.

O happy is that man an' blest!
  Nae wonder that it pride him!
Wha's ain dear lass, that he likes best,
  Comes clinkin down beside him!
Wi' arm repos'd on the chair back,
  He sweetly does compose him;
Which, by degrees, slips round her neck
  An's loof[5] upon her bosom
      Unkend that day.

Now a' the congregation o'er
  Is silent expectation;
For Moodie[6] speels[7] the holy door,
  Wi' tidings o' damnation.
Should Hornie, as in ancient days,
  'Mang sons o' God present him,
The vera sight o' Moodie's face,
  To's ain het hame had sent him
      Wi' fright that day.

Hear how he clears the points o' faith
  Wi' rattlin an' thumpin!
Now meekly calm, now wild in wrath,
  He's stampin an' he's jumpin!
His lengthen'd chin, his turn'd-up snout,
  His eldritch[8] squeel an' gestures,
O how they fire the heart devout,
  Like cantharidian plasters,
      On sic a day!

---

1 Whispering. 2 Weaver.
3 Soiled. 4 Sample.
5 Palm of the hand.
6 Minister of Riccarton. 7 Climbs.
8 Unearthly.

But, hark! the tent has chang'd its voice;
  There's peace and rest nae langer:
For a' the real judges rise,
  They canna sit for anger.
Smith[1] opens out his cauld harangues,
  On practice and on morals;
An' aff the godly pour in thrangs,
  To gie the jars an' barrels
      A lift that day.

What signifies his barren shine
  Of moral pow'rs an' reason?
His English style, an' gesture fine,
  Are a' clean out o' season.
Like Socrates or Antonine,
  Or some auld pagan Heathen,
The moral man he does define,
  But ne'er a word o' faith in
      That's right that day.

In guid time comes an antidote
  Against sic poison'd nostrum;
For Peebles,[2] frae the Water-fit,
  Ascends the holy rostrum:
See, up he's got the word o' God,
  An' meek an' mim[3] has view'd it,
While Common Sense has ta'en the road,
  An' aff, an' up the Cowgate,[4]
      Fast, fast, that day.

Wee Miller,[5] neist, the Guard relieves,
  An' Orthodoxy raibles,[6]
Tho' in his heart he weel believes,
  An' thinks it auld wives' fables:
But, faith! the birkie[7] wants a Manse,
  So cannilie he hums them;
Altho' his carnal wit an' sense
  Like hafflins-ways o'ercomes him
      At times that day.

Now, butt an' ben,[8] the Change-house fills,
  Wi' yill-caup[9] Commentators:
Here's crying out for bakes[10] an' gills,
  An' there the pint-stowp clatters;

---

1 Minister of Galston.
2 Minister of Newtown-upon-Ayr, of which the Water-fit was another name.
3 Prim. 4 A street so called, which faces the *tent* in [Mauchline.]—R. B.
5 Assistant-preacher at Auchenleck.
6 Rattles nonsense. 7 Clever fellow.
8 Kitchen and parlour.
9 Ale-cup. 10 Biscuits.

While thick an' thrang, an' loud an' lang,
Wi' logic, an' wi' Scripture,
They raise a din, that, in the end,
Is like to breed a rupture
O' wrath that day.

Leeze me on Drink! it gie's us mair
Than either School or College:
It kindles Wit, it waukens Lair,
It pangs[1] us fou o' Knowledge.
Be't whisky gill, or penny wheep,
Or ony stronger potion,
It never fails, on drinking deep,
To kittle[2] up our notion
By night or day.

The lads an' lasses, blythely bent
To mind baith saul an' body,
Sit round the table, weel content,
An' steer[3] about the toddy.
On this ane's dress, an' that ane's leuk,
They're makin observations;
While some are cozie i' the neuk,
An' formin assignations
To meet some day.

But now the Lord's ain trumpet touts,
Till a' the hills are rairin,
An' echoes back return the shouts;
Black Russel[4] is na spairin:
His piercing words, like Highlan swords,
Divide the joints an' marrow;
His talk o' Hell, whare devils dwell,
Our vera "sauls does harrow"[5]
Wi' fright that day.

A vast, unbottom'd, boundless pit,
Fill'd fou o' lowin[6] brunstane,
Wha's raging flame, an' scorching heat,
Wad melt the hardest whun-stane![7]
The half asleep start up wi' fear,
An' think they hear it roarin,
When presently it does appear,
'Twas but some neebor snorin
Asleep that day.

[1] Crams. [2] Tickle. [3] Stir.
[4] Minister of Kilmarnock, and described as equally awful in look and language.
[5] Shakspeare's Hamlet.—R. B.
[6] Flaming. [7] Whinstone.

'Twad be owre lang a tale, to tell
How monie stories past,
An' how they crowded to the yill,
When they were a' dismist:
How drink gaed round, in cogs an' caups,
Amang the furms and benches;
An' cheese an' bread, frae women's laps,
Was dealt about in lunches
An' dawds that day.

In comes a gaucie,[1] gash Guidwife,
An' sits down by the fire,
Syne draws her kebbuck[2] an' her knife,
The lasses they are shyer.
The auld Guidmen, about the grace,
Frae side to side they bother,
Till some ane by his bonnet lays,
An' gi'es them' t' like a tether,
Fu' lang that day.

Waesucks![3] for him that gets nae lass,
Or lasses that hae naething!
Sma' need has he to say a grace,
Or melvie[4] his braw claithing!
O Wives be mindfu', ance yoursel
How bonnie lads ye wanted,
An' dinna, for a kebbuck-heel,
Let lasses be affronted
On sic a day!

Now Clinkumbell, wi' rattling tow,
Begins to jow[5] an' croon;
Some swagger hame, the best they dow,[6]
Some wait the afternoon.
At slaps[7] the billies halt a blink,
Till lasses strip their shoon:
Wi' faith an' hope, an' love an' drink,
They're a' in famous tune
For crack that day.

How monie hearts this day converts
O' sinners and o' lasses!
Their hearts o' stane, gin night, are gane
As saft as ony flesh is.
There's some are fou o' love divine,
There's some are fou o' brandy;

[1] Jolly. [2] Cheese. [3] Waes me!
[4] Soil. [5] To peal or roar.
[6] They can. [7] Gates.

An' monie jobs that day begin,
May end in Houghmagandie [1]
Some ither day. [2]

STANZAS ON THE DEATH OF A FAVOURITE DAUGHTER. [3]

WRITTEN IN 1792.

OH! sweet be thy sleep in the land of the grave,
My dear little angel, for ever;
For ever!—oh no! let not man be a slave
His hopes from existence to sever.

Tho' cold be the clay where thou pillow'st thy head
In the dark mansions of sorrow,
The spring shall return to thy low narrow bed,
Like the beam of the day-star to-morrow.

The flower-stem shall bloom like thy sweet seraph form
Ere the Spoiler had nipt thee in blossom;
When thou shrunk from the scowl of the loud winter storm,
And nestled thee close to that bosom.

Oh, still I behold thee all lovely in death,
Reclined on the lap of thy mother,
When the tear trickled bright, when the short, stifled breath,
Told how dear you were aye to each other.

My child, thou art gone to the home of thy rest,
Where suffering no longer can harm ye,
Where the songs of the good, where the hymns of the blest,
Thro' an endless existence shall charm thee:

While he, thy fond parent, must sighing sojourn
Thro' the dire desert regions of sorrow,
O'er the hope and misfortune of being to mourn,
And sigh for life's latest morrow.

[1] Fornication.

[2] Sharp diseases require sharp remedies; and Burns' ridicule is said to have been of considerable use.

[3] The death of his beloved child took place during his temporary absence from home, on which occasion the above heart-speaking lines were written.

DEATH AND DOCTOR HORNBOOK. [1]

A TRUE STORY.

SOME books are lies frae end to end,
And some great lies were never penn'd:
Ev'n Ministers, they hae been kenn'd,
In holy rapture,
A rousing whid, [2] at times to vend,
Wi' faith an' hope, an' love an' drink,
And nail't wi' Scripture.

But this that I am going to tell,
Which lately on a night befell,
Is just as true's the Deil's in hell
Or Dublin city:
That e'er he nearer comes oursel
'S a muckle pity.

The Clachan yill had made me canty,
I wasna fou, but just had plenty:
I stacher'd [3] whyles, but yet took tent ay
To free the ditches;
An' hillocks, stanes, an' bushes, kenn'd ay
Frae' ghaists an' witches.

The rising moon began to glowr
The distant Cumnock hills out-owre;
To count her horns, wi' a' my pow'r,
I set mysel;
But whether she had three or four,
I cou'd na tell.

I was come round about the hill,
And todlin down on Willie's mill,
Setting my staff, wi' a' my skill,
To keep me sicker; [4]
Tho' leeward whyles, against my will,
I took a bicker. [5]

[1] John Wilson, schoolmaster of Tarbolton, who excited the anger of Burns by talking of his medical skill. Wilson sold medicine and gave advice gratis.

[2] Fib. [3] Staggered.

[4] Steady. [5] A short course.

I there wi' Something did forgather,[1]
That put me in an eerie swither;[2]
An awfu' scythe, out-owre ae shouther,
Clear-dangling, hang:
A three-taed leister[3] on the ither
Lay, large an' lang.

Its stature seem'd lang Scotch ells twa,
The queerest shape that e'er I saw,
For fient a wame[4] it had ava,
And then its shanks,
They were as thin, as sharp an' sma'
As cheeks o' branks.[5]

"Guid-een," quo' I; "Friend! hae ye been mawin,
When ither folk are busy sawin?"[6]
It seem'd to mak a kind o' stan',
But naething spak;
At length, says I, "Friend, whare ye gaun,
Will ye go back?"

It spak right howe[7]—"My name is Death,
But be na fley'd."—Quoth I, "Guid faith,
Ye're maybe come to stap my breath;
But tent[8] me, billie;
I red ye weel, tak care o' skaith,[9]
See, there's a gully!"[10]

"Gudeman," quo' he, "put up your whittle,
I'm no design'd to try its mettle;
But if I did, I wad be kittle[11]
To be mislear'd,[12]
I wad na mind it, no that spittle
Out-owre my beard."

"Weel, weel!" says I, "a bargain be't;
Come, gies your hand, an' sae we're gree't;
We'll ease our shanks an' tak a seat,
Come, gies your news,

[1] Meet. [2] Frighted wavering.
[3] Three-pronged dart. [4] Belly.
[5] A kind of wooden curb.
[6] This rencounter happened in seed-time, 1785.—R. B.
[7] Hollow. [8] Be careful. [9] Damage.
[10] A large knife. [11] Difficult.
[12] "Put out of my art."—*Chambers.*

This while[1] ye hae been mony a gate,
At mony a house."

"Ay, ay!" quo' he, an' shook his head,
"It's e'en a lang, lang time, indeed,
Sin' I began to nick the thread,
An' choke the breath:
Folk maun do something for their bread,
An' sae maun Death.

"Sax thousand years are near hand fled,
Sin' I was to the butching bred,
An' mony a scheme in vain's been laid
To stap or scaur me;
Till ane Hornbook's[2] ta'en up the trade,
An' faith, he'll waur[3] me.

"Ye ken Jock Hornbook i' the Clachan,[4]
Deil mak his king's-hood in a spleuchan![5]
He's grown sae well acquaint wi' Buchan[6]
An' ither chaps,
The weans haud out their fingers laughin
And pouk my hips.

"See, here's a scythe, and there's a dart,
They hae pierc'd mony a gallant heart;
But Doctor Hornbook, wi' his art
And cursed skill,
Has made them baith no worth a ——
D—d haet they'll kill.

"'Twas but yestreen, nae farther gaen,
I threw a noble throw at ane;
Wi' less, I'm sure, I've hundreds slain:
But deil-ma-care,
It just play'd dirl[7] on the bane,
But did nae mair.

[1] An epidemical fever was then raging in that country.—R. B.
[2] This gentleman, Dr. Hornbook, is, professionally, a brother of the Sovereign Order of the Ferula; but, by intuition and inspiration, is at once an apothecary, surgeon, and physician.—R. B.
[3] Worse. [4] Small village.
[5] Tobacco-pouch.
[6] "Buchan's Domestic Medicine."—R. B. [7] A slight stroke.

"Hornbook was by, wi' ready art,
And had sae fortify'd the part,
That when I looked to my dart,
It was sae blunt,
Fient haet o't wad hae pierc'd the heart
Of a kail-runt.[1]

"I drew my scythe in sic a fury,
I near-hand cowpit[2] wi' my hurry,
But yet the bauld Apothecary
Withstood the shock;
I might as weel hae try'd a quarry
O' hard whin rock.

"And then, a' doctor's saws and whittles,
Of a' dimensions, shapes, an' mettles,
A' kinds o' boxes, mugs, an' bottles,
He's sure to hae;
Their Latin names as fast he rattles
As A B C.

"Calces o' fossils, earths, and trees;
True Sal-marinum o' the seas;
The Farina of beans and pease,
He has't in plenty;
Aqua-fontis, what you please,
He can content ye.

"Forbye some new, uncommon weapons,
Urinus Spiritus of capons;
Or Mite-horn shavings, filings, scrapings,
Distill'd *per se;*
Sal-alkali o' Midge-tail clippings,
And mony mae."

"Waes me for Johnny Ged's Hole[3] now,"
Quo' I, "if that thae news be true!
His braw calf-ward whare gowans[4] grew,
Sae white and bonnie,
Nae doubt they'll rive it wi' the plew;
They'll ruin Johnnie!"

The creature grain'd an eldritch laugh,
And says, "Ye needna yoke the pleugh,
Kirk-yards will soon be till'd eneugh,
Tak ye nae fear:

[1] A cabbage-root. [2] Tumbled.
[3] The grave-digger.—R. B.
[4] Daisies.

They'll a' be trench'd wi' mony a sheugh[1]
In twa-three year.

"Whare I kill'd ane a fair strae-death,[2]
By loss o' blood or want o' breath,
This night I'm free to tak my aith,
That Hornbook's skill
Has clad a score i' their last claith,
By drap and pill.

"An honest Wabster[3] to his trade,
Whase wife's twa nieves were scarce weel-bred,
Gat tippence-worth to mend her head,
When it was sair;
The wife slade[4] cannie to her bed,
But ne'er spak mair.

"A countra Laird had ta'en the batts,[5]
Or some curmurring[6] in his guts,
His only son for Hornbook sets,
An' pays him well.
The lad, for twa guid gimmer-pets,[7]
Was Laird himsel.

"A bonnie lass, ye kend her name,
Some ill-brewn drink had hov'd[8] her wame:
She trusts hersel, to hide the shame
In Hornbook's care:
Horn sent her aff to her lang hame,
To hide it there.

"That's just a swatch[9] o' Hornbook's way;
Thus goes he on from day to day,
Thus does he poison, kill, an' slay,
An's weel pay'd for't;
Yet stops me o' my lawfu' prey,
Wi' his d—d dirt.

"But, hark! I'll tell you of a plot,
Tho' dinna ye be speaking o't;
I'll nail the self-conceited Sot
As dead's a herrin;
Niest time we meet, I'll wad[10] a groat,
He gets his fairin!"

But just as he began to tell,
The aulk kirk-hammer strak the bell

[1] Ditch. [2] A death in bed.
[3] Weaver. [4] Did slide.
[5] Bots. [6] A rumbling.
[7] Two-year old sheep. [8] Swelled.
[9] Sample. [10] Bet.

Some wee short hour ayont the twal,
Which rais'd us baith:
I took the way that pleas'd mysel,
And sae did Death.

THE BRIGS OF AYR.

A POEM.

INSCRIBED TO JOHN BALLANTYNE, ESQ., OF AYR.

THE simple Bard, rough at the rustic plough,
Learning his tuneful trade from ev'ry bough;
The chanting linnet, or the mellow thrush;
Hailing the setting sun, sweet, in the green thorn bush;
The soaring lark, the perching red-breast shrill,
Or deep-ton'd plovers, grey, wild-whistling o'er the hill;
Shall he, nurst in the Peasant's lowly shed,
To hardy independence bravely bred,
By early poverty to hardship steel'd,
And train'd to arms in stern Misfortune's field:
Shall he be guilty of their hireling crimes,
The servile, mercenary Swiss of rhymes?
Or labour hard the panegyric close,
With all the venal soul of dedicating Prose?
No! though his artless strains he rudely sings,
And throws his hand uncouthly o'er the strings,
He glows with all the spirit of the Bard,
Fame, honest fame, his great, his dear reward.
Still, if some Patron's gen'rous care he trace,
Skill'd in the secret, to bestow with grace;
When Ballantyne befriends his humble name,
And hands the rustic Stranger up to fame,
With heartfelt throes his grateful bosom swells,
The godlike bliss, to give, alone excels.

'Twas when the stacks get on their winter-hap,
And thack[1] and rape secure the toil-won crap;
Potatoe-bings[2] are snugged up frae skaith[3]
O' coming Winter's biting, frosty breath;
The bees, rejoicing o'er their summer toils,
Unnumber'd buds an' flow'rs' delicious spoils,
Seal'd up with frugal care in massive waxen piles,
Are doom'd by man, that tyrant o'er the weak,
The death o' devils, smoor'd[4] wi' brimstone reek;
The thund'ring guns are heard on ev'ry side,
The wounded coveys, reeling, scatter wide;
The feather'd field-mates, bound by Nature's tie,
Sires, mothers, children, in one carnage lie:
(What warm, poetic heart, but inly bleeds,
And execrates man's savage, ruthless deeds!)
Nae mair the flow'r in field or meadow springs;
Nae mair the grove with airy concert rings,
Except perhaps the Robin's whistling glee,
Proud o' the height o' some bit half-lang tree:
The hoary morns precede the sunny days,
Mild, calm, serene, wide spreads the noontide blaze,
While thick the gossamour waves wanton in the rays.

'Twas in that season, when a simple Bard,

---

[1] Thatch. [2] Potato heaps.
[3] Injury. [4] Smothered.

Unknown and poor, simplicity's reward,
Ae night, within the ancient brugh of Ayr,
By whim inspir'd, or haply prest wi' care,
He left his bed and took his wayward rout,
And down by Simpson's[1] wheel'd the left about:
(Whether impell'd by all-directing Fate,
To witness what I after shall narrate;
Or whether, rapt in meditation high,
He wander'd out he knew not where nor why:)
The drowsy Dungeon clock[2] had number'd two,
And Wallace Tow'r[3] had sworn the fact was true;
The tide-swoln Firth, wi' sullen-sounding roar,
Through the still night dash'd hoarse along the shore:
All else was hush'd as Nature's closed e'e;
The silent moon shone high o'er tow'r and tree:
The chilly frost, beneath the silver beam,
Crept, gently-crusting, owre the glittering stream.—
When, lo! on either hand the list'ning Bard,
The clanging sugh[4] of whistling wings is heard;
Two dusky forms dart thro' the midnight air,
Swift as the gos[5] drives on the wheeling hare;
Ane on th' Auld Brig his airy shape uprears,
The ither flutters o'er the rising piers:
Our warlock Rhymer instantly descry'd
The Sprites that owre the Brigs of Ayr preside.
(That Bards are second-sighted is nae joke,

[1] A noted tavern at the Auld Brig End.—R. B.
[2] In the old prison of Ayr.
[3] Which formerly stood in the High-street.
[4] A rushing sound of wind.
[5] The gos-hawk, or falcon.—R. B.

And ken the lingo of the sp'ritual folk;
Fays, Spunkies, Kelpies, a', they can explain them,
And even the vera deils they brawly ken them.)
Auld Brig appear' d o' ancient Pictish race,
The vera wrinkles Gothic in his face:
He seem'd as he wi' Time had warstl'd lang,
Yet, teughly[1] doure, he bade an unco bang.
New Brig was buskit,[2] in a braw new coat,
That he, at Lon'on, frae ane Adams got;
In's hand five taper staves as smooth's a bead,
Wi' virls an' whirlygigums[3] at the head.
The Goth was stalking round with anxious search,
Spying the time-worn flaws in ev'ry arch;
It chanc'd his new-come neebor took his e'e,
And e'en a vex'd and angry heart had he!
Wi' thieveless sneer to see his modish mien,
He down the water, gies him this guid-een:[4]—

AULD BRIG.

I doubt na, Frien', ye'll think ye're nae sheep-shank,
Ance ye were streekit owre frae bank to bank!
But gin ye be a brig as auld as me,
Tho' faith! that date, I doubt, ye'll never see;
There'll be, if that day come, I'll wad a bodle,[5]
Some fewer whigmeleeries[6] in your noddle.

NEW BRIG.

Auld Vandal, ye but show your little mense,[7]
Just much about it wi' your scanty sense;

[1] Toughly stout. [2] Dressed.
[3] Useless ornaments.
[4] Good evening. [5] A small gold coin.
[6] Fancies. [7] Good manners.

Will your poor, narrow foot-path of a street,
Where twa wheel-barrows tremble when they meet,
Your ruin'd, formless bulk o' stane and lime,
Compare wi' bonnie Brigs o' modern time?
There's men of taste wou'd tak the Ducat-stream,[1]
Tho' they should cast the vera sark and swim,
Ere they would grate their feelings wi' the view
O' sic an ugly, Gothic hulk as you.

AULD BRIG.

Conceited gowk![2] puff'd up wi' windy pride!
This mony a year I've stood the flood an' tide;
And tho' wi' crazy eild I'm sair forfairn,[3]
I'll be a Brig, when ye're a shapeless cairn!
As yet ye little ken about the matter,
But twa-three winters will inform ye better.
When heavy, dark, continued, a'-day rains,
Wi' deepening deluges o'erflow the plains:
When from the hills where springs the brawling Coil,
Or stately Lugar's mossy fountains boil,
Or where the Greenock winds his moorland course,
Or haunted Garpal[4] draws his feeble source,
Arous'd by blust'ring winds an' spotting thowes,[5]

[1] A noted ford, just above the Auld Brig.—R. B.
[2] A term of contempt; fool.
[3] Distressed.
[4] The banks of Garpal Water is one of the few places in the West of Scotland where those fancy-scaring beings, known by the name of ghaists, still continue pertinaciously to inhabit.—R. B.
[5] Thaws.

In mony a torrent down his snaw-broo[1] rowes;
While crashing ice, borne on the roaring speat,[2]
Sweeps dams, an' mills, an' brigs, a' to the gate;
And from Glenbuck,[3] down to the Ratton-key,[4]
Auld Ayr is just one lengthen'd, tumbling sea;
Then down ye'll hurl, deil nor ye never rise!
And dash the gumlie[5] jaups[6] up to the pouring skies.
A lesson sadly teaching, to your cost,
That Architecture's noble art is lost!

NEW BRIG.

Fine Architecture, trowth, I needs must say't o't!
The Lord be thankit that we've tint the gate o't![7]
Gaunt, ghastly, ghaist-alluring edifices,
Hanging with threat'ning jut, like precipices:
O'er-arching, mouldy, gloom-inspiring coves,
Supporting roofs fantastic, stony groves:
Windows and doors in nameless sculptures drest,
With order, symmetry, or taste unblest;
Forms like some bedlam Statuary's dream,
The craz'd creations of misguided whim;
Forms might be worshipp'd on the bended knee,
And still the second dread command be free,
Their likeness is not found on earth, in air, or sea.
Mansions that would disgrace the building taste
Of any mason reptile, bird, or beast;

[1] Snow-water. [2] Torrent.
[3] The source of the River Ayr.—R. B.
[4] A small landing-place above the large key.—R. B.
[5] Muddy. [6] Jerks of water.
[7] Lost the way of it.

Fit only for a doited monkish race,
Or frosty maids forsworn the dear embrace;
Or cuifs [1] of later times, wha held the notion
That sullen gloom was sterling, true devotion;
Fancies that our guid Brugh [2] denies protection,
And soon may they expire, unblest with resurrection!

AULD BRIG.

O ye, my dear-remember'd, ancient yearlings,[3]
Were ye but here to share my wounded feelings!
Ye worthy Proveses, an' mony a Bailie,
Wha in the paths o' righteousness did toil ay;
Ye dainty Deacons, an' ye douce Conveeners,
To whom our moderns are but causey-cleaners!
Ye godly Councils wha hae blest this town;
Ye godly Brethren o' the sacred gown,
Wha meekly gie your hurdies to the smiters;
And (what would now be strange) ye godly Writers: [4]
A' ye douce folk I've borne aboon the broo,[5]
Were ye but here, what would ye say or do!
How would your spirits groan in deep vexation,
To see each melancholy alteration;
And agonizing, curse the time and place,
When ye begat the base, degen'rate race!
Nae langer Rev'rend Men, their country's glory,
In plain, braid Scots hold forth a plain, braid story;
Nae langer thrifty Citizens, an' douce,
Meet owre a pint, or in the Council-house;
But staumrel,[6] corky-headed, graceless Gentry,
The herryment [1] and ruin of the country;
Men, three-parts made by Tailors and by Barbers,
Wha waste your weel-hain'd [2] gear on d—d new Brigs and Harbours!

NEW BRIG.

Now haud you there! for faith ye've said enough,
And muckle mair than ye can mak to through;[3]
As for your Priesthood, I shall say but little,
Corbies [4] and Clergy are a shot right kittle:
But, under favour o' your langer beard,
Abuse o' Magistrates might weel be spar'd:
To liken them to your auld-warld squad,
I must needs say, comparisons are odd.
In Ayr, Wag-wits nae mair can have a handle
To mouth "a Citizen," a term o' scandal:
Nae mair the Council waddles down the street,
In all the pomp of ignorant conceit;
Men wha grew wise priggin [5] ower hops an' raisins,
Or gather'd lib'ral views in Bonds and Seisins.
If haply Knowledge, on a random tramp,
Had shor'd [6] them wi' a glimmer of his lamp,
And would to Common-sense for once betray'd them,
Plain, dull Stupidity stept kindly in to aid them.

What farther clishmaclaver [7] might been said,
What bloody wars, if Sprites had blood to shed,
No man can tell; but all before their sight
A fairy train appear'd in order bright:
Adown the glittering stream they featly [8] danc'd;

[1] Blockheads. [2] Burgh.
[3] Coevals. [4] Lawyers. [5] Water.
[6] Half-witted.

[1] Devastation. [2] Well-saved.
[3] Make out. [4] Crows.
[5] Cheapening. [6] Threatened.
[7] Idle conversation. [8] Sprucely.

Bright to the moon their various dresses glanc'd:
They footed o'er the wat'ry glass so neat,
The infant ice scarce bent beneath their feet:
While arts of Minstrelsy among them rung,
And soul-ennobling Bards heroic ditties sung.
O had M'Lauchlan,[1] thairm[2] inspiring sage,
Been there to hear this heavenly band engage,
When thro' his dear strathspeys they bore with Highland rage,
Or when they struck old Scotia's melting airs,
The lover's raptured joys, or bleeding cares;
How would his Highland lug[3] been nobly fir'd,
And ev'n his matchless hand with finer touch inspir'd!
No guess could tell what instrument appear'd,
But all the soul of Music's self was heard;
Harmonious concert rung in every part,
While simple melody pour'd moving on the heart.
The Genius of the Stream in front appears,
A venerable chief, advanc'd in years;
His hoary head with water-lilies crown'd,
His manly leg with garter-tangle[4] bound.
Next came the loveliest pair in all the ring,
Sweet Female Beauty hand in hand with Spring;
Then, crown'd with flow'ry hay, came Rural Joy,
And Summer, with his fervid-beaming eye:
All-cheering Plenty, with her flowing horn,

[1] A well-known performer of Scottish music on the violin.—R. B.
[2] Fiddle-string.
[3] Ear.
[4] Sea-weed.

Led yellow Autumn wreath'd with nodding corn;
Then Winter's time-bleach'd locks did hoary show,
By Hospitality with cloudless brow.
Next followed Courage with his martial stride,
From where the Feal[1] wild-woody coverts hide;
Benevolence, with mild, benignant air,
A Female form, came from the tow'rs of Stair:[2]
Learning and Worth in equal measures trode
From simple Catrine,[3] their long-lov'd abode:
Last, white-rob'd Peace, crown'd with a hazel wreath,
To rustic Agriculture did bequeath
The broken, iron instruments of death:
At sight of whom our Sprites forgat their kindling wrath.

THE ORDINATION.[4]

For sense, they little owe to frugal Heav'n—
To please the mob, they hide the little giv'n.

KILMARNOCK Wabsters,[5] fidge and claw,
An' pour your creeshie[6] nations;

[1] Feal is a small stream that runs near Coilsfield.
[2] The allusion is to Mrs. Stewart, of Stair.
[3] On the banks of Ayr, where Professor Stewart resided, when not occupied by his work at Edinboro'.
[4] The "Ordination" grew out of a Kirk squabble, in Kilmarnock, between the "high-flying" and the "moderate" party, who were vanquished in the fray; a high-flying minister having obtained the appointment. Burns endeavoured to console the defeated "moderates" with a vision of the expected ceremony. "Maggie Lauder," as we are informed by Burns, was the maiden name of the Rev. Mr. Lindsay's wife.
[5] Weavers.
[6] Greasy.

An' ye wha leather rax[1] an' draw,
Of a' denominations,
Swith[2] to the Laigh Kirk, ane an' a',
An' there tak up your stations;
Then aff to Begbie's in a raw,[3]
An' pour divine libations,
For joy this day.

Curst Common-sense, that imp o' hell,
Cam in wi' Maggie Lauder;
But Oliphant aft made her yell,
An' Russel sair misca'd her;
This day M'Kinlay taks the flail,
An' he's the boy will blaud[4] her!
He'll clap a shangan[5] on her tail,
An' set the bairns to daud[6] her
Wi' dirt this day.

Mak haste an' turn king David owre,
An' lilt[7] wi' holy clangor:
O' double verse come gie us four,
An' skirl[8] up the Bangor:
This day the Kirk kicks up a stoure,[9]
Nae mair the knaves shall wrang her,
For Heresy is in her pow'r,
And gloriously she'll whang her
Wi' pith this day.

Come let a proper text be read,
An' touch it off wi' vigour,
How graceless Ham[10] leugh[11] at his Dad,
Which made Canaan a niger:[12]
Or Phineas[13] drove the murdering blade
Wi' w—e-abhorring rigour;
Or Zipporah,[14] the scauldin' jade,
Was like a bluidy tiger
I' th' Inn that day.

There, try his mettle on the creed,
And bind him down wi' caution,
That Stipend is a carnal weed
He taks but for the fashion;

An' gie him o'er the flock, to feed,
And punish each transgression;
Especial, rams that cross the breed,
Gie them sufficient threshin',
Spare them nae day.

Now auld Kilmarnock, cock thy tail,
An' toss thy horns fu' canty;
Nae mair thou'lt rowte[1] out-owre th dale,
Because thy pasture's scanty;
For lapfu's large o' gospel kail
Shall fill thy crib in plenty,
An' runts o' grace the pick an' wale,[2]
No gie'n by way o' dainty,
But ilka day.

Nae mair by Babel streams we'll weep,
To think upon our Zion;
And hing our fiddles up to sleep,
Like baby-clouts a-dryin:
Come, screw the pegs wi' tunefu' cheep,[3]
And o'er the thairms[4] be tryin;
Oh rare! to see our elbucks wheep,[5]
And a' like lamb-tails flyin
Fu' fast this day!

Lang, Patronage, wi' rod o' airn,[6]
Has shor'd the Kirk's undoin,
As lately Fenwick, sair forfairn,
Has proven to its ruin:
Our Patron, honest man! Glencairn,
He saw mischief was brewin;
And like a godly, elect bairn,
He's wal'd[7] us out a true ane,
And sound this day

Now, Robinson, harangue nae mair,
But steek[8] your gab for ever:
Or try the wicked town of Ayr,
For there they'll think you clever;
Or, nae reflection on your lear,
Ye may commence a Shaver;
Or to the Netherton[9] repair,
And turn a Carpet-weaver
Aff-hand this day.

Mutrie and you were just a match,
We never had sic twa drones:
Auld Hornie did the Laigh Kirk watch
Just like a winkin baudrons.[10]

---

[1] Stretch. [2] Get away.
[3] Row. [4] Slap.
[5] A stick cleft at one end. [6] Pelt.
[7] Sing. [8] Shriek. [9] Dust.
[10] Genesis ix. 22.—R. B.
[11] Did laugh. [12] A negro.
[13] Numbers xxv. 8.—R. B.
[14] Exodus iv. 25.—R. B.

[1] Bellow. [2] Choice. [3] Chirp
[4] Strings. [5] Elbows jerk. [6] Iron.
[7] Chosen. [8] Shut.
[9] A district of Kilmarnock. [10] Cat

And ay he catch'd the tither wretch,
  To fry them in his caudrons;
But now his Honor maun detach,
  Wi' a' his brimstone squadrons,
      Fast, fast this day.

See, see auld Orthodoxy's faes
  She's swingein thro' the city:
Hark, how the nine-tail'd cat she plays!
  I vow it's unco pretty!
There Learning, with his Greekish face,
  Grunts out some Latin ditty;
And Common Sense is gaun, she says,
  To mak to Jamie Beattie
      Her plaint this day.

But there's Morality himsel,
  Embracing all opinions;
Hear, how he gies the tither yell,
  Between his twa companions;
See, how she peels the skin an' fell,
  As ane were peelin onions!
Now there,—they're packed aff to hell,
  And banish'd our dominions,
      Henceforth this day.

O happy day! rejoice, rejoice!
  Come bouse about the porter!
Morality's demure decoys
  Shall here nae mair find quarter:
M'Kinlay, Russel are the boys
  That Heresy can torture;
They'll gie her on a rape a hoyse[1]
  And cowe[2] her measure shorter
      By th' head some day.

Come, bring the tither mutchkin[3] in,
  And here's, for a conclusion,
To every New Light[4] mother's son,
  From this time forth, Confusion:
If mair they deave[5] us with their din,
  Or Patronage intrusion,
We'll light a spunk,[6] and, ev'ry skin,
  We'll rin them aff in fusion
      Like oil, some day.

---

[1] A pull upwards. [2] Lop.
[3] An English pint.
[4] New Light is a cant phrase, in the West of Scotland, for those religious opinions which Dr. Taylor, of Norwich, has so strenuously defended.—R. B.
[5] Deafen. [6] A match.

TO THE RIGHT HON. CHARLES JAMES FOX.

(A POLITICAL SKETCH, WRITTEN IN 1789.)

How wisdom and folly meet, mix, and unite;
How virtue and vice blend their black and their white;
How genius, the illustrious father of fiction,
Confounds rule and law, reconciles contradiction—
I sing: if these mortals, the critics, should bustle,
I care not, not I—let the critics go whistle!

  But now for a patron, whose name and whose glory
At once may illustrate and honour my story.

  Thou first of our orators, first of our wits;
Yet whose parts and acquirements seem mere lucky hits;
With knowledge so vast, and with judgment so strong,
No man with the half of 'em e'er went far wrong;
With passions so potent, and fancies so bright,
No man with the half of 'em e'er went quite right;—
A sorry, poor misbegot son of the Muses,
For using thy name offers fifty excuses.

Good Lord, what is man? for as simple he looks,
Do but try to develop his hooks and his crooks;
With his depths and his shallows, his good and his evil;
All in all he's a problem must puzzle the devil.
On his one ruling passion Sir Pope hugely labours,
That, like the old Hebrew walking-switch, eats up its neighbours,
Mankind are his show-box—a friend, would you know him?

Pull the string, ruling passion the picture will show him.
What pity, in rearing so beauteous a system,
One trifling particular truth should have miss'd him;
For, spite of his fine theoretic positions,
Mankind is a science defies definitions.

Some sort all our qualities each to its tribe,
And think human nature they truly describe;
Have you found this, or t'other? there's more in the wind,
As by one drunken fellow his comrades you'll find.
But such is the flaw, or the depth of the plan,
In the make of that wonderful creature call'd man,
No two virtues, whatever relation they claim,
Nor even two different shades of the same,
Though like as was ever twin brother to brother,
Possessing the one shall imply you've the other.

But truce with abstraction, and truce with a Muse,
Whose rhymes you'll perhaps, sir, ne'er deign to peruse:
Will you leave your justings, your jars, and your quarrels,
Contending with Billy for proud-nodding laurels?
My much-honour'd patron, believe your poor poet,
Your courage much more than your prudence you show it;
In vain with Squire Billy for laurels you struggle,
He'll have them by fair trade, if not, he will smuggle;
Not cabinets even of kings would conceal 'em,
He'd up the back-stairs, and by God he would steal 'em.
Then feats like Squire Billy's you ne'er can achieve 'em,
It is not, outdo him, the task is outthieve him.

THE CALF.[1]

TO THE REV. MR. JAMES STEVEN, ON HIS TEXT, MALACHI, CH. IV. VER. 2.

"And they shall go forth, and grow up, like CALVES of the stall."

RIGHT, Sir! your text I'll prove it true,
Tho' Heretics may laugh;
For instance; there's yoursel just now,
God knows, an unco Calf!

And should some Patron be so kind,
As bless you wi' a kirk,
I doubt na, sir, but then we'll find
Ye're still as great a Stirk.[2]

But, if the Lover's raptur'd hour
Shall ever be your lot,
Forbid it, ev'ry heavenly Power,
You e'er should be a Stot![3]

Tho', when some kind, connubial Dear,
Your But-and-ben[4] adorns,
The like has been that you may wear
A noble head of horns.

And, in your lug, most reverend James,
To hear you roar and rowte,[5]
Few men o' sense will doubt your claims
To rank amang the Nowte.[6]

And when ye're number'd wi' the dead,
Below a grassy hillock,
Wi' justice they may mark your head—
"Here lies a famous Bullock!"

STANZAS TO CLARINDA.[7]

CLARINDA, mistress of my soul,[8]
The measured time is run!

---

[1] The Poem was nearly an extemporaneous production on a wager that I would not produce a poem on the subject in a given time.—R. B.

[2] Bullock of a year old. [3] An ox.

[4] Kitchen and parlour. [5] Bellow.

[6] Black cattle.

[7] Written about 1788. Clarinda was the wife of Mr. M'Lehose, from whom she had been separated, but she appears to have had an ardent affection for Burns. Her maiden name was Agnes Craig.

[8] These stanzas appeared in the second volume of the *Musical Museum.*

The wretch beneath the dreary pole
So marks his latest sun.

To what dark cave of frozen night
Shall poor Sylvander hie?
Deprived of thee, his life and light,
The sun of all his joy!

We part—but, by these precious drops
That fill thy lovely eyes!
No other light shall guide my steps
Till thy bright beams arise.

She, the fair sun of all her sex,
Has blest my glorious day;
And shall a glimmering planet fix
My worship to its ray?

TO CLARINDA.

WITH A PRESENT OF A PAIR OF DRINKING GLASSES.

FAIR empress of the poet's soul,
And queen of poetesses;
Clarinda, take this little boon,
This humble pair of glasses.

And fill them high with generous juice,
As generous as your mind;
And pledge me in the generous toast—
"The whole of humankind!"

"To those who love us!"—second fill;
But not to those whom we love;
Lest we love those who love not us!
A third—"To thee and me, love!"

Long may we live! long may we love!
And long may we be happy!
And may we never want a glass
Well charged with generous nappy!

ADDRESS TO THE DEIL.[1]

Oh Prince! Oh Chief of many throned pow'rs,
That led th' embattled Seraphim to war—
Milton.

O THOU! whatever title suit thee,
Auld Hornie, Satan, Nick, or Clootie,
Wha in yon cavern grim an' sootie,
Closed under hatches,
Spairges[1] about the brunstane cootie,[2]
To scaud poor wretches.

Hear me, auld Hangie, for a wee,
An' let poor damned bodies be;
I'm sure sma' pleasure it can gie,
Ev'n to a deil,
To skelp[3] an' scaud poor dogs like me,
An' hear us squeel!

Great is thy pow'r, an' great thy fame;[4]
Far kend an' noted is thy name;
An', tho' yon lowin heugh's[5] thy hame,
Thou travels far;
An', faith! thou's neither lag nor lame,
Nor blate nor scaur.[6]

Whyles, ranging like a roarin lion,
For prey a' holes an' corners tryin;
Whyles on the strong-wing'd tempest flyin,
Tirlin[7] the kirks;
Whyles in the human bosom pryin,
Unseen thou lurks.

I've heard my reverend Graunie say,
In lanely glens ye like to stray;
Or where auld ruin'd castles, gray,
Nod to the moon,
Ye fright the nightly wand'rer's way,
Wi' eldritch croon.[8]

---

[1] It was, I think, in the winter, as we were going together with carts for coal to the family fire (and I could yet point out the particular spot), that the author first repeated to me the "Address to the Deil." The curious idea of such an address was suggested to him by running over in his mind the many ludicrous accounts and representations we have from various quarters of this august personage.—G. B.

[1] Dashest. [2] Wooden dish. [3] Strike.

[4] The third stanza was originally

Lang syne in Eden's happy scene,
When strappin' Adam's days were green,
And Eve was like my bonnie Jean,
My dearest part,
A dancin', sweet, young, handsome quean
Wi' guileless heart.

[5] Flaming pit.

[6] Neither bashful nor apt to be scared.

[7] Uncovering.

[8] Frightful moan.

When twilight did my Graunie summon,
To say her pray'rs, douce, honest woman!
Aft yont the dyke she's heard you bummin,[1]
Wi' eerie drone;
Or, rustlin, thro' the boortries[2] comin,
Wi' heavy groan.

Ae dreary, windy, winter night,
The stars shot down wi' sklentin[3] light,
Wi' you, mysel, I gat a fright,
Ayont the lough;
Ye, like a rash-bush,[4] stood in sight,
Wi' waving sugh.

The cudgel in my nieve[5] did shake,
Each bristl'd hair stood like a stake,
When wi' an eldritch stoor,[6] quaick, quaick,
Amang the springs,
Awa ye squatter'd,[7] like a drake,
On whistling wings.

Let warlocks[8] grim, an' wither'd hags,
Tell how wi' you on ragweed[9] nags,
They skim the muirs, an' dizzy crags,
Wi' wicked speed;
And in kirk-yards renew their leagues,
Owre howkit[10] dead.

Thence, countra wives, wi' toil an' pain,
May plunge an' plunge the kirn[11] in vain;
For, Oh! the yellow treasure's taen
By witching skill;
An' dawtit,[12] twal-pint[13] Hawkie's gaen
As yell's[14] the bill.[15]

Thence, mystic knots mak great abuse,
On young Guidmen, fond, keen, an' crouse;[16]

[1] Humming.
[2] The shrub elder, common in the hedges of barn-yards.
[3] Slanting. [4] A bush of rushes.
[5] Fist. [6] Hoarse. [7] Fluttered.
[8] Wizards. [9] Ragwort.
[10] Digged up. [11] Churn.
[12] Fondled. [13] Twelve-pint.
[14] Barren. [15] Bull. [16] Courageous.

When the best wark-lume[1] i' the house,
By cantraip[2] wit,
Is instant made no worth a ——,
Just at the bit.

When thowes[3] dissolve the snawy hoord,[4]
An' float the jinglin' icy-boord,
Then Water-kelpies haunt the foord,
By your direction,
An' nighted Trav'llers are allur'd
To their destruction.

An' aft your moss-traversing Spunkies[5]
Decoy the wight that late an' drunk is:
The bleezin, curst, mischievous monkies
Delude his eyes,
Till in some miry slough he sunk is,
Ne'er mair to rise.

When Masons' mystic word an' grip,
In storms an' tempests raise you up,
Some cock or cat your rage maun stop,
Or, strange to tell!
The youngest Brother ye wad whip
Aff straught to hell.

Lang syne, in Eden's bonnie yard,
When youthfu' lovers first were pair'd,
An' all the soul of love they shar'd,
The raptur'd hour,
Sweet on the fragrant, flow'ry swaird,
In shady bow'r:

Then you, ye auld, snec-drawing[6] dog!
Ye came to Paradise incog,
An' play'd on man a cursed brogue,[7]
(Black be you fa!)
An' gied the infant warld a shog,[8]
'Maist ruin'd a'.

D'ye mind that day, when in a bizz,[9]
Wi' reekit duds,[10] an' reestit gizz,[11]
Ye did present your smoutie phiz
'Mang better folk,
An' sklented[12] on the man of Uzz
Your spitefu' joke?

An' how ye gat him i' your thrall,
An' brak him out o' house an' hal',

[1] Working tool. [2] Magical.
[3] Thaws. [4] Hoard.
[5] Will-o'-whisp. [6] Trick-contriving.
[7] Trick. [8] Shock. [9] Bustle.
[10] Smoky clothes. [11] Stunted periwig.
[12] Played.

While scabs an' blotches did him gall,
Wi' bitter claw,
An' lows'd[1] his ill-tongu'd, wicked Scawl,[2]
Wast warst ava?[3]

But a' your doings to rehearse,
Your wily snares an' fechtin[4] fierce,
Sin' that day Michael[5] did you pierce,
Down to this time,
Wad ding[6] a' Lallan tongue, or Erse,
In prose or rhyme.

An' now, auld Cloots, I ken ye're thinkin,
A certain Bardie's rantin, drinkin,
Some luckless hour will send him linkin[7]
To your black pit;
But, faith! he'll turn a corner jinkin,[8]
An' cheat you yet.

But, fare you weel, auld Nickie-ben!
O wad ye tak a thought an' men'!
Ye aiblins[9] might—I dinna ken—
Still hae a stake—
I'm wae to think upo' yon den,
Ev'n for your sake!

THE POET'S REPLY TO A GENTLEMAN WHO HAD SENT HIM A NEWSPAPER.[10]

KIND sir, I've read your paper through,
And, faith, to me, 'twas really new!
How guess'd ye, sir, what maist I wanted?
This mony a day I've gran'd and gaunted
To ken what French mischief was brewin',
Or what the drumlie Dutch were doin';
That vile doup-skelper, Emperor Joseph,
If Venus yet had got his nose off;
Or how the collieshangie works
Atween the Russians and the Turks;
Or if the Swede, before he halt,
Would play anither Charles the Twalt:
If Denmark, anybody spak o't;
Or Poland, wha had now the tack o't;
How cut-throat Prussian blades were hingin';
How libbet Italy was singin';
If Spaniards, Portuguese, or Swiss
Were sayin' or takin' aught amiss:
Or how our merry lads at hame,
In Britain's court, kept up the game:
How royal George, the Lord leuk o'er him!
Was managing St Stephen's quorum;
If sleekit Chatham Will was livin',
Or glaikit Charlie got his nieve in;
How Daddie Burke the plea was cookin';
If Warren Hastings' neck was yeukin';
How cesses, stents, and fees were rax'd,
Or if bare a—s yet were tax'd;
The news o' princes, dukes, and earls,
Pimps, sharpers, bawds, and opera girls;
If that daft buckie, Geordie Wales,
Was threshin' still at hizzies' tails;
Or if he was grown oughtlins douser,
And no a perfect kintra cooser.
A' this and mair I never heard of;
And but for you I might despair'd of.
So gratefu', back your news I send you,
And pray, a' guid things may attend you!

THE FIRST KISS OF AFFECTION.

HUMID seal of soft affections,
Tenderest pledge of future bliss,
Dearest tie of young connections,
Love's first snow-drop, virgin kiss!

Speaking silence, dumb confession,
Passion's birth and infant play,
Dove-like fondness, chaste concession,
Glowing dawn of brighter day.

Sorrowing joy, adieu's last action,
When ling'ring lips no more must join,
What words can ever speak affection
So thrilling and sincere as thine!

---

[1] Loosed. [2] Scold. [3] Of all.
[4] Fighting.
[5] Vide Milton, Book vi.—R. B.
[6] Worst. [7] Tripping.
[8] Dodging. [9] Perhaps.
[10] Written at Ellisland, in 1790, in the 32nd year of his age.

THE DEATH AND DYING WORDS OF POOR MAILIE,[1] THE AUTHOR'S ONLY PET YOWE.

AN UNCO MOURNFU' TALE.

As Mailie an' her lambs thegither
Were ae day nibbling on the tether,
Upon her cloot[2] she coost[3] a hitch,[4]
An' owre she warsl'd[5] in the ditch:
There groaning, dying, she did lie,
When Hughoc[6] he cam doytin by.
Wi' glowrin een, an' lifted han's,
Poor Hughoc like a statue stan's;
He saw her days were near-hand ended,
But, waes my heart! he could na mend it.
He gaped wide, but naething spak.
At length poor Mailie silence brak.

"O thou, whase lamentable face
Appears to mourn my woefu' case!
My dying words attentive hear,
An' bear them to my Master dear.
"Tell him, if e'er again he keep
As muckle gear as buy a sheep,
O, bid him never tie them mair
Wi' wicked strings o' hemp or hair!
But ca' them out to park or hill,
An' let them wander at their will;
So may his flocks increase, an' grow
To scores o' lambs, an' packs o' woo'![1]
"Tell him, he was a Master kin',
An' ay was guid to me an' mine;
An' now my dying charge I gie him,
My helpless lambs, I trust them wi' him.
"O, bid him save their harmless lives,
Frae dogs, an' tods, an' butchers' knives!
But gie them guid cow-milk their fill,
Till they be fit to fend[2] themsel:
An' tent them duly, e'en an' morn,
Wi' teats[3] o' hay, an' ripps[4] o' corn.
"An' may they never learn the gaets[5]
Of ither vile, wanrestfu'[6] pets!
To slink thro' slaps,[7] an' reave[8] an' steal,
At stacks o' pease, or stocks o' kail.
So may they, like their great Forbears,[9]
For monie a year come thro' the shears;
So wives will gie them bits o' bread,
An' bairns greet[10] for them when they're dead.
"My poor toop-lamb,[11] my son an' heir,
O, bid him breed him up wi' care!
An' if he live to be a beast,
To pit some havins[12] in his breast!
An' warn him, what I winna name;
To stay content wi' yowes at hame;
An' not to rin an' wear his cloots,
Like ither menseless, graceless brutes.
"An' niest my yowie,[13] silly thing,
Gude keep thee frae a tether string!
O, may thou ne'er forgather up
Wi' ony blastit, moorland toop;
But ay keep mind to moop[14] an' mell,[15]
Wi' sheep o' credit like thysel!
"And now, my bairns, wi' my last breath,
I lea'e my blessin wi' you baith:
An' when you think upo' your Mither,
Mind to be kind to ane anither.
"Now, honest Hughoc, dinna fail,

---

[1] The circumstances of the poor sheep were pretty much as he has described them; he had, partly by way of frolic, bought a ewe and two lambs from a neighbour, and she was tethered in a field adjoining the house at Lochlie. He and I were going out with our teams, and our two younger brothers to drive for us, at mid-day; when Hugh Wilson, a curious-looking, awkward boy, clad in plaiding, came to us, with much anxiety in his face, with the information that the ewe had entangled herself in the tether and was lying in the ditch. Robert was much tickled with Huoc's appearance and postures on the occasion. Poor Mailie was set to rights, and when we returned from the plough in the evening he repeated to me her "Death and Dying Words," pretty much in the way they now stand.—G. B.

[2] Hoof. [3] Cast. [4] Loop.
[5] Wrestled.
[6] A neibor herd-callan.—R. B.

---

[1] Wool. [2] Live comfortably.
[3] Small quantities. [4] Handfuls.
[5] Ways. [6] Restless.
[7] Gates, or breaks in fences.
[8] Rove. [9] Forefathers. [10] Weep.
[11] Ram. [12] Good manners.
[13] Ewe. [14] Nibble. [15] Meddle.

To tell my Master a' my tale;
An' bid him burn this cursed tether,
An', for thy pains, thou'se get my blather."[1]

This said, poor Mailie turn'd her head,
An' clos'd her een amang the dead!

POOR MAILIE'S ELEGY.

LAMENT in rhyme, lament in prose,
Wi' saut tears trickling down your nose;
Our Bardie's fate is at a close,
Past a' remead;
The last, sad cape-stane[2] of his woes;
Poor Mailie's dead!

It's no the loss o' warl's gear,
That could sae bitter draw the tear,
Or mak our Bardie, dowie,[3] wear
The mourning weed:
He's lost a friend and neebor dear,
In Mailie dead.

Thro' a' the toun she trotted by him;
A lang half-mile she could descry him;
Wi' kindly bleat, when she did spy him,
She ran wi' speed:
A friend mair faithfu' ne'er cam nigh him
Than Mailie dead.

I wat she was a sheep o' sense,
An' could behave hersel wi' mense;
I'll say't, she never brak a fence,
Thro' thievish greed.
Our Bardie, lanely, keeps the Spence[4]
Sin' Mailie's dead.

Or, if he wanders up the howe,[6]
Her living image, in her yowe,
Comes bleating to him owre the knowe,[7]
For bits o' bread;
An' down the briny pearls rowe
For Mailie dead.

She was nae get o' moorland tips,[3]
Wi' tawted[6] ket, an' hairy hips;
For her forbears were brought in ships,
Frae yont the Tweed:
A bonnier fleesh ne'er cross'd the clips[9]
Than Mailie dead.

[1] Bladder. [2] Copestone.
[3] Worn with grief. [4] Parlour.
[5] Dell. [6] Hillock. [7] Rams.
[8] Matted wool. [9] Sheers.

Wae worth the man wha first did shape
That vile, wanchancie[1] thing—a rape!
It maks guid fellows girn[2] an' gape,
Wi' chokin dread;
An' Robin's bonnet wave wi' crape,
For Mailie dead.

O, a' ye Bards on bonnie Doon!
An' wha on Ayr your chanters[3] tune!
Come, join the melancholious croon[4]
O' Robin's reed!
His heart will never get aboon
His Mailie dead!

TO JAMES SMITH.[5]

Friendship! mysterious cement of the soul!
Sweet'ner of Life, and solder of Society!
I owe thee much.— *Blair.*

DEAR Smith, the sleest, paukie[6] thief,
That e'er attempted stealth or rief,
Ye surely hae some warlock-breef[7]
Owre human hearts;
For ne'er a bosom yet was prief[8]
Against your arts.

For me, I swear by sun and moon,
And ev'ry star that blinks aboon,
Ye've cost me twenty pair o' shoon
Just gaun to see you;
And ev'ry ither pair that's done,
Mair ta'en I'm wi' you.

That auld, capricious carlin,[9] Nature,
To mak amends for scrimpit[10] stature,
She's turn'd you aff, a human creature
On her first plan,
And in her freaks, on ev'ry feature,
She's wrote, "The Man."

Just now I've taen the fit o' rhyme,
My barmie noddle's working prime,
My fancie yerkit[11] up sublime
Wi' hasty summon:
Hae ye a leisure moment's time
To hear what's comin?

[1] Unlucky. [2] Grin.
[3] Parts of bagpipes. [4] Moan.
[5] Smith kept a shop in Mauchline.
[6] Cunning. [7] Wizard spell. [8] Proof.
[9] Old woman. [10] Scanty. [11] Lashed.

Some rhyme a neebor's name to lash;
Some rhyme (vain thought!) for needfu' cash;
Some rhyme to court the contra clash,
An' raise a din;
For me, an aim I never fash;[1]
I rhyme for fun.

The star that rules my luckless lot,
Has fated me the russet coat,
An' d—d my fortune to the groat;
But, in requit,
Has blest me wi' a random shot
O' countra wit.

This while my notion's taen a sklent,
To try my fate in guid, black prent;
But still the mair I'm that way bent,
Something cries, "Hoolie![2]
I red[3] you, honest man, tak tent!
Ye'll shaw your folly.

"There's ither poets, much your betters,
Far seen in Greek, deep men o' letters,
Hae thought they had ensur'd their debtors,
A' future ages;
Now moths deform in shapeless tatters,
Their unknown pages."

Then fareweel hopes o' laurel-boughs,
To garland my poetic brows!
Henceforth I'll rove where busy ploughs
Are whistling thrang,
An' teach the lanely heights an' howes
My rustic sang.

I'll wander on, wi' tentless[4] heed
How never-halting moments speed,
Till fate shall snap the brittle thread;
Then, all unknown,
I'll lay me with th' inglorious dead,
Forgot and gone!

But why o' Death begin a tale?
Just now we're living, sound an' hale;
Then top and maintop crowd the sail,
Heave Care o'er side!
And large, before Enjoyment's gale,
Let's tak the tide.

[1] Care for. [2] Gently. [3] I warn you. [4] Heedless.

This life, sae far's I understand,[1]
Is a' enchanted fairy-land,
Where pleasure is the magic wand,
That, wielded right,
Maks hours like minutes, hand in hand,
Dance by fu' light.

The magic-wand then let us wield;
For, ance that five-an'-forty's speel'd,[2]
See, crazy, weary, joyless Eild,
Wi' wrinkl'd face,
Comes hostin,[3] hirplin[4] owre the field,
Wi' creepin pace.

When ance life's day draws near the gloamin,
Then fareweel vacant careless roamin;
An' fareweel chearfu' tankards foamin,
An' social noise;
An' fareweel dear deluding woman,
The joy of joys!

O Life! how pleasant in thy morning,
Young Fancy's rays the hills adorning!
Cold-pausing Caution's lesson scorning,
We frisk away,
Like school-boys, at th' expected warning,
To joy and play.

We wander there, we wander here,
We eye the rose upon the brier,
Unmindful that the thorn is near,
Among the leaves;
And tho' the puny wound appear,
Short while it grieves.

Some, lucky, find a flow'ry spot,
For which they never toil'd nor swat;
They drink the sweet and eat the fat,
But care or pain;
And, haply, eye the barren hut
With high disdain.

[1] In your epistle to J. S., the stanzas, from that beginning with this line, "This life," &c. to that which ends with, "Short while it grieves," are easy, flowing, gaily philosophical, and of Horatian elegance. The language is English, with a few Scottish words, and some of those so harmonious as to add to the beauty; for what poet would not prefer *gloaming* to *twilight*?—Dr. Moore, June 10, 1789.

[2] Climbed. [3] Coughing. [4] Limping.

With steady aim, some Fortune chase ;
Keen Hope does ev'ry sinew brace ;
Thro' fair, thro' foul, they urge the race,
And seize the prey :
Then cannie, in some cozie place,
They close the day.

And others, like your humble servan',
Poor wights ! nae rules nor roads observin' ;
To right or left, eternal swervin',
They zig-zag on ;
Till curst with age, obscure an' starvin',
They aften groan.

Alas ! what bitter toil an' straining—
But truce wi' peevish, poor complaining !
Is Fortune's fickle Luna waning ?
E'en let her gang !
Beneath what light she has remaining,
Let's sing our sang.

My pen I here fling to the door,
And kneel, "Ye Pow'rs !" and warm implore,
"Tho' I should wander Terra o'er,
In all her climes,
Grant me but this, I ask no more,
Ay rowth[1] o' rhymes.

"Gie dreeping[2] roasts to countra Lairds,
Till icicles hing frae their beards ;
Gie fine braw claes to fine Life-guards.
And Maids of Honour ;
And yill[3] and whisky gie to Cairds[4]
Until they sconner.[5]

"A Title, Dempster[6] merits it ;
A Garter gie to Willie Pitt ;
Gie Wealth to some be-ledger'd Cit,
In cent per cent ;
But gie me real, sterling Wit,
And I'm content.

"While Ye are pleas'd to keep me hale,
I'll sit down o'er my scanty meal,
Be't water-brose, or muslin-kail,[7]
Wi' cheerfu' face,

[1] Plenty. [2] Dropping. [3] Ale.
[4] Tinkers. [5] Loathe.
[6] An active Member of Parliament, who died in 1818.
[7] Broth made of water, shelled barley, and greens.

As lang's the Muses dinna fail
To say the grace.'

An anxious e'e I never throws
Behint my lug, or by my nose ;
I jouk[1] beneath Misfortune's blows
As weel's I may ;
Sworn foe to Sorrow, Care, and Prose,
I rhyme away.

O ye douce folk, that live by rule,
Grave, tideless-blooded, calm and cool,
Compar'd wi' you—O fool ! fool ! fool !
How much unlike !
Your hearts are just a standing pool,
Your lives, a dyke !

Nae hair-brain'd sentimental traces,
In your unletter'd, nameless faces !
In arioso trills and graces
Ye never stray,
But gravissimo, solemn basses
Ye hum away.

Ye are sae grave, nae doubt ye're wise,
Nae ferly[2] tho' ye do despise
The hairum-scairum, ram-stam[3] boys,
The rattling squad :
I see you upward cast your eyes—
Ye ken the road.—

Whilst I—but I shall haud me there—
Wi' you I'll scarce gang ony where—
Then, Jamie, I shall say nae mair,
But quat[4] my sang,
Content wi' You to mak a pair,
Whare'er I gang.

THE POET'S DREAM.[5]

Guid-mornin to your Majesty !
May heaven augment your blisses,

[1] Stoop.
[2] An expression of contempt.
[3] Thoughtless. [4] Quit.
[5] Written in 1786, in the 28th year of his age. At this period the Rev. Thomas Warton filled the office of Poet Laureate. Burns informs us that on reading in the public papers the Laureate's "Ode," with the other parade of June 4, 1786, he dropt asleep, and then imagined himself transported

On ev'ry new birth-day ye see,
  A humble Poet wishes!
My Bardship here, at your Levee,
  On sic a day as this is,
Is sure an uncouth sight to see,
  Amang thae Birth-day dresses
    Sae fine this day.

I see ye're complimented thrang,
  By many a lord an' lady;
"God save the King!" 's a cuckoo sang
  That's unco easy said ay;
The Poets, too, a venal gang,
  Wi' rhymes weel turn'd and ready,
Wad gar[1] you trow ye ne'er do wrang,
  But ay unerring steady,
    On sic a day.

For me! before a Monarch's face,
  Ev'n there I winna flatter;
For neither pension, post, nor place,
  Am I your humble debtor:
So, nae reflection on Your Grace,
  Your Kingship to bespatter;
There's monie waur been o' the Race,
  And aiblins[2] ane been better
    Than You this day.

'Tis very true, my sovereign King,
  My skill may weel be doubted:
But Facts are cheels[3] that winna ding,[4]
  An' downa[5] be disputed:
Your Royal nest, beneath Your wing,
  Is e'en right reft an' clouted,[6]
And now the third part of the string,
  An' less, will gang about it
    Than did ae day.

Far be't frae me that I aspire
  To blame your legislation,
Or say, ye wisdom want, or fire,
  To rule this mighty nation!
But faith! I muckle doubt, my Sire,
  Ye've trusted Ministration
To chaps, wha, in a barn or byre,[7]
  Wad better filled their station
    Than courts yon day.

---

to the Birth-day Levee; and in his dreaming fancy, made the following ADDRESS.

[1] Make.
[2] Perhaps.
[3] Young fellows.
[4] Will not be beaten.
[5] Cannot.
[6] Torn and patched; the allusion is to the separation of America.
[7] Cow stable.

And now ye've gien auld Britain peace,
  Her broken shins to plaister;
Your sair taxation does her fleece,
  Till she has scarce a tester;
For me, thank God, my life's a lease,
  Nae bargain wearing faster,
Or, faith! I fear, that wi' the geese,
  I shortly boost[1] to pasture
    I' the craft[2] some day.

I'm no mistrusting Willie Pitt,
  When taxes he enlarges,
(An' Will's a true guid fallow's get,[3]
  A name not envy spairges,)[4]
That he intends to pay your debt,
  An' lessen a' your charges;
But, God's sake! let nae saving-fit
  Abridge your bonnie barges
    An' boats this day.

Adieu, my Liege! may freedom geck[5]
  Beneath your high protection;
An' may Ye rax[6] Corruption's neck,
  And gie her for dissection!
But since I'm here, I'll no neglect,
  In loyal, true affection,
To pay your Queen, with due respect,
  My fealty an' subjection
    This great Birth-day.

Hail, Majesty most Excellent!
  While nobles strive to please Ye,
Will Ye accept a compliment
  A simple Poet gies Ye?
Thae bonny bairntime, Heav'n has lent,
  Still higher may they heeze[7] Ye
In bliss, till Fate some day is sent,
  For ever to release Ye
    Frae care that day.

For you, young Potentate o' Wales,
  I tell your Highness fairly,
Down Pleasure's stream, wi' swelling sails,
  I'm tauld ye're driving rarely;
But some day ye may gnaw your nails,
  An' curse your folly sairly,
That e'er ye brak Diana's pales,
  Or rattl'd dice wi' Charlie[8]
    By night or day.

---

[1] Must needs.
[2] Field.
[3] Child.
[4] Bemires.
[5] Exult.
[6] Stretch.
[7] Raise.
[8] Mr Fox.

Yet aft a ragged cowte's[1] been known
To mak a noble aiver;[2]
Sae, ye may doucely fill a Throne,
For a' their clish-ma-claver:[3]
There, Him[4] at Agincourt wha shone,
Few better were or braver;
And yet, wi' funny, queer Sir John,[5]
He was an unco shaver[6]
For monie a day.

For you, right rev'rend Osnaburg,[7]
Nane sets the lawn-sleeves sweeter,
Altho' a ribbon at your lug
Wad been a dress completer:
As ye disown yon paughty[8] dog
That bears the Keys of Peter,
Then, swith![9] an' get a wife to hug,
Or, trouth! ye'll stain the Mitre
Some luckless day.

Young, royal Tarry Breeks,[10] I learn,
Ye've lately come athwart her;
A glorious galley,[11] stem and stern,
Weel rigg'd for Venus' barter;
But first hang out, that she'll discern
Your hymeneal charter.
Then heave aboard your grapple airn,[12]
An', large upon her quarter,
Come full that day.

Ye, lastly, bonnie blossoms a',
Ye royal Lasses dainty,
Heav'n mak you guid as weel as braw,
An' gie you lads a plenty:
But sneer na British boys awa',
For Kings are unco scant ay;
An' German Gentles are but sma',
They're better just than want ay
On onie day.

God bless you a'! consider now
Ye're unco muckle dautet;[13]
But, ere the course o' life be through,
It may be bitter sautet:

[1] Colt. [2] Cart-horse. [3] Idle talk.
[4] King Henry V.—R. B.
[5] Sir John Falstaff; *vide* Shakspeare.—R. B. [6] Wag.
[7] Osnaburg gave the title of Bishop to the second son of George III.
[8] Proud. [9] Get away.
[10] The Royal "Breeks" was the Duke of Clarence.
[11] Alluding to the newspaper account of a certain Royal sailor's amour.—R. B.
[12] Iron. [13] Caressed.

An' I hae seen their coggie[1] fou
That yet hae tarrow't[2] at it;
But or the day was done, I trow,
The laggen[3] they hae clautet[4]
Fu' clean that day.

LINES TO A PAINTER,

WHOM BURNS FOUND AT WORK ON A PICTURE OF JACOB'S DREAM.

DEAR ——, I'll gie ye some advice,
You'll tak it no uncivil;
You shouldna' paint at angels mair,[5]
But try and paint the devil.

To paint an angel's kittle wark,[6]
Wi' auld Nick there's less danger;
You'll easy draw a weel-kent face,
But no sae weel a stranger.

VERSES ON A WAG IN MAUCHLINE.[7]

LAMENT him, Mauchline husbands a';
He often did assist ye;
For had ye staid whole years awa',
Your wives they ne'er had miss'd ye.

Ye Mauchline bairns,[8] as on ye pass
To school in bands thegither,
Oh tread ye lightly on his grass—
Perhaps he was your father.

THE VISION.

DUAN FIRST.[9]

THE sun had closed the winter day,
The Curlers[10] quat their roarin play,
And hunger'd Maukin[11] taen her way
To kail-yards green,

[1] Little wooden dish. [2] Murmured.
[3] The angle between the side and bottom of the dish. [4] Scraped.
[5] More. [6] Ticklish work.
[7] James Smith. [8] Children.
[9] Duan, a term of Ossian's for the different divisions of a digressive poem. See his "Cath-Loda," vol. ii. of M'Pherson's translation.—R. B.
[10] Players at a game on the ice, called curling. [11] Hare.

While faithless snaws ilk step betray
Where she has been.

The thresher's weary flingin-tree
The lee-lang day had tired me;
And when the day had clos'd his e'e,
Far i' the west,
Ben i' the Spence,[1] right pensivelie,
I gaed to rest.

There, lanely, by the ingle-cheek,
I sat and ey'd the spewing reek,
That fill'd, wi' hoast-provoking smeek,
The auld, clay biggin;[2]
An' heard the restless rattons[3] squeak
About the riggin.

All in this mottie, misty clime,
I backward mus'd on wasted time,
How I had spent my youthfu' prime,
An' done nae-thing,
But stringin blethers up in rhyme,
For fools to sing.

Had I to guid advice but harkit,
I might, by this, hae led a market
Or strutted in a bank, and clarkit
My cash-account:
While here, half-mad, half-fed, half-sarkit[4]
Is a' th' amount.

I started, mutt'ring, blockhead! coof![5]
And heav'd on high my waukit loof,[6]
To swear by a' yon starry roof,
Or some rash aith,
That I, henceforth, would be rhyme-proof
Till my last breath—

When, click! the string the snick[7] did draw;
And, jee! the door gaed to the wa';
And by my ingle-lowe[8] I saw,
Now bleezin bright,
A tight, outlandish Hizzie, braw,
Come full in sight.

Ye need na doubt, I held my whist;[9]
The infant aith, half-form'd, was crusht;

[1] The parlour. [2] House.
[3] Rats. [4] Half-provided with shirts.
[5] Ninny.
[6] Thickened or stained palm. [7] Latch.
[8] Hearth-flame. [9] Silence.

I glowr'd as eerie's I'd been dusht[1]
In some wild glen;
When sweet, like modest worth, she blusht,
And stepped ben.[2]

Green, slender, leaf-clad holly-boughs
Were twisted, gracefu', round her brows,
I took her for some Scottish Muse,
By that same token;
And come to stop those reckless vows,
Would soon been broken.

A "hair-brain'd, sentimental trace,"
Was strongly marked in her face;
A wildly-witty, rustic grace
Shone full upon her;
Her eye, ev'n turn'd on empty space,
Beam'd keen with Honour.

Down flow'd her robe, a tartan sheen;
Till half a leg was scrimply[3] seen;
And such a leg! my bonnie Jean
Could only peer it;
Sae straught, sae taper, tight, and clean,
Nane else came near it.

Her mantle large, of greenish hue,
My gazing wonder chiefly drew;
Deep lights and shades, bold-mingling, threw
A lustre grand;
And seem'd, to my astonish'd view,
A well-known land.

Here, rivers in the sea were lost;
There, mountains to the skies were tost:
Here, tumbling billows mark'd the coast,
With surging foam;
There, distant shone Art's lofty boast,
The lordly dome.

Here, Doon pour'd down his far-fetch'd floods;
There, well-fed Irwine stately thuds:[4]
Auld hermit Ayr staw[5] thro' his woods,
On to the shore;
And many a lesser torrent scuds,
With seeming roar.

Low, in a sandy valley spread,
An ancient Borough rear'd her head;
Still, as in Scottish story read,
She boasts a race,

[1] Struck down. [2] Inward.
[3] Partly. [4] Sounds. [5] Did steal.

To ev'ry nobler virtue bred,
And polish'd grace.

By stately tow'r or palace fair,
Or ruins pendent in the air,
Bold stems of Heroes, here and there,
I could discern;
Some seem'd to muse, some seem'd to dare,
With features stern.

My heart did glowing transport feel,
To see a Race[1] heroic wheel,
And brandish round the deep-dy'd steel
In sturdy blows:
While back-recoiling seem'd to reel
Their Suthron foes.

His COUNTRY'S SAVIOUR,[2] mark him well!
Bold Richardton's[3] heroic swell;
The Chief on Sark[4] who glorious fell,
In high command;
And he whom ruthless fates expel
His native land.

There, where a sceptr'd Pictish shade[5]
Stalk'd round his ashes lowly laid,
I mark'd a martial Race, portray'd
In colours strong;
Bold, soldier-featur'd, undismay'd
They strode along.

---

[1] The Wallaces.—R. B.

[2] William Wallace.—R. B.

[3] Adam Wallace, of Richarton, cousin of the immortal preserver of Scottish independence.—R. B.

[4] Wallace, Laird of Craigie, who was second in command, under Douglas Earl of Ormond, at the famous battle on the banks of Sark, fought anno 1448. That glorious victory was principally owing to the judicious conduct and intrepid valour of the gallant Laird of Craigie, who died of his wounds after the action.—R. B.

[5] Coilus, King of the Picts, from whom the district of Kyle is said to take its name, lies buried, as tradition says, near the family-seat of the Montgomeries of Coilsfield, where his burial-place is still shown.—R. B.

Thro' many a wild, romantic grove,[1]
Near many a hermit-fancy'd cove,
(Fit haunts for Friendship or for Love,
In musing mood,)
An aged Judge, I saw him rove,
Dispensing good.

With deep-struck reverential awe
The learned Sire and Son I saw,[2]
To Nature's God and Nature's law
They gave their lore,
This, all its source and end to draw;
That, to adore.

Brydone's brave Ward[3] I well could spy,
Beneath old Scotia's smiling eye;
Who call'd on Fame, low standing by,
To hand him on,
Where many a Patriot name on high,
And Hero shone.

DUAN SECOND.

WITH musing-deep, astonish'd stare,
I view'd the heav'nly-seeming Fair;
A whisp'ring throb did witness bear,
Of kindred sweet,
When with an elder Sister's air
She did me greet.

"All hail! my own inspired Bard!
In me thy native Muse regard!
Nor longer mourn thy fate is hard,
Thus poorly low!
I come to give thee such reward
As we bestow.

"Know, the great Genius of this land
Has many a light, aërial band,
Who, all beneath his high command,
Harmoniously,
As Arts or Arms they understand,
Their labours ply.

"They Scotia's Race among them share;
Some fire the Soldier on to dare:
Some rouse the Patriot up to bare
Corruption's heart:
Some teach the Bard, a darling care,
The tuneful art.

---

[1] Barskimming, the seat of the late Lord Justice Clerk [Miller].—R. B.

[2] Catrine, the seat of the late Doctor and present Professor Stewart.—R. B.

[3] Colonel Fullarton.—R. B.

"'Mong swelling floods of reeking gore,
They, ardent, kindling spirits pour;
Or, 'mid the venal Senate's roar,
They, sightless, stand,
To mend the honest Patriot-lore,
And grace the hand.

"And when the Bard, or hoary Sage,
Charm or instruct the future age,
They bind the wild, Poetic rage
In energy,
Or point the inconclusive page
Full on the eye.

"Hence, Fullarton, the brave and young;
Hence, Dempster's zeal-inspired tongue;
Hence, sweet harmonious Beattie sung
His 'Minstrel lays;'
Or tore, with noble ardour stung,
The Sceptic's bays.

"To lower orders are assign'd
The humbler ranks of human-kind,
The rustic Bard, the lab'ring Hind,
The Artisan:
All chuse, as various they're inclin'd,
The various man.

"When yellow waves the heavy grain,
The threat'ning storm some, strongly, rein;
Some teach to meliorate the plain
With tillage-skill;
And some instruct the Shepherd-train,
Blythe o'er the hill.

"Some hint the Lover's harmless wile;
Some grace the Maiden's artless smile;
Some soothe the Lab'rer's weary toil,
For humble gains,
And make his cottage-scenes beguile
His cares and pains.

"Some, bounded to a district-space,
Explore at large Man's infant race,
To mark the embryotic trace
Of rustic Bard;
And careful note each op'ning grace,
A guide and guard.

"Of these am I—Coila my name;
And this district as mine I claim,
Where once the Campbells, chiefs of fame,
Held ruling pow'r:
I mark'd thy embryo-tuneful flame,
Thy natal hour.

"With future hope, I oft would gaze,
Fond, on thy little early ways,
Thy rudely-caroll'd, chiming phrase,
In uncouth rhymes,
Fir'd at the simple, artless lays
Of other times.

"I saw thee seek the sounding shore,
Delighted with the dashing roar;
Or when the North his fleecy store
Drove thro' the sky,
I saw grim Nature's visage hoar
Struck thy young eye.

"Or when the deep green-mantl'd Earth
Warm-cherish'd ev'ry flow'ret's birth,
And joy and music pouring forth
In ev'ry grove,
I saw thee eye the gen'ral mirth
With boundless love.

"When ripen'd fields, and azure skies,
Call'd forth the Reaper's rustling noise,
I saw thee leave their ev'ning joys,
And lonely stalk,
To vent thy bosom's swelling rise
In pensive walk.

"When youthful Love, warm-blushing strong,
Keen-shivering shot thy nerves along,
Those accents, grateful to thy tongue,
Th' adored Name,
I taught thee how to pour in song,
To soothe thy flame.

"I saw thy pulse's maddening play,
Wild send thee Pleasure's devious way,
Misled by Fancy's meteor ray,
By Passion driven;
But yet the light that led astray
Was light from Heaven.

"I taught thy manners-painting strains,
The loves, the ways of simple swains,
Till now, o'er all my wide domains
Thy fame extends;
And some, the pride of Coila's plains,
Become thy friends.

"Thou canst not learn, nor can I show,
To paint with Thomson's landscape glow;
Or wake the bosom-melting throe,
With Shenstone's art;

Or pour, with Gray, the moving flow
Warm on the heart.

"Yet, all beneath th' unrivall'd rose,
The lowly daisy sweetly blows;
Tho' large the forest's monarch throws
His army shade,
Yet green the juicy hawthorn grows,
Adown the glade.

"Then never murmur nor repine;
Strive in thy humble sphere to shine;
And trust me, not Potosi's mine,
Nor Kings' regard,
Can give a bliss o'ermatching thine,
A rustic Bard.

"To give my counsels all in one,—
Thy tuneful flame still careful fan;
Preserve the dignity of Man,
With Soul erect;
And trust, the Universal Plan
Will all protect.

"And wear thou this"—she solemn said,
And bound the Holly round my head:
The polish'd leaves, and berries red,
Did rustling play;
And, like a passing thought, she fled
In light away.

LINES WRITTEN IN FRIARS-CARSE HERMITAGE.[1]

THOU whom chance may hither lead,
Be thou clad in russet weed,
Be thou deckt in silken stole,
Grave these counsels on thy soul:—

Life is but a day at most,
Sprung from night, in darkness lost;
Hope not sunshine every hour,
Fear not clouds will always lour.

As Youth and Love, with sprightly dance,
Beneath thy morning-star advance,
Pleasure, with her siren air,
May delude the thoughtless pair;
Let Prudence bless Enjoyment's cup,
Then raptured sip, and sip it up.

As thy day grows warm and high,
Life's meridian flaming nigh,
Dost thou spurn the humble vale?
Life's proud summits wouldst thou scale?
Check thy climbing step, elate,
Evils lurk in felon wait:
Dangers, eagle-pinion'd, bold,
Soar around each cliffy hold,
While cheerful Peace, with linnet song,
Chants the lowly dells among.

As the shades of evening close,
Beckoning thee to long repose;
As life itself becomes disease,
Seek the chimney-neuk of ease,
There ruminate with sober thought
On all thou'st seen, and heard, and wrought:
And teach the sportive younkers round,
Saws of experience sage and sound:
Say, man's true, genuine estimate,
The grand criterion of his fate,
Is not—Art thou high or low?
Did thy fortune ebb or flow?
Wast thou cottager or king?
Peer or peasant?—no such thing!
Did many talents gild thy span?
Or frugal Nature grudge thee one?
Tell them, and press it on their mind,
As thou thyself must shortly find,
The smile or frown of awful Heaven
To Virtue or to Vice is given.
Say, "To be just, and kind, and wise,
There solid Self-enjoyment lies;
That foolish, selfish, faithless ways
Lead to the wretched, vile, and base."

Thus resign'd and quiet, creep
To the bed of lasting sleep;
Sleep, whence thou shalt ne'er awake,
Night, where dawn shall never break,
Till future life—future no more—
To light and joy the good restore,
To light and joy unknown before!

Stranger, go! Heaven be thy guide!
Quoth the beadsman of Nithside.

---

[1] The beautiful residence of Captain Riddell, near Ellisland, who was a kind friend of the poet. These lines, which appeared in 1788, were an amended version of one written in 1783.

ADDRESS TO THE UNCO GUID, OR THE RIGIDLY RIGHTEOUS.

My son, these maxims make a rule,
And lump them aye thegither;
The RIGID RIGHTEOUS is a fool,
The RIGID WISE anither:
The cleanest corn that e'er was dight
May hae some pyles o' caff in;
So ne'er a fellow-creature slight
For random fits o' daffin.
Solomon.—Eccles. vii. 16.

O YE wha are sae guid yoursel,
Sae pious and sae holy,
Ye've nought to do but mark and tell
Your Neebour's fauts and folly!
Whase life is like a weel-gaun mill,
Supply'd wi' store o' water,
The heapet happer's ebbing still,
And still the clap plays clatter.

Hear me, ye venerable Core,[1]
As counsel for poor mortals,
That frequent pass douce Wisdom's door,
For glaikit[2] Folly's portals;
I, for their thoughtless, careless sakes,
Would here propone defences,
Their donsie[3] tricks, their black mistakes,
Their failings and mischances.

Ye see your state wi' theirs compar'd
And shudder at the niffer,[4]
But cast a moment's fair regard,
What maks the mighty differ?
Discount what scant occasion gave
That purity ye pride in,
And (what's aft mair than a' the lave)
Your better art o' hidin'.

Think, when your castigated pulse
Gies now and then a wallop,
What raging must his veins convulse,
That still eternal gallop:
Wi' wind and tide fair i' your tail,
Right on ye scud your sea-way:
But in the teeth o' baith to sail,
It maks an unco leeway.

See Social life and Glee sit down,
All joyous and unthinking,
Till, quite transmugrify'd,[1] they're grown
Debauchery and Drinking:
O would they stay to calculate
Th' eternal consequences;
Or your more dreaded hell to state,
Damnation of expenses!

Ye high, exalted, virtuous Dames,
Ty'd up in godly laces,
Before ye gie poor Frailty names,
Suppose a change o' cases;
A dear lov'd lad, convenience snug,
A treacherous inclination—
But let me whisper i' your lug,
Ye're aiblins[2] nae temptation.

Then gently scan your brother Man,
Still gentler sister Woman;
Tho' they may gang a kennie[3] wrang,
To step aside is human:
One point must still be greatly dark,
The moving *Why* they do it;
And just as lamely can ye mark
How far perhaps they rue it.

Who made the heart, 'tis He alone
Decidedly can try us,
He knows each chord—its various tone,
Each spring—its various bias:
Then at the balance let's be mute,
We never can adjust it;
What's *done* we partly may compute,
But know not what's *resisted.*

[1] Corps. [2] Careless. [3] Unlucky. [4] Exchange.

TAM SAMSON'S ELEGY.[4]

An honest man's the noblest work of God.—*Pope.*

HAS auld Kilmarnock seen the Deil?
Or great M'Kinlay[5] thrawn his heel?

[1] Transformed. [2] May be.
[3] Small matter.
[4] When this worthy old sportsman went out last muir-fowl season, he supposed it was to be, in Ossian's phrase, "the last of his fields;" and expressed an ardent wish to die and be buried in the muirs. On this hint the author composed his Elegy and Epitaph.—R. B.
[5] A certain preacher, a great favourite

Or Robinson[1] again grown weel,
To preach an' read?
"Na, waur than a'!" cries ilka chiel,
"Tam Samson's dead!"

Kilmarnock lang may grunt an' grane,
An' sigh, an' sab, an' greet her lane,[2]
An' cleed[3] her bairns, man, wife, an' wean,
In mourning weed;
To Death she's dearly paid the kane,[4]
Tam Samson's dead!

The Brethren o' the mystic level
May hing their head in woefu' bevel,
While by their nose the tears will revel,
Like ony bead;
Death's gien the Lodge an unco devel,
Tam Samson's dead!

When Winter muffles up his cloak,
And binds the mire like a rock;
When to the loughs the Curlers flock
Wi' gleesome speed,
Wha will they station at the cock?
Tam Samson's dead!

He was the king o' a' the Core,
To guard, or draw, or wick a bore,
Or up the rink like Jehu roar
In time o' need;
But now he lags on Death's hog-score,[5]
Tam Samson's dead!

Now safe the stately Sawmont[6] sail,
And Trouts bedropp'd wi' crimson hail,
And Eels weel ken'd for souple tail,
And Geds for greed,
Since dark in Death's fish-creel we wail
Tam Samson's dead!

Rejoice, ye birring Paitricks[7] a';
Ye cootie Moorcocks, crousely craw;[8]
Ye Maukins,[9] cock your fud[10] fu' braw,
Withouten dread;

with the million.—Vide The Ordination, stanza ii.—R. B.

[1] Another preacher, an equal favourite with the few, who was at that time ailing. For him, see also The Ordination, stanza ix.—R. B.

[2] Herself alone. [3] Clothe. [4] Rent.

[5] A distance line in curling, drawn across the *rink*. [6] Salmon.

[7] Partridges. [8] Cheerfully crow.

[9] Hares. [10] Tail.

Your mortal Fae is now awa',—
Tam Samson's dead!

That woefu' morn be ever mourn'd
Saw him in shootin graith[1] adorn'd,
While pointers round impatient burn'd,
Frae couples freed;
But, Och! he gaed and ne'er return'd!
Tam Samson's dead!

In vain auld age his body batters;
In vain the gout his ancles fetters;
In vain the burns cam' down like waters,
An acre braid!
Now ev'ry auld wife, greetin, clatters,
"Tam Samson's dead!"

Owre mony a weary hag he limpit,
An' aye the tither shot he thumpit,
Till coward Death behind him jumpit
Wi' deadly feide;[2]
Now he proclaims, wi' tout o' trumpet,
Tam Samson's dead!

When at his heart he felt the dagger,
He reel'd his wonted bottle-swagger,
But yet he drew the mortal trigger
Wi' weel-aim'd heed;
"Lord, five!" he cry'd, an' owre did stagger;
Tam Samson's dead!

Ilk hoary hunter mourn'd a brither;
Ilk sportsman youth bemoan'd a father;
Yon auld gray stane, amang the heather,
Marks out his head,
Whare Burns has wrote, in rhyming blether,
Tam Samson's dead!

There, low he lies, in lasting rest;
Perhaps upon his mould'ring breast
Some spitefu' muirfowl bigs her nest;
To hatch and breed;
Alas! nae mair he'll them molest!
Tam Samson's dead!

When August winds the heather wave
And sportsmen wander by yon grave,
Three volleys let his mem'ry crave
O' pouther an' lead,
Till Echo answer frae her cave,
Tam Samson's dead!

Heav'n rest his saul, whare'er he be!
Is th' wish o' mony mae than me:

[1] Dress. [2] Feud.

He had twa faults, or maybe three,
Yet what remead?
Ae social, honest man want we:
Tam Samson's dead!

THE EPITAPH.

TAM SAMSON'S weel-worn clay here lies,
Ye canting zealots, spare him!
If honest worth in heaven rise,
Ye'll mend or ye win near him.

PER CONTRA.[1]

Go, Fame, and canter like a filly
Thro' a' the streets an' neuks o' Killie,[2]
Tell ev'ry social, honest billie
To cease his grievin,
For yet, unskaith'd by Death's gleg gullie,[3]
Tam Samson's livin!

THE TREE OF LIBERTY.[4]

HEARD ye o' the tree o' France,
I watna what's the name o't;
Around it a' the patriots dance,
Weel Europe kens the fame o't.
It stands where ance the Bastile stood,
A prison built by kings, man,
When Superstition's hellish brood
Kept France in leading-strings, man.

Upon this tree there grows sic fruit,
Its virtues a' can tell, man;
It raises man aboon the brute,
It maks him ken himsel, man.
Gif ance the peasant taste a bit,
He's greater than a lord, man,
And wi' the beggar shares a mite
Of a' he can afford, man.

This fruit is worth a' Afric's wealth,
To comfort us 'twas sent, man:
To gie the sweetest blush o' health,
And mak us a' content, man.
It clears the een, it cheers the heart,
Maks high and low guid friends, man;
And he wha acts the traitor's part
It to perdition sends, man.

My blessings aye attend the chiel
Wha pitied Gallia's slaves, man,
And staw[1] a branch, spite o' the deil,
Frae yont the western waves, man.
Fair Virtue water'd it wi' care,
And now she sees wi' pride, man,
How weel it buds and blossoms there,
Its branches spreading wide, man.

But vicious folk aye hate to see
The works o' Virtue thrive, man;
The courtly vermin's bann'd the tree,
And grat[2] to see it thrive, man;
King Louis thought to cut it down
When it was unco sma', man;
For this the watchman crack'd his crown,
Cut aff his head and a', man.

A wicked crew syne,[3] on a time,
Did tak a solemn aith, man,
It ne'er should flourish to its prime,
I wat they pledged their faith, man;
Awa' they gaed, wi' mock parade,
Like beagles hunting game, man,
But soon grew weary o' the trade,
And wish'd they'd been at hame, man.

For Freedom, standing by the tree,
Her sons did loudly ca', man;
She sang a sang o' liberty,
Which pleased them ane and a', man.
By her inspired, the new-born race
Soon drew the avenging steel, man;
The hirelings ran—her foes gied chase,
And bang'd the despot weel, man.

Let Britain boast her hardy oak,
Her poplar and her pine, man,
Auld Britain ance could crack her joke,
And o'er her neighbours shine, man.
But seek the forest round and round,
And soon 'twill be agreed, man,
That sic a tree cannot be found
'Twixt London and the Tweed, man.

[1] The "Per Contra" was a peace-offering to the old sportsman, angry at his poetical dissolution. Burns retired to the window in Tam's apartment for a few minutes, and returned with this stanza on his lips.

[2] Killie is a phrase the country-folks sometimes use for the name of a certain town in the west [Kilmarnock].—R. B.

[3] Sharp knife.

[4] Written in 1794, and first printed in Chambers's edition of Burns' works, in 1838.

[1] Stole. [2] Wept. [3] Then.

Without this tree, alake, this life
  Is but a vale o' woe, man ;
A scene o' sorrow mix'd wi' strife,
  Nae real joys we know, man.
We labour soon, we labour late,
  To feed the titled knave, man ;
And a' the comfort we're to get
  Is that ayont the grave, man.

Wi' plenty o' sic trees, I trow,
  The warld would live in peace, man ;
The sword would help to mak a plough,
  The din o' war wad cease, man.
Like brethren in a common cause,
  We'd on each other smile, man ;
And equal rights and equal laws
  Wad gladden every isle, man.

Wae worth the loon wha wadna eat
  Sic halesome dainty cheer, man ;
I'd gie my shoon frae aff my feet,
  To taste sic fruit, I swear, man.
Syne let us pray, auld England may
  Sure plant this far-famed tree, man ;
And blithe we'll sing, and hail the day
  That gives us liberty, man.

HALLOWEEN.[1]

The following Poem will, by many readers, be well enough understood ; but for the sake of those who are unacquainted with the manners and traditions of the country where the scene is cast, notes are added, to give some account of the principal charms and spells of that night, so big with prophecy to the peasantry in the west of Scotland. The passion of prying into futurity makes a striking part of the history of human nature, in its rude state, in all ages and nations ; and it may be some entertainment to a philosophic mind, if any such should honour the Author with a perusal, to see the remains of it, among the more unenlightened in our own.—R. B.

[1] Halloween is thought to be a night when witches, devils, and other mischief-making beings are all abroad on their baneful, midnight errands ; particularly those aërial people, the fairies, are said on that night to hold a grand anniversary.—R. B.

Yes ! let the rich deride, the proud disdain,
The simple pleasures of the lowly train ;
To me more dear, congenial to my heart,
One native charm, than all the gloss of art.—*Goldsmith.*

UPON that night, when Fairies light
  On Cassilis Downans[1] dance,
Or owre the lays,[2] in splendid blaze,
  On sprightly coursers prance ;
Or for Colean the route is ta'en,
  Beneath the moon's pale beams ;
There, up the Cove[3] to stray an' rove,
  Amang the rocks and streams
      To sport that night.

Amang the bonnie, winding banks,
  Where Doon rins, wimplin,[4] clear,
Where Bruce[5] ance rul'd the martial ranks,
  An' shook his Carrick spear,
Some merry, friendly, contra folks,
  Together did convene,
To burn their nits,[6] an' pou their stocks,[7]
  An' haud their Halloween
      Fu' blythe that night.

The lasses feat,[8] an' cleanly neat,
  Mair braw than when they're fine ;
Their faces blythe, fu' sweetly kythe,[9]
  Hearts leal, an' warm, an' kin :

[1] Certain little, romantic, rocky, green hills, in the neighbourhood of the ancient seat of the Earls of Cassilis.—R. B.

[2] Fields.

[3] A noted cavern near Colean-house, called the Cove of Colean ; which, as well as Cassilis Downans, is famed in country story for being a favourite haunt of fairies.—R. B.

[4] Meandering.

[5] The famous family of that name, the ancestors of Robert, the great deliverer of his country, were Earls of Carrick.—R. B.

[6] Nuts.

[7] Plants of kail.

[8] Spruce.

[9] Shewn.

The lads sae trig,[1] wi' wooer-babs,[2]
  Weel knotted on their garten,
Some unco blate, an' some wi' gabs,
  Gar lasses' hearts gang startin
    Whyles fast at night.

Then, first, an' foremost, thro' the kail,
  Their stocks[3] maun a' be sought ance:
They steek their een, an' grape[4] an' wale,[5]
  For muckle anes, an' straught anes.
Poor hav'rel[6] Will fell aff the drift,
  An' wander'd thro' the bow-kail,[7]
An' pow't,[8] for want o' better shift,
  A runt[9] was like a sow-tail,
    Sae bow't[10] that night.

Then, straught or crooked, yird[11] or nane,
  They roar an' cry a' throu'ther;[12]
The vera wee things, toddlin, rin,
  Wi' stocks out-owre their shouther;
An' gif the custocs[13] sweet or sour,
  Wi' joctelegs[14] they taste them;

[1] Smart.
[2] Garters knotted with loops.
[3] The first ceremony of Halloween is, pulling each a stock, or plant of kail. They must go out, hand in hand, with eyes shut, and pull the first they meet with. Its being big or little, straight or crooked, is prophetic of the size and shape of the grand object of all their spells—the husband or wife. If any yird, or earth, stick to the root, that is tocher, or fortune; and the taste of the custoc, that is, the heart of the stem, is indicative of the natural temper and disposition. Lastly, the stems, or, to give them their ordinary appellation, the runts, are placed somewhere above the head of the door; and the Christian names of the people whom chance brings into the house, are, according to the priority of placing the runts, the names in question.—R. B.
[4] Grope. [5] Choose. [6] Half-witted.
[7] Cabbage. [8] Pulled.
[9] A cabbage stem. [10] Crooked.
[11] Earth. [12] In confusion.
[13] Hearts of stems. [14] Knives.

Syne coziely,[1] aboon the door,
  Wi' cannie care, they've plac'd them
    To lie that night.

The lasses staw[2] frae' mang them a'
  To pou their stalks o' corn;[3]
But Rab slips out, an' jinks[4] about,
  Behint the muckle thorn:
He grippet Nelly hard an' fast;
  Loud skirled a' the lasses;
But her tap-pickle maist was lost,
  When kiutlin[5] in the fause-house[6]
    Wi' him that night.

The auld guidwife's weel-hoordet[7] nits[8]
  Are round an' round divided,
An' monie lads' and lasses' fates
  Are there that night decided:
Some kindle, couthie,[9] side by side,
  An' burn thegither trimly;
Some start awa, wi' saucy pride,
  An' jump out-owre the chimlie
    Fu' high that night.

Jean slips in twa wi' tentie[10] e'e;
  Wha 'twas, she wadna tell;

[1] Snugly. [2] Steal.
[3] They go to the barn-yard, and pull each, at three several times, a stalk of oats. If the third stalk wants the top-pickle, that is, the grain at the top of the stalk, the party in question will come to the marriage-bed anything but a maid.—R. B.
[4] Dodges. [5] Cuddling.
[6] When the corn is in a doubtful state, by being too green, or wet, the stack-builder, by means of old timber, &c., makes a large apartment in his stack, with an opening in the side which is fairest exposed to the wind: this he calls a fause-house.—R. B.
[7] Well-hoarded.
[8] Burning the nuts is a famous charm. They name the lad and the lass to each particular nut, as they lay them in the fire; and accordingly as they burn quietly together, or start from beside one another, the course and issue of the courtship will be.—R. B.
[9] Loving. [10] Cautious.

But this is Jock, and this is me,
She says in to hersel:
He bleez'd owre her, an' she owre him,
As they wad never mair part;
Till, fuff! he started up the lum,[1]
An' Jean had e'en a sair heart
To see't that night.

Poor Willie, wi' his bow-kail runt,
Was brunt wi' primsie[2] Mallie,
An' Mary, nae doubt, took the drunt,[3]
To be compared to Willie:
Mall's nit lap out, wi' pridefu' fling,
An' her ain fit it brunt it;
While Willie lap, an' swoor[4] by jing,
'Twas just the way he wanted
To be that night.

Nell had the fause-house in her min',[5]
She pits hersel an' Rob in;
In loving bleeze they sweetly join,
Till white in ase[6] they're sobbin:
Nell's heart was dancin at the view;
She whisper'd Rob to leuk for't:
Rob, stownlins,[7] prie'd[8] her bonnie mou,
Fu' cozie in the neuk for't,
Unseen that night.

But Merran sat behint their backs,
Her thoughts on Andrew Bell;
She lea'es[9] them gashin at their cracks,
An' slips out by hersel:
She thro' the yard the nearest taks,
An' to the kiln she goes then,
An' darklins grapit for the bauks,[10]
And in the blue-clue[11] throws then,
Right fear't that night.

[1] The chimney. [2] Demure.
[3] Pet. [4] Swore. [5] Mind.
[6] Ashes. [7] By stealth.
[8] Tasted. [9] Leaves.
[10] Cross-beams.
[11] Whoever would with success try this spell, must strictly observe these directions:—Steal out, all alone, to the kiln, and, darkling, throw into the pot a clue of blue yarn; wind it in a new clue off the old one; and, towards the latter end, something will hold the thread; demand, Wha hauds? *i. e.* who holds? an answer will be returned from the kiln-pot, by naming the Christian and surname of your future spouse.—R. B.

An' aye she win't, an' ay she swat,
I wat she made nae jaukin;[1]
Till something held within the pat,
Guid Lord! but she was quaukin![2]
But whether 'twas the Deil himsel
Or whether 'twas a bauk-en',
Or whether it was Andrew Bell,
She did na wait on talkin
To spier[3] that night.

Wee Jennie to her Graunie says,
"Will ye go wi' me, Graunie?
I'll eat the apple[4] at the glass,
I gat frae uncle Johnie:"
She fuff't[5] her pipe wi' sic a lunt,[6]
In wrath she was sae vap'rin,
She notic't na, an aizle[7] brunt
Her braw new worset[8] apron
Out thro' that night.

"Ye little skelpie[9]-limmer's face!
I daur you try sic sportin,
As seek the foul Thief onie place,
For him to spae[10] your fortune;
Nae doubt but ye may get a sight!
Great cause ye hae to fear it;
For monie a ane has gotten fright,
An' liv'd an' di'd deleerit,[11]
On sic a night.

"Ae Hairst[12] afore the Sherra-moor,[13]
I mind't as weel's yestreen,
I was a gilpey[14] then, I'm sure
I was na past fyfteen:
The simmer had been cauld an' wat,
An' stuff was unco green;
An' ay a rantin kirn we gat,
An' just on Halloween
It fell that night.

[1] Dallying. [2] Quaking. [3] Inquire.
[4] Take a candle, and go alone to a looking-glass; eat an apple before it, and some traditions say, you should comb your hair all the time; the face of your conjugal companion, to be, will be seen in the glass, as if peeping over your shoulder.—R. B.
[5] Did blow. [6] Column of smoke.
[7] Hot cinder. [8] Worsted.
[9] A word of scolding. [10] Prophesy.
[11] Delirious. [12] Harvest.
[13] Sheriff-moor, the battle fought in the Rebellion, 1715.
[14] A romping girl.

"Our stibble-rig[1] was Rab M'Graen,
A clever, sturdy fallow;
His sin gat Eppie Sim wi' wean,
That liv'd in Auchmacalla;
He gat hemp-seed,[2] I mind it weel,
An' he made unco light o't;
But monie a day was by himsel,
He was sae sairly frighted
That vera night."

Then up gat fechtin Jamie Fleck,
An' he swoor by his conscience,
That he could saw hemp-seed a peck;
For it was a' but nonsense:
The auld guidman raught down the pock,
An' out a handfu' gied him;
Syne bad him slip frae 'mang the folk,
Sometime when nae ane see'd him,
An' try't that night.

He marches thro' amang the stacks,
Tho' he was something sturtin:[3]
The graip[4] he for a harrow taks,
An' haurls[5] at his curpin:[6]
An' ev'ry now an' then, he says,
"Hemp-seed, I saw thee,
An' her that is to be my lass,
Come after me, an' draw thee
As fast this night."

He whistl'd up Lord Lenox' march,
To keep his courage cheary;
Altho' his hair began to arch,
He was sae fley'd[7] an' eerie:

[1] Head reaper.
[2] Steal out unperceived, and sow a handful of hemp-seed; harrowing it with any thing you can conveniently draw after you. Repeat now and then, "Hemp-seed, I saw thee, hemp-seed, I saw thee; and him (or her) that is to be my true-love, come after me and pou thee." Look over your left shoulder, and you will see the appearance of the person invoked, in the attitude of pulling hemp. Some traditions say, "Come after me, and shaw thee," that is, show thyself: in which case it simply appears. Others omit the harrowing, and say, "Come after me, and harrow thee."—R. B.
[3] Frightened. [4] Stable fork.
[5] Drags. [6] Crupper. [7] Scared.

Till presently he hears a squeak,
An' then a grane an' gruntle;
He, by his shouther gae a keek,[1]
An' tumbl'd wi' a wintle[2]
Out-owre that night.

He roar'd a horrid murder-shout,
In dreadfu' desperation!
An' young an' auld came rinnin out,
An' hear the sad narration:
He swoor 'twas hilchin[3] Jean M'Craw,
Or crouchie[4] Merran Humphie,
Till stop! she trotted thro' them a':
An' wha was it but Grumphie
Asteer[5] that night!

Meg fain wad to the barn hae gaen
To winn three wechts o' naething;
But for to meet the Deil her lane,
She put but little faith in:
She gies the herd a pickle nits,
And twa red-cheekit apples,
To watch, while for the barn she sets,
In hopes to see Tam Kipples
That vera night.

She turns the key, wi' cannie thraw,
An' owre the threshold ventures:
But first on Sawnie gies a ca',
Syne bauldly in she enters;
A ratton[7] rattl'd up the wa',
An' she cry'd, Lord preserve her!

[1] A peep. [2] Stagger. [3] Halting.
[4] Crook-backed. [5] Abroad.
[6] This charm must likewise be performed unperceived, and alone. You go to the barn, and open both doors, taking them off the hinges, if possible; for there is danger, that the *being*, about to appear, may shut the doors, and do you some mischief. Then take that instrument used in winnowing the corn, which, in our country dialect, we call a wecht; and go through all the attitudes of letting down corn against the wind. Repeat it three times; and the third time an apparition will pass through the barn, in at the windy door, and out at the other, having both the figure in question, and the appearance or retinue, marking the employment or station in life.—R. B.
[7] Rat.

An' ran thro' midden-hole[1] an' a',
An' pray'd wi' zeal an' fervour,
Fu' fast that night.

They hoy't[2] out Will, wi' sair advice;
They hecht[3] him some fine braw ane;
It chanc'd the stack he faddom't[4] thrice[5]
Was timmer[6]-propt from thrawin:
He taks a swirlie,[7] auld moss-oak,
For some black grousome Carlin;
An' loot a winze,[8] an' drew a stroke,
Till skin in blypes[9] cam haurlin
Aff's nieves[10] that night.

A wanton widow Leezie was,
As cantie[11] as a kittlen;
But, Och! that night, amang the shaws,[12]
She got a fearfu' settlin!
She thro' the wins, an' by the cairn,
An' owre the hill gaed scrievin,
Whare three lairds' lands met at a burn,[13]
To dip her left sark-sleeve in,
Was bent that night.

Whyles owre a linn the burnie plays,
As thro' the glen it whimpl't:
Whyles round a rocky scar it strays;
Whyles in a wiel[14] it dimpl't;

[1] Gutter at the bottom of a dung-hill.
[2] Urged. [3] Foretold. [4] Fathomed.
[5] Take an opportunity of going, unnoticed, to a bean-stack, and fathom it three times round. The last fathom of the last time you will catch in your arms the appearance of your future conjugal yoke-fellow.—R. B.
[6] Timber. [7] Knotty. [8] Oath.
[9] Shreds. [10] Fists. [11] Merry.
[12] Woods.
[13] You go out, one or more, (for this is a social spell,) to a south running spring or rivulet, where "three lairds' lands meet," and dip your left shirt sleeve. Go to bed in sight of a fire and hang your wet sleeve before it to dry. Lie awake; and some time near midnight, an apparition, having the exact figure of the grand object in question, will come and turn the sleeve, as if to dry the other side of it.—R. B.
[14] Small whirlpool, or eddy.

Whyles glitter'd to the nightly rays,
Wi' bickering, dancing dazzle;
Whyles cookit[1] underneath the braes,
Below the spreading hazel,
Unseen that night.

Amang the brachens,[2] on the brae,
Between her an' the moon,
The Deil, or else an outler Quey,
Gat up an' gae a croon:[3]
Poor Leezie's heart maist lap the hool:[4]
Near lav'rock-height she jumpit,
But mist a fit, an' in the pool
Out-owre the lugs[5] she plumpit,
Wi' a plunge that night.

In order, on the clean hearth-stane,
The luggies[6] three[7] are ranged;
And ev'ry time great care is ta'en,
To see them duly changed:
Auld Uncle John, wha wedlock's joys
Sin' Mar's-year did desire,
Because he gat the toom[8] dish thrice,
He heaved them on the fire
In wrath that night.

Wi' merry sangs, an' friendly cracks,
I wat they did na weary;
And unco tales, an' funnie jokes,
Their sports were cheap an' cheary,
Till butter'd So'ns,[9] wi' fragrant lunt,[10]
Set a' their gabs[11] a steerin;[12]

[1] Appeared and vanished.
[2] Fern. [3] A deep moan.
[4] Leaped out of the case. [5] Ears.
[6] Small wooden dishes with handles.
[7] Take three dishes; put clean water in one, foul water in another, leave the third empty: blindfold a person, and lead him to the hearth where the dishes are ranged; he (or she) dips the left hand: if by chance in the clean water, the future husband or wife will come to the bar of matrimony, a maid: if in the foul, a widow: if in the empty dish, it foretells, with equal certainty, no marriage at all. It is repeated three times; and every time the arrangement of the dishes is altered.—R. B. [8] Empty.
[9] Sowens, with butter instead of milk to them, is always the Halloween Supper.—R. B. *Sowens* is a kind of oatmeal pudding. [10] Smoke.
[11] Mouths. [12] A-stirring.

Syne, wi' a social glass o' strunt,[1]
 They parted aff careerin'[2]
  Fu' blythe that night.

THE JOLLY BEGGARS.[3]

A CANTATA.

RECITATIVO.

When lyart[4] leaves bestrew the yird,
Or, wavering like the bauckie[5] bird,
 Bedim cauld Boreas' blast:
When hailstanes drive wi' bitter skyte,
And infant frosts begin to bite,
 In hoary cranreuch[6] drest;

[1] Spirituous liquor of any kind.

[2] Cheerfully.

[3] Sir Walter Scott was unable to conceive any good reason why Dr. Currie did not introduce this Cantata into his collection. For humorous description and nice discrimination of character, he thought it inferior to no poem of the same length in the whole range of English verse; and the mirth of the songs, combined with the vividness of the pictures, he considered to be unequalled. This is very exaggerated praise; and few readers, I should suppose, will admit the truth of Scott's remark, that "even in describing the movements of such a group, the native taste of the poet has never suffered his pen to slide into anything coarse or disgusting." See Scott's "Prose Works," xvii. 244. Mr. Lockhart is yet more profuse of admiration, and doubts if Shakspeare, out of such materials, could have constructed a piece, "in which the sympathy-awakening power could have been displayed more triumphantly." And Allan Cunningham outstrips his predecessors, by affirming that "nothing in the language, in life and character, approaches this song." The "Beggar's Opera" being a "burial, compared to it." Surely this is the burlesque of criticism, and only brings it into contempt.

[4] Discoloured. [5] Bat.

[6] Hoar-frost.

Ae night, at e'en, a merry core
 O' randie, gangrel[1] bodies,
In Poosie-Nansie's held the splore,[2]
 To drink their orra duddies:
  Wi' quaffing and laughing,
   They ranted and they sang;
  Wi' jumping and thumping,
   The vera girdle[3] rang.

First, neist the fire, in auld red rags,
Ane sat, weel brac'd wi' mealy bags,
 And knapsack a' in order;
His doxy lay within his arm,
Wi' usquebae and blankets warm;
 She blinket on her sodger;
An' aye he gies the tozie[4] drab
 The tither skelpin[5] kiss,
While she held up her greedy gab,[6]
 Just like an aumous dish;[7]
  Ilk smack still, did crack still,
   Just like a cadger's whup,
  Then staggering, and swaggering,
   He roar'd this ditty up—

AIR.

TUNE—"SOLDIER'S JOY."

I am a son of Mars, who have been in many wars,
 And show my cuts and scars wherever I come;
This here was for a wench, and that other in a trench,
 When welcoming the French at the sound of the drum.
  Lal de daudle, &c.

My 'prenticeship I past where my leader breath'd his last,
 When the bloody die was cast on the heights of Abram;[8]
I serv'd out my trade when the gallant game was play'd,
 And the Moro[9] low was laid at the sound of the drum.
  Lal de daudle, &c.

[1] Vagrant. [2] Frolic.

[3] The iron plate for baking cakes.

[4] Tipsy. [5] Slapping. [6] Mouth.

[7] The beggar's alms-dish.

[8] Quebec, where Wolfe fell.

[9] A Spanish castle taken by the English army, in 1762.

I lastly was with Curtis, among the floating batt'ries,
And there I left for witnesses an arm and a limb:
Yet let my country need me, with Elliot to head me,
I'd clatter on my stumps at the sound of the drum.
Lal de daudle, &c.

And now, though I must beg, with a wooden arm and leg,
And many a tatter'd rag hanging over my bum,
I'm as happy with my wallet, my bottle, and my callet,
As when I us'd in scarlet to follow the drum.
Lal de daudle, &c.

What tho' with hoary locks, I must stand the winter shocks,
Beneath the woods and rocks, oftentimes for a home;
When the tother bag I sell, and the tother bottle tell,
I could meet a troop of h— at the sound of the drum.

RECITATIVO.

He ended; and the kebars[1] sheuk
Aboon the chorus roar;
While frighted rattons[2] backward leuk,
And seek the benmost[3] bore:

A fairy fiddler frae the neuk,
He skirled out encore!
But up arose the martial chuck,
And laid the loud uproar.

AIR.

TUNE—"SOLDIER LADDIE."

I ONCE was a maid, tho' I cannot tell when,
And still my delight is in proper young men:
Some one of a troop of dragoons was my daddie,
No wonder I'm fond of a sodger laddie.
Sing, Lal de lal, &c.

[1] Rafters. [2] Rats. [3] Innermost.

The first of my loves was a swaggering blade,
To rattle the thundering drum was his trade;
His leg was so tight, and his cheek was so ruddy,
Transported I was with my sodger laddie.
Sing, Lal de lal, &c.

But the goodly old chaplain left him in the lurch,
So the sword I forsook for the sake of the church;
He ventured the soul, and I risked the body,
'Twas then I proved false to my sodger laddie.
Sing, Lal de lal, &c.

Full soon I grew sick of the sanctified sot,
The regiment at large for a husband I got;
From the gilded spontoon to the fife I was ready,
I asked no more but a sodger laddie.
Sing, Lal de lal, &c.

But the peace it reduced me to beg in despair,
Till I met my old boy at Cunningham fair;
His rags regimental they fluttered so gaudy,
My heart it rejoic'd at my sodger laddie.
Sing, Lal de lal, &c.

And now I have liv'd—I know not how long,
And still I can join in a cup or a song
But whilst with both hands I can hold the glass steady,
Here's to thee, my hero, my sodger laddie.
Sing, Lal de lal, &c.

RECITATIVO.

Poor Merry Andrew, in the neuk,
Sat guzzling wi' a tinkler hizzie;
They mind't na wha the chorus took,
Between themselves they were sae bizzy;

At length, wi' drink and courting dizzy,
He stoitered[1] up an' made a face;
Then turn'd, an' laid a smack on Grizzy,
Syne tun'd his pipes wi' grave grimace.

AIR.

TUNE—"AULD SIR SIMON."

SIR Wisdom's a fool when he's fou,
Sir Knave is a fool in a session;
He's there but a 'prentice I trow,
But I am a fool by profession.

My grannie she bought me a beuk,
And I held awa to the school;
I fear I my talent misteuk,
But what will ye hae of a fool?

For drink I would venture my neck;
A hizzie's the half o' my craft;
But what could ye other expect,
Of ane that's avowedly daft?

I ance was ty'd up like a stirk,[2]
For civilly swearing and quaffing;
I ance was abused i' the kirk,
For touzling a lass i' my daffin.[3]

Poor Andrew that tumbles for sport,
Let naebody name wi' a jeer;
There's ev'n, I'm tauld, i' the Court,
A tumbler ca'd the Premier.

Observ'd ye, yon reverend lad
Maks faces to tickle the mob;
He rails at our mountebank squad,
It's rivalship just i' the job.

And now my conclusion I'll tell,
For faith I'm confoundedly dry;
The chiel that's a fool for himsel',
Gude Lord, is far dafter than I.

RECITATIVO.

Then neist outspak a raucle carlin,[4]
Wha kent fu' weel to cleek the sterling,
For monie a pursie she had hooked,
And had in monie a well been ducked;
Her dove had been a Highland laddie,
But weary fa the waefu' woodie![5]
Wi' sighs and sabs, she thus began
To wail her braw John Highlandman:

[1] Staggered.
[2] Bullock. [3] Merriment.
[4] Stout old woman. [5] Rope.

AIR.

TUNE—"O, AN' YE WERE DEAD, GUIDMAN."

A HIGHLAND lad my love was born,
The Lawlan' laws he held in scorn:
But he still was faithful to his clan,
My gallant braw John Highlandman.

CHORUS.

Sing, hey, my braw John Highlandman!
Sing, ho, my braw John Highlandman!
There's no a lad in a' the lan'
Was match for my John Highlandman.

With his philibeg an' tartan plaid,
And gude claymore down by his side,
The ladies' hearts he did trepan,
My gallant braw John Highlandman.
Sing, hey, &c.

We ranged a' from Tweed to Spey,
And liv'd like lords and ladies gay;
For a Lawlan face he feared nane,
My gallant braw John Highlandman.
Sing, hey, &c.

They banish'd him beyond the sea,
But ere the bud was on the tree,
Adown my cheeks the pearls ran,
Embracing my John Highlandman.
Sing, hey, &c.

But, oh! they catch'd him at the last,
And bound him in a dungeon fast;
My curse upon them every ane,
They've hang'd my braw John Highlandman.
Sing, hey, &c.

And now a widow, I must mourn
The pleasures that will ne'er return;
No comfort but a hearty can,
When I think on John Highlandman.
Sing, hey, &c.

RECITATIVO.

A pigmy Scraper wi' his fiddle,
Wha us'd at trysts and fairs to driddle,[1]

[1] Play.

Her strappin limb and gaucy[1] middle
 (He reach'd nae higher),
Had holed his heartie like a riddle,
 And blawn't on fire.

Wi' hand on haunch, and upward e'e,
He croon'd his gamut, ane, twa, three,
Then, in an Arioso key,
 The wee Apollo
Set aff, wi' Allegretto glee,
 His giga solo.

AIR.

TUNE—"WHISTLE O'ER THE LAVE O'T."

LET me ryke[2] up to dight[3] that tear,
And go wi' me and be my dear,
And then your every care and fear
 May whistle owre the lave o't.

CHORUS.

I am a fiddler to my trade,
And a' the tunes that e'er I play'd,
The sweetest still to wife or maid,
 Was whistle o'er the lave o't.

At kirns and weddings we'se be there,
And oh! sae nicely's we will fare;
We'll bouse about, till Daddie Care
 Sings Whistle owre the lave o't.
 I am, &c.

Sae merrily's the banes we'll pyke,[4]
And sun oursels about the dyke,
And at our leisure, when ye like,
 We'll whistle owre the lave o't.
 I am, &c.

But bless me wi' your heav'n o' charms,
And while I kittle[5] hair on thairms,
Hunger, cauld, and a' sic harms,
 May whistle owre the lave o't.
 I am, &c.

RECITATIVO.

Her charms had struck a sturdy caird,[6]
 As well as poor gut-scraper;
He taks the fiddler by the beard,
 And draws a rusty rapier—

He swoor, by a' was swearing worth,
 To speet him like a pliver,
Unless he wad from that time forth
 Relinquish her for ever.

Wi' ghastly ee, poor Tweedle-dee
 Upon his hunkers bended,
And pray'd for grace, wi' ruefu' face,
 And sae the quarrel ended.

But tho' his little heart did grieve
 When round the tinkler prest her,
He feign'd to snirtle[1] in his sleeve,
 When thus the Caird address'd her:

AIR.

TUNE—"CLOUT THE CAUDRON."

MY bonnie lass, I work in brass,
 A tinkler is my station;
I've travell'd round all Christian ground
 In this my occupation;
I've ta'en the gold, I've been enroll'd
 In many a noble squadron;
But vain they search'd, when off I march'd
 To go and clout the caudron.
 I've ta'en the gold, &c.

Despise that shrimp, that wither'd imp,
 Wi' a' his noise and caprin,
And tak a share wi' those that bear
 The budget and the apron;
And by that stoup, my faith and houp,
 And by that dear Kilbagie,[2]
If e'er ye want, or meet wi' scant,
 May I ne'er weet my craigie.[3]
 And by that stoup, &c.

RECITATIVO.

The Caird prevail'd—th' unblushing fair
 In his embraces sunk,
Partly wi' love o'ercome sae sair,
 And partly she was drunk.
Sir Violino, with an air
 That show'd a man o' spunk,
Wish'd unison between the pair,
 And made the bottle clunk,
 To their health that night.

---

[1] Jolly. [2] Reach. [3] Wipe. [4] Pick. [5] While I apply hair to catgut.—*Chambers.* [6] Gipsy.

[1] Laugh. [2] A peculiar sort of whisky. [3] Throat.

But hurchin Cupid shot a shaft
  That play'd a dame a shavie,[1]
The fiddler rak'd her fore and aft,
  Ahint the chicken cavie.
Her lord, a wight o' Homer's craft,
  Tho' limping wi' the spavie,
He hirpl'd[2] up, and lap like daft,
  And shor'd[3] them Dainty Davie
    O' boot that night.

He was a care-defying blade
  As ever Bacchus listed,
Tho' Fortune sair upon him laid,
  His heart she ever miss'd it.
He had nae wish, but—to be glad,
  Nor want but—when he thirsted;
He hated nought but—to be sad,
  And thus the Muse suggested
    His sang that night.

AIR.

TUNE—"FOR A' THAT, AND A' THAT."

I AM a bard of no regard
  Wi' gentlefolks, an' a' that;
But Homer-like, the glowrin byke,[4]
  Frae town to town I draw that.

CHORUS.

For a' that, and a' that,
  And twice as meikle's a' that;
I've lost but ane, I've twa behin',
  I've wife enough for a' that.

I never drank the Muses' stank,[5]
  Castalia's burn, an' a' that:
But there it streams, and richly reams,
  My Helicon I ca' that.
    For a' that, &c.

Great love I bear to a' the fair,
  Their humble slave, an' a' that;
But lordly will, I hold it still
  A mortal sin to thraw that.
    For a' that, &c.

In raptures sweet, this hour we meet,
  Wi' mutual love, an' a' that;
But for how lang the flie may stang,
  Let inclination law that.
    For a' that, &c.

[1] Trick. [2] Crept. [3] Threatened. [4] Staring crowd. [5] Pool.

Their tricks and craft hae put me daft,
  They've ta'en me in, and a' that;
But clear your decks, and "Here's the Sex!"
  I like the jads for a' that.

For a' that, and a' that,
  And twice as meikle's a' that,
My dearest bluid, to do them guid,
  They're welcome till't, for a' that.

RECITATIVO.

So sung the bard—and Nansie's[1] wa's
Shook with a thunder of applause,
  Re-echo'd from each mouth;
They toom'd[2] their pocks, an' pawn'd their duds,[3]
They scarcely left to co'er their fuds,[4]
  To quench their lowan[5] drouth.

Then owre again, the jovial thrang
  The poet did request,
To loose his pack, an' wale[6] a sang,
  A ballad o' the best;
    He, rising, rejoicing,
      Between his twa Deborahs,
    Looks round him, an' found them
      Impatient for the chorus.

AIR.

TUNE—"JOLLY MORTALS, FILL YOUR GLASSES."

SEE! the smoking bowl before us,
  Mark our jovial ragged ring;
Round and round take up the chorus,
  And in raptures let us sing:

[1] Poosie Nansie, otherwise Agnes Gibson, kept a sort of cadger's house, nearly opposite to the church-yard gate in Mauchline. We are told by the biographers of Burns, that passing by the house, one night, in the company of James Smith, he was allured by the mirthful uproar to go in and join the crew. The Cantata gives the poetical experience of the night.
[2] Emptied. [3] Rags. [4] Tails. [5] Flaming. [6] Choose.

CHORUS.

A fig for those by law protected !
  Liberty's a glorious feast !
Courts for cowards were erected,
  Churches built to please the priest.

What is title ? what is treasure ?
  What is reputation's care ?
If we lead a life of pleasure,
  'Tis no matter how or where !
    A fig, &c.

With the ready trick and fable,
  Round we wander all the day ;
And at night, in barn or stable,
  Hug our doxies on the hay.
    A fig, &c.

Does the train-attended carriage
  Thro' the country lighter rove ?
Does the sober bed of marriage
  Witness brighter scenes of love ?
    A fig, &c.

Life is all a variorum,
  We regard not how it goes ;
Let them cant about decorum
  Who have characters to lose.
    A fig, &c.

Here's to budgets, bags, and wallets !
  Here's to all the wandering train !
Here's our ragged brats and callets !
  One and all cry out, Amen !
    A fig, &c.

IMPROMPTU

ADDRESSED TO A YOUNG LADY IN A CHURCH WHO WAS ENGAGED IN SEARCHING FOR A TEXT GIVEN OUT BY THE MINISTER, WHICH CONTAINED A SEVERE DENUNCIATION ON OBSTINATE SINNERS.

FAIR maid, you need not take the hint,
  Nor idle texts pursue ;
'Twas *guilty sinners* that he meant,
  Not *angels* such as you !

CASTLE GORDON.[1]

STREAMS that glide in orient plains,
Never bound by winter's chains !
  Glowing here on golden sands,
There commix'd with foulest stains
  From tyranny's empurpled hands ;
These, their richly-gleaming waves,
I leave to tyrants and their slaves ;
Give me the stream that sweetly laves
  The banks by Castle Gordon.

Spicy forests, ever gay,
Shading from the burning ray
  Hapless wretches sold to toil,
Or the ruthless native's way,
  Bent on slaughter, blood, and spoil ;
Woods that ever verdant wave,
I leave the tyrant and the slave ;
Give me the groves that lofty brave
  The storms by Castle Gordon.

Wildly here, without control,
Nature reigns and rules the whole ;
  In that sober pensive mood,
Dearest to the feeling soul,
  She plants the forest, pours the flood
Life's poor day I'll musin rave,
And find at night a shelt'ring cave,
Where waters flow and wild woods wave,
  By bonnie Castle Gordon.

THE AULD FARMER'S NEW-YEAR MORNING SALUTATION TO HIS AULD MARE MAGGIE, ON GIVING HER THE ACCUSTOMED RIPP OF CORN TO HANSEL IN THE NEW YEAR.

A GUID New-Year I wish thee, Maggie !
Hae, there's a ripp[2] to thy auld baggie :

[1] Written after a brief visit, in 1787. to Gordon Castle, the seat of the Duke of Gordon.
[2] Handful.

Tho' thou's howe-backit[1] now, an' knaggie,[2]
I've seen the day,
Thou could hae gane like onie staggie
Out-owre the lay.

Tho' now thou's dowie,[3] stiff, an' crazy,
An' thy auld hide's as white's a daisie,
I've seen thee dappl't, sleek, an' glaizie,
A bonnie gray:
He should been tight that daur't to raize thee,
Ance in a day.

Thou ance was i' the foremost rank,
A filly buirdly,[4] steeve,[5] an' swank,[6]
An' set weel down a shapely shank,
As e'er tread yird;
An' could hae flown out-owre a stank,[7]
Like onie bird.

It's now some nine-an'-twenty year,
Sin' thou was my guid-father's meere·
He gied me thee, o' tocher[8] clear,
An' fifty mark;
Tho' it was sma', 'twas weel won gear,
An' thou was stark.[9]

When first I gaed to woo my Jenny,
Ye then was trottin wi' your minnie:
Tho' ye was trickie, slee, an' funnie,
Ye ne'er was donsie;[10]
But hamely, tawie, quiet, cannie,
An' unco sonsie.[11]

That day, ye pranc'd wi' muckle pride,
When ye bure[12] hame my bonnie bride;
An' sweet an' gracefu' she did ride,
Wi' maiden air!
Kyle Stewart I could bragged wide,
For sic a pair.

Tho' now ye dow[13] but hoyte and hobble,
An' wintle like a saumont-coble,[14]
That day ye was a jinker noble,
For heels an' win'!
An' ran them till they a' did wauble,[15]
Far, far behin'.

[1] Sunk in the back. [2] Sharp-pointed.
[3] Worn out. [4] Stout-made.
[5] Strong-set. [6] Stately. [7] Morass.
[8] Marriage portion. [9] Stout.
[10] Unlucky. [11] Easily handled.
[12] Did bear. [13] Can.
[14] Salmon fishing boat. [15] Reel.

When thou an' I were young and skeigh,[1]
An' stable-meals at fairs were dreigh,[2]
How thou wad prance, an' snore, an skreigh
An' tak the road!
Town's bodies ran, and stood abeigh,[3]
An' ca't thee mad.

When thou was corn't, an' I was mellow,
We took the road ay like a swallow:
At Brooses[4] thou had ne'er a fellow,
For pith an' speed;
But ev'ry tail thou pay't them hollow,
Whare'er thou gaed.

The sma', droop-rumpl't,[5] hunter cattle,
Might aiblins[6] waur't thee for a brattle;[7]
But sax Scotch miles thou try't their mettle,
An' gart them whaizle:
Nae whip nor spur, but just a wattle
O' saugh or hazel.

Thou was a noble fittie-lan',[8]
As e'er in tug[9] or tow[10] was drawn!
Aft thee an' I, in aught hours gaun,
On guid March-weather,
Hae turn'd sax rood beside our han',
For days thegither.

Thou never braindg't,[11] an' fech't,[12] an fliskit,[13]
But thy auld tail thou wad hae whiskit,
An' spread abreed thy weel-fill'd brisket,
Wi' pith an' pow'r,
Till spritty knowes[14] wad rair't and riskit,
An' slypet[15] owre.

[1] High-mettled. [2] Tedious.
[3] At a safe distance.
[4] A broose is a race at a wedding.
[5] That droops at the crupper.
[6] Perhaps. [7] Short race.
[8] The near horse of the hindmost pair in the plough.
[9] Traces of hide. [10] Rope.
[11] Plunged forward. [12] Pulled by fits.
[13] Fretted. [14] Rushy hillocks.
[15] Fell over.

When frosts lay lang, an' snaws were deep,
An' threaten'd labour back to keep,
I gied thy cog[1] a wee-bit heap
Aboon the timmer;
I ken'd my Maggie wadna sleep
For that, or simmer.

In cart or car thou never reestit;
The steyest[2] brae thou wad hae face't it;
Thou never lap,[3] an' sten't,[4] and breastit,
Then stood to blaw;
But just thy step a wee thing hastit,
Thou snoov't[5] awa.

My pleugh is now thy bairn-time a':
Four gallant brutes as e'er did draw;
Forbye sax mae, I've sell't awa,
That thou has nurst:
They drew me thretteen[6] pund an' twa,
The vera warst.

Monie a sair daurk[7] we twa hae wrought,
An' wi' the weary warl' fought!
An' monie an anxious day, I thought
We wad be beat!
Yet here to crazy age we're brought,
Wi' something yet.

And think na, my auld, trusty servan',
That now perhaps thou's less deservin,
An' thy auld days may end in starvin,
For my last fou,
A heapit stimpart,[8] I'll reserve ane
Laid by for you.

We've worn to crazy years thegither;
We'll toyte[9] about wi' ane anither;
Wi' tentie care I'll flit thy tether
To some hain'd[10] rig,
Whare ye may nobly rax[11] your leather,
Wi' sma' fatigue.

---

[1] Manger. [2] Steepest.
[3] Leaped. [4] Reared.
[5] Went at an even pace.
[6] Thirteen. [7] Day's labour.
[8] Eighth part of a bushel. [9] Totter.
[10] Spared. [11] Stretch.

TO A MOUSE, ON TURNING HER UP IN HER NEST, WITH THE PLOUGH, NOVEMBER, 1785.[1]

Wee, sleekit, cowrin, tim'rous beastie,
O, what a panic's in thy breastie!
Thou need na start awa sae hasty,
Wi' bickering brattle![2]
I wad be laith to rin an' chase thee,
Wi' murd'ring pattle![3]

I'm truly sorry man's dominion
Has broken Nature's social union,
An' justifies that ill opinion,
Which makes thee startle
At me, thy poor, earth-born companion,
An' fellow-mortal!

I doubt na, whyles, but thou may thieve;
What then? poor beastie, thou maun live!
A daimen-icker[4] in a thrave
'S a sma' request:
I'll get a blessin wi' the lave,
And never miss't!

Thy wee bit housie, too, in ruin!
Its silly wa's the win's are strewin!
An' naething, now, to big[5] a new one,
O' foggage green!
An' bleak December's winds ensuin,
Baith snell[6] an' keen!

Thou saw the fields laid bare an' waste,
An' weary winter comin fast,
An' cozie here, beneath the blast,
Thou thought to dwell,
Till, crash! the cruel coulter past
Out thro' thy cell.

---

[1] A farm-servant, lately living, was driving the plough, which Burns held, when a mouse ran across the field. The man's first impulse was to rush after and kill it; but the poet stopped him, and soon turning thoughtful, the verses were conceived and born.
[2] Hurry.
[3] Instrument for clearing the plough.
[4] An ear of corn now and then; thrave is twenty-four sheaves.
[5] Build. [6] Bitter.

That wee bit heap o' leaves an' stibble
Has cost thee mony a weary nibble!
Now thou's turn'd out, for a' thy trouble,
But house or hald,[1]
To thole[2] the winter's sleety dribble,
An' cranreuch[3] cauld!

But, Mousie, thou art no thy lane,[4]
In proving foresight may be vain:
The best-laid schemes o' mice an' men,
Gang aft a-gley,[5]
An' lea'e us nought but grief and pain,
For promis'd joy.

Still thou art blest, compar'd wi' me!
The present only toucheth thee:
But, Och! I backward cast my e'e
On prospects drear!
An' forward, tho' I canna see,
I guess an' fear!

A WINTER NIGHT.

Poor naked wretches, wheresoe'er you are,
That bide the pelting of this pitiless storm!
How shall your houseless heads, and unfed sides,
Your loop'd and window'd raggedness, defend you,
From seasons such as these?—
Shakspeare.

When biting Boreas, fell and doure,[6]
Sharp shivers thro' the leafless bow'r;
When Phœbus gies a short-liv'd glow'r,
Far south the lift,[7]
Dim-dark'ning thro' the flaky show'r,
Or whirling drift:

Ae night the storm the steeples rocked,
Poor labour sweet in sleep was locked,
While burns, wi' snawy wreeths[8] up-choked
Wild-eddying swirl,

[1] Without abiding-place.
[2] Endure. [3] Hoar-frost.
[4] Thyself alone. [5] Wrong.
[6] Sullen. [7] The sky.
[8] Drifted heaps of snow.

Or thro' the mining outlet bocked,[1]
Down headlong hurl.

List'ning the doors an' winnocks[2] rattle,
I thought me on the ourie[3] cattle,
Or silly sheep, wha bide this brattle
O' winter war,
And thro' the drift, deep-lairing,[4] sprattle,[5]
Beneath a scar.

Ilk happing[6] bird, wee, helpless thing!
That, in the merry months o' spring,
Delighted me to hear thee sing,
What comes o' thee?
Whare wilt thou cow'r thy chittering[7] wing,
An' close thy e'e?

Ev'n you on murd'ring errands toil'd,
Lone from your savage homes exil'd,
The blood-stain'd roost, and sheep-cote spoil'd,
My heart forgets,
While pityless the tempest wild
Sore on you beats.

Now Phœbe, in her midnight reign,
Dark muffl'd, view'd the dreary plain:
Still crowding thoughts, a pensive train,
Rose in my soul,
When on my ear this plaintive strain,
Slow, solemn, stole—

"Blow, blow, ye winds, with heavier gust!
And freeze, thou bitter-biting frost!
Descend, ye chilly, smothering snows!
Not all your rage, as now united, shows
More hard unkindness, unrelenting,
Vengeful malice, unrepenting,
Than heav'n-illumin'd man on brother man bestows!
See stern Oppression's iron grip,
Or mad Ambition's gory hand,
Sending, like blood-hounds from the slip,
Woe, want, and murder o'er a land!

[1] Flung out. [2] Windows.
[3] Shivering. [4] Deep wading.
[5] Scramble. [6] Hopping.
[7] Shivering.

Ev'n in the peaceful rural vale,
Truth, weeping, tells the mournful tale,
How pamper'd Luxury, Flatt'ry by her side,
The parasite empoisoning her ear,
With all the servile wretches in the rear,
Looks o'er proud property, extended wide;
And eyes the simple rustic hind,
Whose toil upholds the glitt'ring show,
A creature of another kind,
Some coarser substance, unrefin'd,
Plac'd for her lordly use thus far, thus vile, below!
Where, where is Love's fond, tender throe,
With lordly Honour's lofty brow,
The pow'rs you proudly own?
Is there, beneath Love's noble name,
Can harbour, dark, the selfish aim,
To bless himself alone!
Mark maiden-innocence a prey
To love-pretending snares,
This boasted Honour turns away,
Shunning soft Pity's rising sway,
Regardless of the tears, and unavailing pray'rs!
Perhaps, this hour, in mis'ry's squalid nest
She strains your infant to her joyless breast,
And with a mother's fears shrinks at the rocking blast!
Oh ye! who, sunk in beds of down,
Feel not a want but what yourselves create,
Think, for a moment, on his wretched fate,
Whom friends and fortune quite disown!
Ill-satisfied keen nature's clam'rous call,
Stretch'd on his straw he lays himself to sleep,
While thro' the ragged roof and chinky wall,
Chill o'er his slumbers, piles the drifty heap!
Think on the dungeon's grim confine,
Where Guilt and poor Misfortune pine!
Guilt, erring man, relenting view!
But shall thy legal rage pursue
The wretch, already crushed low
By cruel Fortune's undeserved blow?
Affliction's sons are brothers in distress;
A brother to relieve, how exquisite the bliss!"

I heard nae mair, for Chanticleer
Shook off the pouthery snaw,
And hail'd the morning with a cheer,
A cottage-rousing craw.[1]

But deep this truth impress'd my mind—
Thro' all His works abroad,
The heart benevolent and kind
The most resembles God.

THE TARBOLTON LASSES.[2]

If ye gae up to yon hill-tap,
Ye'll there see bonny Peggy;
She kens her father is a laird,
And she forsooth's a leddy.

There Sophy tight, a lassie bright,
Besides a handsome fortune:
Wha canna win her in a night,
Has little art in courting.

Gae down by Faile, and taste the ale,
And tak a look o' Mysie;
She's dour[3] and din, a deil within,
But aiblins[4] she may please ye.

If she be shy, her sister try,
Ye'll maybe fancy Jenny,
If ye'll dispense wi' want o' sense—
She kens hersel she's bonny.

As ye gae up by yon hill-side,
Speer in for bonny Bessy;
She'll gie ye a beck, and bid ye licht,
And handsomely address ye.

There's few sae bonnie, nane sae guid,
In a' King George's dominion;
If ye should doubt the truth o' this—
It's Bessy's ain opinion.

---

[1] Crow. [2] See p. 8.
[3] Obstinate. [4] Perhaps.

VERSES TO AN OLD SWEETHEART AFTER HER MARRIAGE.[1]

(WRITTEN IN 1786.)

ONCE fondly loved, and still remember'd dear,
Sweet early object of my youthful vows!
Accept this mark of friendship, warm, sincere—
Friendship!—'tis all cold duty now allows.

And when you read the simple, artless rhymes,
One friendly sigh for him,—he asks no more,
Who distant burns in flaming torrid climes,
Or haply lies beneath the Atlantic's roar.

EPISTLE TO DAVIE,[2] A BROTHER POET.

January, 1784.

WHILE winds frae aff Ben-Lomond blaw,
And bar the doors wi' driving snaw,
And hing us owre the ingle,[3]
I set me down, to pass the time,
And spin a verse or twa o' rhyme,
In hamely, westlin jingle.

[1] Written on the fly-leaf of a copy of his poems presented to the lady, whose name is not mentioned. It is supposed that the poet was contemplating emigration.

[2] Davie was David Sillar, the author of a book of Scottish verses. Gilbert Burns writes respecting his brother:—It was, I think, in summer, 1784, when, in the interval of harder labour, he and I were weeding in the garden (kailyard), that he repeated to me the principal part of this Epistle. I believe the first idea of Robert's becoming author was started on this occasion.

[3] Fire-place.

While frosty winds blaw in the drift,
Ben to the chimla-lug,[1]
I grudge a wee the great folks' gift,
That live sae bien[2] an' snug:
I tent[3] less, and want less
Their roomy fire-side;
But hanker and canker,
To see their cursed pride.

It's hardly in a body's pow'r,
To keep, at times, frae being sour,
To see how things are shar'd;
How best o' chiels are whiles in want,
While coofs on countless thousands rant,
And ken na how to wair't;[4]
But, Davie, lad, ne'er fash[5] your head,
Tho' we hae little gear,
We're fit to win our daily bread,
As lang's we're hale and fier:[6]
"Mair spier na, nor fear na,"[7]
Auld age ne'er mind a feg,[8]
The last o't, the warst o't,
Is only for to beg.

To lie in kilns and barns at e'en,
When banes are craz'd, and bluid is thin,
Is, doubtless, great distress!
Yet then content could mak us blest;
Ev'n then, sometimes, we'd snatch a taste
Of truest happiness.
The honest heart that's free frae a'
Intended fraud or guile,
However fortune kick the ba',[9]
Has aye some cause to smile:
And mind still, you'll find still,
A comfort this nae sma';
Nae mair then, we'll care then,
Nae farther can we fa'.

What tho', like commoners of air,
We wander out, we know not where,
But either house or hal'?
Yet nature's charms, the hills and woods,
The sweeping vales, and foaming floods,
Are free alike to all.

[1] To the parlour hearth. [2] Plentiful. [3] Heed. [4] Spend it. [5] Trouble. [6] Sound. [7] Ramsay.—R. B. [8] Fig. [9] Ball.

In days when daisies deck the ground,
  And blackbirds whistle clear,
With honest joy our hearts will bound
  To see the coming year:
    On braes when we please, then,
      We'll sit and sowth[1] a tune;
    Syne[2] rhyme till't,[3] we'll time till't,
      And sing't when we hae done.

It's no in titles nor in rank;
It's no in wealth like Lon'on bank,
  To purchase peace and rest:
It's no in making muckle mair;
It's no in books; it's no in lear,[4]
  To make us truly blest:
If happiness hae not her seat
  And centre in the breast,
We may be wise, or rich, or great,
  But never can be blest:
    Nae treasures, nor pleasures,
      Could make us happy lang;
    The heart aye's the part aye,
      That maks us right or wrang.

Think ye, that sic as you and I,
Wha drudge and drive thro' wet an' dry,
  Wi' never-ceasing toil;
Think ye, are we less blest than they,
Wha scarcely tent[5] us in their way,
  As hardly worth their while?
Alas! how aft in haughty mood,
  God's creatures they oppress!
Or else, neglecting a' that's guid,
  They riot in excess!
    Baith careless, and fearless,
      Of either heav'n or hell!
    Esteeming and deeming
      It's a' an idle tale!

Then let us cheerfu' acquiesce;
Nor make our scanty pleasures less,
  By pining at our state;
And, even should misfortunes come,
I, here wha sit, hae met wi' some,
  An's thanfu' for them yet.
They gie the wit of age to youth;
  They let us ken oursel;
They make us see the naked truth,
  The real guid and ill.

[1] Whistle over. [2] Then. [3] To it. [4] Learning. [5] Heed.

    Tho' losses, and crosses,
      Be lessons right severe,
    There's wit there, ye'll get there,
      Ye'll find nae other where.

But tent me, Davie, ace o' hearts!
(To say aught less wad wrang the cartes,[1]
  And flatt'ry I detest)
This life has joys for you and I;
And joys that riches ne'er could buy;
  And joys the very best.
There's a' the pleasures o' the heart,
  The lover an' the frien';
Ye hae your Meg,[2] your dearest part,
  And I my darling Jean!
    It warms me, it charms me,
      To mention but her name:
    It heats me, it beets me,[3]
      And sets me a' on flame!

O all ye pow'rs who rule above!
O Thou, whose very self art love!
  Thou know'st my words sincere!
The life-blood streaming thro' my heart,
Or my more dear immortal part,
  Is not more fondly dear!
When heart-corroding care and grief
  Deprive my soul of rest,
Her dear idea brings relief
  And solace to my breast
    Thou Being, All-seeing,
      O hear my fervent pray'r;
    Still take her, and make her
      Thy most peculiar care!

All hail, ye tender feelings dear!
The smile of love, the friendly tear,
  The sympathetic glow!
Long since, this world's thorny ways
Had number'd out my weary days,
  Had it not been for you!
Fate still has blest me with a friend,
  In every care and ill;
And oft a more endearing band,
  A tie more tender still,
    It lightens, it brightens
      The tenebrific scene,
    To meet with, and greet with
      My Davie, or my Jean.

[1] Cards.
[2] "Meg" was Margaret Orr, the nursery-maid of Mrs. Stewart of Stair.—A. C.
[3] Adds fuel.

O, how that name inspires my style!
The words come skelpin,[1] rank and file,
Amaist before I ken!
The ready measure rins as fine,
As Phœbus and the famous Nine
Were glowrin owre my pen.
My spaviet[2] Pegasus will limp,
Till ance he's fairly het;
And then he'll hilch,[3] and stilt, and jimp,
An' rin an unco fit:
But lest then, the beast then,
Should rue this hasty ride,
I'll light now, and dight[4] now
His sweaty, wizen'd[5] hide.

THE LAMENT.[6]

OCCASIONED BY THE UNFORTUNATE ISSUE OF A FRIEND'S AMOUR.

Alas! how oft does Goodness wound itself,
And Sweet AFFECTION prove the spring of woe! *Home.*

O THOU pale Orb, that silent shines,
While care-untroubled mortals sleep!
Thou seest a wretch that inly pines,
And wanders here to wail and weep!
With woe I nightly vigils keep,
Beneath thy wan unwarming beam;
And mourn, in lamentation deep,
How life and love are all a dream.

I joyless view thy rays adorn
The faintly-marked, distant hill:
I joyless view thy trembling horn,
Reflected in the gurgling rill:
My fondly-fluttering heart, be still!
Thou busy pow'r, Remembrance, cease!
Ah! must the agonizing thrill
For ever bar returning peace!

No idly-feign'd poetic pains,
My sad, love-lorn lamentings claim;
No shepherd's pipe—Arcadian strains;
No fabled tortures, quaint and tame:
The plighted faith; the mutual flame;
The oft-attested pow'rs above;
The promis'd father's tender name:
These were the pledges of my love!

Encircled in her clasping arms,
How have the raptur'd moments flown!
How have I wish'd for fortune's charms,
For her dear sake, and hers alone!
And must I think it! is she gone,
My secret heart's exulting boast?
And does she heedless hear my groan?
And is she ever, ever lost?

Oh! can she bear so base a heart,
So lost to honour, lost to truth,
As from the fondest lover part,
The plighted husband of her youth!
Alas! life's path may be unsmooth!
Her way may lie thro' rough distress!
Then, who her pangs and pains will soothe,
Her sorrows share, and make them less?

Ye winged hours that o'er us past,
Enraptur'd more, the more enjoy'd,
Your dear remembrance in my breast,
My fondly-treasur'd thoughts employ'd.
That breast, how dreary now, and void,
For her too scanty once of room!
Ev'n ev'ry ray of hope destroy'd,
And not a wish to gild the gloom!

The morn that warns th' approaching day,
Awakes me up to toil and woe:
I see the hours in long array,
That I must suffer, lingering, slow.
Full many a pang, and many a throe,
Keen recollection's direful train,
Must wring my soul, ere Phœbus, low,
Shall kiss the distant, western main.

---

[1] Marching lightly.
[2] Spavined. [3] Hobble.
[4] Wipe. [5] Shrunk.
[6] It is scarcely necessary to mention, that "The Lament" was composed on that unfortunate passage in his matrimonial history, which I have mentioned in my letter to Mrs. Dunlop, after the first distraction of his feelings had a little subsided.—G. B.

And when my nightly couch I try,
Sore harass'd out with care and grief,
My toil-beat nerves, and tear-worn eye,
Keep watchings with the nightly thief;
Or if I slumber, fancy, chief,
Reigns, haggard-wild, in sore affright:
Ev'n day, all-bitter, brings relief,
From such a horror-breathing night.

O! thou bright Queen, who o'er the expanse
Now highest reign'st, with boundless sway!
Oft has thy silent-marking glance
Observ'd us, fondly-wand'ring, stray!
The time, unheeded, sped away,
While love's luxurious pulse beat high,
Beneath thy silver-gleaming ray,
To mark the mutual-kindling eye.

Oh! scenes in strong remembrance set!
Scenes, never, never to return!
Scenes, if in stupor I forget,
Again I feel, again I burn!
From ev'ry joy and pleasure torn,
Life's weary vale I wander thro';
And hopeless, comfortless, I'll mourn
A faithless woman's broken vow.

DESPONDENCY.

AN ODE.

Oppress'd with grief, oppress'd with care,
A burden more than I can bear,
I sit me down and sigh:
O life! thou art a galling load,
Along a rough, a weary road,
To wretches such as I!
Dim backward as I cast my view,
What sick'ning scenes appear!
What sorrows yet may pierce me thro',
Too justly I may fear!
Still caring, despairing,
Must be my bitter doom;
My woes here shall close ne'er,
But with the closing tomb!

Happy, ye sons of busy life,
Who, equal to the bustling strife,
No other view regard!
Ev'n when the wished end's deny'd,
Yet while the busy means are ply'd,
They bring their own reward:
Whilst I, a hope-abandon'd wight,
Unfitted with an aim,
Meet ev'ry sad returning night,
And joyless morn the same;
You, bustling, and justling,
Forget each grief and pain;
I, listless, yet restless,
Find every prospect vain.

How blest the Solitary's lot,
Who, all-forgetting, all-forgot,
Within his humble cell,
The cavern wild with tangling roots,
Sits o'er his newly-gather'd fruits,
Beside his crystal well!
Or, haply, to his ev'ning thought,
By unfrequented stream,
The ways of men are distant brought,
A faint-collected dream:
While praising, and raising
His thoughts to Heav'n on high,
As wand'ring, meand'ring,
He views the solemn sky.

Than I, no lonely hermit plac'd
Where never human footstep trac'd,
Less fit to play the part;
The lucky moment to improve,
And just to stop, and just to move,
With self-respecting art:
But, ah! those pleasures, loves, and joys
Which I too keenly taste,
The Solitary can despise,
Can want, and yet be blest!
He needs not, he heeds not,
Or human love or hate,
Whilst I here must cry here,
At perfidy ingrate!

Oh! enviable, early days,
When dancing thoughtless pleasure's maze,
To care, to guilt unknown!
How ill exchang'd for riper times,
To feel the follies, or the crimes,
Of others, or my own!
Ye tiny elves that guiltless sport,
Like linnets in the bush,

Ye little know the ills ye court,
When manhood is your wish!
The losses, the crosses,
That active man engage!
The fears all, the tears all,
Of dim-declining age!

LINES TO MY BED.

Thou bed, in which I first began
To be that varied creature—*Man!*
And when again the fates decree,
The place where I must cease to be;
When sickness comes, to whom I fly
To soothe my pain or close mine eye;
When cares surround me, where I weep,
Or lose them all in balmy sleep;
When sore with labour, whom I court,
And to thy downy breast resort;
Where too ecstatic joys I find,
When deigns my Delia to be kind;
And full of love, in all her charms,
Thou giv'st the fair one to my arms:
The centre thou, where grief and pain,
Disease and rest, alternate reign.
Oh, since within thy little space
So many various scenes take place,
Lessons as useful shalt thou teach,
As sages dictate—churchmen preach;
And man, convinced by thee alone,
This great important truth shall own,
That thin partitions do divide
The bounds where good and ill reside;
That naught is perfect here below,
But *bliss* still bordering upon *woe!*

WINTER.

A DIRGE.

The wintry west extends his blast,
And hail and rain does blaw;
Or the stormy north sends driving forth
The blinding sleet and snaw:
While, tumbling brown, the burn comes down,
And roars frae bank to brae;
And bird and beast in covert rest,
And pass the heartless day.

"The sweeping blast, the sky o'ercast,"[1]
The joyless winter-day,
Let others fear, to me more dear
Than all the pride of May:
The tempest's howl, it soothes my soul,
My griefs it seems to join:
The leafless trees my fancy please,
Their fate resembles mine!

Thou Pow'r Supreme, whose mighty scheme
These woes of mine fulfil,
Here, firm, I rest, they must be best,
Because they are Thy will!
Then all I want (Oh! do thou grant
This one request of mine!)
Since to enjoy thou dost deny,
Assist me to resign.

THE COTTER'S SATURDAY NIGHT.

INSCRIBED TO ROBERT AIKEN, ESQ.,[2] OF AYR.

Let not ambition mock their useful toil,
Their homely joys, and destiny obscure;
Nor Grandeur hear, with a disdainful smile,
The short but simple annals of the Poor.—*Gray.*

My lov'd, my honour'd, much respected friend!
No mercenary bard his homage pays;
With honest pride, I scorn each selfish end:
My dearest meed, a friend's esteem and praise:

[1] Dr. Young.—R. B.

[2] Mr. Aiken was a "writer" in Ayr; Gilbert Burns affectionately notices him in a letter to Currie, as a man of worth and taste, and warm affections, and who eagerly spread among his friends the merits of the new Poet.

To you I sing, in simple Scottish lays,
The lowly train in life's sequester'd scene;
The native feelings strong, the guileless ways;
What Aiken in a cottage would have been;
Ah! though his worth unknown, far happier there I ween.

November chill blaws loud wi' angry sugh;[1]
The short'ning winter-day is near a close;
The miry beasts retreating frae the pleugh;
The black'ning trains o' craws to their repose;
The toil-worn Cotter frae his labour goes,
This night his weekly moil is at an end,
Collects his spades, his mattocks, and his hoes,
Hoping the morn in ease and rest to spend,
And weary, o'er the moor, his course does hameward bend.

At length his lonely cot appears in view,
Beneath the shelter of an aged tree;
Th' expectant wee-things, toddlin, stacher[2] thro',
To meet their Dad, wi' flichterin[3] noise an' glee.
His wee bit ingle, blinkin bonnily,
His clane hearth-stane, his thriftie wifie's smile,
The lisping infant prattling on his knee,
Does a' his weary carking cares beguile,
An' makes him quite forget his labour an' his toil.

Belyve,[4] the elder bairns come drapping in,
At service out, amang the farmers roun';[5]

[1] Rushing sound. [2] Stagger.
[3] Fluttering. [4] By and by.
[5] Although the "Cotter," in the Saturday Night, is an exact copy of my father in his manners, his family devotions, and exhortations, yet the other parts of the description do not apply to our family. None of us ever were "At service out amang the neebors roun'." Instead of our depositing our "sair-won penny-fee" with our parents, my father laboured hard, and lived with the most rigid economy, that he might be able to keep his children at home. —*Gilbert Burns to Dr. Currie.* Oct. 24, 1800.

Some ca' the pleugh, some herd, some tentie[1] rin
A cannie errand to a neebor town:
Their eldest hope, their Jenny, woman grown,
In youthfu' bloom, love sparkling in her e'e,
Comes hame, perhaps, to show a braw new gown,
Or deposite her sair-won penny-fee,
To help her parents dear, if they in hardship be.

Wi' joy unfeign'd brothers and sisters meet,
An' each for other's welfare kindly spiers:
The social hours, swift-wing'd, unnoticed fleet;
Each tells the uncos[2] that he sees or hears;
The parents, partial, eye their hopeful years,
Anticipation forward points the view.
The mother, wi' her needle an' her shears,
Gars[3] auld claes look amaist as weel's the new;
The father mixes a' wi' admonition due.

Their master's an' their mistress's command,
The younkers a' are warned to obey;
An' mind their labours wi' an eydent[4] hand,
An' ne'er, tho' out o' sight, to jauk or play:

[1] Cautious. [2] News.
[3] Makes. [4] Diligent.

"An', oh! be sure to fear the Lord alway,
An' mind your duty, duly, morn an' night!
Lest in temptation's path ye gang astray,
Implore His counsel and assisting might:
They never sought in vain that sought the Lord aright!"

But, hark! a rap comes gently to the door;
Jenny, wha kens the meaning o' the same,
Tells how a neebor lad cam o'er the moor,
To do some errands, and convoy her hame.
The wily mother sees the conscious flame
Sparkle in Jenny's e'e, and flush her cheek;
Wi' heart-struck anxious care, inquires his name,
While Jenny hafflins[1] is afraid to speak;
Weel pleas'd the mother hears, it's nae wild worthless rake.

Wi' kindly welcome Jenny brings him ben;
A strappan youth; he takes the mother's eye;
Blythe Jenny sees the visit's no ill ta'en;
The father cracks[2] of horses, pleughs, and kye.
The youngster's artless heart o'erflows wi' joy,
But, blate[3] and laithfu',[4] scarce can weel behave;
The woman, wi' a woman's wiles, can spy
What makes the youth sae bashfu' an' sae grave;
Weel pleas'd to think her bairn's respected like the lave.[5]

O happy love! where love like this is found!
O heart-felt raptures! bliss beyond compare!

[1] Half. [2] Talks. [3] Bashful.
[4] Sheepish. [5] The rest.

I've paced much this weary, mortal round,
And sage experience bids me this declare—
"If Heav'n a draught of heav'nly pleasure spare,
One cordial in this melancholy vale,
'Tis when a youthful, loving, modest pair,
In other's arms breathe out the tender tale,
Beneath the milk-white thorn that scents the ev'ning gale!"

Is there, in human form, that bears a heart—
A wretch! a villain! lost to love and truth!
That can, with studied, sly, ensnaring art,
Betray sweet Jenny's unsuspecting youth?
Curse on his perjur'd arts! dissembling smooth!
Are honour, virtue, conscience, all exil'd?
Is there no pity, no relenting ruth,
Points to the parents fondling o'er their child?
Then paints the ruin'd maid, and their distraction wild!

But now the supper crowns their simple board,
The halesome parritch, chief o' Scotia's food:
The soupe their only hawkie[1] does afford,
That 'yont the hallan[2] snugly chows her cood;
The dame brings forth in complimental mood,
To grace the lad, her weel-hain'd[3] kebbuck,[4] fell,
An' aft he's prest, an' aft he ca's it guid:
The frugal wifie, garrulous, will tell
How 'twas a towmond[5] auld, sin' lint was i' the bell.[6]

[1] Cow. [2] Partition wall.
[3] Well-saved. [4] Cheese.
[5] A twelvemonth.
[6] Since the flax was in flower.

The cheerfu' supper done, wi' serious face,
They, round the ingle, form a circle wide;
The sire turns o'er, wi' patriarchal grace,
The big ha'-Bible, ance his father's pride:
His bonnet rev'rently is laid aside,
His lyart haffets[1] wearing thin an' bare;
Those strains that once did sweet in Zion glide,
He wales[2] a portion with judicious care;
And "Let us worship God!" he says, with solemn air.

They chant their artless notes in simple guise;
They tune their hearts, by far the noblest aim:
Perhaps "Dundee's" wild warbling measures rise,
Or plaintive "Martyrs," worthy of the name;
Or noble "Elgin" beets the heav'nward flame,
The sweetest far of Scotia's holy lays:
Compar'd with these, Italian trills are tame;
The tickl'd ears no heart-felt raptures raise;
Nae unison hae they with our Creator's praise.

The priest-like father reads the sacred page,
How Abram was the friend of God on high;
Or Moses bade eternal warfare wage
With Amalek's ungracious progeny;
Or how the royal Bard did groaning lie
Beneath the stroke of Heaven's avenging ire;
Or Job's pathetic plaint, and wailing cry;
Or rapt Isaiah's wild, seraphic fire;
Or other holy seers that tune the sacred lyre.

[1] Grey locks. [2] Chooses.

Perhaps the Christian volume is the theme,
How guiltless blood for guilty man was shed;
How He, who bore in Heav'n the second name,
Had not on earth whereon to lay His head:
How His first followers and servants sped;
The precepts sage they wrote to many a land:
How he, who lone in Patmos banished,
Saw in the sun a mighty angel stand;
And heard great Bab'lon's doom pronounced by Heav'n's command.

Then kneeling down, to Heaven's Eternal King,
The saint, the father, and the husband prays:
Hope "springs exulting on triumphant wing,"[1]
That thus they all shall meet in future days:
There ever bask in uncreated rays,
No more to sigh, or shed the bitter tear,
Together hymning their Creator's praise,
In such society, yet still more dear;
While circling time moves round in an eternal sphere.

Compar'd with this, how poor Religion's pride,
In all the pomp of method, and of art,
When men display to congregations wide
Devotion's ev'ry grace, except the heart!
The Pow'r, incens'd, the pageant will desert,
The pompous strain, the sacerdotal stole;
But haply, in some cottage far apart,
May hear, well pleas'd, the language of the soul;
And in His book of life the inmates poor enrol.

[1] Pope's "Windsor Forest."—R. B.

Then homeward all take off their sev'ral way;
The youngling cottagers retire to rest:
The parent-pair their secret homage pay,
And proffer up to Heav'n the warm request,
That He, who stills the raven's clam'rous nest,
And decks the lily fair in flow'ry pride,
Would, in the way His wisdom sees the best,
For them, and for their little ones provide;
But chiefly, in their hearts with grace divine preside.

From scenes like these old Scotia's grandeur springs,
That makes her lov'd at home, rever'd abroad:
Princes and lords are but the breath of kings;
"An honest man's the noblest work of God:"
And certes, in fair virtue's heav'nly road,
The cottage leaves the palace far behind;
What is a lordling's pomp? a cumbrous load,
Disguising oft the wretch of human kind,
Studied in arts of hell, in wickedness refin'd!

O Scotia! my dear, my native soil!
For whom my warmest wish to Heaven is sent!
Long may thy hardy sons of rustic toil
Be blest with health, and peace, and sweet content!
And, oh, may Heaven their simple lives prevent
From luxury's contagion, weak and vile!
Then, howe'er crowns and coronets be rent,
A virtuous populace may rise the while,
And stand a wall of fire around their much-lov'd Isle.

O Thou! who pour'd the patriotic tide
That stream'd thro' Wallace's undaunted heart;
Who dar'd to nobly stem tyrannic pride,
Or nobly die, the second glorious part,
(The patriot's God, peculiarly Thou art,
His friend, inspirer, guardian, and reward!)
O never, never Scotia's realm desert;
But still the patriot, and the patriot-bard,
In bright succession raise, her ornament and guard!

MAN WAS MADE TO MOURN.[1]

A DIRGE.

When chill November's surly blast
Made fields and forests bare,
One ev'ning, as I wander'd forth
Along the banks of Ayr,
I spy'd a man, whose aged step
Seem'd weary, worn with care;
His face was furrow'd o'er with years,
And hoary was his hair.

Young stranger, whither wand'rest thou?
Began the rev'rend sage;
Does thirst of wealth thy step constrain,
Or youthful pleasure's rage?
Or, haply, prest with cares and woes,
Too soon thou hast began
To wander forth, with me, to mourn
The miseries of Man.

The sun that overhangs yon moors,
Outspreading far and wide,
Where hundreds labour to support
A haughty lordling's pride;
I've seen yon weary winter-sun
Twice forty times return;
And ev'ry time has added proofs
That Man was made to mourn.

[1] Several of the poems were produced for the purpose of bringing forward some favourite sentiment of the author. He used to remark to me, that he could not well conceive a more mortifying picture of human life than a man seeking work. In casting about in his mind how this sentiment might be brought forward, the elegy, "Man was made to mourn," was composed.—G. B.

O man! while in thy early years,
  How prodigal of time!
Mis-spending all thy precious hours,
  Thy glorious youthful prime!
Alternate follies take the sway;
  Licentious passions burn;
Which tenfold force give nature's law,
  That Man was made to mourn.

Look not alone on youthful prime,
  Or manhood's active might;
Man then is useful to his kind,
  Supported is his right.
But see him on the edge of life,
  With cares and sorrows worn;
Then age and want, oh! ill-match'd pair!
  Show Man was made to mourn.

A few seem favourites of fate,
  In pleasure's lap carest;
Yet, think not all the rich and great
  Are likewise truly blest.
But, oh! what crowds in ev'ry land
  Are wretched and forlorn.
Thro' weary life this lesson learn,
  That Man was made to mourn.

Many and sharp the num'rous ills
  Inwoven with our frame!
More pointed still we make ourselves,
  Regret, remorse, and shame!
And man, whose heav'n-erected face
  The smiles of love adorn,
Man's inhumanity to man
  Makes countless thousands mourn!

See yonder poor, o'erlabour'd wight,
  So abject, mean, and vile,
Who begs a brother of the earth
  To give him leave to toil;
And see his lordly fellow-worm
  The poor petition spurn,
Unmindful, tho' a weeping wife
  And helpless offspring mourn.

If I'm design'd yon lordling's slave—
  By Nature's law design'd,—
Why was an independent wish
  E'er planted in my mind?
If not, why am I subject to
  His cruelty or scorn?
Or why has man the will and pow'r
  To make his fellow mourn?

Yet, let not this too much, my son,
  Disturb thy youthful breast:
This partial view of human kind
  Is surely not the last!
The poor, oppressed, honest man
  Had never, sure, been born,
Had there not been some recompence
  To comfort those that mourn!

O death! the poor man's dearest friend.
  The kindest and the best!
Welcome the hour my aged limbs
  Are laid with thee at rest!
The great, the wealthy, fear thy blow
  From pomp and pleasure torn;
But, oh! a blest relief to those
  That weary-laden mourn![1]

ON THE ILLNESS OF A BELOVED CHILD.

Now health forsakes that angel face
  Nae mair my deary smiles;
Pale sickness withers ilka grace,
  And a' my hopes beguiles.

The cruel Powers reject the prayer
  I hourly mak for thee!
Ye heavens, how great is my despair,
  How can I see him die!

A PRAYER IN THE PROSPECT OF DEATH.[2]

O Thou unknown, Almighty Cause
  Of all my hope and fear!
In whose dread presence, ere an hour,
  Perhaps I must appear!

[1] Whatever might be the casual idea that set the poet to work, it is but too evident that he wrote from the habitual feelings of his own bosom. The indignation with which he contemplated the inequality of human condition, and particularly the contrast between his own worldly circumstances and intellectual rank, was never more bitterly nor more loftily expressed, than in some of these stanzas.—*Lockhart*.

[2] Burns has entitled his verses, "A prayer, when fainting fits, and other

f I have wander'd in those paths
Of life I ought to shun;
ls something, loudly in my breast,
Remonstrates I have done;

Thou know'st that thou hast formed me,
With passions wild and strong;
And list'ning to their witching voice
Has often led me wrong.

Where human weakness has come short,
Or frailty stept aside,
Do thou, All-Good! for such Thou art,
In shades of darkness hide.

Where with intention I have err'd,
No other plea I have,
But Thou art good; and Goodness still
Delighteth to forgive.

STANZAS ON THE SAME OCCASION.[1]

Why am I loth to leave this earthly scene!
Have I so found it full of pleasing charms?
Some drops of joy with draughts of ill between:
Some gleams of sunshine 'mid renewing storms;
Is it departing pangs my soul alarms?
Or death's unlovely, dreary, dark abode?
For guilt, for guilt, my terrors are in arms:
I tremble to approach an angry God,
And justly smart beneath his sin-avenging rod.

Fain would I say, "Forgive my foul offence!"
Fain promise never more to disobey;

larming symptoms of pleurisy, or ome other dangerous disorder, which ndeed still threatens me, first put na-ure on the alarm."

[1] August, [1784,] Misgivings in the our of Despondency and Prospect of Death.

But, should my Author health again dispense,
Again I might desert fair virtue's way;
Again in folly's path might go astray;
Again exalt the brute, and sink the man;
Then how should I for Heav'nly mercy pray,
Who act so counter Heav'nly mercy's plan?
Who sin so oft have mourn'd, yet to temptation ran?

O Thou, great Governor of all below!
If I may dare a lifted eye to Thee,
Thy nod can make the tempest cease to blow,
And still the tumult of the raging sea;
With that controlling pow'r assist ev'n me,
Those headlong furious passions to confine,
For all unfit I feel my powers to be,
To rule their torrent in th' allowed line;
O, aid me with thy help, Omnipotence Divine!

LYING AT A REVEREND FRIEND'S HOUSE ONE NIGHT, THE AUTHOR LEFT THE FOLLOWING

VERSES

IN THE ROOM WHERE HE SLEPT.[1]

O Thou dread Pow'r, who reign'st above!
I know Thou wilt me hear;

[1] The first time Robert heard the spinnet played upon was at the house of Dr. Lawrie, then minister of the parish of Loudon, now in Glasgow, having given up the parish in favour of his son. Dr. Lawrie has several daughters; one of them played; the father and mother led down the dance; the rest of the sisters, the brother, the poet, and the other guests, mixed in

When for this scene of peace and love
  I make my pray'r sincere.

The hoary sire—the mortal stroke,
  Long, long, be pleas'd to spare:
To bless his little filial flock,
  And show what good men are.

She, who her lovely offspring eyes
  With tender hopes and fears,
Oh, bless her with a mother's joys,
  But spare a mother's tears!

Their hope, their stay, their darling youth,
  In manhood's dawning blush;
Bless him, thou God of love and truth,
  Up to a parent's wish.

The beauteous, seraph sister-band,
  With earnest tears I pray,
Thou know'st the snares on ev'ry hand,
  Guide Thou their steps alway.

When soon or late they reach that coast,
  O'er life's rough ocean driv'n,
May they rejoice, no wand'rer lost,
  A family in Heav'n!

THE FIRST PSALM.

The man, in life wherever plac'd,
  Hath happiness in store,
Who walks not in the wicked's way,
  Nor learns their guilty lore!

Nor from the seat of scornful pride
  Casts forth his eyes abroad,
But with humility and awe
  Still walks before his God.

That man shall flourish like the trees
  Which by the streamlets grow;
The fruitful top is spread on high,
  And firm the root below.

But he, whose blossom buds in guilt,
  Shall to the ground be cast,
And like the rootless stubble tost,
  Before the sweeping blast.

For why? that God the good adore
  Hath giv'n them peace and rest,
But hath decreed that wicked men
  Shall ne'er be truly blest.

A PRAYER, UNDER THE PRES SURE OF VIOLENT ANGUISH.

O Thou Great Being! what Thou ar
  Surpasses me to know:
Yet sure I am, that known to Thee
  Are all Thy works below.

Thy creature here before Thee stands
  All wretched and distrest;
Yet sure those ills that wring my sou
  Obey Thy high behest.

Sure, Thou, Almighty, canst not act
  From cruelty or wrath!
O, free my weary eyes from tears,
  Or close them fast in death!

But if I must afflicted be,
  To suit some wise design;
Then man my soul with firm resolves
  To bear and not repine!

STANZAS WRITTEN WHIL UNDER EXCESSIVE GRIEF.[2]

Accept the gift of a friend sincere
  Wad on thy worth be pressin';

---

it. It was a delightful family scene for our poet, then lately introduced to the world. His mind was roused to a poetic enthusiasm, and the Stanzas were left in the room where he slept. —G. B.

March, 1784.

[1] There was a certain period of m life that my spirit was broke b repeated losses and disasters, whic threatened, and indeed effected, th utter ruin of my fortune. My bod too was attacked by that most dreadf disorder, a hypochondria, or confirm melancholy. In this wretched stat the recollection of which makes me y shudder, I hung my harp on the willo trees, except in some lucid interval in one of which I composed the fo lowing.—R. B.

[2] Written in 1786, and first print in the *Sun* newspaper of April, 1823.

ℓemembrance oft may start a tear,
ℑut oh that tenderness forbear,
Tho' 'twad my sorrows lessen.

ℳy morning rose sae clear and fair,
I thought sair storms wad never
ℬedew the scene; but grief and care
n wildest fury hae made bare
My peace, my hope, for ever!

'ou think I'm glad; oh, I pay weel
For a' the joy I borrow,
n solitude—then, then I feel'
canna to myself conceal
My deeply ranklin' sorrow.

'arewell! within thy bosom free
A sigh may whiles awaken;
. tear may wet thy laughin' ee,
'or Scotia's son—once gay like thee—
Now hopeless, comfortless, forsaken!

THE FIRST SIX VERSES OF THE NINETIETH PSALM.

) Thou, the first, the greatest friend
Of all the human race!
Vhose strong right hand has ever been
Their stay and dwelling place!

'efore the mountains heav'd their heads
Beneath Thy forming hand,
'efore this pond'rous globe itself
Arose at Thy command;

'hat pow'r, which rais'd and still upholds
This universal frame,
'rom countless, unbeginning time
Was ever still the same.

'hose mighty periods of years,
Which seem to us so vast,
.ppear no more before Thy sight
Than yesterday that's past.

'hou giv'st the word; Thy creature, man,
Is to existence brought;
.gain Thou say'st, "Ye sons of men,
Return ye into nought!"

'hou layest them, with all their cares,
In everlasting sleep;
As with a flood thou tak'st them off
With overwhelming sweep.

They flourish like the morning flow'r,
In beauty's pride array'd;
But long ere night cut down, it lies
All wither'd and decay'd.

TO A MOUNTAIN DAISY,

ON TURNING ONE DOWN WITH THE PLOUGH, IN APRIL, 1786.[1]

Wee, modest, crimson-tipped flow'r,
Thou's met me in an evil hour;
For I maun crush amang the stoure
Thy slender stem:
To spare thee now is past my pow'r,
Thou bonnie gem.

Alas! it's no thy neebor sweet,
The bonnie Lark,[2] companion meet!
Bending thee 'mang the dewy weet!
Wi' spreckl'd breast,
When upward-springing, blythe, to greet
The purpling east.

Cauld blew the bitter-biting north
Upon thy early, humble birth;
Yet cheerfully thou glinted forth
Amid thy storm,
Scarce rear'd above the parent-earth
Thy tender form.

The flaunting flow'rs our gardens yield,
High shelt'ring woods and wa's maun shield,

---

[1] The Daisy grew in the field next to that in which the plough had turned up the mouse's nest.

[2] I have seldom met with an image more truly pastoral than that of the lark in the second stanza. Such strokes as these mark the pencil of the poet, which delineates Nature with the precision of intimacy, yet with the delicate colouring of beauty and taste.—H. Mackenzie, in "The Lounger," No. 97.

But thou beneath the random bield[1]
O' clod, or stane,
Adorns the histie[2] stibble-field,
Unseen, alane.

There, in thy scanty mantle clad,
Thy snawy bosom sunward spread,
Thou lifts thy unassuming head
In humble guise;
But now the share uptears thy bed,
And low thou lies!

Such is the fate of artless Maid,
Sweet flow'ret of the rural shade!
By love's simplicity betray'd,
And guileless trust,
Till she, like thee, all soil'd, is laid
Low i' the dust.

Such is the fate of simple Bard,
On life's rough ocean luckless starr'd!
Unskilful he to note the card
Of prudent lore,
Till billows rage, and gales blow hard,
And whelm him o'er!

Such fate to suffering worth is giv'n,
Who long with wants and woes has striv'n,
By human pride or cunning driv'n
To mis'ry's brink,
Till, wrench'd of ev'ry stay but Heav'n,
He, ruin'd, sink!

Ev'n thou who mourn'st the Daisy's fate,
That fate is thine—no distant date;
Stern Ruin's ploughshare drives, elate,
Full on thy bloom,
Till crush'd beneath the furrow's weight
Shall be thy doom!

TO RUIN.[3]

All hail! inexorable lord!
At whose destruction-breathing word
The mightiest empires fall!
Thy cruel, woe-delighted train,
The ministers of grief and pain,
A sullen welcome, all!
With stern-resolv'd, despairing eye,
I see each aimed dart;
For one has cut my dearest tie,
And quivers in my heart.
Then low'ring, and pouring,
The storm no more I dread:
Tho' thick'ning and black'ning
Round my devoted head.

And thou grim pow'r, by life abhorr'd,
While life a pleasure can afford,
Oh! hear a wretch's pray'r!
No more I shrink appall'd, afraid;
I court, I beg thy friendly aid,
To close this scene of care!
When shall my soul, in silent peace,
Resign life's joyless day:
My weary heart its throbbing cease,
Cold mould'ring in the clay?
No fear more, no tear more,
To stain my lifeless face,
Enclasped, and grasped
Within thy cold embrace!

STANZAS ON THE DESTRUCTION OF THE WOODS NEAR DRUMLANRIG.[1]

(WRITTEN IN 1796.)

As on the banks o' wand'ring Nith
Ae smiling summer morn I stray'd,

---

[1] Shelter. [2] Dry.

[3] I have here enclosed a small piece, the very latest of my productions. I am a good deal pleased with some sentiments myself, as they are just the native querulous feelings of a heart which, as the elegantly melting Gray says, "Melancholy has marked for her own."—To Mr. Kennedy, April 20, 1786.

[1] According to Mr. Chambers, the Duke of Queensberry, who was no great favourite with Burns, "had stripped his domains of Drumlanrig, in Dumfriesshire, and Neldpath, in Peeblesshire, of all the wood fit for being cut, in order to enrich the Countess of Yarmouth, whom he supposed to be his daughter."

And traced its bonny howes and haughs[1]
  Where linties sang and lambkins play'd,
I sat me down upon a craig,
  And drank my fill o' fancy's dream,
When, from the eddying deep below,
  Uprose the genius of the stream.

Dark, like the frowning rock, his brow,
  And troubled like his wintry wave,
And deep, as sughs[2] the boding wind
  Amang his eaves, the sigh he gave—
"And came ye here, my son," he cried,
  "To wander in my birken shade?
To muse some favourite Scottish theme,
  Or sing some favourite Scottish maid!

"There was a time, it's nae lang syne,
  Ye might hae seen me in my pride,
When a' my banks sae bravely saw
  Their woody pictures in my tide;
When hanging beech and spreading elm
  Shaded my stream sae clear and cool;
And stately oaks their twisted arms
  Threw broad and dark across the pool;

"When glinting through the trees appear'd
  The wee white cot aboon the mill,
And peacefu' rose its ingle reek,[3]
  That slowly curled up the hill.
But now the cot is bare and cauld,
  Its branchy shelter's lost and gane,
And scarce a stinted birk is left
  To shiver in the blast its lane."

"Alas!" said I, "what ruefu' chance
  Has twin'd ye o' your stately trees?
Has laid your rocky bosom bare?
  Has stripp'd the cleeding o' your braes?
Was it the bitter eastern blast,
  That scatters blight in early spring?
Or was't the wil'-fire scorch'd their boughs,
  Or canker-worm wi' secret sting?"

"Nae eastlin blast," the sprite replied;
  "It blew na here sae fierce and fell;
And on my dry and halesome banks
  Nae canker-worms get leave to dwell:
Man! cruel man!" the genius sigh'd—
  As through the cliffs he sank him down—
"The worm that gnaw'd my bonny trees,
  That reptile wears a ducal crown!"

[1] Valleys. [2] Moans. [3] Smoke.

TO MISS LOGAN, WITH BEATTIE'S POEMS,

AS A NEW YEAR'S GIFT, JANUARY 1, 1787.

AGAIN the silent wheels of time
  Their annual round have driv'n,
And you, tho' scarce in maiden prime,
  Are so much nearer Heav'n.

No gifts have I from Indian coasts
  The infant year to hail;
I send you more than India boasts,
  In Edwin's simple tale.

Our sex with guile and faithless love
  Is charg'd, perhaps, too true;
But may, dear Maid, each lover prove
  An Edwin still to you!

EPISTLE TO A YOUNG FRIEND.[1]

MAY, 1786.

I LANG hae thought, my youthfu' friend,
  A something to have sent you,
Tho' it should serve nae ither end
  Than just a kind memento;
But how the subject-theme may gang,
  Let time and chance determine;
Perhaps, it may turn out a sang,
  Perhaps turn out a sermon.

Ye'll try the world soon, my lad,
  And Andrew dear, believe me,
Ye'll find mankind an unco squad,
  And muckle they may grieve ye:

[1] Andrew Aiken, of Ayr, son of the friend to whom Burns inscribed "The Cotter's Saturday Night."

For care and trouble set your thought,
  Ev'n when your end's attained;
And a' your views may come to nought,
  Where ev'ry nerve is strained.

I'll no say, men are villains a';
  The real, harden'd wicked,
Wha hae nae check but human law,
  Are to a few restricked;
But, Och! mankind are unco weak,
  An' little to be trusted;
If self the wavering balance shake,
  It's rarely right adjusted!

Yet they wha[1] fa'[2] in fortune's strife,
  Their fate we should na censure,
For still th' important end of life
  They equally may answer;
A man may hae an honest heart,
  Tho' poortith[3] hourly stare him;
A man may tak a neebor's part,
  Yet hae nae cash to spare him.

Aye free, aff-han'[4] your story tell,
  When wi' a bosom crony;
But still keep something to yoursel
  Ye scarcely tell to ony.
Conceal yoursel as weel's ye can
  Frae critical dissection;
But keek[5] thro' ev'ry other man,
  Wi' sharpen'd, sly inspection.

The sacred lowe[6] o' weel-plac'd love,
  Luxuriantly indulge it;
But never tempt th' illicit rove,
  Tho' naething should divulge it;
I wave the quantum o' the sin,
  The hazard o' concealing;
But, Och! it hardens a' within,
  And petrifies the feeling!

To catch dame Fortune's golden smile,
  Assiduous wait upon her;
And gather gear by ev'ry wile
  That's justify'd by honour;
Not for to hide it in a hedge,
  Nor for a train attendant;
But for the glorious privilege
  Of being independent.

The fear o' hell's a hangman's whip,
  To haud the wretch in order;
But where ye feel your honour grip,
  Let that aye be your border;

[1] Who. [2] Fall. [3] Poverty.
[4] Off-hand. [5] Peep. [6] Flame.

Its slightest touches, instant pause—
  Debar a' side pretences;
And resolutely keep its laws,
  Uncaring consequences.

The great Creator to revere,
  Must sure become the creature;
But still the preaching cant forbear,
  And ev'n the rigid feature;
Yet ne'er with wits profane to range,
  Be complaisance extended;
An Atheist-laugh's a poor exchange
  For Deity offended!

When ranting round in pleasure's ring,
  Religion may be blinded;
Or, if she gie a random sting,
  It may be little minded;
But when on life we're tempest-driv'n,
  A conscience but a canker—
A correspondence fix'd wi' Heav'n
  Is sure a noble anchor!

Adieu, dear, amiable Youth!
  Your heart can ne'er be wanting!
May prudence, fortitude, and truth,
  Erect your brow undaunting!
In ploughman phrase, "God send you speed,"
  Still daily to grow wiser;
And may you better reck the rede,[1]
  Than ever did th' Adviser!

ON A SCOTCH BARD, GONE TO THE WEST INDIES.

A' YE wha live by sowps[2] o' drink,
A' ye wha live by crambo-clink,[3]
A' ye wha live an' never think,
    Come mourn wi' me!
Our billie's[4] gien us a' a jink,[5]
    An' owre the sea.

Lament him a' ye rantin core,[6]
Wha dearly like a random-splore,[7]
Nae mair he'll join the merry roar,
    In social key;
For now he's taen anither shore,
    An' ower the sea!

[1] Heed the counsel. [2] Spoonsful.
[3] Rhymes. [4] Our brother. [5] Dodge.
[6] Corps. [7] Riot.

The bonnie lasses weel may wiss him,
And in their dear petitions place him;
The widows, wives, an' a' may bless him
Wi' tearfu' e'e;
For weel I wat they'll sairly miss him,
That's ower the sea!

O Fortune, they hae room to grumble!
Hadst thou ta'en aff some drowsy bummle,[1]
Wha can do nought but fyke[2] an' fumble,
'Twad been nae plea;
But he was gleg[3] as ony wumble,[4]
That's owre the sea!

Auld, cantie Kyle[5] may weepers wear,
An' stain them wi' the saut, saut tear;
'Twill mak her poor auld heart, I fear,
In flinders[6] flee;
He was her Laureat monie a year,
That's owre the sea!

He saw misfortune's cauld Nor-west
Lang mustering up a bitter blast;
A jillet[7] brak his heart at last,
Ill may she be!
So, took a berth afore the mast,
An' owre the sea.

To tremble under Fortune's cummock,[8]
On scarce a bellyfu' o' drummock,[9]
Wi' his proud, independent stomach,
Could ill agree;
So, row't[10] his hurdies in a hammock,
An' owre the sea.

He ne'er was gi'en to great misguiding,
Yet coin his pouches wad na bide in;
Wi' him it ne'er was under hiding,
He dealt it free:
The Muse was a' that he took pride in,
That's owre the sea.

Jamaica bodies, use him weel,
An' hap[11] him in a cozie biel;[12]
Ye'll find him ay' a dainty chiel,
And fu' o' glee;
He wad na wrang'd the vera deil,
That's owre the sea.

1 Blunderer. 2 Fuss. 3 Sharp.
4 A wimble. 5 Kilmarnock.
6 Shreds. 7 Jilt. 8 Staff.
9 Meal and water. 10 Wrapped.
11 Cover. 12 Shelter.

Fareweel, my rhyme-composing billie!
Your native soil was right ill-willie;
But may ye flourish like a lily,
Now bonnilie!
I'll toast ye in my hindmost gillie,[1]
Tho' owre the sea!

TO A HAGGIS.[2]

Fair fa' your honest, sonsie face,
Great chieftain o' the pudding-race!
Aboon them a' ye tak your place,
Painch, tripe,[3] or thairm:
Weel are ye wordy o' a grace
As lang's my arm.

The groaning trencher there ye fill,
Your hurdies like a distant hill,
Your pin wad help to mend a mill
In time o' need,
While thro' your pores the dews distil
Like amber bead.

His knife see rustic Labour dight,[4]
An' cut you up wi' ready slight,
Trenching your gushing entrails bright
Like onie ditch;
And then, O what a glorious sight,
Warm-reekin, rich!

Then, horn for horn they stretch an' strive,
Deil tak the hindmost, on they drive,
Till a' their weel-swall'd[5] kytes[6] belyve
Are bent like drums;
Then auld guidman, maist like to rive,[7]
"Bethankit" hums.

Is there that o'er his French ragout,
Or olio that wad staw[8] a sow,
Or fricassee wad mak her spew
Wi' perfect sconner,[9]

1 Diminutive of gill.
2 A dish which is only known or relished in Scotland. It is said to be composed of minced mutton, oatmeal, and suet; but a Southron reader will not desire a particular receipt.
3 Small entrails. 4 Wipe.
5 Swelled. 6 Stomachs. 7 Burst.
8 Surfeit. 9 Loathing.

Looks down wi' sneering, scornfu' view
On sic a dinner!

Poor devil! see him owre his trash,
As feckless[1] as a wither'd rash,
His spindle shank a guid whip-lash,
His nieve[2] a nit;[3]
Thro' bloody flood or field to dash,
O how unfit!

But mark the rustic, haggis-fed,
The trembling earth resounds his tread,
Clap in his walie[4] nieve a blade,
He'll mak it whissle;
An' legs, an' arms, an' heads will sned,[5]
Like taps o' thrissle.

Ye pow'rs wha mak mankind your care,
And dish them out their bill o' fare,
Auld Scotland wants nae skinking ware
That jaups in luggies;[6]
But, if ye wish her gratefu' prayer,
Gie her a Haggis.

A DEDICATION TO GAVIN HAMILTON, ESQ.

EXPECT na, Sir, in this narration
A fleechin,[7] fleth'rin[8] Dedication,
To roose you up, an' ca' you guid,
An' sprung o' great an' noble bluid,
Because ye're surnam'd like His Grace,
Perhaps related to the race;
Then when I'm tir'd—and sae are ye,
Wi' mony a fulsome, sinfu' lie,
Set up a face, how I stop short
For fear your modesty be hurt.

This may do—maun do, Sir, wi' them wha
Maun please the great folk for a wamefou;[9]
For me! sae laigh I needna bow,
For, Lord be thankit, I can plough;
And when I downa yoke a naig,[10]
Then, Lord be thankit, I can beg;
Sae I shall say, an' that's nae flatt'rin,
It's just sic Poet, an' sic Patron.

[1] Weak. [2] Fist. [3] Nut. [4] Large.
[5] Lop. [6] Splashes in wooden dishes.
[7] Supplicating. [8] Flattering.
[9] Bellyful. [10] Horse.

The Poet, some guid angel help him,
Or else, I fear some ill ane skelp[1] him!
He may do weel for a' he's done yet,
But only he's no just begun yet.

The Patron (Sir, ye maun forgie me,
I winna lie, come what will o' me),
On ev'ry hand it will allow'd be,
He's just—nae better than he should be.

I readily and freely grant,
He downa see a poor man want;
What's no his ain he winna tak it,
What ance he says he winna break it;
Aught he can lend he'll no refus't,
Till aft his guidness is abus'd;
And rascals whyles that do him wrang,
Ev'n that, he does na mind it lang:
As master, landlord, husband, father,
He does na fail his part in either.

But then, nae thanks to him for a that;
Nae godly symptom ye can ca' that;
It's naething but a milder feature
Of our poor, sinfu', corrupt nature:
Ye'll get the best o' moral works,
'Mang black Gentoos and pagan Turks
Or hunters wild on Ponotaxi,
Wha never heard of orthodoxy.
That's he's the poor man's friend i need,
The gentleman in word and deed,
It's no thro' terror of damnation;
It's just a carnal inclination.

Morality, thou deadly bane,
Thy tens o' thousands thou hast slain
Vain is his hope, whose stay and trust
In moral mercy, truth, and justice!

No—stretch a point to catch a plack;
Abuse a brother to his back;
Steal thro' a winnock[3] frae a ——
But point the rake that taks the doo
Be to the poor like onie whunstane,[4]
And haud their noses to the grunstan
Ply ev'ry art o' legal thieving;
Nae matter, stick to sound believing

Learn three-mile pray'rs, and ha mile graces,
Wi' weel-spread looves,[5] an' lang, w faces;

[1] Strike. [2] An old Scotch co
[3] Window. [4] Whinstone. [5] Hanc

Grunt up a solemn, lengthen'd groan,
And damn a' parties but your own;
I'll warrant then, ye're nae deceiver,
A steady, sturdy, staunch believer.

O ye wha leave the springs of Calvin,
For gumlie[1] dubs[2] of your ain delvin!
Ye sons of heresy and error,
Ye'll some day squeel in quaking terror!
When Vengeance draws the sword in wrath,
And in the fire throws the sheath;
When Ruin, with his sweeping besom,
Just frets till Heav'n commission gies him:
While o'er the harp pale Mis'ry moans,
And strikes the ever-deep'ning tones,
Still louder shrieks, and heavier groans!

Your pardon, Sir, for this digression,
I maist forgat my Dedication;
But when divinity comes cross me,
My readers still are sure to lose me.

So, Sir, ye see 'twas nae daft vapour,
But I maturely thought it proper,
When a' my works I did review,
To dedicate them, Sir, to you:
Because (you need na tak it ill)
I thought them something like yoursel.

Then patronize them wi' your favour,
And your petitioner shall ever—
I had amaist said, ever pray:
But that's a word I need na say:
For prayin I hae little skill o't;
I'm baith dead-sweer,[3] an' wretched ill o't;[4]
But I'se repeat each poor man's pray'r,
That kens or hears about you, Sir,—

"May ne'er misfortune's gowling bark
Howl thro' the dwelling o' the Clerk!
May ne'er his gen'rous, honest heart,
For that same gen'rous spirit smart!
May Kennedy's far honoured name
Lang beet[5] his hymeneal flame;
Till Hamiltons, at least a dizen,
Are frae their nuptial labours risen:
Five bonnie lasses round their table,
And seven braw fellows, stout and able,
To serve their King and Country weel,
By word, or pen, or pointed steel!
May health and peace, with mutual rays,
Shine on the evening o' his days;
Till his wee, curlie John's ier-oe,[1]
When ebbing life nae mair shall flow,
The last sad mournful rites bestow!"

I will not wind a lang conclusion,
Wi' complimentary effusion:
But whilst your wishes and endeavours
Are blest with Fortune's smiles and favours,
I am, dear Sir, with zeal most fervent,
Your much indebted, humble servant.

But if (which Pow'rs above prevent)
That iron-hearted carl, Want,
Attended in his grim advances,
By sad mistakes, and black mischances,
While hopes, and joys, and pleasures fly him,
Make you as poor a dog as I am,
Your humble servant then no more;
For who would humbly serve the poor?
But, by a poor man's hopes in Heav'n!
While recollection's pow'r is given,
If, in the vale of humble life,
The victim sad of fortune's strife,
I, thro' the tender gushing tear,
Should recognise my Master dear,
If friendless, low, we meet together,
Then, Sir, your hand—my Friend and Brother!

[1] Muddy. [2] Ponds.
[3] Extremely averse. [4] Of it.
[5] Add fuel to.

[1] Great grandchild.

TO A ——, ON SEEING ONE ON A LADY'S BONNET AT CHURCH.

Ha! whare ye gaun, ye crowlin ferlie![2]
Your impudence protects you sairly:
I canna say but ye strunt[3] rarely,
Owre gauze and lace;
Tho', faith, I fear ye dine but sparely
On sic a place.

[2] Wonder. [3] Strut.

Ye ugly, creepin, blastit wonner,
Detested, shunn'd by saunt an' sinner,
How dare ye set your fit [1] upon her,
Sae fine a lady!
Gae somewhere else, and seek your dinner
On some poor body.

Swith,[2] in some beggar's haffet [3] squattle;
There ye may creep, and sprawl, and sprattle [4]
Wi' ither kindred, jumping cattle,
In shoals and nations:
Whare horn nor bane ne'er dare unsettle
Your thick plantations.

Now haud ye there, ye're out o' sight,
Below the fatt'rils,[5] snug an' tight;
Na, faith ye yet! ye'll no be right
Till ye've got on it,
The vera tapmost, tow'ring height
O' Miss's bonnet.

My sooth! right bauld ye set your nose out,
As plump and gray as onie grozet: [6]
O for some rank, mercurial rozet,
Or fell, red smeddum,[7]
I'd gie you sic a hearty doze o't,
Wad dress your droddum! [8]

I wad na been surpris'd to spy
You on an auld wife's flainen toy; [9]
Or aiblins some bit duddie boy,
On 's wyliecoat: [10]
But Miss's fine Lunardi! [11] fie,
How daur ye do't?

O Jenny, dinna toss your head,
An' set your beauties a' abread!
Ye little ken what cursed speed
The blastie's [12] makin!
Thae winks and finger-ends, I dread,
Are notice takin!

O wad some Pow'r the giftie gie us
To see oursels as others see us!
It wad frae monie a blunder free us
And foolish notion:
What airs in dress an' gait wad lea'e us,
And ev'n Devotion!

[1] Foot. [2] Get away. [3] Temple. [4] Scramble. [5] Ribbon-ends. [6] Gooseberry. [7] Powder. [8] Breech. [9] An old-fashioned head-dress. [10] Flannel vest.
[11] A bonnet, named after Lunardi, whose balloon made him notorious in Scotland about 1785.
[12] The shrivelled dwarf.

LINES WRITTEN AT KENMORE, TAYMOUTH.[1]

Admiring Nature in her wildest grace,
These northern scenes with weary feet I trace;
O'er many a winding dale and painful steep,
The abodes of covey'd grouse and timid sheep,
My savage journey, curious, I pursue,
Till fam'd Breadalbane opens to my view,—
The meeting cliffs each deep-sunk glen divides,
The woods, wild scatter'd, clothe their ample sides;
Th' outstretching lake, embosom'd 'mong the hills,
The eye with wonder and amazement fills.
The Tay, meand'ring sweet in infant pride,
The palace, rising on its verdant side
The lawns, wood-fring'd in Nature's native taste,
The hillocks, dropt in Nature's careless haste;

[1] Professor Walker informs us that "Burns passed two or three days with the Duke of Athole, and was highly delighted by the attention he received and the company to whom he was introduced. By the Duke's advice he visited the falls of Bruar, and in a few days I received a letter from Inverness with the above verses inclosed." The lines were first written over the chimney-piece in the parlour of the inn Kenmore.

The arches, striding o'er the new-born stream,
The village, glittering in the noon-tide beam.

* * * * * *

Here Poesy might wake her heaven-taught lyre,
And look through Nature with creative fire;
Here, to the wrongs of Fate half reconciled,
Misfortune's lighten'd steps might wander wild;
And Disappointment, in these lonely bounds,
Find balm to soothe her bitter, rankling wounds;
Here heart-struck Grief might heavenward stretch her scan,
And injured Worth forget and pardon man.

ADDRESS TO EDINBURGH.

Edina! Scotia's darling seat!
All hail thy palaces and tow'rs,
Where once beneath a monarch's feet
Sat Legislation's sov'reign pow'rs!
From marking wildly-scatter'd flow'rs,
As on the banks of Ayr I stray'd,
And singing, lone, the ling'ring hours,
I shelter in thy honour'd shade.

Here wealth still swells the golden tide,
As busy Trade his labours plies;
There Architecture's noble pride
Bids elegance and splendour rise;
Here Justice, from her native skies,
High wields her balance and her rod;
There Learning, with his eagle eyes,
Seeks Science in her coy abode.

Thy sons, Edina, social, kind,
With open arms the stranger hail;
Their views enlarg'd, their lib'ral mind,
Above the narrow, rural vale;
Attentive still to sorrow's wail,
Or modest merit's silent claim:
And never may their sources fail!
And never envy blot their name!

Thy daughters bright thy walks adorn,
Gay as the gilded summer sky,
Sweet as the dewy milk-white thorn,
Dear as the raptur'd thrill of joy!
Fair Burnet[1] strikes th' adoring eye,
Heav'n's beauties on my fancy shine;
I see the Sire of Love on high,
And own his work indeed divine!

There watching high the least alarms,
Thy rough rude fortress gleams afar:
Like some bold vet'ran, gray in arms,
And mark'd with many a seamy scar:
The pond'rous wall and massy bar,
Grim-rising o'er the rugged rock,
Have oft withstood assailing war,
And oft repell'd th' invader's shock.

With awe-struck thought, and pitying tears,
I view that noble, stately dome,
Where Scotia's kings of other years,
Fam'd heroes, had their royal home:
Alas, how chang'd the times to come!
Their royal name low in the dust!
Their hapless racewild-wand'ring roam!
Tho' rigid law cries out, 'twas just!

Wild beats my heart,to trace your steps,
Whose ancestors, in days of yore,
Thro' hostile ranks and ruin'd gaps
Old Scotia's bloody lion bore:
Ev'n I who sing in rustic lore,
Haply my sires have left their shed,
And fac'd grim danger's loudest roar,
Bold-following where your fathers led!

Edina! Scotia's darling seat!
All hail thy palaces and towr's,
Where once beneath a monarch's feet
Sat Legislation's sovereign pow'rs!
From marking wildly-scatter'd flow'rs,
As on the banks of Ayr I stray'd,
And singing, lone, the ling'ring hours,
I shelter in thy honour'd shade.

---

[1] Daughter of Lord Monboddo. Burns said there had not been anything like her,in beauty, grace, and goodness, since Eve on the first day of her existence.

EPISTLE TO JOHN LAPRAIK, AN OLD SCOTTISH BARD.[1]

April 1st, 1785.

WHILE briers an' woodbines budding green,
An' paitricks[2] scraichin loud at e'en,
An' morning poussie[3] whiddin[4] seen,
Inspire my Muse,
This freedom in an unknown frien'
I pray excuse.

On Fasten-een we had a rockin,
To ca' the crack and weave our stockin:
And there was muckle fun and jokin,
Ye need na doubt;
At length we had a hearty yokin[5]
At sang about.

[1] The "Epistle to John Lapraik" was produced exactly on the occasion described by the author. He says in that poem, "On fasten-e'en we had a rockin." I believe he has omitted the word *rocking* in the glossary. It is a term derived from those primitive times, when the country-women employed their spare hours in spinning on the rock, or distaff. This simple implement is a very portable one, and well fitted to the social inclination of meeting in a neighbour's house; hence the phrase of *going a-rocking*, or *with the rock*. As the connexion the phrase had with the implement was forgotten when the rock gave place to the spinning-wheel, the phrase came to be used by both sexes on social occasions, and men talk of going with their rocks as well as women. It was at one of these *rockings* at our house, when we had twelve or fifteen young people with their *rocks*, that Lapraik's song, beginning, "When I upon thy bosom lean," was sung, and we were informed who was the author. Upon this Robert wrote his first Epistle to Lapraik; and his second in reply to his answer.—G. B.

[2] Partridges. [3] Hare.
[4] Running. [5] A bout.

There was ae sang, amang the rest,
Aboon them a' it pleas'd me best,
That some kind husband had addrest
To some sweet wife:
It thirl'd[1] the heart-strings thro' the breast,
A' to the life.

I've scarce heard aught describes sae weel,
What gen'rous, manly bosoms feel:
Thought I, "Can this be Pope, or Steele,
Or Beattie's wark?"
They tauld me 'twas an odd kind chiel
About Muirkirk.

It pat me fidgin-fain[2] to hear't,
And sae about him there I spier't,
Then a' that ken'd him round declar'd
He had ingine,[3]
That nane excell'd it, few cam near't
It was sae fine;

That, set him to a pint of ale,
An' either douce or merry tale,
Or rhymes an' sangs he'd made himsel,
Or witty catches,
'Tween Inverness and Tiviotdale
He had few matches.

Then up I gat, an' swoor an aith,
Tho' I should pawn my pleugh and graith,[4]
Or die a cadger pownie's[5] death,
At some dyke-back,
A pint an' gill I'd gie them baith
To hear your crack.

But, first an' foremost, I should tell,
Amaist as soon as I could spell,
I to the crambo-jingle fell,
Tho' rude an' rough,
Yet crooning[6] to a body's sel
Does weel eneugh.

I am nae Poet, in a sense,
But just a Rhymer like, by chance,
An' hae to learning nae pretence,
Yet, what the matter?
Whene'er my Muse does on me glance
I jingle at her.

[1] Thrilled. [2] Very anxious.
[3] Genius. [4] And gear.
[5] Carrier pony. [6] Humming.

Your critic-folk may cock their nose,
And say, "How can you e'er propose,
You wha ken hardly verse frae prose,
To mak a sang?"
But, by your leaves, my learned foes,
Ye're maybe wrang.

What's a' your jargon o' your schools,
Your Latin names for horns an' stools;
If honest nature made you fools,
What sairs[1] your grammars?
Ye'd better taen up spades and shools,
Or knappin[2]-hammers.

A set o' dull, conceited hashes,[3]
Confuse their brains in college classes!
They gang in stirks,[4] and come out asses,
Plain truth to speak;
An' syne[5] they think to climb Parnassus
By dint o' Greek!

Gie me ae spark o' Nature's fire,
That's a' the learning I desire;
Then tho' I drudge thro' dub[6] an' mire
At pleugh or cart,
My Muse, though hamely in attire,
May touch the heart.

O for a spunk[7] o' Allan's glee,
Or Fergusson's, the bauld and slee,
Or bright Lapraik's, my friend to be,
If I can hit it!
That would be lear[8] eneugh for me,
If I could get it.

Now, Sir, if ye hae friends enow,
Tho' real friends, I b'lieve, are few,
Yet, if your catalogue be fou,[9]
I'se no insist,
But gif ye want ae friend that's true,
I'm on your list.

I winna blaw about mysel;
As ill I like my fauts to tell;
But friends and folk that wish me well,
They sometimes roose[10] me;
Tho' I maun own, as monie still
As far abuse me.

There's ae wee faut they whiles lay to me,
I like the lasses—Gude forgie me!

[1] Serves. [2] Stone-breaking.
[3] Louts. [4] Cows. [5] Then.
[6] Pond. [7] Spark. [8] Learning.
[9] Full. [10] Praise.

For monie a plack they wheedle frae me,
At dance or fair;
Maybe some ither thing they gie me
They weel can spare.

But Mauchline race, or Mauchline fair,
I should be proud to meet you there;
We'se gie ae night's discharge to care,
If we forgather,[1]
An' hae a swap[2] o' rhymin-ware
Wi' ane anither.

The four-gill chap, we'se gar him clatter,
An' kirsen[3] him wi' reekin water:
Syne we'll sit down an' tak our whitter,[4]
To cheer our heart;
An' faith, we'se be acquainted better
Before we part.

Awa ye selfish warly[5] race,
Wha think that havins,[6] sense, an' grace,
Ev'n love an' friendship, should give place
To catch-the-plack!
I dinna like to see your face,
Nor hear your crack.

But ye whom social pleasure charms,
Whose hearts the tide of kindness warms,
Who hold your being on the terms,
'Each aid the others,'
Come to my bowl, come to my arms,
My friends, my brothers!

But to conclude my lang epistle,
As my auld pen's worn to the grissle;
Twa lines frae you wad gar me fissle,
Who am, most fervent,
While I can either sing or whissle,
Your friend and servant.

TO THE SAME.[7]

April 21st, 1785.

While new-ca'd kye[8] rout[9] at the stake,
An' pownies reek in pleugh or braik,[10]

[1] Meet. [2] Exchange.
[3] Christen. [4] Hearty draught.
[5] Worldly. [6] Good manners.
[7] In answer to verses which Lapraik had sent.
[8] Cows. [9] Low. [10] Harrow.

This hour on e'enin's[1] edge I take,
To own I'm debtor
To honest-hearted, auld Lapraik,
For his kind letter.

Forjesket[2] sair, with weary legs,
Rattlin the corn out-owre the rigs,
Or dealing thro' amang the naigs
Their ten-hours' bite,
My awkwart Muse sair pleads and begs,
I would na write.

The tapetless,[3] ramfeezl'd[4] hizzie,
She's saft at best, and something lazy,
Quo' she, "Ye ken, we've been sae busy,
This month an' mair,
That trouth my head is grown right dizzie,
An' something sair."

Her dowff[5] excuses pat me mad;
"Conscience," says I, "ye thowless[6] jad!
I'll write, an' that a hearty blaud,
This vera night;
So dinna ye affront your trade,
But rhyme it right.

"Shall bauld Lapraik, the king o' hearts,
Tho' mankind were a pack o' cartes,[7]
Roose you sae weel for your deserts,
In terms sae friendly,
Yet ye'll neglect to shaw your parts,
An' thank him kindly!"

Sae I gat paper in a blink,
An' down gaed stumpie in the ink:
Quoth I, "Before I sleep a wink,
I vow I'll close it;
An' if ye winna mak it clink,
By Jove, I'll prose it!"

Sae I've begun to scrawl, but whether
In rhyme, or prose, or baith thegither,
Or some hotch-potch that's rightly neither,
Let time mak proof;
But I shall scribble down some blether[8]
Just clean aff-loof.[9]

1 Evening's. 2 Jaded. 3 Foolish. 4 Tired. 5 Silly. 6 Lazy. 7 Cards. 8 Nonsense. 9 Unpremeditated.

My worthy friend, ne'er grudge an carp,
Tho' fortune use you hard an' sharp;
Come, kittle[1] up your moorland harp
Wi' gleesome touch!
Ne'er mind how fortune waft an' warp;
She's but a b—h.

She's gien me monie a jirt an' fleg,[2]
Sin' I could striddle owre a rig;
But, by the Lord, tho' I should beg
Wi' lyart pow,
I'll laugh, and sing, an' shake my leg,
As lang's I dow![3]

Now comes the sax an' twentieth simmer,
I've seen the bud upo' the timmer,
Still persecuted by the limmer
Frae year to year;
But yet, despite the kittle kimmer,[4]
I, Rob, am here.

Do ye envy the city Gent,
Behint a kist[5] to lie and sklent,[6]
Or purse-proud, big wi' cent per cent,
An' muckle wame,[7]
In some bit Brugh to represent
A Bailie's name?

Or is't the paughty,[8] feudal Thane,
Wi' ruffled sark an' glancing cane,
Wha thinks himsel nae sheep-shank bane,
But lordly stalks,
While caps and bonnets aff are ta'en,
As by he walks?

"O Thou wha gies us each guid gift!
Gie me o' wit an' sense a lift,
Then turn me, if Thou please, adrift,
Thro' Scotland wide;
Wi' cits nor lairds I wadna shift,
In a' their pride!"

Were this the charter of our state,
"On pain o' hell be rich an' great,"
Damnation then would be our fate,
Beyond remead;
But, thanks to Heav'n! that's no the gate
We learn our creed.

1 Tickle. 2 Kick. 3 Can. 4 Skittish girl. 5 Counter. 6 Deceive. 7 Belly. 8 Haughty.

For thus the royal mandate ran,
When first the human race began,
"The social, friendly, honest man,
Whate'er he be,
'Tis he fulfils great Nature's plan,
And none but he!"

O mandate glorious and divine!
The ragged followers of the Nine,
Poor, thoughtless devils! yet may shine,
In glorious light,
While sordid sons of Mammon's line
Are dark as night.

Tho' here they scrape, an' squeeze, an' growl,
Their worthless nievefu'[1] of a soul
May in some future carcase howl,
The forest's fright;
Or in some day-detesting owl
May shun the light.

Then may Lapraik and Burns arise,
To reach their native, kindred skies,
And sing their pleasures, hopes, an' joys,
In some mild sphere,
Still closer knit in friendship's ties
Each passing year!

THE TWO LAWYERS,

IN THE PARLIAMENT HOUSE AT EDINBURGH.[2]

LORD ADVOCATE.

He clench'd his pamphlets in his fist,
He quoted and he hinted,
Till in a declamation mist
His argument he tint o't,[3]
He gaped for't, he graped[4] for't,
He found it was awa', man;
But what his common sense cam short
He eked out wi' law, man.

DEAN OF FACULTY.

Collected Harry stood a wee,
Then open'd out his arm, man;
His lordship sat, wi' ruefu' e'e,
And eyed the gath'ring storm, man;
Like wind-driven hail, it did assail,
Or torrents ow're a linn, man;
The Bench, sae wise, lift up their eyes,
Half-waken'd wi' the din, man.

[1] Handful.
[2] Mr. Hay Campbell, the Lord Advocate (afterwards Lord President), and Harry Erskine, the Dean of Faculty.
[3] Lost. [4] Groped.

TO WILLIAM SIMPSON,[1]

OCHILTREE.

May, 1785.

I gat your letter, winsome Willie;
Wi' gratefu' heart I thank you brawlie;
Tho' I maun say't, I wad be silly,
An' unco vain,
Should I believe, my coaxin billie,[2]
Your flatterin strain.

But I'se believe ye kindly meant it,
I sud be laith to think ye hinted
Ironic satire, sidelins sklented[3]
On my poor Musie;
Tho' in sic phraisin terms ye've penn'd it,
I scarce excuse ye.

My senses wad be in a creel,[4]
Should I but dare a hope to speel,[5]
Wi' Allan, or wi' Gilbertfiel',[6]
The braes o' fame;
Or Fergusson, the writer-chiel,
A deathless name.

(O Fergusson! thy glorious parts
Ill suited law's dry, musty arts!
My curse upon your whunstane hearts,
Ye Enbrugh Gentry!
The tythe o' what ye waste at cartes
Wad stow'd his pantry!)

Yet when a tale comes i' my head,
Or lasses gie my heart a screed,[7]
As whiles they're like to be my deed,
(O sad disease!)
I kittle up my rustic reed;
It gies me ease.

[1] Schoolmaster of Ochiltree.
[2] Brother. [3] Sidelong flung.
[4] Be crazed. [5] Climb.
[6] Allan Ramsay and Hamilton of Gilbertfield. [7] Rent.

Auld Coila, now, may fidge [1] fu' fain,
She's gotten Poets o' her ain,
Chiels wha their chanters winna hain,[2]
But tune their lays,
Till echoes a' resound again
Her weel-sung praise.

Nae Poet thought her worth his while,
To set her name in measur'd style ;
She lay like some unkend-of isle,
Beside New Holland,
Or whare wild-meeting oceans boil
Besouth Magellan.

Ramsay an' famous Fergusson
Gied Forth an Tay a lift aboon ;
Yarrow an' Tweed, to monie a tune,
Ower Scotland rings,
While Irwin, Lugar, Ayr, an' Doon,
Nae body sings.

Th' Illissus, Tiber, Thames, an' Seine,
Glide sweet in monie a tunefu' line !
But, Willie, set your fit to mine,
An' cock your crest,
We'll gar our streams an' burnies shine
Up wi' the best.

We'll sing auld Coila's plains an' fells,
Her moors red-brown wi' heather bells,
Her banks an' braes, her dens an' dells,
Whare Glorious Wallace
Aft bure [3] the gree, as story tells,
Frae southron billies.

At Wallace' name, what Scottish blood
But boils up in a spring-tide flood !
Oft have our fearless fathers strode
By Wallace' side,
Still pressing onward, red-wat-shod,[4]
Or glorious dy'd.

O, sweet are Coila's haughs [5] an' woods,
When lintwhites [6] chant amang the buds,
And jinkin [7] hares, in amorous whids,
Their loves enjoy,
While thro' the braes the cushat croods [8]
Wi' wailfu' cry !

[1] Be right glad.
[2] Will not spare their bagpipes.
[3] Did bear.
[4] Walking in blood over the shoe-tops.
[5] Valleys. [6] Linnets.
[7] Dodging. [8] Coos.

Ev'n winter bleak has charms to me,
When winds rave thro' the naked tree ;
Or frosts on hills of Ochiltree
Are hoary gray ;
Or blinding drifts wild-furious flee,
Dark'ning the day !

O Nature ! a' thy shews an' forms
To feeling, pensive hearts hae charms !
Whether the summer kindly warms,
Wi' life an' light,
Or winter howls, in gusty storms,
The lang, dark night !

The Muse, nae Poet ever fand [1] her,
Till by himsel he learn'd to wander,
Adown some trotting burn's meander,
An' no think lang ;
O sweet, to stray an' pensive ponder
A heart-felt sang !

The war'ly race may drudge an' drive,
Hog-shouther,[2] jundie,[3] stretch, an' strive,—
Let me fair Nature's face descrive,
And I, wi' pleasure,
Shall let the busy, grumbling hive
Bum [4] owre their treasure.

Fareweel, " my rhyme-composing brither ! "
We've been owre lang unkenn'd to ither :
Now let us lay our heads thegither,
In love fraternal :
May Envy wallop in a tether,
Black fiend, infernal !

While highlandmen hate tolls an' taxes ;
While moorlan' herds [5] like guid, fat braxies ; [6]
While terra firma, on her axis
Diurnal turns,
Count on a friend, in faith an' practice,
In Robert Burns.

POSTSCRIPT.

My memory's no worth a preen ; [7]
I had amaist forgotten clean,

[1] Found. [2] Push with the shoulder.
[3] Jostle. [4] Hum. [5] Shepherds.
[6] Diseased sheep. [7] Pin.

Ye bade me write you what they mean
By this New-Light,
'Bout which our herds sae aft hae been
Maist like to fight.

In days when mankind were but callans[1]
At grammar, logic, an' sic talents,
They took nae pains their speech to balance,
Or rules to gie,
But spak their thoughts in plain, braid Lallans,[2]
Like you or me.

In thae auld times, they thought the moon,
Just like a sark, or pair o' shoon,
Wore by degrees, till her last roon,[3]
Gaed past their viewing,
An' shortly after she was done,
They gat a new one.

This past for certain, undisputed;
It ne'er cam i' their heads to doubt it,
Till chiels gat up an' wad confute it,
An' ca'd it wrang;
An' muckle din there was about it,
Baith loud an' lang.

Some herds, weel learn'd upo' the beuk,[4]
Wad threap[5] auld folk the thing misteuk;
For 'twas the auld moon turn'd a neuk,
An' out o' sight,
An' backlins[6]-comin, to the leuk
She grew mair bright.

This was deny'd, it was affirm'd;
The herds an' hirsels[7] were alarm'd;
The rev'rend gray-beards rav'd an' storm'd,
That beardless laddies
Should think they better were inform'd
Than their auld daddies.

Frae less to mair it gaed to sticks;
Frae words an' aiths to clours[8] an' nicks;
An' monie a fallow gat his licks,
Wi' hearty crunt;[9]

[1] Boys. [2] Lowland speech. [3] Shred. [4] Book. [5] Maintain. [6] Returning. [7] Flocks. [8] Bumps. [9] Blow.

An' some, to learn them for their tricks,
Were hang'd an' brunt.[1]

This game was play'd in monie lands,
An' Auld-light caddies bure sic hands,
That, faith, the youngsters took the sands
Wi' nimble shanks,
The lairds farbade, by strict commands,
Sic bluidy pranks.

But New-light herds gat sic a cowe,
Folk thought them ruined stick-an-stowe,[2]
Till now amaist on ev'ry knowe[3]
Ye'll find ane plac'd;
An' some their New-light fair avow,
Just quite barefac'd.

Nae doubt the Auld-light flocks are bleatin;
Their zealous herds are vex'd an' sweatin;
Mysel, I've even seen them greetin
Wi' girnin[4] spite,
To hear the moon sae sadly lied on
By word an' write.

But shortly they will cowe the louns![5]
Some Auld-light herds in neebor towns
Are mind't, in things they ca' balloons,
To tak a flight,
An' stay ae month amang the moons,
An' see them right.

Guid observation they will gie them:
An' when the auld moon's gaun to lea'e them,
The hindmost shaird,[6] they'll fetch it wi' them,
Just i' their pouch,
An' when the New-light billies see them,
I think they'll crouch!

Sae, ye observe that a' this clatter
Is naething but a "moonshine matter;"
But tho' dull-prose folk Latin splatter
In logic tulzie,[7]
I hope we Bardies ken some better
Than mind sic brulzie.[8]

[1] Burnt. [2] Totally. [3] Hillock. [4] Grinning. [5] Fellows. [6] Shred. [7] Quarrel. [8] A broil.

EPISTLE TO JOHN RANKINE, ENCLOSING SOME POEMS.

O ROUGH, rude, ready-witted Rankine,
The wale[2] o' cocks for fun an' drinkin!
There's monie godly folks are thinkin,
Your dreams an' tricks
Will send you, Korah-like, a-sinkin,
Straught to auld Nick's.

Ye hae sae monie cracks an' cants,
And in your wicked, drucken rants,
Ye mak a devil o' the saunts,
An' fill them fou:
And then their failings, flaws, an' wants,
Are a' seen thro'.

Hypocrisy, in mercy spare it!
That holy robe, O dinna tear it!
Spare 't for their sakes wha aften wear it,
The lads in black!
But your curst wit, when it comes near it,
Rives 't aff their back.

Think, wicked sinner, wha ye're skaithing,[3]
It's just the blue-gown badge an' claithing
O' saunts; tak that, ye lea'e them naithing
To ken them by,
Frae ony unregenerate heathen
Like you or I.

I've sent you here some rhyming ware,
A' that I bargain'd for an' mair;
Sae, when ye hae an hour to spare,
I will expect,
Yon sang,[4] ye'll sen 't[5] wi' cannie care,
And no neglect.

Tho', faith, sma' heart hae I to sing!
My Muse dow scarcely spread her wing!
I've play'd mysel a bonnie spring,
An' danc'd my fill!

[1] According to Allan Cunningham, "an out-spoken, ready-witted man, and a little of a scoffer."
[2] Choice. [3] Damaging.
[4] A song he had promised the author.—R. B. [5] Send it.

I'd better gaen an' sair't[1] the king
At Bunker's Hill.

'Twas ae night lately, in my fun,
I gaed a roving wi' the gun,
An' brought a paitrick to the grun,[2]
A bonnie hen;
And, as the twilight was begun,
Thought nane wad ken.

The poor wee thing was little hurt;
I straikit[3] it a wee for sport,
Ne'er thinkin they wad fash me for't;
But, Deil-ma-care!
Somebody tells the poacher-court
The hale[4] affair.

Some auld us'd hands had ta'en a note,
That sic a hen had got a shot;
I was suspected for the plot;
I scorn'd to lie;
So gat the whissle o' my groat,
An' pay't the fee.

But, by my gun, o' guns the wale,
An' by my pouther an' my hail,
An' by my hen, an' by her tail,
I vow an' swear!
The game shall pay, o'er moor an' dale,
For this, niest year.

As soon's the clockin-time[5] is by,
An' the wee pouts[6] begun to cry,
L—d, I'se hae sportin by an' by,
For my gowd guinea;
Tho' I should herd the Buckskin[7] kye
For't, in Virginia.

Trowth, they had muckle for to blame!
'Twas neither broken wing nor limb,
But twa-three draps about the wame,[8]
Scarce thro' the feathers;
An' baith a yellow George to claim,
An' thole their blethers![9]

It pits[10] me aye as mad's a hare;
So I can rhyme nor write nae mair;

[1] Served. [2] Partridge to the ground.
[3] Stroked. [4] Whole.
[5] Hatching time. [6] Chicks.
[7] Buckskin, an inhabitant of Virginia.
[8] Belly.
[9] And endure their foolish talk.
[10] Puts.

But pennyworths again is fair,
When time's expedient:
Meanwhile I am, respected Sir,
Your most obedient.

ELEGY ON CAPTAIN MATTHEW HENDERSON,[1]

A GENTLEMAN WHO HELD THE PATENT FOR HIS HONOURS IMMEDIATELY FROM ALMIGHTY GOD.

But now his radiant course is run,
For Matthew's course was bright:
His soul was like the glorious sun,
A matchless, Heav'nly Light.

O DEATH! thou tyrant fell and bloody!
The meikle devil wi' a woodie[2]
Haurl thee hame to his black smiddie,[3]
O'er hurcheon[4] hides,
And like stock-fish come o'er his studdie[5]
Wi' thy auld sides!

He's gane, he's gane! he's frae us torn,
The ae best fellow e'er was born!
Thee, Matthew, Nature's sel[6] shall mourn
By wood and wild,
Where, haply, Pity strays forlorn,
Frae man exil'd.

Ye hills, near neebors o' the starns,
That proudly cock your cresting cairns![7]
Ye cliffs, the haunts of sailing yearns,[8]
Where echo slumbers!
Come join, ye Nature's sturdiest bairns,
My wailing numbers!

Mourn, ilka grove the cushat[1] kens!
Ye haz'lly shaws and briery dens!
Ye burnies, wimplin[2] down your glens,
Wi' toddlin din,
Or foaming strang, wi' hasty stens,[3]
Frae lin to lin.[4]

Mourn, little harebells o'er the lea;
Ye stately foxgloves fair to see;
Ye woodbines hanging bonnilie,
In scented bow'rs;
Ye roses on your thorny tree,
The first o' flow'rs.

At dawn, when ev'ry grassy blade
Droops with a diamond at his head,
At ev'n, when beans their fragrance shed,
I' th' rustling gale,
Ye maukins[5] whiddin[6] thro' the glade,
Come join my wail.

Mourn, ye wee songsters o' the wood;
Ye grouse that crap the heather-bud;
Ye curlews calling thro' a clud;[7]
Ye whistling plover;
And mourn, ye whirring paitrick brood;
He's gane for ever!

Mourn, sooty coots, and speckled teals,
Ye fisher herons, watching eels;
Ye duck and drake, wi' airy wheels
Circling the lake;
Ye bitterns, till the quagmire reels,
Rair[8] for his sake.

Mourn, clam'ring craiks at close o' day,
'Mang fields o' flow'ring claver gay;
And when ye wing your annual way
Frae our cauld shore,
Tell thae far warlds, wha lies in clay,
Wham we deplore.

Ye houlets,[9] frae your ivy bow'r,
In some auld tree, or eldritch[10] tow'r,
What time the moon, wi' silent glow'r,
Sets up her horn,

---

[1] The Elegy on Captain Henderson is a tribute to the memory of a man I loved much. Poets have in this the same advantage as Roman Catholics; they can be of service to their friends after they have passed that bourne where all other kindness ceases to be of any avail.—*To Dr. Moore*, (Feb. 28, 1791,) who remarked, in reply, that the chief merit of the Elegy lies in its lively pictures of country scenes and things, which none but a Scottish poet, and a close observer of Nature, could have so described.

[2] Rope. [3] Smithy. [4] Hedgehog. [5] Anvil. [6] Self. [7] Heaps of stones. [8] Eagles.

[1] Wood-pigeon. [2] Meandering. [3] Plunges. [4] Pool to pool. [5] Hares. [6] Running. [7] Cloud. [8] Boom. [9] Owls. [10] Dismal.

Wail thro' the dreary midnight hour
Till waukrife[1] morn!

O rivers, forests, hills, and plains!
Oft have ye heard my canty[2] strains:
But now, what else for me remains
But tales of woe;
And frae my een the drapping rains
Maun ever flow.

Mourn, Spring, thou darling of the year!
Ilk cowslip cup shall kep a tear:
Thou, Simmer, while each corny spear
Shoots up its head,
Thy gay, green, flow'ry tresses shear
For him that's dead!

Thou, Autumn, wi' thy yellow hair,
In grief thy sallow mantle tear!
Thou, Winter, hurling thro' the air
The roaring blast,
Wide o'er the naked world declare
The worth we've lost!

Mourn him, thou Sun, great source of light!
Mourn, Empress of the silent night!
And you, ye twinkling starnies bright,
My Matthew mourn!
For through your orbs he's ta'en his flight,
Ne'er to return.

O Henderson! the man! the brother!
And art thou gone, and gone for ever!
And hast thou crost that unknown river,
Life's dreary bound!
Like thee, where shall I find another,
The world around?

Go to your sculptur'd tombs, ye Great,
In a' the tinsel trash o' state!
But by thy honest turf I'll wait,
Thou man of worth!
And weep the ae[3] best fellow's fate
E'er lay in earth.

[1] Wakeful. [2] Merry. [3] One.

THE EPITAPH.

Stop, passenger! my story's brief,
And truth I shall relate, man;
I tell nae common tale o' grief,—
For Matthew was a great man.

If thou uncommon merit hast,
Yet spurn'd at fortune's door, man;
A look of pity hither cast,—
For Matthew was a poor man.

If thou a noble sodger art,
That passest by this grave, man,
There moulders here a gallant heart,—
For Matthew was a brave man.

If thou on men, their works and ways,
Canst throw uncommon light, man;
Here lies wha weel had won thy praise,—
For Matthew was a bright man.

If thou at friendship's sacred ca'
Wad life itself resign, man;
Thy sympathetic tear maun fa',—
For Matthew was a kind man.

If thou art staunch without a stain,
Like the unchanging blue, man;
This was a kinsman o' thy ain,—
For Matthew was a true man.

If thou hast wit, and fun, and fire,
And ne'er gude wine did fear, man;
This was thy billie, dam, and sire,—
For Matthew was a queer man.

If ony whiggish whingin[1] sot,
To blame poor Matthew dare, man
May dool[2] and sorrow be his lot,—
For Matthew was a rare man.

LAMENT OF MARY, QUEEN OF SCOTS, ON THE APPROACH OF SPRING.[3]

Now Nature hangs her mantle green
On every blooming tree,

[1] Complaining. [2] Mourning.
[3] Whether it is that the story of our Mary, Queen of Scots, has a peculiar effect on the feelings of a poet, or whether I have, in the enclosed ballad, succeeded beyond my usual poetic success, I know not; but it has pleased me beyond any effort of my muse for a good while past.—R. B.

And spreads her sheets o' daisies white
Out owre the grassy lea:
Now Phœbus cheers the crystal streams,
And glads the azure skies;
But nought can glad the weary wight
That fast in durance lies.

Now lav'rocks[1] wake the merry morn,
Aloft on dewy wing;
The merle, in his noontide bow'r,
Makes woodland echoes ring;
The mavis[2] mild, wi' many a note,
Sings drowsy day to rest:
In love and freedom they rejoice,
Wi' care nor thrall opprest.

Now blooms the lily by the bank,
The primrose down the brae;
The hawthorn's budding in the glen,
And milk-white is the slae:
The meanest hind in fair Scotland
May rove their sweets amang:
But I, the Queen of a' Scotland,
Maun lie in prison strang.

I was the Queen o' bonnie France,
Where happy I hae been,
Fu' lightly rase I in the morn,
As blythe lay down at e'en:
And I'm the sov'reign of Scotland,
And mony a traitor there;
Yet here I lie in foreign bands,
And never-ending care.

But as for thee, thou false woman,
My sister and my fae,
Grim vengeance, yet, shall whet a sword
That thro' thy soul shall gae:
The weeping blood in woman's breast
Was never known to thee;
Nor th' balm that draps on wounds of woe
Frae woman's pitying e'e.

My son! my son! may kinder stars
Upon thy fortune shine;
And may those pleasures gild thy reign,
That ne'er wad blink on mine!
God keep thee frae thy mother's faes,
Or turn their hearts to thee;
And where thou meet'st thy mother's friend,
Remember him for me!

Oh! soon, to me, may summer suns
Nae mair light up the morn!
Nae mair, to me, the autumn winds
Wave o'er the yellow corn!
And in the narrow house o' death
Let winter round me rave;
And the next flow'rs, that deck the spring,
Bloom on my peaceful grave!

---

[1] Larks. [2] Thrush.

ODE,[1] SACRED TO THE MEMORY OF MRS. OSWALD.

Dweller in yon dungeon dark,
Hangman of creation! mark

---

[1] Ellisland, March 23, 1789.

The enclosed Ode is a compliment to the memory of the late Mrs. Oswald, of Auchencruive. You probably knew her personally, an honour which I cannot boast; but I spent my early years in her neighbourhood, and among her servants and tenants. I know that she was detested with the most heartfelt cordiality. However, in the particular part of her conduct which roused my poetic wrath, she was much less blameable. In January last, on my road to Ayrshire, I had put up at Bailie Wigham's, in Sanquhar, the only tolerable inn in the place. The frost was keen, and the grim evening and howling wind were ushering in a night of snow and drift. My horse and I were both much fatigued with the labours of the day, and just as my friend the Bailie and I were bidding defiance to the storm, over a smoking bowl, in wheels the funeral pageantry of the late great Mrs. —, and poor I am forced to brave all the horrors of the tempestuous night, and jade my horse, my young favourite horse, whom I had just christened Pegasus, twelve miles farther on, through the wildest muirs and hills of Ayrshire, to New Cumnock the next inn. The powers of poesy and prose sink under me, when I would describe what I felt. Suffice it to say, that when

Who in widow-weeds appears,
Laden with unhonour'd years,
Noosing with care a bursting purse,
Baited with many a deadly curse !

STROPHE.

View the wither'd beldam's face—
Can thy keen inspection trace
Aught of humanity's sweet melting grace?
Note that eye, 'tis rheum o'erflows,
Pity's flood there never rose.
See those hands, ne'er stretch'd to save,
Hands that took—but never gave.
Keeper of Mammon's iron chest,
Lo, there she goes, unpitied and unblest—
She goes, but not to realms of everlasting rest!

ANTISTROPHE.

Plunderer of armies, lift thine eyes
(A while forbear, ye tort'ring fiends),
Seest thou whose step, unwilling, hither bends?
No fallen angel, hurl'd from upper skies;
'Tis thy trusty quondam mate,
Doom'd to share thy fiery fate,
She, tardy, hell-ward plies.

EPODE.

And are they of no more avail,
Ten thousand glitt'ring pounds a year?
In other worlds can Mammon fail,
Omnipotent as he is here?
Oh, bitter mock'ry of the pompous bier,
While down the wretched vital part is driv'n!
The cave-lodg'd beggar, with a conscience clear,
Expires in rags, unknown, and goes to Heav'n.

---

a good fire at New Cumnock had so far recovered my frozen sinews, I sat down and wrote the enclosed Ode.—BURNS *to Dr. Moore, March* 23, 1789.

EPISTLE TO R. GRAHAM, ESQ.[1]

WHEN Nature her great master-piece design'd,
And fram'd her last, best work, the human mind,
Her eye intent on all the mazy plan,
She form'd of various parts the various man.
Then first she calls the useful many forth;
Plain plodding industry, and sober worth:
Thence peasants, farmers, native sons of earth,
And merchandise' whole genus take their birth:
Each prudent cit a warm existence finds,
And all mechanics' many-apron'd kinds.
Some other rarer sorts are wanted yet,
The lead and buoy are needful to the net:
The caput mortuum of gross desires
Makes a material for mere knights and squires;
The martial phosphorus is taught to flow,
She kneads the lumpish philosophic dough,
Then marks th' unyielding mass with grave designs,
Law, physic, politics, and deep divines:
Last, she sublimes th' Aurora of the poles,
The flashing elements of female souls.
The order'd system fair before her stood,
Nature, well-pleas'd, pronounc'd it very good;
But ere she gave creating labour o'er,
Half-jest, she try'd one curious labour more.
Some spumy, fiery, *ignis fatuus* matter;
Such as the slightest breath of air might scatter;
With arch alacrity and conscious glee
(Nature may have her whim as well as we,

---

[1] Robert Graham, of Fintry, Esq., one of the Commissioners of Excise.

Her Hogarth-art perhaps she meant to show it)
She forms the thing, and christens it—a Poet,
Creature, tho' oft the prey of care and sorrow,
When blest to-day, unmindful of to-morrow.
A being form'd t' amuse his graver friends,
Admir'd and prais'd—and there the homage ends:
A mortal quite unfit for Fortune's strife,
Yet oft the sport of all the ills of life;
Prone to enjoy each pleasure riches give,
Yet haply wanting wherewithal to live:
Longing to wipe each tear, to heal each groan,
Yet frequent all unheeded in his own.
But honest Nature is not quite a Turk,
She laugh'd at first, then felt for her poor work.
Pitying the propless climber of mankind,
She cast about a standard tree to find;
And, to support his helpless woodbine-state,
Attach'd him to the generous truly great,
A title, and the only one I claim,
To lay strong hold for help on bount'ous Graham.
Pity the tuneful muses' hapless train,
Weak, timid landsmen on life's stormy main!
Their hearts no selfish stern absorbent stuff,
That never gives—tho' humbly takes enough;
The little fate allows, they share as soon,
Jnlike sage, proverb'd, wisdom's hard-wrung boon.
'he world were blest did bliss on them depend,
.h, that "the friendly e'er should want a friend!"
et prudence number o'er each sturdy son,
'ho life and wisdom at one race begun,
'ho feel by reason, and who give by rule,
(Instinct's a brute, and sentiment a fool!)
Who make poor "will do" wait upon "I should"—
We own they're prudent, but who feels they're good?
Ye wise ones, hence! ye hurt the social eye!
God's image rudely etch'd on base alloy!
But come ye, who the godlike pleasure know,
Heaven's attribute distinguish'd—to bestow!
Whose arms of love would grasp the human race:
Come thou who giv'st with all a courtier's grace;
Friend of my life, true patron of my rhymes!
Prop of my dearest hopes for future times.
Why shrinks my soul half blushing, half afraid,
Backward, abash'd to ask thy friendly aid?
I know my need, I know thy giving hand,
I crave thy friendship at thy kind command;
But there are such who court the tuneful Nine—
Heavens! should the branded character be mine!
Whose verse in manhood's pride sublimely flows,
Yet vilest reptiles in their begging prose.
Mark, how their lofty independent spirit
Soars on the spurning wing of injur'd merit!
Seek not the proofs in private life to find;
Pity the best of words should be but wind!
So, to heaven's gates the lark's shrill song ascends,
But grovelling on the earth the carol ends.
In all the clam'rous cry of starving want,
They dun benevolence with shameless front;

Oblige them, patronise their tinsel lays,
They persecute you all your future days!
Ere my poor soul such deep damnation stain,
My horny fist assume the plough again;
The piebald jacket let me patch once more;
On eighteen-pence a week I've liv'd before.
Tho', thanks to Heaven, I dare e'en that last shift!
I trust, meantime, my boon is in thy gift;
That, plac'd by thee upon the wish'd-for height,
Where, man and nature fairer in her sight,
My muse may imp her wing for some sublimer flight.

TO ROBERT GRAHAM, OF FINTRY, ESQ.

LATE crippl'd of an arm, and now a leg,
About to beg a pass for leave to beg;
Dull, listless, teas'd, dejected, and deprest
(Nature is adverse to a cripple's rest):
Will generous Graham list to his Poet's wail?
(It soothes poor Misery, heark'ning to her tale),
And hear him curse the light he first survey'd,
And doubly curse the luckless rhyming trade?
Thou, Nature, partial Nature, I arraign;
Of thy caprice maternal I complain.
The lion and the bull thy care have found,
One shakes the forests, and one spurns the ground:
Thou giv'st the ass his hide, the snail his shell,
Th' envenom'd wasp, victorious, guards his cell.—
Thy minions, kings defend, controu', devour,
In all th' omnipotence of rule and power.
Foxes and statesmen, subtile wiles ensure;
The cit and polecat stink, and are secure.
Toads with their poison, doctors with their drug,
The priest and hedgehog in their robes are snug.
Ev'n silly woman has her warlike arts,
Her tongue and eyes, her dreaded spear and darts.
But oh! thou bitter step-mother and hard,
To thy poor, fenceless, naked child—the Bard!
A thing unteachable in world's skill,
And half an idiot too, more helpless still.
No heels to bear him from the op'ning dun;
No claws to dig, his hated sight to shun;
No horns, but those by luckless Hymen worn,
And those, alas! not Amalthea's horn:
No nerves olfact'ry, Mammon's trusty cur,
Clad in rich Dulness' comfortable fur;
In naked feeling, and in aching pride,
He bears th' unbroken blast from ev'ry side:
Vampyre booksellers drain him to the heart,
And scorpion critics cureless venom dart.
Critics—appall'd I venture on the name,
Those cut-throat bandits in the paths of fame:
Bloody dissectors, worse than ten Monroes;—
He hacks to teach, they mangle to expose.
His heart by causeless, wanton malice wrung,
By blockheads' daring into madness stung;
His well-won bays, than life itself more dear,
By miscreants torn, who ne'er one sprig must wear:

Foil'd, bleeding, tortur'd in th' unequal strife,
The hapless Poet flounders on thro' life.
Till fled each hope that once his bosom fir'd,
And fled each Muse that glorious once inspir'd,
Low sunk in squalid, unprotected age,
Dead, even resentment for his injur'd page,
He heeds or feels no more the ruthless critic's rage?
So, by some hedge, the generous steed deceas'd,
For half-starv'd snarling curs a dainty feast,
By toil and famine wore to skin and bone,
Lies, senseless of each tugging bitch's son.
O Dulness! portion of the truly blest!
Calm shelter'd haven of eternal rest!
Thy sons ne'er madden in the fierce extremes
Of Fortune's polar frost, or torrid beams.
If mantling high she fills the golden cup,
With sober selfish ease they sip it up;
Conscious the bounteous meed they well deserve,
They only wonder "some folks" do not starve.
The grave sage hern thus easy picks his frog,
And thinks the mallard a sad worthless dog.
When disappointment snaps the clue of hope,
And thro' disastrous night they darkling grope,
With deaf endurance sluggishly they bear,
And just conclude that "fools are Fortune's care."
So, heavy, passive to the tempest's shocks,
Strong on the sign-post stands the stupid ox.
Not so the idle Muses' mad-cap train,
Not such the workings of their moonstruck brain:
In equanimity they never dwell,
By turns in soaring heav'n, or vaulted hell.
I dread thee, Fate, relentless and severe,
With all a poet's, husband's, father's fear!
Already one stronghold of hope is lost,
Glencairn, the truly noble, lies in dust;
(Fled, like the sun eclips'd as noon appears,
And left us darkling in a world of tears:)
Oh! hear my ardent, grateful, selfish pray'r!
Fintry, my other stay, long bless and spare!
Thro' a long life his hopes and wishes crown,
And bright in cloudless skies his sun go down!
May bliss domestic smooth his private path;
Give energy to life; and soothe his latest breath,
With many a filial tear circling the bed of death!

LAMENT FOR JAMES, EARL OF GLENCAIRN.[1]

The wind blew hollow frae the hills,
By fits the sun's departing beam

---

[1] "Had the wing of my fancy been equal to the ardour of my heart, the enclosed had been much more worthy your perusal: as it is, I beg leave to lay it at your ladyship's feet. As all the world knows my obligations to the late Earl of Glencairn, I would wish to show as openly that my heart glows, and shall ever glow, with the most grateful sense and remembrance of his lordship's goodness. The sables I did myself the honour to wear to his lordship's memory were not the 'mockery of woe.' Nor shall my gratitude perish with me:—If, among my children, I shall have a son that has a heart, he shall hand it down to his child as a

Look'd on the fading yellow woods
  That wav'd o'er Lugar's winding stream:
Beneath a craigy steep, a Bard,
  Laden with years and meikle pain,
In loud lament bewail'd his lord,
  Whom death had all untimely ta'en.

He lean'd him to an ancient aik,[1]
  Whose trunk was mould'ring down with years;
His locks were bleached white with time,
  His hoary cheek was wet wi' tears;
And as he touch'd his trembling harp,
  And as he tun'd his doleful sang,
The winds, lamenting thro' their caves,
  To echo bore the notes alang.

"Ye scatter'd birds that faintly sing,
  The reliques of the vernal quire!
Ye woods that shed on a' the winds
  The honours of the aged year!
A few short months, and glad and gay,
  Again ye'll charm the ear and e'e;
But nocht[2] in all revolving time
  Can gladness bring again to me.

"I am a bending aged tree,
  That long has stood the wind and rain;
But now has come a cruel blast,
  And my last hold of earth is gane:
Nae leaf o' mine shall greet the spring,
  Nae simmer sun exalt my bloom;
But I maun lie before the storm,
  And ithers[3] plant them in my room.

"I've seen sae mony changefu' years,
  On earth I am a stranger grown;
I wander in the ways of men,
  Alike unknowing and unknown;

family honour and a family debt, that my dearest existence I owe to the noble house of Glencairn! I was about to say, my lady, that if you think the poem may venture to see the light, I would, in some way or other, give it to the world."—Lord Glencairn died January 30, 1791, and Burns sent the "Lament" to the Earl's sister, Lady Elizabeth Cunningham, with a letter, of which the above passage is an extract.

[1] Oak. [2] Nought. [3] Others.

Unheard, unpitied, unreliev'd,
  I bear alane my lade o' care,
For silent, low, on beds of dust,
  Lie a' that would my sorrows share

"And last (the sum of a' my griefs!
  My noble master lies in clay;
The flow'r amang our barons bold,
  His country's pride, his country's stay:
In weary being now I pine,
  For a' the life of life is dead,
And hope has left my aged ken,
  On forward wing for ever fled.

"Awake thy last sad voice, my harp!
  The voice of woe and wild despair!
Awake, resound thy latest lay,
  Then sleep in silence evermair!
And thou, my last, best, only friend,
  That fillest an untimely tomb,
Accept this tribute from the Bard
  Thou brought from fortune's mirkest[1] gloom.

"In Poverty's low barren vale
  Thick mists, obscure, involv'd me round;
Though oft I turn'd the wistful eye,
  No ray of fame was to be found:
Thou found'st me, like the morning sun
  That melts the fogs in limpid air,
The friendless Bard, and rustic song,
  Became alike thy fostering care.

"Oh! why has worth so short a date?
  While villains ripen grey with time
Must thou, the noble, gen'rous, great,
  Fall in bold manhood's hardy prime?
Why did I live to see that day—
  A day to me so full of woe?
O! had I met the mortal shaft
  Which laid my benefactor low!

"The bridegroom may forget the bride
  Was made his wedded wife yestreen;
The monarch may forget the crown
  That on his head an hour has been;
The mother may forget the child
  That smiles sae sweetly on her knee;
But I'll remember thee, Glencairn,
  And a' that thou hast done for me!"

[1] Darkest.

LINES, SENT TO SIR JOHN WHITEFORD, OF WHITEFORD, BART.,[1] WITH THE FOREGOING POEM.

THOU, who thy honour as thy God rever'st,
Who, save thy mind's reproach, nought earthly fear'st,
To thee this votive off'ring I impart,
The tearful tribute of a broken heart.
The Friend thou valued'st, I the Patron lov'd ;
His worth, his honour, all the world approv'd.
We'll mourn till we too go as he has gone,
And tread the dreary path to that dark world unknown.

TAM O' SHANTER.[2]

A TALE.

Brownyis and of Bogilis full is this Buke.—*Gawin Douglas.*

WHEN chapman billies leave the street,
And drouthy neebors, neebors meet,
As market-days are wearing late,
An' folk begin to tak the gate ;
While we sit bousing at the nappy,[1]
An' getting fou and unco happy,
We thinkna on the lang Scots miles,
The mosses, waters, slaps, and stiles,
That lie between us and our hame,
Whare sits our sulky sullen dame,
Gath'ring her brows like gath'ring storm,
Nursing her wrath to keep it warm.
This truth fand honest Tam O' Shanter,
As he frae Ayr ae night did canter
(Auld Ayr, wham ne'er a town surpasses,
For honest men and bonnie lasses).
O Tam ! hadst thou but been sae wise,
As ta'en thy ain wife Kate's advice !
She tauld thee weel thou wast a skellum,[2]
A blethering, blustering, drunken blellum ;[3]
That frae November till October,
Ae market-day thou was nae sober ;
That ilka melder,[4] wi' the miller,
Thou sat as lang as thou had siller ;
That ev'ry naig was ca'd a shoe on,
The smith and thee gat roaring fou on ;
That at the Lord's house, ev'n on Sunday,
Thou drank wi' Kirkton[5] Jean till Monday.
She prophesy'd that, late or soon,
Thou would be found deep drown'd in Doon ;
Or catch'd wi' warlocks[6] i' the mirk,[7]
By Alloway's auld haunted kirk.
Ah, gentle dames ! it gars me greet,[8]
To think how mony counsels sweet,
How mony lengthen'd, sage advices,
The husband frae the wife despises !

---

[1] An early friend of Burns', who gratefully acknowledged his interest in his fate as a man, and his fame as a poet.

[2] This poem was written to illustrate a drawing of Alloway Kirk, by Captain Grose, in whose "Antiquities of Scotland" it was published. The poet versified the chief circumstances of the historical story. Gilbert Burns specifies those of "a man riding home very late from Ayr in a stormy night, his seeing a light in Alloway Kirk, his having the curiosity to look in, his seeing a dance of witches with the Devil playing on the bagpipe to them, the scanty covering of one of the witches, which made him so far forget himself as to cry—'Weel loupen, short sark !' with the melancholy catastrophe of the piece." The poet has given a fuller and racier description of the original scene in a letter to Grose.

[1] Ale. [2] Worthless fellow.

[3] Idle talker.

[4] Every time that corn was sent to be ground.

[5] Kirkton is the distinctive name of a village in which the parish kirk stands.

[6] Wizards. [7] Dark.

[8] Makes me weep.

But to our tale: Ae market night,
Tam had got planted unco right;
Fast by an ingle, bleezing finely,
Wi' reaming swats,[1] that drank divinely;
And at his elbow, Souter Johnny,
His ancient, trusty, drouthy crony;
Tam lo'ed him like a vera brither;
They had been fou for weeks thegither.
The night drave on wi' sangs and clatter;
And ay the ale was growing better:
The landlady and Tam grew gracious,
Wi' favours, secret, sweet, and precious:
The souter[2] tauld his queerest stories;
The landlord's laugh was ready chorus:
The storm without might rair and rustle,
Tam did na mind the storm a whistle.
Care, mad to see a man sae happy,
E'en drowned himself amang the nappy!
As bees flee hame wi' lades o' treasure,
The minutes wing'd their way wi' pleasure:
Kings may be blest, but Tam was glorious,
O'er a' the ills o' life victorious!
But pleasures are like poppies spread,
You seize the flow'r, its bloom is shed;
Or like the snow falls in the river,
A moment white—then melts for ever;
Or like the borealis race,
That flit ere you can point their place;
Or like the rainbow's lovely form
Evanishing amid the storm.
Nae man can tether time or tide;—
The hour approaches Tam maun ride;
That hour, o' night's black arch the key-stane,
That dreary hour he mounts his beast in;
And sic a night he taks the road in,
As ne'er poor sinner was abroad in.
The wind blew as 'twad blawn its last;
The rattling show'rs rose on the blast;
The speedy gleams the darkness swallow'd;
Loud, deep, and lang, the thunder bellow'd:
That night, a child might understand,
The Deil had business on his hand.
Weel mounted on his grey mare, Meg,
A better never lifted leg,

[1] Frothing ale. [2] Shoemaker.

Tam skelpit[1] on thro' dub and mire,
Despising wind, and rain, and fire;
Whiles holding fast his gude blue bonnet;
Whiles crooning o'er some auld Scots sonnet;
Whiles glow'ring round wi' prudent cares,
Lest bogles catch him unawares;
Kirk Alloway was drawing nigh,
Whare ghaists and houlets nightly cry.
By this time he was cross the ford,
Whare in the snaw the chapman smoor'd;[2]
And past the birks[3] and meikle[4] stane,
Whare drunken Charlie brak's neck-bane;
And thro' the whins, and by the cairn,
Whare hunters fand the murder'd bairn;
And near the thorn, aboon the well,
Whare Mungo's mither hang'd hersel.
Before him Doon pours all his floods;
The doubling storm roars thro' the woods;
The lightnings flash from pole to pole;
Near and more near the thunders roll:
When, glimmering thro' the groaning trees,
Kirk Alloway seem'd in a bleeze;
Thro' ilka bore[5] the beams were glancing;
And loud resounded mirth and dancing.
Inspiring bold John Barleycorn!
What dangers thou canst make us scorn!
Wi' tippenny, we fear nae evil;
Wi' usquebae, we'll face the Devil!
The swats sae ream'd in Tammie's noddle,
Fair play, he car'd na deils a boddle.
But Maggie stood right sair astonish'd,
Till, by the heel and hand admonish'd,
She ventur'd forward on the light;
And, wow! Tam saw an unco sight!
Warlocks and witches in a dance;
Nae cotillion brent new frae France,
But hornpipes, jigs, strathspeys, and reels,
Put life and mettle in their heels.

[1] Went at a smart pace. [2] Smothered. [3] Birches. [4] Big. [5] Hole in the wall.

At winnock-bunker[1] in the east,
There sat auld Nick, in shape o' beast;
A towzie[2] tyke, black, grim, and large,
To gie them music was his charge:
He screw'd the pipes and gart[3] them skirl,[4]
Till roof and rafters a' did dirl.—
Coffins stood round, like open presses,
That shaw'd the dead in their last dresses;
And by some devilish cantrip[5] slight
Each in its cauld hand held a light,—
By which heroic Tam was able
To note upon the haly table,
A murderer's banes in gibbet airns;[6]
Twa span-lang, wee, unchristen'd bairns;
A thief, new-cutted frae a rape,
Wi' his last gasp his gab did gape;
Five tomahawks, wi' blude red rusted;
Five scymitars, wi' murder crusted;
A garter, which a babe had strangled;
A knife, a father's throat had mangled,
Whom his ain son o' life bereft,
The grey hairs yet stack to the heft;
Wi' mair o' horrible and awfu',
Which ev'n to name wad be unlawfu'.
As Tammie glowr'd, amaz'd and curious,
The mirth and fun grew fast and furious:
The piper loud and louder blew;
The dancers quick and quicker flew;
They reel'd, they set, they cross'd, they cleekit,
Till ilka carlin swat and reekit,
And coost her duddies[7] to the wark,
And linket[8] at it in her sark!
Now Tam, O Tam! had thae been queans
A' plump and strapping in their teens;
Their sarks, instead o' creeshie[9] flannen,
Been snaw-white seventeen-hunder linnen![10]
Thir[11] breeks o' mine, my only pair,
That ance were plush, o' gude blue hair,

[1] Window-seat. [2] Shaggy.
[3] Forced. [4] Scream. [5] Magic.
[6] Irons. [7] Clothes.
[8] Tripped along. [9] Greasy.
[10] The manufacturing term for a fine linen, woven in a reed of 1700 divisions.
—*Cromek.* [11] These.

I wad hae gi'en them off my hurdies,[1]
For ae blink o' the bonnie burdies!
But wither'd beldams, auld and droll,
Rigwoodie hags, wad spean a foal,
Lowping and flinging on a crummock,[2]
I wonder didna turn thy stomach.
But Tam kend what was what fu' brawlie,
"There was ae winsome wench and walie,"
That night enlisted in the core,
(Lang after kend on Carrick shore;
For mony a beast to dead she shot,
And perish'd mony a bonnie boat,
And shook baith meikle corn and bear,[3]
And kept the country-side in fear,)
Her cutty[4] sark, o' Paisley harn,[5]
That, while a lassie, she had worn,
In longitude tho' sorely scanty,
It was her best, and she was vauntie.—
Ah! little kend thy reverend grannie,
That sark she coft[6] for her wee Nannie,
Wi' twa pund Scots, ('twas a' her riches,)
Wad ever grac'd a dance of witches!
But here my muse her wing maun cour;
Sic flights are far beyond her pow'r;
To sing how Nannie lap and flang
(A souple jade she was, and strang),
And how Tam stood, like ane bewitch'd,
And thought his very e'en enrich'd;
Even Satan glowr'd, and fidg'd fu' fain,
And hotch'd and blew wi' might and main:
Till first ae caper, syne[7] anither,
Tam tint[8] his reason a' thegither,
And roars out, "Weel done, Cutty-sark!"
And in an instant all was dark;
And scarcely had he Maggie rallied,
When out the hellish legion sallied.
As bees bizz out wi' angry fyke,[9]
When plundering herds assail their byke;[10]
As open pussie's mortal foes,
When, pop! she starts before their nose;
As eager runs the market-crowd,

[1] Loins. [2] Short staff.
[3] Barley. [4] Short.
[5] Very coarse linen. [6] Bought.
[7] Then. [8] Lost. [9] Bustle. [10] Hive.

When, "Catch the thief!" resounds aloud;
So Maggie runs, the witches follow,
Wi' monie an eldritch skreech and hollow.
Ah, Tam! ah, Tam! thou'll get thy fairin!
In hell they'll roast thee like a herrin!
In vain thy Kate awaits thy comin!
Kate soon will be a woefu' woman!
Now, do thy speedy utmost, Meg,
And win the key-stane[1] of the brig;
There at them thou thy tail may toss,
A running stream they dare na cross.
But ere the key-stane she could make,
The fient a tail she had to shake!
For Nannie, far before the rest,
Hard upon noble Maggie prest,
And flew at Tam wi' furious ettle;[2]
But little wist she Maggie's mettle—
Ae spring brought off her master hale,
But left behind her ain gray tail:
The carlin claught her by the rump,
And left poor Maggie scarce a stump.
Now, wha this tale o' truth shall read,
Ilk man and mother's son, tak heed;
Whene'er to drink you are inclin'd,
Or cutty-sarks run in your mind,
Think, ye may buy the joys o'er dear,
Remember Tam o' Shanter's mare.

STANZAS

INTENDED TO BE WRITTEN BELOW THE PICTURE OF A NOBLE EARL.[3]

(WRITTEN IN 1787.)

Whose is that noble, dauntless brow?
And whose that eye of fire?
And whose that generous princely mien,
Ev'n rooted foes admire?

Stranger, to justly show that brow,
And mark that eye of fire,
Would take *his* hand, whose vernal tints
His other works inspire.

Bright as a cloudless summer sun,
With stately port he moves;
His guardian seraph eyes with awe
The noble ward he loves.

Among th' illustrious Scottish sons
That chief thou mayst discern;
Mark Scotia's fond returning eye—
It dwells upon Glencairn.

ON THE LATE CAPTAIN GROSE'S PEREGRINATIONS THROUGH SCOTLAND, COLLECTING THE ANTIQUITIES OF THAT KINGDOM.

Hear, Land o' Cakes, and brither Scots,
Frae Maidenkirk to Johnny Groat's;—
If there's a hole in a' your coats,
I rede you tent it:[1]
A chield's amang you, taking notes,
And, faith, he'll prent it.

If in your bounds ye chance to light
Upon a fine, fat, fodgel[2] wight,
O' stature short, but genius bright,
That's he, mark weel—
And wow! he has an unco slight
O' cauk and keel.[3]

By some auld, houlet-haunted biggin,[4]
Or kirk deserted by its riggin,
It's ten to ane ye'll find him snug in
Some eldritch part,

---

[1] It is a well-known fact, that witches, or any evil spirits, have no power to follow a poor wight any farther than the middle of the next running stream. It may be proper likewise to mention to the benighted traveller, that when he falls in with bogles, whatever danger may be in his going forward, there is much more hazard in turning back.—R. B.

[2] Effort.

[3] The Earl of Glencairn, a kind patron of Burns. See the poet's "Lament," p. 89.

[1] I advise you to look to it.

[2] Plump.

[3] Chalk and red clay.

[4] Building.—Vide his "Antiquities of Scotland."—R. B.

Wi' deils, they say, Lord safe's! colleaguin
At some black art.—

Ilk ghaist that haunts auld ha' or chamer,
Ye gipsy-gang that deal in glamor,
And you deep read in hell's black grammar,
Warlocks and witches;
Ye'll quake at his conjuring hammer,
Ye midnight bitches.

It's tauld he was a sodger bred,
And ane wad rather fa'n than fled;
But now he's quat[1] the spurtle-blade,
And dog-skin wallet,
And ta'en the—Antiquarian trade,
I think they call it.

He has a fouth[2] o' auld nick-nackets;
Rusty airn caps and jinglin jackets,[3]
Wad haud the Lothians three in tackets,[4]
A towmont[5] gude,
And parritch-pats, and auld saut-backets,
Before the Flood.

Of Eve's first fire he has a cinder;
Auld Tubalcain's fire-shool and fender;
That which distinguished the gender
O' Balaam's ass;
A broom-stick o' the witch of Endor,
Weel shod wi' brass.

Forbye, he'll shape you aff, fu' gleg,
The cut of Adam's philibeg;
The knife that nicket Abel's craig
He'll prove you fully,
It was a faulding jocteleg,[6]
Or lang-kail gullie.[7]—

But wad ye see him in his glee—
For meikle glee and fun has he,—
Then set him down, and twa or three
Gude fellows wi' him;
And port, O port! shine thou a wee,
And then ye'll see him!

[1] Has quitted. [2] Plenty.
[3] Vide his "Treatise on Ancient Armour and Weapons."—R. B.
[4] Nails. [5] A twelvemonth.
[6] Clasp-knife. [7] Large knife.

Now, by the Pow'rs o' verse and prose!
Thou art a dainty chiel, O Grose!—
Whae'er o' thee shall ill suppose,
They sair misca' thee;
I'd take the rascal by the nose,
Wad say, Shame fa' thee!

ON SEEING A WOUNDED HARE LIMP BY ME, WHICH A FELLOW HAD JUST SHOT AT.[1]

April, 1789.

INHUMAN man! curse on thy barb'rous art,
And blasted be thy murder-aiming eye;
May never pity soothe thee with a sigh,
Nor ever pleasure glad thy cruel heart!

Go, live, poor wanderer of the wood and field,
The bitter little that of life remains;
No more the thickening brakes and verdant plains
To thee shall home, or food, or pastime yield.

Seek, mangled wretch, some place of wonted rest,
No more of rest, but now thy dying bed!
The sheltering rushes whistling o'er thy head,
The cold earth with thy bloody bosom prest.

Oft as by winding nith, I, musing, wait
The sober eve, or hail the cheerful dawn,

[1] I have just put the last hand to a little poem, which I think will be something to your taste. One morning lately as I was out pretty early in the fields sowing some grass seeds, I heard the burst of a shot from a neighbouring plantation, and presently a poor little wounded hare came crippling by me. —R. B.

I'll miss thee sporting o'er the dewy lawn,
And curse the ruffian's aim, and mourn thy hapless fate.

ADDRESS TO THE SHADE OF THOMSON, ON CROWNING HIS BUST AT EDNAM, ROXBURGHSHIRE, WITH BAYS.

While virgin Spring, by Eden's flood,
Unfolds her tender mantle green,
Or pranks the sod in frolic mood,
Or tunes Æolian strains between:

While Summer, with a matron grace,
Retreats to Dryburgh's cooling shade,
Yet oft, delighted, stops to trace
The progress of the spiky blade:

While Autumn, benefactor kind,
By Tweed erects his aged head,
And sees, with self-approving mind,
Each creature on his bounty fed:

While maniac Winter rages o'er
The hills whence classic Yarrow flows,
Rousing the turbid torrent's roar,
Or sweeping, wild, a waste of snows:—

So long, sweet Poet of the year,
Shall bloom that wreath thou well hast won;
While Scotia, with exulting tear,
Proclaims that Thomson was her son.

TO MISS CRUIKSHANK, A VERY YOUNG LADY; WRITTEN ON THE BLANK LEAF OF A BOOK PRESENTED TO HER BY THE AUTHOR.

Beauteous rose-bud, young and gay,
Blooming in thy early May,[1]
Never may'st thou, lovely Flow'r,
Chilly shrink in sleety show'r!
Never Boreas' hoary path,
Never Eurus' pois'nous breath,
Never baleful stellar lights,
Taint thee with untimely blights!
Never, never reptile thief
Riot on thy virgin leaf!
Nor even Sol too fiercely view
Thy bosom blushing still with dew!
May'st thou long, sweet crimson gem,
Richly deck thy native stem;
Till some ev'ning, sober, calm,
Dropping dews, and breathing balm,
While all around the woodland rings,
And ev'ry bird thy requiem sings,
Thou, amid the dirgeful sound,
Shed thy dying honours round,
And resign to parent earth
The loveliest form she e'er gave birth.

[1] The "dear little Jeanie" of one of his letters; her father was a Master in the High School at Edinburgh.

ON READING, IN A NEWSPAPER, THE DEATH OF JOHN M'LEOD, ESQ., BROTHER TO A YOUNG LADY, A PARTICULAR FRIEND OF THE AUTHOR.

Sad thy tale, thou idle page,
And rueful thy alarms:
Death tears the brother of her love
From Isabella's arms.

Sweetly deckt with pearly dew,
The morning rose may blow;
But cold successive noontide blasts
May lay its beauties low.

Fair on Isabella's morn
The sun propitious smil'd;
But, long ere noon, succeeding clouds
Succeeding hopes beguil'd.

Fate oft tears the bosom chords,
That Nature finest strung;
So Isabella's heart was form'd,
And so that heart was wrung.

Dread Omnipotence, alone,
Can heal the wound He gave;

Can point the brimful grief-worn eyes
  To scenes beyond the grave.
Virtue's blossoms there shall blow,
  And fear no withering blast;
There Isabella's spotless worth
  Shall happy be at last.

THE HUMBLE PETITION OF BRUAR WATER[1] TO THE NOBLE DUKE OF ATHOLE.

My Lord, I know your noble ear
  Woe ne'er assails in vain;
Embolden'd thus, I beg you'll hear
  Your humble slave complain,
How saucy Phœbus' scorching beams,
  In flaming summer-pride,
Dry-withering waste my foamy streams
  And drink my crystal tide.

The lightly-jumping glowrin trouts,
  That thro' my waters play,
If, in their random, wanton spouts,
  They near the margin stray;
If, hapless chance! they linger lang,
  I'm scorching up so shallow,
They're left the whitening stanes amang,
  In gasping death to wallow.

Last day I grat[2] wi' spite and teen,
  As Poet Burns came by,
That to a Bard I should be seen
  Wi' half my channel dry:
A panegyric rhyme, I ween,
  Even as I was he shor'd[3] me;
But had I in my glory been,
  He, kneeling, wad ador'd me.

Here, foaming down the shelvy rocks,
  In twisting strength I rin;
There, high my boiling torrent smokes,
  Wild-roarin o'er a linn:
Enjoying large each spring and well
  As Nature gave them me,
I am, altho' I say't mysel,
  Worth gaun[4] a mile to see.

Would then my noble master please
  To grant my highest wishes,
He'll shade my banks wi' tow'ring trees,
  And bonnie spreading bushes.
Delighted doubly then, my Lord,
  You'll wander on my banks,
And listen mony a grateful bird
  Return you tuneful thanks.

The sober laverock, warbling wild,
  Shall to the skies aspire;
The gowdspink, Music's gayest child,
  Shall sweetly join the choir:
The blackbird strong, the lintwhite clear,
  The mavis mild and mellow;
The robin pensive Autumn cheer,
  In all her locks of yellow:

This, too, a covert shall ensure,
  To shield them from the storm;
And coward maukin[1] sleep secure,
  Low in her grassy form:
Here shall the shepherd make his seat,
  To weave his crown of flow'rs;
Or find a sheltering safe retreat,
  From prone-descending show'rs.

And here, by sweet endearing stealth,
  Shall meet the loving pair,
Despising worlds with all their wealth
  As empty, idle care:
The flow'rs shall vie in all their charms
  The hour of heav'n to grace,
And birks extend their fragrant arms,
  To screen the dear embrace.

Here haply too, at vernal dawn,
  Some musing bard may stray,
And eye the smoking, dewy lawn,
  And misty mountain, grey;
Or, by the reaper's nightly beam,
  Mild-chequering thro' the trees,
Rave to my darkly dashing stream,
  Hoarse-swelling on the breeze.

Let lofty firs, and ashes cool,
  My lowly banks o'erspread,
And view, deep-bending in the pool,
  Their shadows' wat'ry bed!
Let fragrant birks in woodbines drest
  My craggy cliffs adorn;
And, for the little songster's nest,
  The close embow'ring thorn.

---

[1] Bruar Falls, in Athole, are exceedingly picturesque and beautiful; but their effect is much impaired by the want of trees and shrubs.—R. B.

[2] Wept. [3] Offered. [4] Going.

[1] Hare.

So may Old Scotia's darling hope,
Your little angel band,
Spring, like their fathers, up to prop
Their honour'd native land!
So may thro' Albion's farthest ken,
To social-flowing glasses,
The grace be—"Athole's honest men,
And Athole's bonny lasses!"

LAMENT ON FERGUSSON.[1]

(WRITTEN IN 1792.—INSCRIBED BY THE POET ON A COPY OF THE PERIODICAL CALLED "THE WORLD.")

ILL-FATED genius! Heav'n-taught Fergusson!
What heart that feels, and will not yield a tear,
To think life's sun did set, ere well begun
To shed its influence on thy bright career.

Oh, why should truest worth and genius pine
Beneath the iron grasp of Want and Woe,
While titled knaves and idiot greatness shine
In all the splendour Fortune can bestow!

[1] This was Robert Fergusson, the lyric poet, who was born at Edinburgh about 1750, and died in 1774. He was buried in Canongate churchyard, Edinburgh, where his friend Burns erected a monument to his memory. His poems, written in the Scottish dialect, and originally published in Ruddiman's "Weekly Magazine," possess considerable merit. His talents and conversational powers rendered his company extremely attractive; and the excesses into which he was led impaired his constitution, and eventually rendered him the inmate of a lunatic asylum, where he died at the early age of twenty-four. That Burns held him in great esteem is evident from what he says in the preface to the first edition of his works:—"To the genius of a Ramsay or the glorious dawnings of the poor unfortunate Fergusson, he, with equal unaffected sincerity, declares that, even in his highest pulse of vanity, he has not the most distant pretension."

WHEN GUILFORD GOOD OUR PILOT STOOD.

A FRAGMENT.

TUNE—"GILLICRANKIE."

WHEN Guilford good our Pilot stood,
An' did our hellim thraw, man,
Ae night, at tea, began a plea,
Within America, man:
Then up they gat the maskin-pat,[1]
And in the sea did jaw,[2] man;
An' did nae less, in full Congress,
Than quite refuse our law, man.

Then thro' the lakes Montgomery takes,
I wat he was na slaw, man;
Down Lowrie's burn he took a turn,
And Carleton did ca', man:
But yet, what-reck, he, at Quebec,
Montgomery like did fa', man,
Wi' sword in hand, before his band,
Amang his en'mies a', man.

Poor Tammy Gage, within a cage
Was kept at Boston ha', man;
Till Willie Howe took o'er the knowe
For Philadelphia, man:
Wi' sword an' gun he thought a sin
Guid Christian bluid to draw, man;
But at New York, wi' knife an' fork,
Sir-loin he hacked sma', man.

Burgoyne gaed up, like spur an' whip,
Till Fraser brave did fa', man;
Then lost his way, ae misty day,
In Saratoga shaw, man.

[1] Tea-pot.
[2] Jerk. The English Parliament having imposed an excise duty upon tea imported into North America, the East India Company sent several ships laden with that article to Boston, and the natives went on board by force of arms and emptied the cargo into the sea.

Cornwallis fought as lang's he dought,[1]
An' did the buckskins claw, man;
But Clinton's glaive frae rust to save,
He hung it to the wa', man.

Then Montague, an' Guilford too,
Began to fear a fa', man:
And Sackville doure, wha stood the stoure,
The German Chief to thraw, man:
For Paddy Burke, like ony Turk,
Nae mercy had at a', man;
An' Charlie Fox threw by the box,
An' lows'd his tinkler[2] jaw, man.

Then Rockingham took up the game;
Till death did on him ca', man:
When Shelburne meek held up his cheek,
Conform to Gospel law, man;
Saint Stephen's boys, wi' jarring noise,
They did his measures thraw, man;
For North an' Fox united stocks,
An' bore him to the wa', man.

Then Clubs an' Hearts were Charlie's cartes,
He swept the stakes awa', man,
Till the Diamond's Ace, of Indian race,
Led him a sair faux pas, man:
The Saxon lads, wi' loud placads,
On Chatham's boy did ca', man;
An' Scotland drew her pipe, an' blew,
"Up, Willie, waur them a', man!"

Behind the throne then Grenville's gone,
A secret word or twa, man;
While slee Dundas arous'd the class
Be-north the Roman wa', man:
An' Chatham's wraith, in heavenly graith
(Inspired Bardies saw, man),
Wi' kindling eyes cry'd, "Willie, rise!
Would I hae fear'd them a', man?"

But, word an' blow, North, Fox, and Co.,
Gowff'd[3] Willie like a ba', man,
Till Suthrons raise, an' coost their claise
Behind him in a raw, man;
An' Caledon threw by the drone,
An' did her whittle draw, man;
An' swoor fu' rude, thro' dirt an' bluid,
To make it guid in law, man.

* * * * *

[1] He was able. [2] Tinker. [3] Struck.

MY TOCHER'S THE JEWEL.

O MEIKLE thinks my luve o' my beauty,
And meikle thinks my luve o' my kin;
But little thinks my luve I ken brawlie
My Tocher's the jewel has charms for him.
It's a' for the apple he'll nourish the tree;
It's a' for the hiney he'll cherish the bee;
My laddie's sae meikle in luve wi' the siller,
He canna hae luve to spare for me.

Your proffer o' luve's an airl-penny,
My Tocher's the bargain you wad buy;
But an ye be crafty, I am cunnin',
Sae ye wi' anither your fortune maun try.
Ye're like to the timmer o' yon rotten wood,
Ye're like to the bark o' yon rotten tree,
Ye'll slip frae me like a knotless thread,
And ye'll crack your credit wi' mae nor me.

ADDRESS TO THE TOOTH-ACHE; WRITTEN WHEN THE AUTHOR WAS GRIEVOUSLY TORMENTED BY THAT DISORDER.

MY curse upon thy venom'd stang,
That shoots my tortur'd gums alang;
And thro' my lugs[1] gies monie a twang,
Wi' gnawing vengeance;
Tearing my nerves wi' bitter pang,
Like racking engines!

When fevers burn, or ague freezes,
Rheumatics gnaw, or cholic squeezes;
Our neighbour's sympathy may ease us,
Wi' pitying moan;
But thee—thou hell o' a' diseases,
Aye mocks our groan!

[1] Ears.

Adown my beard the slavers trickle !
I kick the wee stools o'er the mickle,
As round the fire the giglets[1] keckle
To see me loup ;
While, raving mad, I wish a heckle
Were in their doup.

O' a' the num'rous human dools,[2]
Ill har'sts, daft bargains, cutty-stools,
Or worthy friends rak'd i' the mools,[3]
Sad sight to see !
The tricks o' knaves, or fash[4] o' fools,
Thou bear'st the gree.[5]

Where'er that place be priests ca' hell,
Whence a' the tones o' mis'ry yell,
And ranked plagues their numbers tell,
In dreadfu' raw,[6]
Thou, Tooth-ache, surely bear'st the bell
Amang them a' !

O thou grim mischief-making chiel,
That gars the notes of discord squeel,
Till daft mankind aft dance a reel
In gore a shoe-thick ;—
Gie a' the faes o' Scotland's weal
A towmond's Tooth-ache !

ON THE BIRTH OF A POSTHUMOUS CHILD, BORN IN PECULIAR CIRCUMSTANCES OF FAMILY DISTRESS.[7]

SWEET flow'ret, pledge o' meikle love,
And ward o' mony a prayer,
What heart o' stane wad thou na move,
Sae helpless, sweet, and fair.

November hirples[1] o'er the lea,
Chill on thy lovely form ;
And gane, alas ! the shelt'ring tree
Should shield thee frae the storm.

May He, who gives the rain to pour,
And wings the blast to blaw,
Protect thee frae the driving show'r,
The bitter frost and snaw.

May He, the friend of woe and want,
Who heals life's various stounds,[2]
Protect and guard the mother plant,
And heal her cruel wounds.

But late she flourish'd, rooted fast,
Fair on the summer morn :
Now, feebly bends she in the blast,
Unshelter'd and forlorn.

Blest be thy bloom, thou lovely gem,
Unscath'd by ruffian hand !
And from thee many a parent stem
Arise to deck our land.

WRITTEN WITH A PENCIL, STANDING BY THE FALL OF FYERS, NEAR LOCH-NESS.

AMONG the heathy hills and ragged woods
The roaring Fyers pours his mossy floods,

[1] Young girls. [2] Griefs. [3] Clods. [4] Care. [5] The palm. [6] Row.

[7] "As cold waters to a thirsty soul, so is good news from a far country." Fate has long owed me a letter of good news from you, in return for the many tidings of sorrow which I have received. In this instance I most cordially obey the Apostle—"Rejoice with them that do rejoice"—for me to *sing* for joy is no new thing; but to *preach* for joy, as I have done in the commencement of this epistle, is a pitch of extravagant rapture to which I never rose before. I read your letter—I literally jumped for joy—how could such a mercurial creature as a poet lumpishly keep his seat on the receipt of the best news from his best friend? I seized my gilt-headed wangee rod, an instrument indispensably necessary, in my left hand, in the moment of inspiration and rapture ; and stride, stride—quick and quicker—out skipped I among the broomy banks of Nith, to muse over my joy by retail. To keep within the bounds of prose was impossible. Mrs Little's is a more elegant, but not a more sincere compliment to the sweet little fellow than I, *extempore* almost, poured out to him, in the following verses."—BURNS *to Mrs. Dunlop*, Nov. 1790. [1] Creeps. [2] Heart-pangs.

Till full he dashes on the rocky mounds,
Where, thro' a shapeless breach, his stream resounds.
As high in air the bursting torrents flow,
As deep recoiling surges foam below,
Prone down the rock the whitening sheet descends,
And viewless Echo's ear, astonish'd, rends.
Dim-seen, thro' rising mists, and ceaseless show'rs,
The hoary cavern, wide-surrounding, low'rs.
Still, thro' the gap the struggling river toils,
And still, below, the horrid cauldron boils—

* * * * *

SECOND EPISTLE TO DAVIE, A BROTHER POET.

AULD NEIBOR,

I'M three times, doubly, o'er your debtor,
For your auld-farrant,[1] frien'ly letter;
Tho' I maun say't, I doubt ye flatter,
Ye speak sae fair,
For my puir, silly, rhymin clatter
Some less maun sair.[2]

Hale be your heart, hale be your fiddle;
Lang may your elbuck[3] jink and diddle,
Tae cheer you thro' the weary widdle
O' war'ly cares,
Till bairns' bairns kindly cuddle
Your auld, gray hairs.

But Davie, lad, I'm red ye're glaikit;[4]
I'm tauld the Muse ye hae negleckit;
An' gif it's sae, ye sud be licket
Until ye fyke;
Sic hauns as you sud ne'er be faiket,[5]
Be hain't[6] wha like.

For me, I'm on Parnassus' brink,
Rivin' the words tae gar them clink;
Whyles daez't wi' love, whyles daez't wi' drink,
Wi' jads or masons;
An' whyles, but aye owre late, I think,
Braw sober lessons.

Of a' the thoughtless sons o' man,
Commen' me to the Bardie clan;
Except it be some idle plan
O' rhymin clink,
The devil-haet, that I sud ban,[1]
They ever think.

Nae thought, nae view, nae scheme o' livin',
Nae cares tae gie us joy or grievin';
But just the pouchie put the nieve in,
An' while ought's there,
Then hiltie, skiltie, we gae scrievin',
An' fash nae mair.

Leeze me on rhyme![2] it 's aye a treasure,
My chief, amaist my only pleasure,
At hame, a-fiel', at wark, or leisure,
The Muse, poor hizzie!
Tho' rough an' raploch[3] be her measure,
She's seldom lazy.

Haud to the Muse, my dainty Davie:
The warl' may play you monie a shavie;
But for the Muse, she'll never leave ye,
Tho' e'er sae puir,
Na, even tho' limpin' wi' the spavie
Frae door ta door.

THE INVENTORY;

IN ANSWER TO THE USUAL MANDATE SENT BY A SURVEYOR OF THE TAXES, REQUIRING A RETURN OF THE NUMBER OF HORSES, SERVANTS, CARRIAGES, ETC., KEPT.

SIR, as your mandate did request,
I send you here a faithfu' list,

---

[1] Sagacious. [2] Serve. [3] Elbow. [4] Inattentive. [5] Unknown. [6] Spared.

[1] Swear.
[2] A phrase of endearment.
[3] Coarse.

My horses, servants, carts, and graith,
To which I'm free to tak my aith.
Imprimis, then, for carriage cattle,
I ha'e four brutes o' gallant mettle,
As ever drew afore a pettle;[1]
My hand-afore,[2] a gude auld *has-been*,
An' wight an' wilfu' a' his days been;
My hand-ahin,[3] a weel gaun fillie,
That aft has borne me hame frae Killie,[4]
An' your auld borough mony a time,
In days when riding was nae crime—
But ance, whan in my wooing pride,
I, like a blockhead, boost to ride,
The wilfu' creature sae I pat to,
(Lord, pardon a' my sins, an' that too!)
I played my fillie sic a shavie,
She's a' bedevil'd wi' the spavie.
My fur-ahin[5] 's a gude, grey beast,
As e'er in tug or tow was trac'd,—
The fourth, a Highland Donald hastie,
A d—d red-wud, Kilburnie blastie;
Foreby a Cowte, o' Cowtes the wale,
As ever ran afore a tail;
If he be spar'd to be a beast,
He'll draw me fifteen pund at least.—
Wheel carriages I ha'e but few,
Three carts, an' twa are feckly new;
Ae auld wheelbarrow, mair for token,
Ae leg an' baith the trams are broken;
I made a poker o' the spindle,
An' my auld mither brunt the trindle.
For men, I've three mischievous boys,
Run-de'ils for rantin' an' for noise;
A gaudsman[6] ane, a thrasher t' other,
Wee Davoc hauds the nowte in fother.[7]
I rule them, as I ought, discreetly,
An' aften labour them completely.
An' ay on Sundays duly, nightly,
I on the questions targe them tightly;
Till faith, wee Davoc's turn'd sae gleg,
Tho' scarcely langer than your leg,

[1] Plough-staff.
[2] The fore-horse on the left-hand in the plough.—R. B.
[3] The hindmost on the left-hand in the plough.—R. B.
[4] Kilmarnock.—R. B.
[5] The hindmost horse on the right-hand in the plough.—R. B.
[6] Plough-driver.
[7] Black cattle in fodder.

He'll screed you aff Effectual Calling,
As fast as ony in the dwalling.—
I've nane in female servan' station,
(Lord keep me ay frae a' temptation!)
I ha'e nae wife; and that my bliss is,
An' ye ha'e laid nae tax on misses;
An' then if kirk folks dinna clutch me,
I ken the devils darena touch me.
Wi' weans I'm mair than weel contented,
Heav'n sent me ane mae than I wanted.
My sonsie, smirking, dear-bought Bess,
She stares the daddy in her face,
Enough of ought ye like but grace.
But her, my bonny sweet wee lady,
I've paid enough for her already,
An' gin ye tax her or her mither,
B' the L—d! ye'se get them a' thegither.
And now, remember, Mr. Aiken,
Nae kind of license out I'm takin';
Frae this time forth, I do declare,
I'se ne'er ride horse nor hizzie mair;
Thro' dirt and dub for life I'll paidle,
Ere I sae dear pay for a saddle;
My travel a' on foot I'll shank it,
I've sturdy bearers, Gude be thankit!—
The Kirk an' you may tak' you that,
It puts but little in your pat;[1]
Sae dinna put me in your buke,
Nor for my ten white shillings luke.
This list wi' my ain han' I wrote it,
Day an' date as under notit:
Then know all ye whom it concerns,
Subscripsi huic,

ROBERT BURNS.

Mossgiel, February 22nd, 1786.

THE WHISTLE.[2]

A BALLAD.

I SING of a Whistle, a Whistle of worth,
I sing of a Whistle, the pride of the North,

[1] Pot.
[2] "The highest gentry of the county," writes Mr. J. G. Lockhart, "whenever they had especial merriment in

Was brought to the court of our good Scottish king,
And long with this Whistle all Scotland shall ring.

Old Loda,[1] still rueing the arm of Fingal,
The god of the bottle sends down from his hall—
"This Whistle's your challenge, in Scotland get o'er,
And drink them to hell, Sir, or ne'er see me more!"

Old poets have sung, and old chronicles tell,
What champions ventur'd, what champions fell;
The son of great Loda was conqueror still,
And blew on the Whistle his requiem shrill.

Till Robert, the lord of the Cairn and the Scaur,
Unmatch'd at the bottle; unconquer'd in war,
He drank his poor god-ship as deep as the sea,
No tide of the Baltic e'er drunker than he.

Thus Robert, victorious, the trophy has gain'd,
Which now in his house has for ages remain'd;

---

view, called in the wit and eloquence of Burns to enliven their carousals. The famous song of 'The Whistle of Worth' commemorates a scene of this kind, more picturesque in some of its circumstances than every day occurred, yet strictly in character with the usual tenor of life among this jovial *squirearchy*. These gentlemen, of ancient descent, had met to determine, by a solemn drinking match, who should possess the Whistle, which a common ancestor of them all had earned ages before in a Bacchanalian contest of the same sort with a noble toper from Denmark; and the poet was summoned to watch over and celebrate the issue of the debate." The following is Burns' description of the prize and the struggle. He seems, however, to have fallen into some error as to the date:—"As the authentic prose history of the Whistle is curious, I shall here give it.—In the train of Anne of Denmark, when she came to Scotland with our James the Sixth, there came over also a Danish gentleman of gigantic stature and great prowess, and a matchless champion of Bacchus. He had a little ebony Whistle, which at the commencement of the orgies he laid on the table, and whoever was last able to blow it, everybody else being disabled by the potency of the bottle, was to carry off the Whistle as a trophy of victory. The Dane produced credentials of his victories, without a single defeat, at the courts of Copenhagen, Stockholm, Moscow, Warsaw, and several of the petty courts in Germany; and challenged the Scots Bacchanalians to the alternative of trying his prowess, or else of acknowledging their inferiority. —After many overthrows on the part of the Scots, the Dane was encountered by Sir Robert Lowrie of Maxwelton, ancestor of the present worthy Baronet of that name, who, after three days and three nights' hard contest, left the Scandinavian under the table,

'And blew on the Whistle his requiem shrill.'

"Sir Walter, son to Sir Robert, before mentioned, afterwards lost the Whistle to Walter Riddel of Glenriddel, who had married a sister of Sir Walter. On Friday, the 16th October, 1790, at Friars-Carse, the Whistle was once more contended for, as related in the ballad, by the present Sir Robert Lowrie of Maxwelton; Robert Riddel, Esq., of Glenriddel, lineal descendant and representative of Walter Riddel, who won the Whistle, and in whose family it had continued; and Alexander Ferguson, Esq., of Craigdarroch, likewise descended of the great Sir Robert, which last gentleman carried off the hard-won honours of the field."

[1] See Ossian's "Caric-thura."—R. B.

Till three noble chieftains, and all of his blood,
The jovial contest again have renew'd.

Three joyous good fellows, with hearts clear of flaw:
Craigdarroch, so famous for wit, worth, and law;
And trusty Glenriddel, so skill'd in old coins;
And gallant Sir Robert, deep-read in old wines.

Craigdarroch began with a tongue smooth as oil,
Desiring Glenriddel to yield up the spoil;
Or else he would muster the heads of the clan,
And once more, in claret, try which was the man.

"By the gods of the ancients!" Glenriddel replies,
"Before I surrender so glorious a prize,
I'll conjure the ghost of the great Rorie More,[1]
And bumper his horn with him twenty times o'er."

Sir Robert, a soldier, no speech would pretend,
But he ne'er turn'd his back on his foe—or his friend,
Said, toss down the Whistle, the prize of the field,
And, knee-deep in claret, he'd die ere he'd yield.

To the board of Glenriddel our heroes repair,
So noted for drowning of sorrow and care;
But for wine and for welcome not more known to fame,
Than the sense, wit, and taste of a sweet lovely dame.

A bard was selected to witness the fray,
And tell future ages the feats of the day;
A bard who detested all sadness and spleen,
And wish'd that Parnassus a vineyard had been.

The dinner being over, the claret they ply,
And ev'ry new cork is a new spring of joy,
In the bands of old friendship and kindred so set,
And the bands grew the tighter the more they were wet.

Gay Pleasure ran riot as bumpers ran o'er;
Bright Phœbus ne'er witness'd so joyous a core,
And vow'd that to leave them he was quite forlorn,
Till Cynthia hinted he'd see them next morn.

Six bottles a-piece had well wore out the night,
When gallant Sir Robert, to finish the fight,
Turn'd o'er in one bumper a bottle of red,
And swore 'twas the way that their ancestors did.

Then worthy Glenriddel, so cautious and sage,
No longer the warfare, ungodly, would wage;
A high-ruling elder to wallow in wine!
He left the foul business to folks less divine.

The gallant Sir Robert fought hard to the end;
But who can with Fate and quart bumpers contend?
Though Fate said, a hero should perish in light;
So uprose bright Phœbus—and down fell the knight.

Next uprose our bard, like a prophet in drink:—
"Craigdarroch, thou'lt soar when creation shall sink!
But if thou would flourish immortal in rhyme,
Come—one bottle more—and have at the sublime!

[1] See Johnson's "Tour to the Hebrides."—R. B.

"Thy line, that have struggled for
Freedom with Bruce,
Shall heroes and patriots ever produce:
So thine be the laurel, and mine be the
bay;
The field thou hast won, by yon bright
god of day!"

TO DR. BLACKLOCK.

Ellisland, 21st Oct. 1789.

Wow,[1] but your letter made me vaun-
tie!
And are ye hale, and weel, and cantie?
I kenn'd it still your wee bit jauntie
Wad bring ye to:
Lord send you aye as weel's I want ye,
And then ye'll do.

The ill-thief blaw the Heron[2] south!
And never drink be near his drouth!
He tald mysel by word o' mouth,
He'd tak my letter;
I lippen'd to the chiel in trouth,
And bade nae better.

But aiblins honest Master Heron
Had at the time some dainty fair one,
To ware his theologic care on,
And holy study;
And tir'd o' sauls to waste his lear[3] on,
E'en tried the body.

But what d'ye think, my trusty fier,[4]
I'm turn'd a gauger—Peace be here!
Parnassian queans, I fear, I fear
Ye'll now disdain me!
And then my fifty pounds a year
Will little gain me.

Ye glaikit, gleesome, dainty damies,
Wha, by Castalia's wimplin' streamies,
Lowp, sing, and lave your pretty
limbies,
Ye ken, ye ken,
That strang necessity supreme is
'Mang sons o' men.

I hae a wife and twa wee laddies,
They maun hae brose and brats o'
duddies;[1]
Ye ken yoursels my heart right proud
is—
I need na vaunt
But I'll sned[2] besoms—thraw saugh
woodies,[3]
Before they want.

Lord, help me thro' this warld o' care!
I'm weary sick o't late and air!
Not but I hae a richer share
Than monie ithers;
But why should ae man better fare,
And a' men brithers?

Come, firm Resolve, take thou the van—
Thou stalk o' carl-hemp[4] in man!
And let us mind, faint heart ne'er wan
A lady fair;
Wha does the utmost that he can,
Will whyles the mair.

But to conclude my silly rhyme
(I'm scant o' verse, and scant o' time),
To make a happy fire-side clime
To weans and wife,
That's the true pathos and sublime
Of human life.

My compliments to sister Beckie;
And eke the same to honest Lucky,
I wat she is a dainty chuckie,
As e'er tread clay!
And gratefully, my guid auld cockie,
I'm yours for ay,

ROBERT BURNS.

PROLOGUE, SPOKEN AT THE THEATRE, ELLISLAND.[5]

No song nor dance I bring from yon
great city
That queens it o'er our taste—the more's
the pity;

---

[1] An exclamation of pleasure.
[2] Robert Heron, who wrote a History of Scotland, and a Life of Burns.
[3] Learning. [4] Brother.

[1] Rags of clothes. [2] Lop.
[3] Twist willow ropes.
[4] The male, or stronger stalk of hemp.
[5] We have gotten a set of very decent players here just now. I have seen them an evening or two. David

Tho', by-the-by, abroad why will you roam?
Good sense and taste are natives here at home:
But not for panegyric I appear,
I come to wish you all a good new-year!
Old Father Time deputes me here before ye,
Not for to preach, but tell his simple story:
The sage grave ancient cough'd, and bade me say,
"You're one year older this important day."
If wiser too—he hinted some suggestion,
But 'twould be rude, you know, to ask the question;
And with a would-be roguish leer and wink,
He bade me on you press this one word —"think!"
Ye sprightly youths, quite flush'd with hope and spirit,
Who think to storm the world by dint of merit,
To you the dotard has a deal to say,
In his sly, dry, sententious, proverb way;
He bids you mind, amid your thoughtless rattle,
That the first blow is ever half the battle;
That tho' some by the skirt may try to snatch him,
Yet by the forelock is the hold to catch him;
That whether doing, suffering, or forbearing,
You may do miracles by persevering.
Last, tho' not least in love, ye youthful fair,
Angelic forms, high Heaven's peculiar care!

Campbell, in Ayr, wrote to me by the manager of the company, a Mr. Southerland, who is a man of apparent worth. On New-year-day evening I gave him the following Prologue, which he spouted to his audience with applause.—R. B.

To you old Bald-pate smooths his wrinkled brow,
And humbly begs you'll mind the important *now!*
To crown your happiness he asks your leave,
And offers bliss to give and to receive.
For our sincere, tho' haply weak, endeavours,
With grateful pride we own your many favours;
And howsoe'er our tongues may ill reveal it,
Believe our glowing bosoms truly feel it.

ELEGY ON THE LATE MISS BURNET, OF MONBODDO.

Life ne'er exulted in so rich a prize
As Burnet, lovely from her native skies;
Nor envious death so triumph'd in a blow,
As that which laid th' accomplish'd Burnet low.

Thy form and mind, sweet maid, can I forget?
In richest ore the brightest jewel set!
In thee, high Heaven above was truest shown,
As by his noblest work the Godhead best is known.

In vain, ye flaunt in summer's pride, ye groves;
Thou crystal streamlet with thy flowery shore,
Ye woodland choir that chant your idle loves,
Ye cease to charm—Eliza is no more!

Ye heathy wastes, immix'd with reedy fens;
Ye mossy streams, with sedge and rushes stor'd;
Ye rugged cliffs o'erhanging dreary glens,
To you I fly, ye with my soul accord.

Princes, whose cumbrous pride was all their worth,
Shall venal lays their pompous exit hail?

And thou, sweet excellence! forsake our earth,
  And not a Muse in honest grief bewail?

We saw thee shine in youth and beauty's pride,
And virtue's light, that beams beyond the spheres;
But, like the sun eclips'd at morning tide,
  Thou left'st us darkling in a world of tears.

The parent's heart that nestled fond in thee,
  That heart how sunk, a prey to grief and care;
So deckt the woodbine sweet yon aged tree;
  So, from it ravish'd, leaves it bleak and bare.

LINES
TO A MEDICAL FRIEND,[1]

INVITING HIM TO ATTEND AN ANNUAL MASONIC MEETING.[2]

Friday first's the day appointed,
By our right worshipful anointed,
  To hold our grand procession;
To get a blade o' Johnny's morals,
And taste a swatch[3] o' Manson's[4] barrels,
  I' the way of our profession.

Our Master and the Brotherhood
  Wad a' be glad to see you;
For me, I would be mair than proud
  To share the mercies wi' you.
    If death, then, wi' skaith, then,
      Some mortal heart is hetchin,[5]
    Inform him, and storm him,
      That Saturday ye'll fecht[6] him.

Robert Burns.

[1] Mr. Mackenzie.
[2] The Saint James's Masonic Lodge at Mauchline. [3] Sample.
[4] The name of a landlord, at whose house the Masonic Lodge assembled.
[5] Threatening. [6] Fight.

LINES ON AN INTERVIEW WITH LORD DAER.[1]

This wot ye all whom it concerns,
I, Rhymer Robin, alias Burns,
    October twenty-third,
A ne'er to be forgotten day!
Sae far I sprackled[2] up the brae,
    I dinner'd wi' a Lord.

I've been at drucken writers' feasts,
Nay, been bitch-fou 'mang godly priests
    (Wi' rev'rence be it spoken);
I've even join'd the honour'd jorum,
When mighty Squireships of the quorum,
    Their hydra drouth did sloken.

But wi' a Lord—stand out my shin,
A Lord—a Peer—an Earl's son,
    Up higher yet, my bonnet!
And sic a Lord—lang Scotch ells twa,
Our Peerage he o'erlooks them a',
    As I look o'er my sonnet.

But, oh! for Hogarth's magic pow'r!
To show Sir Bardie's willyart glow'r,[3]
    And how he star'd and stammer'd,
When goavan,[4] as if led wi' branks,[5]
An' stumpan on his ploughman shanks,
    He in the parlour hammer'd.

I sidling shelter'd in a nook,
An' at his Lordship steal't a look,
    Like some portentous omen;
Except good sense and social glee,
An' (what surprised me) modesty,
    I marked nought uncommon.

I watch'd the symptoms o' the great,
The gentle pride, the lordly state,
    The arrogant assuming;
The fient a pride, nae pride had he,
Nor sauce, nor state that I could see,
    Mair than an honest ploughman.

Then from his lordship I shall learn,
Henceforth to meet with unconcern
    One rank as weel's another;

[1] Son of the Earl of Selkirk. Burns was introduced to him by Dugald Stewart.
[2] Clambered. [3] Frightened stare
[4] Walking with stupid wonder.
[5] A curb bridle.

Nae honest worthy man need care
To meet with noble, youthful Daer,
For he but meets a brother.

THE RIGHTS OF WOMAN.

PROLOGUE SPOKEN BY MISS FONTENELLE ON HER BENEFIT NIGHT.

WHILE Europe's eye is fix'd on mighty things,
The fate of Empires and the fall of Kings;
While quacks of State must each produce his plan,
And even children lisp The Rights of Man;
Amid the mighty fuss, just let me mention,
The Rights of Woman merit some attention.
First, in the Sexes' intermixed connexion,
One sacred Right of Woman is, Protection.—
The tender flower that lifts its head, elate,
Helpless, must fall before the blasts of Fate,
Sunk on the earth, defac'd its lovely form,
Unless your shelter ward th' impending storm.
Our second Right—but needless here is caution,
To keep that Right inviolate's the fashion,
Each man of sense has it so full before him,
He'd die before he'd wrong it—'tis Decorum.
There was, indeed, in far less polish'd days,
A time, when rough rude man had naughty ways;
Would swagger, swear, get drunk, kick up a riot,
Nay, even thus invade a Lady's quiet!—
Now, thank our stars! those Gothic times are fled;
Now, well-bred men—and you are all well-bred!
Most justly think (and we are much the gainers)
Such conduct, neither spirit, wit, nor manners.
For Right the third, our last, our best, our dearest,
That Right to fluttering female hearts the nearest,
Which ev'n the Rights of Kings in low prostration
Most humbly own—'tis dear, dear Admiration!
In that blest sphere alone we live and move;
There taste that life of life—immortal Love.—
Sighs, tears, smiles, glances, fits, flirtations, airs,
'Gainst such an host what flinty savage dares—
When awful Beauty joins with all her charms,
Who is so rash as rise in rebel arms?
Then truce with kings, and truce with constitutions,
With bloody armaments and revolutions!
Let Majesty your first attention summon,
Ah! Ça ira! THE MAJESTY OF WOMAN!

ADDRESS,

SPOKEN BY MISS FONTENELLE, ON HER BENEFIT-NIGHT, DECEMBER 4, 1795, AT THE THEATRE, DUMFRIES.

STILL anxious to secure your partial favour,
And not less anxious, sure, this night, than ever,
A Prologue, Epilogue, or some such matter,
'Twould vamp my bill, said I, if nothing better;
So sought a poet, roosted near the skies,
Told him I came to feast my curious eyes;

Said, nothing like his works was ever printed;
And last, my Prologue-business slily hinted.
"Ma'am, let me tell you," quoth my man of rhymes,
"I know your bent—these are no laughing times;
Can you—but, Miss, I own I have my fears—
Dissolve in pause,—and sentimental tears,
With laden sighs, and solemn-rounded sentence,
Rouse from his sluggish slumbers fell Repentance;
Paint Vengeance, as he takes his horrid stand,
Waving on high the desolating brand,
Calling the storms to bear him o'er a guilty land?"
I could no more—askance the creature eyeing,
D'ye think, said I, this face was made for crying?
I'll laugh, that's poz—nay, more, the world shall know it;
And so, your servant! gloomy Master Poet!
Firm as my creed, Sirs, 'tis my fix'd belief,
That Misery's another word for Grief;
I also think—so may I be a bride!
That so much laughter, so much life enjoy'd.
Thou man of crazy care and ceaseless sigh,
Still under bleak Misfortune's blasting eye;
Doom'd to that sorest task of man alive—
To make three guineas do the work of five:
Laugh in misfortune's face—the beldam witch!
Say, you'll be merry, tho' you can't be rich.
Thou other man of care, the wretch in love,
Who long with jiltish hearts and airs hast strove;
Who, as the boughs all temptingly project,
Measur'st in desperate thought—a rope—thy neck—
Or, where the beetling cliff o'erhangs the deep,
Peerest to meditate the healing leap:
Would'st thou be cur'd, thou silly, moping elf?
Laugh at her follies—laugh e'en at thyself:
Learn to despise those frowns now so terrific,
And love a kinder—that's your grand specific.
To sum up all, be merry, I advise;
And as we're merry, may we still be wise.

STANZAS

ADDRESSED TO MISS FERRIER,[1] INCLOSING AN ELEGY ON SIR JAMES HUNTER BLAIR.[2]

(WRITTEN IN 1787.)

NAE heathen name shall I prefix
Frae Pindus or Parnassus;
Auld Reekie dings them a' to sticks,
For rhyme-inspiring lasses.

Jove's tunefu' dochters three times three
Made Homer deep their debtor;
But, gien the body half an ee,
Nine Ferriers wad done better!

Last day my mind was in a bog,
Down George's Street I stoited,[3]
A creeping, cauld, prosaic fog
My very senses doited.[4]

Do what I dought to set her free,
My saul lay in the mire;
Ye turned a neuk[5]—I saw your ee—
She took the wing like fire!

---

[1] The accomplished novellist, and daughter of Mr. J. Ferrier, one of Burns' warmest patrons.
[2] A great friend and patron of the poet.
[3] Tottered. [4] Stupefied. [5] Corner.

The mournfu' sang I here inclose,
In gratitude I send you;
And wish and pray in rhyme sincere,
A' guid things may attend you.

VERSES TO A YOUNG LADY,[1]

WITH A PRESENT OF SONGS.

Here, where the Scottish Muse immortal lives,
In sacred strains and tuneful numbers join'd,
Accept the gift; tho' humble he who gives,
Rich is the tribute of the grateful mind.

So may no ruffian feeling in thy breast
Discordant jar thy bosom-chords among!
But Peace attune thy gentle soul to rest,
Or Love, ecstatic, wake his seraph song;

Or Pity's notes, in luxury of tears,
As modest Want the tale of woe reveals;
While conscious Virtue all the strain endears,
And heaven-born Piety her sanction seals!

POEM ON PASTORAL POETRY.[2]

Hail, Poesie! thou Nymph reserv'd![3]
In chase o' thee, what crowds hae swerv'd
Frae common sense, or sunk enerv'd
'Mang heaps o' clavers;
And och! owre aft thy joes hae starv'd,
'Mid a' thy favours!

Say, Lassie, why thy train amang,
While loud the trump's heroic clang,
And sock or buskin skelp alang
To death or marriage;
Scarce ane has tried the shepherd-sang
But wi' miscarriage?

In Homer's craft Jock Milton thrives;
Eschylus' pen Will Shakespeare drives;
Wee Pope, the knurlin,[1] till him rives
Horatian fame;
In thy sweet sang, Barbauld, survives
Ev'n Sappho's flame.

But thee, Theocritus, wha matches?
They're no herd's ballats, Maro's catches;
Squire Pope but busks[2] his skinklin[3] patches
O' heathen tatters:
I pass by hunders, nameless wretches,
That ape their betters.

In this braw age o' wit and lear,
Will nane the Shepherd's whistle mair
Blaw sweetly in its native air
And rural grace;
And wi' the far-fam'd Grecian share
A rival place?

Yes! there is ane; a Scottish callan—
There's ane; come forrit, honest Allan!
Thou need na jouk[4] behint the hallan,
A chiel sae clever;
The teeth o' Time may gnaw Tantallan,[5]
But thou's for ever!

Thou paints auld Nature to the nines,
In thy sweet Caledonian lines;
Nae gowden stream thro' myrtles twines,
Where Philomel,
While nightly breezes sweep the vines,
Her griefs will tell!

In gowany glens[6] thy burnie strays,
Where bonnie lasses bleach their claes;
Or trots by hazelly shaws and braes,
Wi' hawthorns grey,

---

[1] Daughter of Mr. Graham, of Fintry.
[2] Gilbert Burns doubted the authenticity of these verses, but surely without reason. [3] Collins.

[1] Dwarf. [2] Dresses.
[3] Small. [4] Stoop.
[5] The name of a castle.
[6] Daisied dales.

Where blackbirds join the shepherd's lays
At close o' day.

Thy rural loves are nature's sel';
Nae bombast spates[1] o' nonsense swell;
Nae snap conceits, but that sweet spell
O' witchin' love;
That charm that can the strongest quell,
The sternest move.

WRITTEN ON THE BLANK LEAF OF

THE

LAST EDITION OF HIS POEMS,

PRESENTED TO THE LADY WHOM HE HAD OFTEN CELEBRATED UNDER THE NAME OF CHLORIS.[2]

'Tis Friendship's pledge, my young fair friend,
Nor thou the gift refuse,
Nor with unwilling ear attend
The moralizing muse.

Since thou, in all thy youth and charms,
Must bid the world adieu,
(A world 'gainst peace in constant arms)
To join the friendly few.

Since, thy gay morn of life o'ercast,
Chill came the tempest's lower,
(And ne'er misfortune's eastern blast
Did nip a fairer flower.)

Since life's gay scenes must charm no more,
Still much is left behind;
Still nobler wealth hast thou in store—
The comforts of the mind!

Thine is the self-approving glow,
On conscious honour's part;
And, dearest gift of Heaven below,
Thine friendship's truest heart.

The joys refin'd of sense and taste,
With ev'ry muse to rove:
And doubly were the poet blest,
These joys could he improve.

[1] Torrents. [2] Jean Lorimer.

POETICAL ADDRESS TO MR. WILLIAM TYTLER,

WITH THE PRESENT OF THE BARD'S PICTURE.

Revered defender of beauteous Stuart,
Of Stuart, a name once respected,
A name, which to love was the mark of a true heart,
But now 'tis despis'd and neglected!

Tho' something like moisture conglobes in my eye,
Let no one misdeem me disloyal;
A poor friendless wand'rer may well claim a sigh,
Still more, if that wand'rer were royal.

My fathers that name have rever'd on a throne;
My fathers have fallen to right it;
Those fathers would spurn their degenerate son;
That name should he scoffingly slight it.

Still in prayers for King George I most heartily join,
The Queen, and the rest of the gentry;
Be they wise, be they foolish, is nothing of mine;
Their title's avow'd by my country.

But why of this epocha make such a fuss,
That gave us the Hanover stem?
If bringing them over was lucky for us,
I'm sure 'twas as lucky for them.

But, loyalty, truce! we're on dangerous ground,
Who knows how the fashions may alter?
The doctrine, to-day, that is loyalty sound,
To-morrow may bring us a halter.

I send you a trifle, a head of a bard,
A trifle scarce worthy your care;
But accept it, good Sir, as a mark of regard,
Sincere as a saint's dying prayer.

Now life's chilly evening dim shades in your eye,
And ushers the long dreary night;
But you like the star that athwart gilds the sky,
Your course to the latest is bright.

SKETCH.—NEW-YEAR DAY.

TO MRS. DUNLOP.

This day Time winds th' exhausted chain,
To run the twelvemonth's length again:
I see the old, bald-pated fellow,
With ardent eyes, complexion sallow,
Adjust the unimpair'd machine
To wheel the equal, dull routine.
The absent lover, minor heir,
In vain assail them with their prayer,
Deaf, as my friend, he sees them press,
Nor makes the hour one moment less.
Will you (the Major's[1] with the hounds,
The happy tenants share his rounds;
Coila's fair Rachel's[2] care to-day,
And blooming Keith's[3] engaged with Gray)
From housewife cares a minute borrow—
—That grandchild's cap will make to-morrow—
And join with me a-moralizing;
This day's propitious to be wise in.
First, what did yesternight deliver?
"Another year is gone for ever."
And what is this day's strong suggestion?
"The passing moment's all we rest on!"
Rest on—for what? what do we here?
Or why regard the passing year?
Will Time, amus'd with proverb'd lore,
Add to our date one minute more?
A few days may, a few years must,
Repose us in the silent dust;
Then is it wise to damp our bliss?
Yes—all such reasonings are amiss!
The voice of Nature loudly cries,
And many a message from the skies
That something in us never dies;
That on this frail, uncertain state
Hang matters of eternal weight;
That future life in worlds unknown
Must take its hue from this alone;
Whether as Heavenly glory bright,
Or dark as Misery's woful night.—
Since then, my honour'd, first of friends,
On this poor being all depends;
Let us th' important Now employ,
And live as those that never die.
Tho' you, with days and honours crown'd,
Witness that filial circle round,
(A sight life's sorrows to repulse;
A sight pale Envy to convulse;)
Others now claim your chief regard;
Yourself, you wait your bright reward.

[1] Major, afterwards General Andrew Dunlop, second son of Mrs. Dunlop.
[2] Miss Rachel Dunlop.
[3] Miss Keith Dunlop, the youngest daughter.

EXTEMPORE, ON MR. WILLIAM SMELLIE,

AUTHOR OF THE PHILOSOPHY OF NATURAL HISTORY, AND MEMBER OF THE ANTIQUARIAN AND ROYAL SOCIETIES OF EDINBURGH.

Shrewd Willie Smellie to Crochallan[1] came,
The old cock'd hat, the gray surtout the same;
His bristling beard just rising in its might;
'Twas four long nights and days to shaving night;
His uncomb'd grizzly locks, wild staring, thatch'd
A head, for thought profound and clear, unmatch'd:

[1] There was a club in Edinburgh—the Crochallan Fencibles—of which Burns and Smellie were members.

Yet tho' his caustic wit was biting, rude,
His heart was warm, benevolent, and good.

INSCRIPTION FOR AN ALTAR TO INDEPENDENCE, AT KERROUGHTRY, SEAT OF MR. HERON;

WRITTEN IN SUMMER, 1795.

Thou of an independent mind,
With soul resolv'd, with soul resign'd;
Prepar'd Power's proudest frown to brave,
Who wilt not be nor have a slave;
Virtue alone who dost revere,
Thy own reproach alone dost fear,
Approach this shrine, and worship here.

MONODY ON A LADY FAMED FOR HER CAPRICE.[1]

How cold is that bosom which folly once fir'd;
How pale is that cheek where the rouge lately glisten'd!
How silent that tongue which the echoes oft tir'd;
How dull is that ear which to flattery so listen'd!

If sorrow and anguish their exit await,
From friendship and dearest affection remov'd;
How doubly severer, Eliza, thy fate!
Thou diedst unwept, as thou livedst unlov'd.

Loves, Graces, and Virtues, I call not on you;
So shy, grave, and distant, ye shed not a tear:
But come, all ye offspring of Folly so true,
And flowers let us cull for Eliza's cold bier.

We'll search thro' the garden for each silly flower,
We'll roam thro' the forest for each idle weed;
But chiefly the nettle, so typical, shower,
For none e'er approach'd her but rued the rash deed.

We'll sculpture the marble, we'll measure the lay;
Here Vanity strums on her idiot lyre;
There keen Indignation shall dart on her prey,
Which spurning Contempt shall redeem from his ire.

THE EPITAPH.

Here lies, now a prey to insulting neglect,
What once was a butterfly, gay in life's beam:
Want only of wisdom denied her respect!
Want only of goodness denied her esteem.

[1] The lady was the Mrs. Riddel, whose name so often occurs in the Poet's history.

SONNET, ON THE DEATH OF ROBERT RIDDEL, ESQ., OF GLENRIDDEL;

APRIL, 1794.

No more, ye warblers of the wood—no more!
Nor pour your descant, grating, on my soul;
Thou young-eyed Spring, gay in thy verdant stole,
More welcome were to me grim Winter's wildest roar.

How can ye charm, ye flow'rs, with all your dyes?
Ye blow upon the sod that wraps my friend:
How can I to the tuneful strain attend?
The strain flows round th' untimely tomb where Riddel lies.

Yes, pour, ye warblers, pour the notes of woe!
And soothe the Virtues weeping on this bier:
The Man of Worth, who has not left his peer,
Is in his "narrow house" for ever darkly low.

Thee, Spring, again with joy shall others greet;
Me, mem'ry of my loss will only meet.

IMPROMPTU, ON MRS. RIDDEL'S BIRTH-DAY,

NOVEMBER 4, 1793.

OLD Winter, with his frosty beard,
Thus once to Jove his prayer preferr'd—
What have I done, of all the year,
To bear this hated doom severe?
My cheerless suns no pleasure know;
Night's horrid car drags, dreary, slow;
My dismal months no joys are crowning,
But spleeny English, hanging, drowning.
Now, Jove, for once be mighty civil,
To counterbalance all this evil;
Give me, and I've no more to say,
Give me Maria's natal day!
That brilliant gift will so enrich me,
Spring, Summer, Autumn, cannot match me.
'Tis done! says Jove; so ends my story,
And Winter once rejoic'd in glory.

TO MISS JESSY LEWARS, DUMFRIES,

WITH BOOKS WHICH THE BARD PRESENTED HER.

THINE be the volumes, Jessy fair,
And with them take the Poet's prayer—
That Fate may in her fairest page,
With every kindliest, best presage
Of future bliss, enrol thy name;
With native worth, and spotless fame,
And wakeful caution still aware
Of ill—but chief, man's felon snare;
All blameless joys on earth we find,
And all the treasures of the mind—
These be thy guardian and reward;
So prays thy faithful friend, the Bard.

EXTEMPORE TO MR. SYME,

ON REFUSING TO DINE WITH HIM, AFTER HAVING BEEN PROMISED THE FIRST OF COMPANY AND THE FIRST OF COOKERY.

DECEMBER 17TH, 1795.

No more of your guests, be they titled or not,
And cook'ry the first in the nation;
Who is proof to thy personal converse and wit,
Is proof to all other temptation.

TO MR. SYME,

WITH A PRESENT OF A DOZEN OF PORTER.

O, HAD the malt thy strength of mind,
Or hops the flavour of thy wit,
'Twere drink for first of human kind,
A gift that e'en for Syme were fit.

Jerusalem Tavern, Dumfries.

SONNET, ON HEARING A THRUSH SING IN A MORNING WALK;

WRITTEN JANUARY 25TH, 1793, THE BIRTH-DAY OF THE AUTHOR, R. B., AGED 34.

SING on, sweet Thrush, upon the leafless bough;
Sing on, sweet bird, I listen to thy strain:
See aged Winter, 'mid his surly reign
At thy blithe carol clears his furrow'd brow.

So in lone Poverty's dominion drear
Sits meek Content with light unanxious heart,
Welcomes the rapid moments, bids them part,
Nor asks if they bring aught to hope or fear.

I thank thee, Author of this opening day!
Thou whose bright sun now gilds the orient skies!
Riches denied, thy boon was purer joys,
What wealth could never give, nor take away!

Yet come, thou child of poverty and care;
The mite high Heav'n bestow'd, that mite with thee I'll share.

POEM, ADDRESSED TO MR. MITCHELL,

COLLECTOR OF EXCISE, DUMFRIES, 1796.

Friend of the Poet, tried and leal,
Wha, wanting thee, might beg or steal;
Alake, alake, the meikle Deil
Wi' a' his witches
Are at it, skelpin! jig and reel,
In my poor pouches.

I modestly fu' fain wad hint it,
That one pound one, I sairly want it:
If wi' the hizzie down ye sent it,
It would be kind;
And while my heart wi' life-blood dunted,[1]
I'd bear't in mind.

So may the auld year gang out moaning
To see the new come laden, groaning,
Wi' double plenty o'er the loanin
To thee and thine;
Domestic peace and comforts crowning
The hale design.

[1] Beat.

POSTSCRIPT.

Ye've heard this while how I've been licket,
And by fell Death was nearly nicket:
Grim loun! he gat me by the fecket,[1]
And sair me sheuk;
But by guid luck I lap a wicket,
And turn'd a neuk.

But by that health, I've got a share o't,
And by that life, I'm promis'd mair o't,
My heal and weal I'll take a care o't
A tentier[2] way:
Then fareweel folly, hide and hair o't,
For ance and aye.

SENT TO A GENTLEMAN WHOM HE HAD OFFENDED.

The friend whom wild from wisdom's way
The fumes of wine infuriate send;
(Not moony madness more astray;)
Who but deplores that hapless friend?

Mine was th' insensate frenzied part,
Ah why should I such scenes outlive?
Scenes so abhorrent to my heart!
'Tis thine to pity and forgive.

POEM ON LIFE, ADDRESSED TO COLONEL DE PEYSTER;[3] DUMFRIES, 1796.

My honour'd Colonel, deep I feel
Your interest in the Poet's weal;
Ah! how sma' heart hae I to speel[4]
The steep Parnassus,
Surrounded thus by bolus pill,
And potion glasses.

[1] Waistcoat. [2] Wiser.
[3] Colonel of the Dumfries Volunteers. [4] Climb.

O what a canty warld were it,
Would pain, and care, and sickness spare it;
And fortune favour worth and merit,
As they deserve:
(And aye a rowth,[1] roast beef and claret;
Syne, wha wad starve?)

Dame Life, though fiction out may trick her,
And in paste gems and fripp'ry deck her;
Oh! flick'ring, feeble, and unsicker[2]
I've found her still,
Aye wav'ring like the willow wicker,
'Tween good and ill.

Then that curst carmagnole, auld Satan,
Watches, like baudrons[3] by a rattan,[4]
Our sinfu' saul to get a claut[5] on
Wi' felon ire;
Syne, whip! his tail ye'll ne'er cast saut on,—
He's aff like fire.

Ah Nick! ah Nick! it is na fair,
First showing us the tempting ware,
Bright wines and bonnie lasses rare,
To put us daft;
Syne[6] weave, unseen, thy spider snare
O' hell's d—d waft.[7]

Poor man, the flie, aft bizzes by,
And aft, as chance he comes thee nigh,
Thy auld d—d elbow yeuks with joy,
And hellish pleasure;
Already, in thy fancy's eye,
Thy sicker[8] treasure.

Soon, heels-o'er-gowdy![9] in he gangs,
And like a sheep-head on a tangs,
Thy girning[10] laugh enjoys his pangs,
And murd'ring wrestle
As, dangling in the wind, he hangs
A gibbet's tassel.

But lest you think I am uncivil,
To plague you with this draunting drivel,
Abjuring a' intentions evil,
I quat my pen:
The Lord preserve us frae the Devil!
Amen! amen!

[1] Plenty. [2] Unsteady. [3] Cat. [4] Rat. [5] A scrape. [6] Then. [7] Woof. [8] Sure. [9] Topsy-turvy. [10] Grinning.

TO ROBERT GRAHAM, ESQ., OF FINTRY, ON RECEIVING A FAVOUR.

I CALL no Goddess to inspire my strains,
A fabled Muse may suit a Bard that feigns;
Friend of my life! my ardent spirit burns,
And all the tribute of my heart returns,
For boons recorded, goodness ever new,
The gift still dearer, as the giver you.
Thou orb of day! thou other paler light!
And all ye many sparkling stars of night;
If aught that giver from my mind efface;
If I that giver's bounty e'er disgrace;
Then roll to me, along your wand'ring spheres,
Only to number out a villain's years!

EPITAPH ON A FRIEND.

AN honest man here lies at rest,
As e'er God with his image blest;
The friend of man, the friend of truth;
The friend of age, and guide of youth:
Few hearts like his, with virtue warm'd,
Few heads with knowledge so inform'd:
If there's another world, he lives in bliss;
If there is none, he made the best of this.

EPISTLE TO WILLIAM CREECH.[1]

AULD chuckie Reekie's[2] sair distrest,
Down drops her ance weel burnisht crest,

[1] The inclosed I have just wrote, nearly extempore, in a solitary inn in Selkirk, after a miserable wet day's riding.—R. B.
[2] Edinburgh.

Nae joy her bonnie buskit[1] nest
Can yield ava,
Her darling bird that she lo'es best,
Willie's awa!

O Willie was a witty wight,
And had o' things an unco slight;
Auld Reekie ay he keepit tight,
An' trig[2] an' braw.
But now they'll busk her like a fright,
Willie's awa!

The stiffest o' them a' he bow'd;
The bauldest o' them a' he cow'd;
They durst nae mair than he allow'd,
That was a law:
We've lost a birkie[3] weel worth gowd,
Willie's awa!

Now gawkies, tawpies,[4] gowks, and fools,
Frae colleges and boarding-schools,
May sprout like simmer puddock-stools
In glen or shaw;[5]
He wha could brush them down to mools,
Willie's awa!

The brethren o' the Commerce-Chaumer[6]
May mourn their loss wi' doolfu' clamour;
He was a dictionar and grammar
Amang them a';
I fear they'll now mak mony a stammer,
Willie's awa!

Nae mair we see his levee door
Philosophers and Poets pour,
And toothy critics by the score,
In bloody raw;
The adjutant o' a' the core,
Willie's awa!

Now worthy Gregory's Latin face,
Tytler's and Greenfield's modest grace:
M'Kenzie, Stewart—such a brace
As Rome ne'er saw;
They a' maun meet some ither place,
Willie's awa!

[1] Ornamented. [2] Neat.
[3] Clever fellow. [4] Silly girls.
[5] Wood in a hollow.
[6] The Chamber of Commerce in Edinburgh.

Poor Burns e'en Scotch drink canna quicken,
He cheeps[1] like some bewildered chicken
Scar'd frae its minnie and the cleckin
By hoodie-craw;[2]
Grief's gien his heart an unco kickin',
Willie's awa!

Now ev'ry sour-mou'd girnin' blellum,[3]
And Calvin's fock, are fit to fell him;
And self-conceited critic skellum[4]
His quill may draw;
He wha could brawlie ward their bellum,
Willie's awa!

Up whimpling stately Tweed I've sped,
And Eden scenes on crystal Jed,
And Ettrick banks now roaring red,
While tempests blaw;
But every joy and pleasure's fled,
Willie's awa!

May I be slander's common speech;
A text for infamy to preach;
And lastly, streekit out to bleach
In winter snaw;
When I forget thee, WILLIE CREECH,[5]
Tho' far awa!

May never wicked fortune touzle him!
May never wicked men bamboozle him!
Until a pow[6] as auld's Methusalem
He canty claw![7]
Then to the blessed New Jerusalem,
Fleet wing awa!

A GRACE BEFORE DINNER.

O THOU, who kindly dost provide
For every creature's want!
We bless thee, God of Nature wide,
For all thy goodness lent:
And, if it please thee, Heavenly Guide,
May never worse be sent;

[1] Chirps. [2] Blood-crow.
[3] Talking fellow. [4] Scamp.
[5] Creech was the chief publisher in Edinburgh.
[6] Head. [7] Cheerful scratch.

But whether granted or denied,
Lord, bless us with content!
Amen!

INSCRIPTION ON THE TOMBSTONE ERECTED BY BURNS TO THE MEMORY OF FERGUSSON.[1]

"Here lies Robert Fergusson, Poet, born September 5th, 1751—Died, 16th October, 1774."

No sculptur'd marble here, nor pompous lay,
"No storied urn, nor animated bust;"
This simple stone directs pale Scotia's way
To pour her sorrows o'er her Poet's dust.

A VERSE COMPOSED AND REPEATED BY BURNS, TO THE MASTER OF THE HOUSE, ON TAKING LEAVE AT A PLACE IN THE HIGHLANDS, WHERE HE HAD BEEN HOSPITABLY ENTERTAINED.

When death's dark stream I ferry o'er,
A time that surely shall come;
In Heaven itself I'll ask no more,
Than just a Highland welcome.

LIBERTY—A FRAGMENT.[2]

Thee, Caledonia, thy wild heaths among,
Thee, famed for martial deed and sacred song,
To thee I turn with swimming eyes;
Where is that soul of Freedom fled?
Immingled with the mighty dead!
Beneath the hallow'd turf where Wallace lies!
Hear it not, Wallace, in thy bed of death!
Ye babbling winds, in silence sweep;
Disturb not ye the hero's sleep,
Nor give the coward secret breath.
Is this the power in Freedom's war,
That wont to bid the battle rage?
Behold that eye which shot immortal hate,
Crushing the despot's proudest bearing,
That arm which, nerved with thundering fate,
Brav'd usurpation's boldest daring!
One quench'd in darkness, like the sinking star,
And one the palsied arm of tottering, powerless age.

ELEGY ON THE DEATH OF ROBERT RUISSEAUX.[1]

Now Robin lies in his last lair,
He'll gabble rhyme, nor sing nae mair,
Cauld poverty, wi' hungry stare,
Nae mair shall fear him:
Nor anxious fear, nor cankert care
E'er mair come near him.

To tell the truth, they seldom fasht him,
Except the moment that they crusht him;
For sune as chance, or fate, had husht 'em,
Tho' e'er sae short,
Then wi' a rhyme, or sang, he lasht 'em,
And thought it sport.

Tho' he was bred to kintra wark,
And counted was baith wight and stark,[2]
Yet that was never Robin's mark
To mak a man;

[1] Burns had asked permission of the Bailies of Canongate, to "lay a simple stone over the revered ashes" of Fergusson.

[2] The Fragment was the amusement of a lonely hour at a village inn, in the summer of 1794.

[1] In *Ruisseaux*, Burns plays on his own name.

[2] Stout and enduring.

But tell him, he was learn'd and clark,
Ye roos'd him than!

ANSWER

TO VERSES ADDRESSED TO THE POET BY THE GUIDWIFE OF WAUCHOPE-HOUSE.[1]

GUIDWIFE,

I MIND it weel, in early date,
When I was beardless, young, and blate,
An' first could thrash the barn,
Or haud a yokin at the pleugh.
An' tho' forfoughten[2] sair eneugh,
Yet unco' proud to learn:
When first amang the yellow corn
A man I reckon'd was,
And wi' the lave ilk merry morn
Could rank my rig and lass,
Still shearing and clearing
The tither stooked raw,[3]
Wi' claivers, an' haivers,[4]
Wearing the day awa:

Ev'n then a wish (I mind its power),
A wish that, to my latest hour,
Shall strongly heave my breast;
That I for poor auld Scotland's sake,
Some usefu' plan, or beuk could make,
Or sing a sang at least.
The rough bur-thistle, spreading wide
Amang the bearded bear,[5]
I turn'd the weeding-hook aside,
An' spar'd the symbol dear:
No nation, no station,
My envy e'er could raise;
A Scot still, but blot still,
I knew nae higher praise.

But still the elements o' sang
In formless jumble, right an' wrang,
Wild floated in my brain;
Till on that har'st I said before,
My partner in the merry core,
She rous'd the forming strain:
I see her yet, the sonsie quean,
That lighted up my jingle,

[1] Mrs. Scott, who had some skill in rhyming and painting.
[2] Tired. [3] The other row of shocks.
[4] Nonsense. [5] Barley.

Her witching smile, her pauky een,
That gart my heart-strings tingle;
I fired, inspired,
At ev'ry kindling keek,[1]
But bashing, and dashing,
I feared aye to speak.

Health to the sex! ilk guid chiel says,
Wi' merry dance in winter days,
An' we to share in common:
The gust o' joy, the balm of woe,
The saul o' life, the heav'n below,
Is rapture-giving woman.
Ye surly sumphs, who hate the name,
Be mindfu' o' your mither:
She, honest woman, may think shame
That ye're connected with her.
Ye're wae men, ye're nae men,
That slight the lovely dears:
To shame ye, disclaim ye,
Ilk honest birkie swears.

For you, no bred to barn and byre,[2]
Wha sweetly tune the Scottish lyre,
Thanks to you for your line:
The marled plaid ye kindly spare,
By me should gratefully be ware;
'Twad please me to the Nine.
I'd be mair vauntie o' my hap,[3]
Douce hingin' owre my curple,
Than ony ermine ever lap,
Or proud imperial purple.
Fareweel then, lang heal then,
An' plenty be your fa':
May losses and crosses
Ne'er at your hallan ca'.

March, 1787.

LINES ON VIEWING STIRLING CASTLE.[4]

HERE Stuarts once in glory reign'd,
And laws for Scotland's weal ordain'd,

[1] Look. [2] Stable, or sheep-pen.
[3] Mantle.
[4] Scratched with a diamond on a pane of glass at the inn where Burns was staying. As the lines were afterwards quoted to his prejudice, he smashed the pane of glass on his next visit to Stirling.

But now unroof'd their palace stands,
Their sceptre sway'd by other hands.
The injur'd Stuart line is gone,—
A race outlandish fills their throne;—
An idiot race, to honour lost;
Who know them best despise them most.

TO J. LAPRAIK.

Sept. 13th, 1785.

GUID speed an' furder to you, Johnny,
Guid health, hale hans, and weather bonny;
Now when ye're nickan down fu' canny
The staff, o' bread,
May ye ne'er want a stoup o' bran'y
To clear your head.

May Boreas never thresh your rigs,
Nor kick your rickles aff their legs,
Sendin' the stuff o'er muirs an' haggs
Like drivin' wrack;
But may the tapmast grain that wags
Come to the sack.

I'm bizzie too, an' skelpin' at it,
But bitter, daudin showers hae wat it,
Sae my auld stumpie pen I gat it
Wi' muckle wark,
An' took my jocteleg[1] an' what it,
Like ony clark.

It's now twa month that I'm your debtor,
For your braw, nameless, dateless letter,
Abusin' me for harsh ill-nature
On holy men,
While Deil a hair yoursel ye're better,
But mair profane.

But let the kirk-folk ring their bells,
Let's sing about our noble sels;
We'll cry nae jads frae heathen hills
To help, or roose us,
But browster wives[2] an' whiskie stills,
They are the Muses.

Your friendship, Sir, I winna quat it,
An' if ye mak objections at it,
Then han' in nieve some day we'll knot it,
An' witness take,
An' when wi' Usquebae we've wat it
It winna break.

But if the beast and branks be spar'd
Till kye be gaun without the herd,
An' a' the vittel in the yard,
An' theekit right,
I mean your ingle-side to guard
Ae winter night.

The muse-inspirin' aqua-vitæ
Shall make us baith sae blithe an' witty,
Till ye forget ye're auld an' gatty,
An' be as canty
As ye were nine years less than thretty,
Sweet ane an' twenty!

But stooks are cowpet[1] wi' the blast,
An' now the sinn keeks[2] in the west,
Then I maun rin amang the rest
An' quit my chanter;
Sae I subscribe mysel in haste
Your's, Rab the Ranter.[3]

[1] Clasp-knife. [2] Alehouse wives.

TO THE REV. JOHN M'MATH.

ENCLOSING A COPY OF HOLY WILLIE'S PRAYER, WHICH HE HAD REQUESTED.

Sept. 17th, 1785.

WHILE at the stook the shearers cow'r
To shun the bitter blaudin'[4] show'r,
Or in gulravage rinnin scour,[5]
To pass the time,
To you I dedicate the hour
In idle rhyme.

My musie, tir'd wi' monie a sonnet
On gown, an' ban', an' douse black bonnet,

[1] Tumbled over. [2] Sun peeps.
[3] It is very probable that the Poet thus named himself after the *Border Piper*, so spiritedly introduced in the popular song of "Maggie Lauder."—*Cromek.*
[4] Driving.
[5] Running in confusion, like boys leaving school.

Is grown right eerie[1] now she's done it,
Lest they shou'd blame her,
An' rouse their holy thunder on it,
And anathem her.

I own 'twas rash, and rather hardy,
That I, a simple countra bardie,
Shou'd meddle wi' a pack so sturdy,
Wha, if they ken me,
Can easy, wi' a single wordie,
Loose hell upon me.

But I gae mad at their grimaces,
Their sighin', cantin', grace-proud faces,
Their three-mile prayers, and hauf-mile graces,
Their raxin'[2] conscience,
Whase greed, revenge, an' pride disgraces
Waur nor their nonsense.

There's Gawn,[3] miska't waur than a beast,
Wha has mair honour in his breast
Than monie scores as guid 's the priest
Wha sae abus'd him;
An' may a bard no crack his jest
What way they've us'd him?

See him, the poor man's friend in need,
The gentleman in word an' deed,
An' shall his fame an' honour bleed
By worthless skellums,
An' no a muse erect her head
To cowe the blellums?

O Pope, had I thy satire's darts
To gie the rascals their deserts,
I'd rip their rotten, hollow hearts,
An' tell aloud
Their jugglin' hocus-pocus arts
To cheat the crowd.

God knows, I'm no the thing I shou'd be,
Nor am I even the thing I cou'd be,
But, twenty times, I rather wou'd be
An atheist clean,
Than under Gospel colours hid be,
Just for a screen.

An honest man may like a glass,
An honest man may like a lass,

[1] Frighted. [2] Stretching.
[3] Gavin Hamilton.

But mean revenge, an' malice fause,
He'll still disdain,
An' then cry zeal for Gospel laws,
Like some we ken.

They tak religion in their mouth;
They talk o' mercy, grace, an' truth,
For what? to gie their malice skouth[1]
On some puir wight,
An' hunt him down, o'er right an' ruth,
To ruin straight.

All hail, Religion! maid divine!
Pardon a muse sae mean as mine,
Who in her rough imperfect line
Thus daurs to name thee;
To stigmatise false friends of thine
Can n'er defame thee.

Tho' blotch't an' foul wi' monie a stain,
An' far unworthy of thy train,
Wi' trembling voice I tune my strain,
To join wi' those,
Who boldly daur thy cause maintain
In spite o' foes;

In spite o' crowds, in spite o' mobs,
In spite o' undermining jobs,
In spite o' dark banditti stabs
At worth an' merit,
By scoundrels, ev'n wi' holy robes,
But hellish spirit.

O Ayr! my dear, my native ground!
Within thy presbytereal bound,
A candid lib'ral band is found
Of public teachers,
As men, as Christians too, renown'd,
An' manly preachers.

Sir, in that circle you are nam'd;
Sir, in that circle you are fam'd;
An' some, by whom your doctrine's blam'd,
(Which gies you honour,)
Ev'n, Sir, by them your heart's esteem'd,
An' winning manner.

Pardon this freedom I have ta'en,
An' if impertinent I've been,
Impute it not, good Sir, in ane
Whase heart ne'er wrang'd ye,
But to his utmost would befriend
Ought that belang'd t' ye.

[1] Vent.

TO GAVIN HAMILTON, ESQ., MAUCHLINE.

RECOMMENDING A BOY.

Mosgaville, May 3, 1786.

I HOLD it, Sir, my bounden duty,
To warn you how that Master Tootie,
Alias, Laird M'Gaun,[1]
Was here to lure the lad away
'Bout whom ye spak the tither day,
An' wad hae don 't aff han':[2]
But lest he learn the callan tricks,
As, faith, I muckle doubt him,
Like scrapin' out auld Crummie's nicks,
An' tellin' lies about them;
As lieve then, I'd have then,
Your clerkship he should sair,
If sae be, ye may be
Not fitted otherwhere.

Altho' I say't, he's gleg[3] enough,
An' 'bout a house that's rude an' rough,
The boy might learn to swear;
But then wi' you, he'll be sae taught,
An' get sic fair example straught,
I hae na ony fear.
Ye'll catechise him every quirk,
An' shore[4] him weel wi' hell;
An' gar[5] him follow to the kirk—
—Aye when ye gang yoursel.
If ye then, maun be then
Frae hame this comin' Friday,
Then please, Sir, to lea'e, Sir,
The orders wi' your lady.

My word of honour I hae gi'en,
In Paisley John's, that night at e'en,
To meet the warld's worm:
To try to get the twa to gree,
An' name the airles[6] an' the fee,
In legal mode an' form:
I ken he weel a snick can draw,[1]
When simple bodies let him;
An' if a Devil be at a',
In faith he's sure to get him.
To phrase you, an' praise you,
Ye ken your Laureat scorns:
The pray'r still, your share still,
Of grateful Minstrel—BURNS.

[1] Master Tootie then lived in Mauchline; a dealer in cows. It was his common practice to cut the nicks or markings from the horns of cattle, to disguise their age. He was an artful trick-contriving character; hence he is called a snick-drawer. Burns styles the Devil, in his address to that personage, an auld, *snick-drawing* dog."—*Cromek.*

[2] Off hand. [3] Sharp. [4] Threaten. [5] Make. [6] Earnest money.

[1] Contrive a trick.

EPISTLE TO MR. M'ADAM OF CRAIGEN-GILLAN,

IN ANSWER TO AN OBLIGING LETTER HE SENT IN THE COMMENCEMENT OF MY POETIC CAREER.

SIR, o'er a gill I gat your card,
I trow it made me proud;
"See wha taks notice o' the Bard!"
I lap and cry fu' loud.

"Now deil-ma-care about their jaw,
The senseless, gawky million;
I'll cock my nose aboon them a',
I'm roos'd by Craigen-Gillan!"

'Twas noble, Sir; 'twas like yoursel,
To grant your high protection:
A great man's smile, ye ken fu' weel,
Is aye a blest infection.

Tho', by his[2] banes wha in a tub
Match'd Macedonian Sandy!
On my ain legs, thro' dirt and dub,
I independent stand aye.—

And when those legs to gude, warm kail,
Wi' welcome canna bear me;
A lee dyke-side, a sybow-tail,
And barley scone shall cheer me.

Heaven spare you lang to kiss the breath
O' mony flow'ry simmers!
And bless your bonnie lasses baith,
I'm tald they're loosome kimmers![3]

And God bless young Dunaskin's laird,
The blossom of our gentry!
And may he wear an auld man's beard
A credit to his country.

[2] Diogenes. [3] Girls.

TO CAPTAIN RIDDEL, GLENRIDDEL.

EXTEMPORE LINES ON RETURNING A NEWSPAPER.

Ellisland, Monday Evening.

YOUR News and Review, Sir, I've read through and through, Sir,
With little admiring or blaming:
The papers are barren of home-news or foreign,
No murders or rapes worth the naming.

Our friends the Reviewers, those chippers and hewers,
Are judges of mortar and stone, Sir;
But of meet, or unmeet, in a fabrick complete,
I'll boldly pronounce they are none, Sir.

My goose-quill too rude is, to tell all your goodness
Bestow'd on your servant, the Poet;
Would to God I had one like a beam of the sun,
And then all the world, Sir, should know it!

TO JOHN MAXWELL,[1] OF TERRAUGHTY, ON HIS BIRTHDAY.

(WRITTEN IN 1791.)

HEALTH to the Maxwells' vet'ran Chief!
Health, aye unsour'd by care or grief:
Inspir'd, I turn'd Fate's sibyl leaf
This natal morn;
I see thy life is stuff o' prief,[2]
Scarce quite half worn.

This day thou metes threescore eleven,
And I can tell that bounteous Heaven
(The second-sight, ye ken, is given
To ilka Poet)

[1] An able but eccentric man, who had a great admiration for the poet's social qualities and conversational powers.
[2] Proof.

On thee a tack o' seven times seven
Will yet bestow it.

If envious buckies view wi' sorrow
Thy lengthen'd days on this blest morrow,
May Desolation's lang-teeth'd harrow,
Nine miles an hour,
Rake them, like Sodom and Gomorrah,
In brunstane stoure![1]

But for thy friends, and they are monie,
Baith honest men and lasses bonnie,
May couthie[2] fortune, kind and cannie,
In social glee,
Wi' mornings blythe and e'enings funny
Bless them and thee!

Fareweel, auld birkie![3] Lord be near ye,
And then the Deil he daur na steer[4] ye:
Your friends aye love, your faes aye fear ye;
For me, shame fa' me!
If neist my heart I dinna wear ye
While BURNS they ca' me.

THE VOWELS.

A TALE.

'TWAS where the birch and sounding thong are ply'd,
The noisy domicile of pedant pride;
Where ignorance her darkening vapour throws,
And cruelty directs the thickening blows;
Upon a time, Sir Abece the great,
In all his pedagogic powers elate,
His awful chair of state resolves to mount,
And call the trembling Vowels to account.
First enter'd A, a grave, broad, solemn wight,
But ah! deform'd, dishonest to the sight!
His twisted head look'd backward on his way,

[1] Dust. [2] Loving.
[3] A clever fellow. [4] Molest.

And flagrant from the scourge, he grunted, *ai!*
 Reluctant, E stalk'd in; with piteous race
The jostling tears ran down his honest face!
That name, that well-worn name, and all his own,
Pale he surrenders at the tyrant's throne!
The pedant stifles keen the Roman sound
Not all his mongrel diphthongs can compound;
And, next, the title following close behind,
He to the nameless, ghastly wretch assign'd.
 The cobweb'd gothic dome resounded, Y!
In sullen vengeance, I disdain'd reply:
The pedant swung his felon cudgel round,
And knock'd the groaning vowel to the ground!
 In rueful apprehension enter'd O,
The wailing minstrel of despairing woe;
Th' Inquisitor of Spain, the most expert,
Might there have learnt new mysteries of his art:
So grim, deform'd, with horrors entering, U
His dearest friend and brother scarcely knew!
 As trembling U stood staring all aghast,
The pedant in his left hand clutch'd him fast,
In helpless infants' tears he dipp'd his right,
Baptis'd him *eu*, and kick'd him from his sight.

PROLOGUE
FOR MR. SUTHERLAND'S BENEFIT-NIGHT, DUMFRIES.

WHAT needs this din about the town o' Lon'on,
How this new play, an' that new sang, is comin'?
Why is outlandish stuff sae meikle courted?
Does nonsense mend like whisky, when imported?
Is there nae poet, burning keen for fame,
Will try to gie us sangs and plays at hame?
For comedy abroad he need na toil,
A fool and knave are plants of every soil:
Nor need he hunt as far as Rome and Greece,
To gather matter for a serious piece;
There's themes enow in Caledonian story,
Would show the tragic muse in a' her glory.
 Is there no daring Bard will rise and tell
How glorious Wallace stood, how hapless fell?
Where are the Muses fled that could produce
A drama worthy o' the name o' Bruce;
How here, even here, he first unsheath'd the sword
'Gainst mighty England and her guilty lord;
And after monie a bloody, deathless doin',
Wrench'd his dear country from the jaws of ruin?
O for a Shakespeare, or an Otway scene,
To draw the lovely, hapless Scottish Queen!
Vain all the omnipotence of female charms
'Gainst headlong, ruthless, mad Rebellion's arms,
She fell, but fell with spirit truly Roman,
To glut the vengeance of a rival woman:
A woman, tho' the phrase may seem uncivil,
As able and as cruel as the Devil!
One Douglas lives in Home's immortal page,
But Douglases were heroes every age:
And tho' your fathers, prodigal of life,
A Douglas follow'd to the martial strife,

Perhaps, if bowls row right, and right succeeds,
Ye yet may follow where a Douglas leads!
As ye hae generous done, if a' the land
Would tak the Muses' servants by the hand;
Not only hear, but patronize, befriend them,
And where ye justly can commend, commend them;
And aiblins when they winna stand the test,
Wink hard and say, the folks hae done their best!
Would a' the land do this, then I'll be caution
Ye'll soon hae Poets, o' the Scottish nation,
Will gar fame blaw until her trumpet crack,
And warsle[1] time an' lay him on his back!
For us and for our stage should onie spier,
"Whase aught thae chiels maks a' this bustle here?"
My best leg foremost, I'll set up my brow,
We hae the honour to belong to you!
We're your ain bairns, e'en guide us as ye like,
But, like good mithers, shore before ye strike—
And gratefu' still I hope ye'll ever find us,
For a' the patronage and meikle kindness
We've got frae a' professions, sets, and ranks:
God help us! we're but poor—ye'se get but thanks.

ELEGY ON THE YEAR 1788.

SKETCH.

For Lords or Kings I dinna mourn,
E'en let them die—for that they're born;

[1] Wrestle.

But oh! prodigious to reflec'!
A Towmont,[1] Sirs, is gane to wreck!
O Eighty-eight, in thy sma' space
What dire events hae taken place!
Of what enjoyments thou hast reft us!
In what a pickle thou hast left us!
The Spanish empire's tint[2] a head,
And my auld teethless Bawtie's dead!
The tulzie's[3] sair between Pitt an' Fox,
And 'tween our Maggie's twa wee cocks;
The tane is game, a bludie devil,
But to the hen-birds unco civil;
The tither's something dour o' treadin',
But better stuff ne'er claw'd a midden.[4]
Ye ministers, come mount the poupit[5]
An' cry till ye be haerse[6] an' roupet,
For Eighty-eight he wisn'd you weel,
And gied you a' baith gear an' meal;
E'en monie a plack, and monie a peck,
Ye ken yoursels, for little feck.
Ye bonnie lasses, dight your een,[7]
For some o' you hae tint a frien;
In Eighty-eight, ye ken, was ta'en
What ye'll ne'er hae to gie again.
Observe the vera nowte[8] an' sheep,
How dowf[9] and daviely they creep:
Nay, even the yirth itsel does cry,
For E'mbrugh wells are grutten dry.
O Eighty-nine, thou's but a bairn,
An' no owre auld, I hope, to learn!
Thou beardless boy, I pray tak care,
Thou now has got thy daddy's chair,
Nae hand-cuff'd, mizzl'd, hap-shackl'd Regent,
But, like himsel, a full free agent.
Be sure ye follow out the plan
Nae waur than he did, honest man:
As muckle better as you can.

January 1, 1789.

DELIA.[10]

AN ODE.

Fair the face of orient day,
Fair the tints of op'ning rose;

[1] Twelvemonth. [2] Lost.
[3] Quarrel. [4] Dunghill.
[5] Pulpit. [6] Hoarse.
[7] Wipe your eyes. [8] Cattle.
[9] Languid.
[10] Said to have been written at the

But fairer still my Delia dawns,
More lovely far her beauty blows.

Sweet the lark's wild-warbled lay,
Sweet the tinkling rill to hear;
But, Delia, more delightful still
Steal thine accents on mine ear.

The flower-enamour'd busy bee
The rosy banquet loves to sip;
Sweet the streamlet's limpid lapse
To the sun-brown'd Arab's lip;

But, Delia, on thy balmy lips
Let me, no vagrant insect, rove!
O let me steal one liquid kiss!
For, oh! my soul is parch'd with love!

SKETCH.[1]

A LITTLE, upright, pert, tart, tripping wight,
And still his precious self his dear delight;
Who loves his own smart shadow in the streets
Better than e'er the fairest she he meets;
A man of fashion too, he made his tour,
Learn'd vive la bagatelle, et vive l'amour;
So travell'd monkeys their grimace improve,
Polish their grin, nay, sigh for ladies' love.
Much specious lore, but little understood;
Veneering oft outshines the solid wood:
His solid sense—by inches you must tell,
But mete his cunning by the old Scots ell;
His meddling vanity, a busy fiend,
Still making work his selfish craft must mend.

inn of Brownhill, in the parish of Closeburn, "a favourite resting-place of Burns."

[1] The piece inscribed, "R. G., Esq.," is a copy of verses I sent Mr. Graham, of Fintry, accompanying a request for his assistance in a matter to me of very great moment. This poem is a species of composition new to me, but I do not intend it shall be my last essay of the kind, as you will see by the "Poet's Progress." These fragments, if my design succeed, are but a small part of the intended whole. I propose it shall be the work of my utmost exertions, ripened by years. The fragment beginning, "A little, upright, pert, tart," &c., forms the postulate, the axioms, the definition of a character, which, if it appear at all, shall be placed in a variety of lights. This particular part I send you merely as a sample of my hand at portrait-sketching.—*To Professor D. Stewart,* Jan. 20, 1789.

VERSES

WRITTEN UNDER THE PORTRAIT OF FERGUSSON, THE POET, IN A COPY OF THAT AUTHOR'S WORKS, PRESENTED TO A YOUNG LADY IN EDINBURGH, MARCH 19TH, 1787.

CURSE on ungrateful man, that can be pleas'd,
And yet can starve the author of the pleasure!
O thou, my elder brother in misfortune,
By far my elder brother in the Muses,
With tears I pity thy unhappy fate!
Why is the Bard unpitied by the world,
Yet has so keen a relish of its pleasures?

LAMENT,

WRITTEN AT A TIME WHEN THE POET WAS ABOUT TO LEAVE SCOTLAND.[1]

O'ER the mist-shrouded cliffs of the lone mountain straying,
Where the wild winds of winter incessantly rave,

[1] Originally published in the Dum

What woes wring my heart while intently surveying
The storm's gloomy path on the breast of the wave.

Ye foam-crested billows, allow me to wail,
Ere ye toss me afar from my lov'd native shore;
Where the flower which bloom'd sweetest in Coila's green vale,
The pride of my bosom, my Mary's no more.

No more by the banks of the streamlet we'll wander,
And smile at the moon's rimpled face in the wave;
No more shall my arms cling with fondness around her,
For the dew-drops of morning fall cold on her grave.

No more shall the soft thrill of love warm my breast,
I haste with the storm to a far distant shore;
Where unknown, unlamented, my ashes shall rest,
And joy shall revisit my bosom no more.

ON THE DEATH OF SIR JAMES HUNTER BLAIR.[1]

The lamp of day, with ill-presaging glare,
Dim, cloudy, sunk beneath the western wave;
Th' inconstant blast howl'd thro' the dark'ning air,
And hollow whistl'd in the rocky cave.

Lone as I wander'd by each cliff and dell,
Once the lov'd haunts of Scotia's royal train;[2]
Or mus'd where limpid streams, once hallow'd, well,[1]
Or mould'ring ruins mark the sacred fane.[2]

Th' increasing blast roar'd round the beetling rocks,
The clouds swift-wing'd flew o'er the starry sky,
The groaning trees untimely shed their locks,
And shooting meteors caught the startled eye.

The paly moon rose in the livid east,
And 'mong the cliffs disclos'd a stately form,
In weeds of woe that frantic beat her breast,
And mix'd her wailings with the raving storm.

Wild to my heart the filial pulses glow,
'Twas Caledonia's trophied shield I view'd:
Her form majestic droop'd in pensive woe,
The lightning of her eye in tears imbued.

Revers'd that spear, redoubtable in war,
Reclin'd that banner, erst in fields unfurl'd,
That like a deathful meteor gleam'd afar,
And brav'd the mighty monarchs of the world.—

"My patriot son fills an untimely grave!"
With accents wild and lifted arms she cried;
"Low lies the hand that oft was stretch'd to save,
Low lies the heart that swell'd with honest pride.

"A weeping country joins a widow's tear,
The helpless poor mix with the orphan's cry;
The drooping Arts surround their patron's bier,
And grateful Science heaves the heartfelt sigh.—

---

fries Journal, July 5th, 1815, but doubtfully ascribed to Burns.

[1] Sir James Blair died July 1, 1787: he was a partner in Forbes' Bank, at Edinburgh.

[2] The King's Park, at Holyrood House.—R. B.

[1] St. Anthony's Well.—R. B.

[2] St. Anthony's Chapel.—R. B.

"I saw my sons resume their ancient fire;
I saw fair Freedom's blossoms richly blow;
But, ah! how hope is born but to expire!
Relentless fate has laid their guardian low.—

"My patriot falls, but shall he lie unsung,
While empty greatness saves a worthless name?
No; every Muse shall join her tuneful tongue,
And future ages hear his growing fame.

"And I will join a mother's tender cares,
Thro' future times to make his virtues last,
That distant years may boast of other Blairs,"—
She said, and vanish'd with the sweeping blast.

THE POET'S WELCOME TO HIS ILLEGITIMATE CHILD.[1]

Thou's welcome, wean! mischanter[2] fa' me,
If ought of thee, or of thy mammy,
Shall ever danton me, or awe me,
My sweet wee lady,
Or if I blush when thou shalt ca' me
Tit-ta, or daddy.

Wee image of my bonnie Betty,
I, fatherly, will kiss and daut[3] thee,
As dear an' near my heart I set thee
Wi' as gude will,
As a' the priests had seen me get thee
That's out o' h—ll.

What tho' they ca' me fornicator,
An' tease my name in kintra clatter:

[1] The mother was Elizabeth Paton, of Largieside, and her daughter died in 1817, the wife of the overseer at Polkemmet.
[2] Accident. [3] Fondle.

The mair they talk I'm kent the better,
E'en let them clash;
An auld wife's tongue's a feckless matter
To gie ane fash.

Sweet fruit o' monie a merry dint,
My funny toil is now a' tint,
Sin' thou came to the warld asklent,[1]
Which fools may scoff at;
In my last plack thy part's be in't—
The better half o't.

An' if thou be what I wad hae thee,
An' tak the counsel I shall gie thee,
A lovin' father I'll be to thee,
If thou be spar'd;
Thro' a' thy childish years I'll e'e thee,
An' think 't weel war'd.

Gude grant that thou may aye inherit
Thy mither's person, grace, an' merit,
An' thy poor worthless daddy's spirit,
Without his failins,
'Twill please me mair to hear an' see't,
Than stockit mailins.[2]

LETTER TO JOHN GOUDIE, KILMARNOCK, ON THE PUBLICATION OF HIS ESSAYS.

O Goudie! terror o' the Whigs,
Dread o' black coats and rev'rend wigs,
Sour Bigotry, on her last legs,
Girnin'[3] looks back,
Wishin' the ten Egyptian plagues
Wad seize you quick.

Poor gapin', glowrin' Superstition,
Waes me! she's in a sad condition;
Fy, bring Black-Jock, her state physician,
To see her water;
Alas! there's ground o' great suspicion
She'll ne'er get better.

Auld Orthodoxy lang did grapple,
But now she's got an unco ripple;[4]

[1] Asquint. [2] Farms.
[3] Grinning. [4] Death-pain.

Haste, gie her name up i' the chapel,
Nigh unto death;
See how she fetches at the thrapple,[1]
An' gasps for breath.

Enthusiasm's past redemption,
Gaen in a galloping consumption,
Not a' the quacks, wi' a' their gumption,
Will ever mend her;
Her feeble pulse gies strong presumption,
Death soon will end her.

'Tis you and Taylor[2] are the chief,
Wha are to blame for this mischief;
But gin the Lord's ain focks gat leave,
A toom[3] tar-barrel
An' twa red peats wad send relief,
An' end the quarrel.

LETTER TO JAMES TAIT, GLENCONNER.[4]

AULD comrade dear, and brither sinner,
How's a' the folk about Glenconner;
How do you this blae eastlin win',
That's like to blaw a body blin'?
For me, my faculties are frozen,
My dearest member nearly dozen'.
I've sent you here by Johnnie Simson,
Twa sage philosophers to glimpse on;
Smith, wi' his sympathetic feeling,
An' Reid, to common sense appealing,
Philosophers have fought an' wrangled,
An' meikle Greek an' Latin mangled,
Till wi' their logic-jargon tir'd,
An' in the depth of Science mir'd,
To common sense they now appeal,
What wives an' wabsters[5] see an' feel.
But, hark ye, friend, I charge you strictly,
Peruse them, an' return them quickly,
For now I'm grown sae cursed douse,
I pray an' ponder but the house,

[1] Throat. [2] Dr. Taylor, of Norwich.
[3] Empty.
[4] According to Burns, "the most intelligent farmer in the country."
[5] Weavers.

My shins, my lane,[1] I there sit roastin',
Perusing Bunyan, Brown, an' Boston;
Till by an' by, if I haud on,
I'll grunt a real Gospel-groan:
Already I begin to try it,
To cast my een up like a pyet,[2]
When by the gun she tumbles o'er,
Flutt'ring an' gaspin' in her gore:
Sae shortly you shall see me bright,
A burning an' a shining light.

My heart-warm love to guid auld Glen,
The ace an' wale[3] of honest men:
When bending down wi' auld grey hairs,
Beneath the load of years and cares,
May he who made him still support him,
An' views beyond the grave comfort him.
His worthy fam'ly far and near,
God bless them a' wi' grace and gear!

My auld school-fellow, Preacher Willie,
The manly tar,[4] my mason Billie,
An' Auchenbay, I wish him joy;
If he's a parent, lass or boy,
May he be dad, and Meg the mither,
Just five-and-forty years thegither!
An' no forgetting wabster Charlie,
I'm tauld he offers very fairly.
An' Lord remember singing Sannock,
Wi' hale-breeks, saxpence, an' a bannock.
An' next, my auld acquaintance, Nancy,
Since she is fitted to her fancy;
An' her kind stars hae airted till her
A good chiel wi' a pickle[5] siller.
My kindest, best respects I sen' it,
To cousin Kate an' sister Janet;
Tell them frae me, wi' chiels be cautious,
For, faith, they'll aiblins fin' them fashious:
To grant a heart is fairly civil.—
An' lastly, Jamie, for yoursel,
May guardian angels tak a spell,

[1] Myself alone.
[2] Magpie. [3] Choice.
[4] The "manly tar" was probably Richard Brown.—CUNNINGHAM.
[5] Small quantity.

An' steer you seven miles south o' hell:
But first, before ye see heav'n's glory,
May ye get monie a merry story,
Monie a laugh, and monie a drink,
An' aye eneugh o' needfu' clink.
Now fare ye weel, an' joy be wi' you,
For my sake this I beg it o' you,
Assist poor Simson a' ye can,
Ye'll fin' him just an honest man;
Sae I conclude and quat my chanter,
Yours, saint or sinner,
ROB THE RANTER.

EPISTLE FROM ESOPUS[1] TO MARIA.

FROM those drear solitudes and frowzy cells,
Where infamy with sad repentance dwells;
Where turnkeys make the jealous portal fast,
And deal from iron hands the spare repast;
Where truant 'prentices, yet young in sin,
Blush at the curious stranger peeping in;
Where strumpets, relics of the drunken roar,
Resolve to drink, nay half to w—e, no more;
Where tiny thieves, not destin'd yet to swing,
Beat hemp for others, riper for the string:
From these dire scenes my wretched lines I date,
To tell Maria her Esopus' fate.

"Alas! I feel I am no actor here!"
'Tis real hangmen, real scourges bear!
Prepare, Maria, for a horrid tale
Will turn thy very rouge to deadly pale;
Will make thy hair, tho' erst from gipsy poll'd,
By barber woven, and by barber sold,
Though twisted smooth with Harry's nicest care,
Like hoary bristles to erect and stare.
The hero of the mimic scene, no more
I start in Hamlet, in Othello roar;
Or haughty Chieftain, 'mid the din of arms,
In Highland bonnet woo Malvina's charms:
While sans culottes stoop up the mountain high,
And steal from me Maria's prying eye.
Bless'd Highland bonnet! Once my proudest dress,
Now prouder still, Maria's temples press.
I see her wave thy towering plumes afar,
And call each coxcomb to the wordy war.
I see her face the first of Ireland's sons,
And even out-Irish his Hibernian bronze;
The crafty colonel leaves the tartan'd lines,
For other wars, where he a hero shines:
The hopeful youth, in Scottish senate bred,
Who owns a Bushby's heart without the head,
Comes, 'mid a string of coxcombs to display
That *veni, vidi, vici,* is his way;
The shrinking bard adown an alley skulks,
And dreads a meeting worse than Woolwich hulks;
Though there his heresies in church and state
Might well award him Muir and Palmer's fate:
Still she undaunted reels and rattles on,
And dares the public like a noontide sun
(What scandal called Maria's janty stagger
The ricket reeling of a crooked swagger
Whose spleen, e'en worse than Burns's venom—when
He dips in gall unmix'd his eager pen
And pours his vengeance in the burning line,—

---

[1] The *Esopus* of this strange epistle was Williamson the actor, and the *Maria* to whom it is addressed was Mrs. Riddel.—ALLAN CUNNINGHAM.

Who christen'd thus Maria's lyre divine;
The idiot strum of vanity bemused,
And even th' abuse of poesy abused!
Who call'd her verse, a parish workhouse made
For motley, foundling fancies, stolen or stray'd?)
A workhouse! ah, that sound awakes my woes,
And pillows on the thorn my rack'd repose!
In durance vile here must I wake and weep,
And all my frowzy couch in sorrow steep;
That straw where many a rogue has lain of yore,
And vermin'd gipsies litter'd heretofore.

Why, Lonsdale, thus thy wrath on vagrants pour,
Must earth no rascal, save thyself, endure?
Must thou alone in guilt immortal swell,
And make a vast monopoly of hell?
Thou know'st the virtues cannot hate thee worse;
The vices also, must they club their curse?
Or must no tiny sin to others fall,
Because thy guilt's supreme enough for all?

Maria, send me too thy griefs and cares;
In all of thee sure thy Esopus shares.
As thou at all mankind the flag unfurls,
Who on my fair-one satire's vengeance hurls?
Who calls thee pert, affected, vain coquette,
A wit in folly, and a fool in wit?
Who says that fool alone is not thy due,
And quotes thy treacheries to prove it true?
Our force united on thy foes we'll turn,
And dare the war with all of woman born:
For who can write and speak as thou and I?
My periods that decyphering defy,
And thy still matchless tongue that conquers all reply.

ON A SUICIDE.[1]

EARTH'D up here lies an imp o' hell,
 Planted by Satan's dibble—
Poor silly wretch, he's d—d himsel'
 To save the Lord the trouble.

A FAREWELL.[2]

FAREWELL, dear Friend! may guid luck hit you,
And, 'mang her favourites admit you!
If e'er Detraction shore to smit you,
 May nane believe him!
And ony Deil that thinks to get you,
 Good Lord, deceive him.

THE FAREWELL.

FAREWELL old Scotia's bleak domains,
Far dearer than the torrid plains
 Where rich ananas blow!
Farewell, a mother's blessing dear!
A brother's sigh! a sister's tear!
 My Jean's heart-rending throe!
Farewell, my Bess! tho' thou'rt bereft
 Of my parental care;
A faithful brother I have left,
 My part in him thou'lt share!

---

[1] A melancholy person of the name of Glendinning, having taken away his own life, was interred at a place called "The Old Chapel," close beside Dumfries. My friend Dr. Copland Hutchinson happened to be walking out that way: he saw Burns with his foot on the grave, his hat on his knee, and paper laid on his hat, on which he was writing. He then took the paper, thrust it with his finger into the red mould of the grave, and went away. This was the above epigram, and such was the Poet's mode of publishing it. —A. CUNNINGHAM.

[2] The friend was Mr. John Kennedy.

Adieu too, to you too,
My Smith, my bosom frien';
When kindly you mind me,
O then befriend my Jean!

When bursting anguish tears my heart!
From thee, my Jeannie, must I part!
Thou weeping answ'rest, "No!"
Alas! misfortune stares my face,
And points to ruin and disgrace,
I, for thy sake, must go!
Thee Hamilton, and Aiken dear,
A grateful, warm adieu!
I, with a much-indebted tear,
Shall still remember you!
All-hail then, the gale then,
Wafts me from thee, dear shore!
It rustles, and whistles—
I'll never see thee more!

EPISTLE TO ROBERT GRAHAM, ESQ., OF FINTRY; ON THE CLOSE OF THE DISPUTED ELECTION BETWEEN SIR JAMES JOHNSTONE AND CAPTAIN MILLER, FOR THE DUMFRIES DISTRICT OF BOROUGHS.

FINTRY, my stay in worldly strife,
Friend o' my Muse, friend o' my life,
Are ye as idle's I am?
Come then, wi' uncouth, kintra fleg,[1]
O'er Pegasus I'll fling my leg,
And ye shall see me try him.

I'll sing the zeal Drumlanrig bears
Who left the all-important cares
Of princes and their darlings;
And, bent on winning borough towns,
Came shaking hands wi' wabster lowns,
And kissing barefit carlins.[2]

Combustion thro' our boroughs rode
Whistling his roaring pack abroad
Of mad unmuzzled lions;

[1] Kick. [2] Old women.

As Queensberry buff and blue unfurl'd,
And Westerha' and Hopeton hurl'd
To every Whig defiance.

But cautious Queensberry left the war,
Th' unmanner'd dust might soil his star;
Besides, he hated bleeding;
But left behind him heroes bright,
Heroes in Cæsarean fight,
Or Ciceronian pleading.

O! for a throat like huge Mons-meg,
To muster o'er each ardent Whig
Beneath Drumlanrig's banner;
Heroes and heroines commix,
All in the field of politics,
To win immortal honour.

M'Murdo and his lovely spouse,
(Th' enamour'd laurels kiss her brows!)
Led on the loves and graces:
She won each gaping burgess' heart,
While, he, all-conquering, play'd his part
Among their wives and lasses.

Craigdarroch led a light-arm'd corps,
Tropes, metaphors, and figures pour,
Like Hecla streaming thunder:
Glenriddel, skill'd in rusty coins,
Blew up each Tory's dark designs,
And bared the treason under.

In either wing two champions fought,
Redoubted Staig, who set at nought
The wildest savage Tory:
And Welsh, who ne'er yet flinch'd his ground,
High-waved his magnum-bonum round
With Cyclopeian fury.

Miller brought up th' artillery ranks,
The many-pounders of the Banks,
Resistless desolation!
While Maxwelton, that baron bold,
'Mid Lawson's port entrench'd his hold,
And threaten'd worse damnation.

To these what Tory hosts oppos'd,
With these what Tory warriors clos'd,
Surpasses my descriving:
Squadrons, extended long and large,
With furious speed rush to the charge,
Like raging devils driving.

What verse can sing, what prose narrate,
The butcher deeds of bloody fate
Amid this mighty tulzie!
Grim Horror girn'd—pale Terror roar'd,
As Murther at his thrapple[1] shor'd,
And Hell mix'd in the brulzie.[2]

As highland crags by thunder cleft,
When lightnings fire the stormy lift,
Hurl down with crashing rattle:
As flames among a hundred woods;
As headlong foam a hundred floods;
Such is the rage of battle!

The stubborn Tories dare to die;
As soon the rooted oaks would fly
Before th' approaching fellers:
The Whigs come on like Ocean's roar,
When all his wintry billows pour
Against the Buchan Bullers.[3]

Lo, from the shades of Death's deep night,
Departed Whigs enjoy the fight,
And think on former daring:
The muffled murtherer of Charles
The Magna Charta flag unfurls,
All deadly gules its bearing.

Nor wanting ghosts of Tory fame,
Bold Scrimgeour follows gallant Graham,
Auld Covenanters shiver.
(Forgive, forgive, much-wrong'd Montrose!
Now death and hell engulf thy foes,
Thou liv'st on high for ever!)

Still o'er the field the combat burns,
The Tories, Whigs, give way by turns;
But Fate the word has spoken.
For woman's wit and strength o' man,
Alas! can do but what they can!
The Tory ranks are broken.

O that my een were flowing burns!
My voice a lioness that mourns
Her darling cubs' undoing!
That I might greet, that I might cry,
While Tories fall, while Tories fly,
And furious Whigs pursuing!

What Whig but melts for good Sir James?
Dear to his country by the names
Friend, patron, benefactor!
Not Pulteney's wealth can Pulteney save!
And Hopeton falls, the generous brave!
And Stewart, bold as Hector.

Thou, Pitt, shalt rue this overthrow;
And Thurlow growl a curse of woe;
And Melville melt in wailing!
How Fox and Sheridan rejoice!
And Burke shall sing, O Prince, arise,
Thy power is all-prevailing!

For your poor friend, the Bard, afar
He only hears and sees the war,
A cool spectator purely!
So, when the storm the forest rends,
The robin in the hedge descends,
And sober chirps securely.

Now for my friends' and brethren's sakes,
And for my dear-loved Land o' Cakes,
I pray with holy fire:
Lord, send a rough-shod troop o' hell,
O'er a' wad Scotland buy or sell,
To grind them in the mire!

EPISTLE TO MAJOR LOGAN.

[Major Logan was a skilful player of the violin, and a man after Burns' own heart. He was a retired military officer, and well known to the celebrated Neil Gow. He resided at Park House, near Ayr, and lived with his sister and mother. This sister was the Miss Logan to whom the poet addressed some verses, with a present of Beattie's Poems (see p. 69). The Major was a jovial friend and a great favourite of the poet's, and, besides being a first-rate violinist, was a capital companion. He abounded in anecdote and humorous sallies of good-humoured wit. This Epistle shows the high esteem in which he was held, and especially by Burns.]

---

[1] Throat. [2] The broil.

[3] A rocky opening on the coast of Aberdeenshire.

HAIL, thairm[1]-inspirin', rattlin' Willie!
Though Fortune's road be rough an' hilly
To every fiddling, rhyming billie,
We never heed,
But tak it like the unback'd filly,
Proud o' her speed.

When idly goavan[2] whyles we saunter,
Yirr[3] fancy barks, awa' we canter
Uphill, down brae, till some mischanter,[4]
Some black bog-hole,
Arrests us, then the scathe[5] an' banter
We're forced to thole.[6]

Hale be your heart! Hale be your fiddle!
Lang may your elbuck jink and diddle,
To cheer you through the weary widdle
O' this wild warl',
Until you on a crummock driddle[7]
A grey-hair'd carl.

Come wealth, come poortith, late or soon,
Heaven send your heart-strings aye in tune,
And screw your temper-pins aboon,
A fifth or mair,
The melancholious, lazy croon
O' cankrie care.

May still your life from day to day
Nae "lente largo" in the play,
But "allegretto forte" gay
Harmonious flow:

[1] Fiddle-string.
[2] Walking without an object.
[3] Lively.
[4] Accident.
[5] Injury.
[6] To bear.
[7] Hobble on a stick.

A sweeping, kindling, bauld strathspey—
Encore! Bravo!

A blessing on the cheery gang
Wha dearly like a jig or sang,
An' never think o' right an' wrang
By square an' rule,
But as the clegs[1] o' feeling stang[2]
Are wise or fool.

My hand-waled curse keep hard in chase
The harpy, hoodock,[3] purse-proud race,
Wha count on poortith as disgrace—
Their tuneless hearts!
May fire-side discords jar a base
To a' their parts!

But come, your hand, my careless brither,
I' th' ither warl'—if there's anither,
An' that there is I've little swither[4]
About the matter,—
We cheek for chow shall jog thegither,
I'se ne'er bid better.

We've faults and failings—granted clearly,
We're frail backsliding mortals merely,
Eve's bonny squad priests wyte[5] them sheerly
For our grand fa';
But still, but still, I like them dearly—
God bless them a'!

Ochon for poor Castalian drinkers,
When they fa' foul o' earthly jinkers,
The witching curs'd delicious blinkers
Hae put me hyte,[6]
And gart me weet my waukrife winkers,[7]
Wi' girnin spite.

But by yon moon!—and that's high swearin'—
An' every star within my hearin'!
An' by her een wha was a dear ane!
I'll ne'er forget;
I hope to gie the jads[8] a clearin'
In fair play yet.

[1] Gadflies. [2] Sting.
[3] Miserly. [4] Doubt.
[5] Blame. [6] Frantic.
[7] Wet my sleepless eyes. [8] Jades.

My loss I mourn, but not repent it,
I'll seek my pursie whare I tint[1] it,
Ance to the Indies I were wonted,
Some cantraip[2] hour,
By some sweet elf I'll yet be dinted,
Then, *vive l'amour!*

Faites mes baissemains respectueuses,
To sentimental sister Susie,
An' honest Lucky; no to roose ye,
Ye may be proud,
That sic a couple fate allows ye
To grace your blood.

Nae mair at present can I measure,
An' trowth my rhymin' ware's nae treasure;
But when in Ayr, some half-hour's leisure,
Be't light, be't dark,
Sir Bard will do himsel' the pleasure
To call at Park.

ROBERT BURNS.

Mossgiel, 30th October, 1786.

EPITAPH ON THE POET'S DAUGHTER.[3]

HERE lies a rose, a budding rose,
Blasted before its bloom;
Whose innocence did sweets disclose
Beyond that flower's perfume.
To those who for her loss are grieved,
This consolation's given—
She's from a world of woe relieved,
And blooms a rose in Heaven.

EPITAPH ON GABRIEL RICHARDSON.[1]

HERE Brewer Gabriel's fire's extinct,
And empty all his barrels:
He's blest—if, as he brew'd, he drink
In upright honest morals.

EPISTLE TO HUGH PARKER.[2]

IN this strange land, this uncouth clime,
A land unknown to prose or rhyme;
Where words ne'er crost the Muse's heckles,[3]
Nor limpet in poetic shackles;
A land that prose did never view it,
Except when drunk he stachert through it;

---

[1] Lost. [2] Charmed.

[3] These lines are said to have been written by Burns on the loss of his daughter, who died in the autumn of 1795, and of whom he thus speaks in his letter to Mrs. Dunlop, from Dumfries, January 31, 1796: "These many months you have been two packets in my debt—what sin of ignorance I have committed against so highly valued a friend I am utterly at a loss to guess. Alas! madam, ill can I afford, at this time, to be deprived of any of the small remnant of my pleasures. I have lately drunk deep of the cup of affliction. The autumn robbed me of my only daughter and darling child, and that at a distance too, and so rapidly, as to put it out of my power to pay the last duties to her. I had scarcely begun to recover from that shock when I became myself the victim of a most severe rheumatic fever, and long the die spun doubtful; until, after many weeks of sick bed, it seems to have turned up life, and I am beginning to crawl across my room, and once indeed have been before my own door in the street.

"When pleasure fascinates the mental sight,
Affliction purifies the visual ray,
Religion hails the drear, the untried night,
That shuts, for ever shuts, life's doubtful day."

[1] A brewer in Dumfries.

[2] A merchant of Kilmarnock, and a generous patron of Burns at the beginning of his poetical career.

[3] Instrument for dressing flax.

Here, ambush'd by the chimla[1] cheek,
Hid in an atmosphere of reek,
I hear a wheel thrum i' the neuk,
I hear it—for in vain I leuk.—
The red peat gleams, a fiery kernel,
Enhusked by a fog infernal:
Here, for my wonted rhyming raptures,
I sit and count my sins by chapters;
For life and spunk, like ither Christians,
I'm dwindled down to mere existence,
Wi' nae converse but Gallowa' bodies,
Wi' nae kend face but Jenny Geddes.
Jenny, my Pegasean pride!
Dowie[2] she saunters down Nithside,
And aye a westlin leuk she throws,
While tears hap o'er her auld brown nose!
Was it for this, wi' canny care,
Thou bure the Bard through many a shire?
At howes or hillocks never stumbled,
And late or early never grumbled?
Oh, had I power like inclination,
I'd heeze[3] thee up a constellation,
To canter with the Sagitarre,
Or loup the ecliptic like a bar,
Or turn the pole like any arrow:
Or, when auld Phœbus bids good-morrow,
Down the zodiac urge the race,
And cast dirt on his godship's face:
For I could lay my bread and kail,
He'd ne'er cast saut upo' thy tail.—
Wi' a' this care and a' this grief,
And sma', sma' prospect of relief,
And nought but peat reek i' my head,
How can I write what ye can read?—
Tarbolton, twenty-fourth o' June,
Ye'll find me in a better tune;
But till we meet and weet our whistle,
Tak this excuse for nae epistle.

ROBERT BURNS.

---

[1] Fire-place. [2] Weary. [3] Raise. [4] The Earl of Breadalbane.

ADDRESS OF BEELZEBUB TO THE PRESIDENT[4] OF THE HIGHLAND SOCIETY.

LONG life, my Lord, an' health be yours,
Unskaith'd by hunger'd Highland boors;
Lord grant nae duddie[1] desperate beggar,
Wi' dirk, claymore, or rusty trigger,
May twin[2] auld Scotland o' a life
She likes—as lambkins like a knife.
Faith you and A——s were right
To keep the Highland hounds in sight;
I doubt na'! they wad bid nae better
Than let them ance out owre the water;
Then up amang thae lakes and seas
They'll mak what rules and laws they please;
Some daring Hancock, or a Franklin,
May set their Highland bluid a ranklin';
Some Washington again may head them,
Or some Montgomery fearless lead them,
Till God knows what may be effected,
When by such heads and hearts directed—
Poor dunghill sons of dirt and mire
May to Patrician rights aspire!
Nae sage North, now, nor sager Sackville,
To watch and premier o'er the pack vile;
An' whare will ye get Howes and Clintons
To bring them to a right repentance,
To cowe the rebel generation,
An' save the honour o' the nation?
They an' be——! what right hae they
To meat or sleep, or light o' day?
Far less to riches, pow'r, or freedom,
But what your Lordship likes to gie them?

But hear, my Lord! Glengarry, hear!
Your hand's owre light on them, I fear;
Your factors, grieves, trustees, and bailies,
I canna' say but they do gaylies;[3]
They lay aside a' tender mercies,
An' tirl the hallions to the birses;
Yet while they're only poind't and herriet,[4]
They'll keep their stubborn Highland spirit;

---

[1] Ragged. [2] Deprive. [3] Pretty well. [4] Seized and plundered.

But smash them! crash them a' to
spails![1]
An' rot the dyvors[2] i' the jails!
The young dogs, swinge[3] them to the
labour;
Let wark and hunger mak them sober!
The hizzies, if they're aughtlins faw-
sont,[4]
Let them in Drury-lane be lesson'd!
An' if the wives an' dirty brats
E'en thigger[5] at your doors an' yetts[6]
Flaffan wi' duds[7] an' grey wi' beas',
Frightin' awa your deucks an' geese,
Get out a horsewhip, or a jowler,
The langest thong, the fiercest growler,
An' gar the tatter'd gypsies pack
Wi' a' their bastarts on their back!
Go on, my Lord! I lang to meet you,
An' in my house at hame to greet you;
Wi' common lords ye shanna mingle,
The benmost neuk beside the ingle,
At my right han' assign'd your seat
'Tween Herod's hip and Polycrate,—
Or if you on your station tarrow,[8]
Between Almagro and Pizarro,
A seat, I'm sure ye're weel deservin 't;
An' till ye come—Your humble servant,
BEELZEBUB.

June 1, Anno Mundi, 5790.

TO MR. JOHN KENNEDY.

Now, Kennedy, if foot or horse
E'er bring you in by Mauchline Corse,
Lord, man, there's lasses there wad
force
A hermit's fancy,
And down the gate, in faith, they're
worse,
An' mair unchancy.

But, as I'm sayin', please step to Dow's,
And taste sic gear as Johnnie brews,
Till some bit callan bring me news
That you are there,
And if we dinna haud a bouze,
I'se ne'er drink mair.

It's no I like to sit an' swallow,
Then like a swine to puke an' wallow;
But gie me just a true good fallow
Wi' right ingine,[1]
And spunkie ance to make us mellow,
And then we'll shine.

Now, if ye're ane o' warl's folk,
Wha rate the wearer by the cloak,
An' sklent on poverty their joke,
Wi' bitter sneer,
Wi' you no friendship will I troke,
Nor cheap nor dear.

But if, as I'm informed weel,
Ye hate, as ill's the vera Deil,
The flinty heart that canna feel—
Come, Sir, here's tae you;
Hae, there's my haun', I wiss[2] you
weel,
And guid be wi' you.

ON THE DEATH OF ROBERT DUNDAS, ESQ., OF ARNISTON, LATE LORD PRESIDENT OF THE COURT OF SESSION.

LONE on the bleaky hills the straying
flocks
Shun the fierce storms among the shel-
tering rocks:
Down from the rivulets, red with dash-
ing rains,
The gathering floods burst o'er the
distant plains;
Beneath the blasts the leafless forests
groan;
The hollow caves return a sullen moan.

Ye hills, ye plains, ye forests, and ye
caves,
Ye howling winds, and wintry swelling
waves!
Unheard, unseen, by human ear or
eye,
Sad to your sympathetic scenes I fly;
Where to the whistling blast and
waters' roar,
Pale Scotia's recent wound I may de-
plore.

---

1 Chips. 2 Bankrupts.
3 Whip. 4 Decent. 5 Crowd.
6 Farm-yard gates.
7 Fluttering with rags. 8 Murmur.

1 Genius, or disposition. 2 Wish.

O heavy loss, thy country ill could bear!
A loss these evil days can ne'er repair!
Justice, the high vicegerent of her God,
Her doubtful balance eyed, and sway'd her rod;
Hearing the tidings of the fatal blow
She sunk, abandon'd to the wildest woe.

Wrongs, injuries from many a darksome den,
Now gay in hope explore the paths of men:
See from his cavern grim Oppression rise,
And throw on Poverty his cruel eyes;
Keen on the helpless victim see him fly,
And stifle, dark, the feebly-bursting cry:

Mark ruffian Violence, distain'd with crimes,
Rousing elate in these degenerate times;
View unsuspecting Innocence a prey,
As guileful Fraud points out the erring way:
While subtile Litigation's pliant tongue
The life-blood equal sucks of Right and Wrong:
Hark, injured Want recounts th' unlisten'd tale,
And much-wrong'd Mis'ry pours th' unpitied wail!

Ye dark waste hills, and brown unsightly plains,
To you I sing my grief-inspired strains:
Ye tempests, rage! ye turbid torrents, roll!
Ye suit the joyless tenor of my soul.
Life's social haunts and pleasures I resign,
Be nameless wilds and lonely wanderings mine,
To mourn the woes my country must endure,
That wound degenerate ages cannot cure.

TO JOHN M'MURDO, ESQ.

O, COULD I give thee India's wealth,
As I this trifle send!
Because thy joy in both would be
To share them with a friend.

But golden sands did never grace
The Heliconian stream;
Then take what gold could never buy—
An honest Bard's esteem.

ON THE DEATH OF A LAP-DOG, NAMED ECHO.

IN wood and wild, ye warbling throng,
Your heavy loss deplore;
Now half-extinct your powers of song,
Sweet Echo is no more.

Ye jarring, screeching things around,
Scream your discordant joys;
Now half your din of tuneless sound
With Echo silent lies.

THE KIRK'S ALARM.[2]

A SATIRE.

ORTHODOX, orthodox,
Wha believe in John Knox,

---

[1] Steward to the Duke of Queensberry.

[2] It is impossible to look back now to the civil war which then raged among the churchmen of the west of Scotland, without confessing that on either side there was much to regret, and not a little to blame; and no one can doubt that, in the, at best, unsettled state of Robert Burns' principles, the unhappy effect must have been powerful indeed, as to him. M'Gill and Dalrymple, the two ministers of the town of Ayr, had long been suspected of entertaining heterodox opinions. The gentry of the country took, for the most part, the side of M'Gill; the bulk of the lower orders espoused the cause of those who conducted the prosecution against this erring Doctor.

Let me sound an alarm to your conscience—
There's a heretic blast,
Has been blawn i' the wast,
That what is not sense must be nonsense.

Doctor Mac, Doctor Mac,
Ye should stretch on a rack,
To strike evil-doers wi' terror;
To join faith and sense,
Upon any pretence,
Is heretic, damnable error.

Town of Ayr, town of Ayr,
It was mad, I declare,
To meddle wi' mischief a-brewing;
Provost John is still deaf
To the Church's relief,
And orator Bob[1] is its ruin.

D'rymple mild, D'rymple mild,
Tho' your heart's like a child,
And your life like the new-driven snaw,
Yet that winna save ye,
Old Satan must have ye,
For preaching that three's ane an' twa.

Calvin's sons, Calvin's sons,
Seize your spiritual guns,
Ammunition ye never can need;
Your hearts are the stuff,
Will be powder enough,
And your skulls are storehouses of lead.

Rumble John, Rumble John,[2]
Mount the steps wi' a groan,
Cry, the book is with heresy cramm'd;
Then lug out your ladle,
Deal brimstone like adle,[1]
And roar every note o' the damn'd.

Simper James, Simper James,[2]
Leave the fair Killie dames,
There's a holier chase in your view;
I'll lay on your head,
That the pack ye'll soon lead,
For puppies like you there's but few.

Singet Sawnie, Singet Sawnie,[3]
Are ye herding the penny,
Unconscious what danger awaits?
With a jump, yell, and howl,
Alarm every soul,
For Hannibal's just at your gates.

Andrew Gowk, Andrew Gowk,[4]
Ye may slander the book,
And the book nought the waur—let me tell you;
Tho' ye're rich and look big,
Yet lay by hat and wig,
And ye'll hae a calf's-head o' sma' value.

Barr Steenie, Barr Steenie,[5]
What mean ye? what mean ye?
If ye'll meddle nae mair wi' the matter,
Ye may hae some pretence
To havins and sense
Wi' people wha ken ye nae better.

Jamie Goose, Jamie Goose,[6]
Ye hae made but toom roose,
In hunting the wicked Lieutenant;
But the Doctor's your mark,—
For the Lord's haly ark,
He has cooper'd and ca'd a wrang pin in 't.

Davie Bluster, Davie Bluster,[7]
For a saunt if ye muster,
It's a sign they're no nice o' recruits,
Yet to worth let's be just,
Royal blood ye might boast,
If the ass was the king o' the brutes.

Muirland Jock, Muirland Jock,[8]
When the L—— makes a rock,

Gavin Hamilton, and all persons of his stamp, were, of course, on the side of M'Gill; Auld, and the Mauchline Elders, with his enemies. Mr. Robert Aiken, a writer in Ayr, had the principal management of M'Gill's cause. He was an intimate friend of Hamilton, and through him had formed an acquaintance which now ripened into a warm friendship with Burns. M'Gill, Dalrymple, and their brethren, were the New-Light Pastors of his earliest "Satires."—*Lockhart's Life of Burns*, p. 60.

[1] Robert Aiken, agent, or, as we should say, attorney for Dr. M'Gill.

[2] John Russell, with the loud voice.

[1] Stagnant water. [2] James M'Kinla.

[3] Alexander Moodie. [4] Dr. Mitchell.

[5] Stephen Young, Barr.

[6] Mr. Young. [7] Mr. Grant.

[8] Mr. John Sheppard.

To crush Common Sense for her sins;
If ill manners were wit,
There's no mortal so fit,
To confound the poor Doctor at ance.

Cessnockside, Cessnockside,[1]
Wi' your turkey-cock pride,
O' manhood but sma' is your share;
Ye've the figure, it's true,
Ev'n our faes maun allow,
And your friends daurna say ye hae mair.

Daddie Auld, Daddie Auld,[2]
There's a tod[3] i' the fauld,
A tod meikle waur than the clerk;[4]
Tho' ye downa do skaith,
Ye'll be in at the death,
And if ye canna bite, ye can bark.

Poet Burns, Poet Burns,
Wi' your priest-skelping turns,
Why desert ye your auld native shire?
Tho' your Muse is a gipsy,
Yet were she ev'n tipsy,
She could ca' us nae waur than we are.[5]

DAINTIE DAVIE.

Now rosy May comes in wi' flowers,
To deck her gay, green-spreading bowers;
And now come in my happy hours,
To wander wi' my Davie.

CHORUS.

Meet me on the warlock-knowe,[1]
Daintie Davie, daintie Davie,
There I'll spend the day wi' you,
My ain dear daintie Davie.

The crystal waters round us fa',
The merry birds are lovers a',
The scented breezes round us blaw,
A wandering wi' my Davie.
Meet me, &c.

When purple morning starts the hare,
To steal upon her early fare,
Then through the dews I will repair,
To meet my faithfu' Davie.
Meet me, &c.

When day, expiring in the west,
The curtain draws o' Nature's rest,
I flee to his arms I lo'e best,
And that's my ain dear Davie.
Meet me, &c.

THE SELKIRK GRACE.[2]

Some hae meat, and canna eat,
And some wad eat that want it
But we hae meat and we can eat,
And sae the Lord be thankit.

ELEGY ON THE DEATH OF PEG NICHOLSON.

Peg Nicholson was a gude bay mare,
As ever trode on airn;
But now she's floating down the Nith,
An' past the mouth o' Cairn.

Peg Nicholson was a gude bay mare,
An' rode thro' thick an' thin;
But now she's floating down the Nith,
An' wanting ev'n the skin.

Peg Nicholson was a gude bay mare,
An' ance she bare a priest;

[1] Mr. G. Smith. [2] Of Mauchline.
[3] Fox. [4] Gavin Hamilton.
[5] The chosen champions of the *Auld Light*, in Ayrshire, presented, in many particulars of personal conduct and demeanour, as broad a mark as ever tempted the shafts of a satirist. That Burns has grossly overcharged the portraits of them, deepening the shadows that were sufficiently dark, and excluding altogether those brighter, and perhaps softer, traits of character which redeemed the originals within the sympathies of many of the worthiest and best of men, seems equally clear.—*Lockhart*, p. 62.

[1] A knoll where wizards have held tryste.
[2] Said by Burns, at the request of the Earl of Selkirk.

But now she's floating down the Nith,
For Solway fish a feast.
Peg Nicholson was a gude bay mare,
An' the priest he rode her sair;
An' meikle oppress'd an' bruised she was,
As priest-rid cattle are.

ON SEEING MISS FONTENELLE IN A FAVOURITE CHARACTER.

SWEET naïveté of feature,
Simple, wild, enchanting elf,
Not to thee, but thanks to Nature,
Thou art acting but thyself.

Wert thou awkward, stiff, affected,
Spurning nature, torturing art;
Loves and graces all rejected,
Then indeed thou'd'st act a part.

THE LEAGUE AND COVENANT.[1]

THE Solemn League and Covenant
Cost Scotland blood—cost Scotland tears:
But it seal'd Freedom's sacred cause—
If thou 'rt a slave, indulge thy sneers.

ON MISS JESSY LEWARS.

TALK not to me of savages,
From Afric's burning sun,
No savage e'er could rend my heart,
As, Jessy, thou hast done.

But Jessy's lovely hand in mine,
A mutual faith to plight,
Not ev'n to view the Heavenly choir,
Would be so blest a sight.

[1] In reply to a gentleman who undervalued the sufferings of Scotland "for conscience' sake."

EPITAPH ON MISS JESSY LEWARS.[1]

SAY, Sages, what's the charm on earth
Can turn Death's dart aside?
It is not purity and worth,
Else Jessy had not died.

THE RECOVERY OF JESSY LEWARS.

BUT rarely seen since Nature's birth,
The natives of the sky,
Yet still one Seraph's left on earth,
For Jessy did not die.

THE TOAST.

FILL me with the rosy wine,
Call a toast, a toast divine;
Give the Poet's darling flame,
Lovely Jessy be the name;
Then thou mayest freely boast,
Thou hast given a peerless toast.

THE KIRK OF LAMINGTON.

As cauld a wind as ever blew,
A caulder kirk, and in't but few;
As cauld a minister's e'er spak,
Ye'se a' be het[2] ere I come back.

INSCRIPTION ON A GOBLET.

THERE's death in the cup—sae beware!
Nay, more—there is danger in touching;
But wha can avoid the fell snare?
The man and his wine sae bewitching!

[1] Playfully written, when she was indisposed.
[2] Hot.

TO MISS C.—WRITTEN ON A BLANK LEAF OF ONE OF MISS HANNAH MORE'S WORKS.

THOU flattering mark of friendship kind,
Still may thy pages call to mind
The dear, the beauteous donor:
Though sweetly female every part,
Yet such a head, and more the heart,
Does both the sexes honour.
She show'd her taste refined and just
When she selected thee,
Yet deviating, own I must,
For so approving me.
But kind still, I'll mind still
The giver in the gift;
I'll bless her and wiss her
A Friend above the Lift.[1]

THE BOOK-WORMS.[2]

THROUGH and through the inspired leaves,
Ye maggots, make your windings;
But, oh! respect his Lordship's taste,
And spare his golden bindings.

WILLIE CHALMERS.[3]

WI' braw new branks in mickle pride,
And eke a braw new brechan,[4]
My Pegasus I'm got astride,
And up Parnassus pechin;[5]

[1] Sky.
[2] Suggested by a splendidly bound, but worm-eaten copy of Shakspeare.
[3] Mr. Chalmers, a gentleman in Ayrshire, a particular friend of mine, asked me to write a poetic epistle to a young lady, his Dulcinea. I had seen her, but was scarcely acquainted with her, and wrote as follows.—R. B.
[4] With new bridle and collar.
[5] Panting.

Whiles owre a bush wi' downward crush,
The doited beastie stammers;
Then up he gets, and off he sets,
For sake o' Willie Chalmers.

I doubt na, lass, that weel-kenn'd name
May cost a pair o' blushes;
I am nae stranger to your fame,
Nor his warm-urged wishes.
Your bonnie face sae mild and sweet,
His honest heart enamours,
And, faith, ye'll no be lost a whit,
Tho' waired on Willie Chalmers.

Auld Truth hersel' might swear ye're fair,
And Honour safely back her,
And Modesty assume your air,
And ne'er a ane mistak her:
And sic twa love-inspiring een
Might fire ev'n holy Palmers;
Nae wonder then they've fatal been
To honest Willie Chalmers.

I doubt nae fortune may you shore
Some mim-mou'd[1] pouthered priestie;
Fu' lifted up wi' Hebrew lore,
And band upon his breastie:
But, oh! what signifies to you,
His lexicons and grammars;
The feeling heart's the royal blue,
And that's wi' Willie Chalmers.

Some gapin' glowrin' countra laird
May warsle for your favour;
May claw his lug, and straik his beard,
And hoast up some palaver;
My bonny maid, before ye wed
Sic clumsy-witted hammers,
Seek Heaven for help, and barefit skelp
Awa' wi' Willie Chalmers.

Forgive the Bard! my fond regard,
For ane that shares my bosom,
Inspires my Muse to gie 'm his dues,
For deil a hair I roose[2] him.
May powers aboon unite you soon,
And fructify your amours,—
And every year come in mair dear
To you and Willie Chalmers.

[1] Gentle-mouthed. [2] Praise.

ON ROBERT RIDDEL.

To Riddel, much-lamented man,
This ivied cot was dear;
Reader, dost value matchless worth?
The ivied cot revere.

TO JOHN TAYLOR.[1]

With Pegasus upon a day,
Apollo, weary flying,—
Through frosty hills the journey lay,
On foot the way was plying.

Poor slip-shod giddy Pegasus
Was but a sorry walker;
To Vulcan then Apollo goes,
To get a frosty calker.

Obliging Vulcan fell to work,
Threw by his coat and bonnet,
And did Sol's business in a crack;
Sol paid him with a sonnet.

Ye Vulcan's sons of Wanlockhead,
Pity my sad disaster;
My Pegasus is poorly shod—
I'll pay you like my master.

LINES WRITTEN ON A BANK-NOTE.

The following verses, in the handwriting of Burns, were copied from a bank-note, in the possession of Mr. James F. Gracie, of Dumfries. The note is of the Bank of Scotland, and is dated on the 1st of March, 1780.

Wae worth thy power, thou cursed leaf!
Fell source o' a' my woe and grief!
For lack o' thee I've lost my lass!
For lack o' thee I scrimp my glass.
I see the children of affliction
Unaided, thro' thy curs'd restriction.
I've seen the oppressor's cruel smile,
Amid his hapless victim's spoil,
And for thy potence vainly wish'd,
To crush the villain in the dust.
For lack o' thee I leave this much-lov'd shore,
Never, perhaps, to greet old Scotland more.

[1] Burns, during one of his excise journeys, on a winter day, found it necessary to get his horse's shoes "roughed." The blacksmith was very busy; and the Poet sought Mr. Taylor's influence in obtaining his aid.

BURNS—EXTEMPORE.

Ye true 'Loyal Natives,'[1] attend to my song,
In uproar and riot rejoice the night long;
From envy and hatred your corps is exempt:
But where is your shield from the darts of contempt?

REMORSE.[2]

Of all the numerous ills that hurt our peace,
That press the soul, or wring the mind with anguish,
Beyond comparison, the worst are those
That to our folly, or our guilt, we owe.

[1] The political fever ran high in 1794, and a member of a club at Dumfries, called the Loyal Natives, in a violent paroxysm, produced some verses to which Burns gave the extempore reply.

[2] I entirely agree with that judicious philosopher, Mr. Smith, in his excellent "Theory of Moral Sentiments," that remorse is the most painful sentiment that can embitter the human bosom. Any ordinary pitch of fortitude may bear up tolerably well under those calamities in the procurement of which we ourselves have had no hand; but when our own follies or crimes have made us miserable and wretched, to bear up with manly firmness, and at the same time have a proper penitential sense of our misconduct, is a glorious effort of self-command.—R. B.

In every other circumstance, the mind
Has this to say—"It was no deed of mine;"
But when to all the evil of misfortune
This sting is added—"Blame thy foolish self!"
Or worser far, the pangs of keen Remorse;
The torturing, gnawing consciousness of guilt—
Of guilt, perhaps, where we've involved others;
The young, the innocent, who fondly lov'd us;
Nay, more, that very love their cause of ruin!
O burning hell! in all thy store of torments,
There's not a keener lash!
Lives there a man so firm, who, while his heart
Feels all the bitter horrors of his crime,
Can reason down its agonizing throbs;
And, after proper purpose of amendment,
Can firmly force his jarring thoughts to peace?
O, happy! happy! enviable man!
O glorious magnanimity of soul!

TO ———.

Mossgiel, ——, 1786.

Sir,
Yours this moment I unseal,
And faith I'm gay and hearty!
To tell the truth an' shame the Deil,
I am as fu' as Bartie:[1]
But foorsday, Sir, my promise leal
Expect me o' your party,
If on a beastie I can speel,[2]
Or hurl in a cartie. R. B.

IN VAIN WOULD PRUDENCE.

In vain would Prudence, with decorous sneer,
Point out a cens'ring world, and bid me fear;
Above that world on wings of love I rise,
I know its worst—and do that worst despise.
"Wrong'd, injur'd, shunn'd, unpitied, unredrest,—
The mock'd quotation of the scorner's jest,"
Let Prudence' direst bodements on me fall,
Clarinda, rich reward! o'erpays them all!

[1] A proverb for a drinker. [2] Climb.

THOUGH FICKLE FORTUNE.[1]

Though fickle Fortune has deceiv'd me,
She promis'd fair and perform'd but ill;
Of mistress, friends, and wealth bereav'd me,
Yet I bear a heart shall support me still.—

I'll act with prudence as far's I'm able,
But if success I must never find,
Then come, Misfortune, I bid thee welcome,
I'll meet thee with an undaunted mind.

[1] The above was an extempore, under the pressure of a heavy train of misfortunes, which, indeed, threatened to undo me altogether. It was just at the close of that dreadful period before mentioned (March, 1784); and though the weather has brightened up a little with me since, yet there has always been a tempest brewing round me in the grim sky of futurity, which I pretty plainly see will some time or other, perhaps ere long, overwhelm me, and drive me into some doleful dell, to pine in solitary, squalid wretchedness. However, as I hope my poor country Muse, who, all rustic, awkward, and unpolished as she is, has more charms for me than any other of the pleasures of life beside—as I hope she will not then desert me, I may even then learn to be, if not happy, at least easy, and *sowth a sang* to soothe my misery.—R. B.

I BURN, I BURN.[1]

"I BURN, I burn, as when thro' ripen'd corn,
By driving winds the crackling flames are borne,"
Now maddening, wild, I curse that fatal night;
Now bless the hour which charm'd my guilty sight.
In vain the laws their feeble force oppose:
Chain'd at his feet they groan, Love's vanquish'd foes;
In vain Religion meets my sinking eye;
dare not combat—but I turn and fly;
Conscience in vain upbraids th' unhallowed fire;
ove grasps his scorpions—stifled they expire!
Reason drops headlong from his sacred throne,
Your dear idea reigns and reigns alone:
Each thought intoxicated homage yields,
and riots wanton in forbidden fields!

By all on high adoring mortals know!
By all the conscious villain fears below!
By your dear self!—the last great oath I swear;
For life nor soul were ever half so dear!

TAM THE CHAPMAN.[2]

s Tam, the Chapman, on a day
Wi' Death forgather'd by the way,
'eel pleas'd, he greets a wight sae famous,
nd Death was nae less pleased wi' Thomas,
ha cheerfully lays down the pack,
d there blaws up a hearty crack;
His social, friendly, honest heart,
Sae tickled Death they could na part:
Sae after viewing knives and garters,
Death takes him hame to gie him quarters.

TO DR. MAXWELL, ON MISS JESSY STAIG'S RECOVERY.[1]

MAXWELL, if merit here you crave,
That merit I deny:
You save fair Jessy from the grave!
An Angel could not die.

THE PARVENU,

WRITTEN IN REPLY TO THE BOASTINGS OF AN ILL-EDUCATED COXCOMB, WHO WAS BORING THE COMPANY WITH AN ACCOUNT OF THE MANY GREAT PEOPLE HE HAD BEEN VISITING.

No more of your titled acquaintances boast,
And in what lordly circles you've been;
An insect is still but an insect at most,
Tho' it crawl on the head of a queen

TO THE OWL.

BY JOHN M'CREDDIE.[2]

SAD Bird of Night, what sorrow calls thee forth,
To vent thy plaints thus in the midnight hour;
Is it some blast that gathers in the north,
Threat'ning to nip the verdure of thy bow'r?

Is it, sad Owl, that Autumn strips the shade,
And leaves thee here, unshelter'd and forlorn?

---

[1] To Clarinda.

[2] Mr. Kennedy, who is styled "Chapman," in allusion to his connexion with mercantile house, as agent.

[1] "Dr. Maxwell," says Burns in a letter to Thomson, "was the physician who seemingly saved her from the grave;" and accordingly the poet wrote the above epigram.

[2] Mr. M'Creddie is supposed to be a mythical personage, the verses having been found in the hand-writing of Burns.

Or fear that Winter will thy nest invade?
Or friendly Melancholy bids thee mourn?

Shut out, lone Bird, from all the feather'd train,
To tell thy sorrows to th' unheeding gloom;
No friend to pity when thou dost complain,
Grief all thy thought, and solitude thy home.

Sing on, sad mourner! I will bless thy strain,
And pleased in sorrow listen to thy song:
Sing on, sad mourner! to the night complain,
While the lone echo wafts thy notes along.

Is beauty less, when down the glowing cheek
Sad piteous tears in native sorrows fall?
Less kind the heart, when Sorrow bids it break?
Less happy he who lists to Pity's call?

Ah no, sad Owl! nor is thy voice less sweet,
That Sadness tunes it, and that Grief is there;
That Spring's gay notes, unskill'd, thou canst repeat;
And Sorrow bids thee to the gloom repair.

Nor that the treble songsters of the day,
Are quite estranged, sad Bird of night! from thee;
Nor that the thrush deserts the evening spray,
When darkness calls thee from thy reverie.

From some old tower, thy melancholy dome,
While the grey walls and desert solitudes
Return each note, responsive, to the gloom
Of ivied coverts and surrounding woods;

There hooting, I will list more pleased to thee,
Than ever lover to the nightingale;
Or drooping wretch, oppress'd with misery,
Lending his ear to some condoling tale.

WAS E'ER PUIR POET.[1]

"WAS e'er puir Poet sae befitted,
The maister drunk—the horse committed:
Puir harmless beast! tak thee nae care
Thou'lt be a horse, when he's nae mai (mayor)."

THERE'S NAETHING LIKE THE HONEST NAPPY.

THERE'S naething like the hone: nappy!
Whaur'll ye e'er see men sae happy,
Or women sonsie, saft, an' sappy,
'Tween morn and morn,
As them wha like to taste the drappi
In glass or horn.

I've seen me daez't upon a time;
I scarce could wink or see a styme;[2]
Just ae hauf muchkin[3] does me prim
Ought less is little;
Then back I rattle on the rhyme
As gleg's a whittle!

TO THE RUINS OF LINCLU DEN ABBEY.[4]

YE holy walls, that still sublime
Resist the crumbling touch of Time,

---

[1] Burns once visited Carlisle; a while he was in the condition wh his verses describe, the Mayor put horse, which had trespassed on a c poration meadow, into the "pound.

[2] Glimmer. [3] Half-a-pi

[4] On the banks of the river Clud near Dumfries. The verses w

:Iow strongly still your form displays
['he piety of ancient days.
\s through your ruins, hoar and grey—
Ruins, yet beauteous in decay—
[he silvery moonbeams trembling fly,
[he forms of ages long gone by
Crowd thick on Fancy's wond'ring eye,
\nd wake the soul to musings high.
:v'n now, as lost in thought profound,
: view the solemn scene around,
\nd pensive gaze with wistful eyes,
['he past returns, the present flies;
\gain the dome, in pristine pride,
.ifts high its roof, and arches wide,
:hat, knit with curious tracery
Each Gothic ornament display;
:he high-arched windows, painted fair,
;how many a saint and martyr there;
\s on their slender forms I gaze,
/Iethinks they brighten to a blaze;
Vith noiseless step and taper bright,
Vhat are yon forms that meet my sight?
·lowly they move, while every eye
s heavenward raised in ecstasy:—
['is the fair, spotless, vestal train,
'hat seeks in prayer the midnight fane.
.nd hark! what more than mortal sound
)f music breathes the pile around?
['is the soft-chaunted choral song,
/hose tones the echoing aisles prolong:
'ill thence return'd they softly stray
'er Cluden's wave with fond delay;
[ow on the rising gale swell high,
n'd now in fainting murmurs die:
he boatmen on Nith's gentle stream,
hat glistens in the pale moon's beam,
uspend their dashing oars to hear
he holy anthem, loud and clear;
ach worldly thought awhile forbear,
nd mutter forth a half-formed prayer.
ut as I gaze, the vision fails,
ike frost-work touch'd by southern gales;
he altar sinks, the tapers fade,
nd all the splendid scene's decay'd.
ı window fair the painted pane
o longer glows with holy stain,
.ıt, through the broken glass, the gale
.ows chilly from the misty vale.

cribed to Burns by an anonymous :iter, and are included in later editions his works.

The bird of eve flits sullen by,
Her home, these aisles and arches high:
The choral hymn, that erst so clear
Broke softly sweet on Fancy's ear,
Is drown'd amid the mournful scream,
That breaks the magic of my dream:
Roused by the sound, I start and see
The ruin'd, sad reality.

PROLOGUE,[1]

SPOKEN BY MR. WOODS, ON HIS BENEFIT NIGHT,

MONDAY, APRIL 16, 1787.

When by a generous Public's kind acclaim,
That dearest meed is granted—honest fame:
When here your favour is the actor's lot,
Nor ev'n the man in private life forgot;
What breast, so dead to heav'nly virtue's glow,
But heaves impassion'd with the grateful throe?
Poor is the task to please a barb'rous throng,
It needs no Siddons' power in Southern's song:
But here an ancient nation, fam'd afar
For genius, learning high, as great in war—
Hail, Caledonia! name for ever dear!
Before whose sons I'm honour'd to appear!
Where every science, every nobler art—
That can inform the mind, or mend the heart,
Is known; as grateful nations oft have found,
Far as the rude barbarian marks the bound.
Philosophy, no idle, pedant dream,
Here holds her search, by heaven-taught Reason's beam;

[1] Ascribed to Burns on very slight evidence.

Here History paints, with elegance and force,
The tide of Empire's fluctuating course;
Here Douglas forms wild Shakespeare into plan,
And Harley rouses all the God in man.
When well-form'd taste and sparkling wit unite,
With manly lore, or female beauty bright
(Beauty, where faultless symmetry and grace,
Can only charm us in the second place),
Witness my heart, how oft with panting fear,
As on this night, I've met these judges here!
But still the hope Experience taught to live,
Equal to judge—you're candid to forgive.
No hundred-headed Riot here we meet,
With decency and law beneath his feet,
Nor Insolence assumes fair Freedom's name;
Like Caledonians, you applaud or blame.
  O Thou, dread Power! whose empire-giving hand
Has oft been stretch'd to shield the honour'd land!
Strong may she glow with all her ancient fire;
May every son be worthy of his sire;
Firm may she rise with generous disdain
At Tyranny's, or direr Pleasure's, chain;
Still self-dependent in her native shore,
Bold may she brave grim Danger's loudest roar
Till Fate the curtain drop on worlds to be no more!

TRAGIC FRAGMENT.[1]

"ALL devil as I am, a damned wretch,
A harden'd, stubborn, unrepenting villain,
Still my heart melts at human wretchedness;
And with sincere, tho' unavailing, sigh
I view the helpless children of distress
With tears indignant I behold the oppressor
Rejoicing in the honest man's destruction,
Whose unsubmitting heart was all hi crime.
Ev'n you, ye helpless crew, I pity you
Ye, whom the seeming good think si to pity;
Ye poor, despis'd, abandon'd vagabonds
Whom Vice, as usual, has turn'd o'e to Ruin.
O but for kind, tho' ill-requited friends
I had been driven forth like you, for lorn,
The most detested, worthless wretc among you!
O injur'd God! thy goodness has en dow'd me
With talents passing most of my com peers,
Which I in just proportion have abus'
As far surpassing other common vil lains,
As Thou in natural parts hadst give me more."

O CAN YE LABOUR LEA.

O CAN ye labour lea, young man,
  An' can ye labour lea;
Gae back the gate ye cam' again,
  Ye'se never scorn me.

[1] In my early years nothing less would serve me than courting the Tragic Muse. I was, I think, about eightee or nineteen when I sketched the ou lines of a tragedy, forsooth: but tl bursting of a cloud of family misfo tunes, which had for some time threa ened us, prevented my further pr gress. In those days I never wro down anything; so, except a speec or two, the whole has escaped m memory. The following, which I mo distinctly remember, was an exclar ation from a great character—great occasional instances of generosity, ar daring at times in villanies.—R. B.

I feed a man at Martinmas,
  Wi' airl[1]-pennies three;
An' a' the faut I fan' wi' him,
  He couldna labour lea.

The stibble rig is easy plough'd,
  The fallow land is free;
But wha wad keep the handless coof,
  That couldna labour lea?

O Thou, in whom we live and move,
  Who mad'st the sea and shore;
Thy goodness constantly we prove,
  And grateful would adore.

And if it please thee, Pow'r above!
  Still grant us with such store,
The friend we trust, the fair we love,
  And we desire no more.

---

[1] Silver penny given as hiring money.

SONGS.

THE LASS O' BALLOCHMYLE.[1]

TUNE—"MISS FORBES'S FAREWELL TO BANFF."

'TWAS even—the dewy fields were green,
On every blade the pearls hang,
The Zephyrs wanton'd round the bean,
And bore its fragrant sweets alang:
In every glen the Mavis sang,
All nature listening seem'd the while,
Except where green-wood echoes rang,
Amang the braes o' Ballochmyle.

With careless step I onward stray'd,
My heart rejoic'd in nature's joy,
When musing in a lonely glade,
A maiden fair I chanc'd to spy;
Her look was like the morning's eye,
Her air like nature's vernal smile,
Perfection whisper'd, passing by,
"Behold the Lass o' Ballochmyle!"

Fair is the morn in flowery May,
And sweet is night in Autumn mild,
When roving thro' the garden gay,
Or wandering in a lonely wild:
But Woman, Nature's darling child!
There all her charms she does compile;
Ev'n there her other works are foil'd
By the bonnie Lass o' Ballochmyle.

O, had she been a country maid,
And I the happy country swain,
Tho' shelter'd in the lowest shed
That ever rose in Scotland's plain:
Thro' weary Winter's wind and rain,
With joy, with rapture, I would toil
And nightly to my bosom strain
The bonnie Lass o' Ballochmyle.

Then pride might climb the slipp'ry steep,
Where fame and honours lofty shine
And thirst of gold might tempt th deep,
Or downward seek the Indian mine
Give me the cot below the pine,
To tend the flocks, or till the soil,
And every day have joys divine
With the bonnie Lass o' Ballochmyle.[1]

---

[1] "The Lass of Ballochmyle" was Miss Alexander, whose brother had recently come to reside in Ballochmyle House, of which the pleasure grounds extend along the north bank of the Ayr. The farm of Burns, Mossgiel, was in the immediate neighbourhood.—He inclosed a copy of the song to Miss Alexander, and was extremely indignant at the lady's silence respecting his letter. Of the verses his own opinion was justly high:—"I think myself," he told Mrs. Stewart of Stair, "it has some merit, both as a tolerable description of one of Nature's scenes—a July evening, and one of the finest pieces of Nature's workmanship,—the finest indeed we know anything of—an amiable, beautiful young woman."

[1] Under the above song is writte "Miss Willie Alexander."

SONG OF DEATH.[1]

A GAELIC AIR.

Scene—A field of battle. Time of the day—Evening. The wounded and dying of the victorious army are supposed to join in the song.

FAREWELL, thou fair day, thou green earth, and ye skies,
Now gay with the broad setting sun!
Farewell, loves and friendships, ye dear, tender ties,
Our race of existence is run!

Thou grim King of Terrors, thou life's gloomy foe!
Go, frighten the coward and slave!
Go, teach them to tremble, fell tyrant! but know,
No terrors hast thou for the brave!

Thou strik'st the dull peasant — he sinks in the dark,
Nor saves e'en the wreck of a name;
Thou strik'st the young hero—a glorious mark!
He falls in the blaze of his fame!

In the field of proud honour—our swords in our hands,
Our King and our Country to save—
While victory shines on life's last ebbing sands,
O! who would not die with the brave!

MY AIN KIND DEARIE! O.

WHEN o'er the hill the eastern star
Tells bughtin-time[2] is near, my jo;

[1] When the pressing nature of public affairs called, in 1795, for a general arming of the people, Burns appeared in the ranks of the "Dumfries Volunteers," employed his poetical talents in stimulating their patriotism; and at this season of alarm he brought forward the following hymn.—(CURRIE.) The song was written in 1791.

[2] Time of collecting the sheep.

And owsen[1] frae the furrow'd field
Return sae dowf and wearie, O;
Down by the burn, where scented birks
Wi' dew are hanging clear, my jo,
I'll meet thee on the lea-rig,
My ain kind dearie! O.

In mirkest glen, at midnight hour,
I'd rove, and ne'er be eerie, O.
If thro' that glen I gaed to thee,
My ain kind dearie, O.
Altho' the night were ne'er sae wild,
And I were ne'er sae wearie, O,
I'd meet thee on the lea-rig,
My ain kind dearie! O.

The hunter lo'es the morning sun,
To rouse the mountain deer, my jo;
At noon the fisher seeks the glen,
Along the burn to steer, my jo;
Gie me the hour o' gloamin' grey,
It maks my heart sae cheery, O,
To meet thee on the lea-rig,
My ain kind dearie! O.

AULD ROB MORRIS.

THERE'S auld Rob Morris that wons[2] in yon glen,
He's the king o' guid fellows and wale of auld men;
He has gowd in his coffers, he has owsen and kine,
And ae bonnie lassie, his darling and mine.

She's fresh as the morning, the fairest in May;
She's sweet as the evening amang the new hay;
As blythe and as artless as lamb on the lea,
And dear to my heart, as the light to my e'e.

But oh! she's an heiress, auld Robin's a laird,
And my daddie has nought but a cot-house and yard;
A wooer like me maunna hope to come speed;
The wound I must hide that will soon be my dead.

[1] Oxen. [2] Dwells.

The day comes to me, but delight brings me nane;
The night comes to me, but my rest it is gane:
I wander my lane, like a night-troubled ghaist,
And I sigh as my heart it wad burst in my breast.

O had she but been of a lower degree,
I then might hae hop'd she wad smil'd upon me;
O how past describing had then been my bliss,
As now my distraction no words can express!

NAEBODY.

I HAE a wife o' my ain,
I'll partake wi' naebody;
I'll tak cuckold frae nane,
I'll gie cuckold to naebody.

I hae a penny to spend,
There—thanks to naebody;
I hae naething to lend,
I'll borrow frae naebody.

I am naebody's lord,
I'll be slave to naebody;
I hae a guid braid sword,
I'll tak dunts[1] frae naebody.

I'll be merry and free,
I'll be sad for naebody;
If naebody care for me,
I'll care for naebody.

MY WIFE'S A WINSOME WEE THING.[2]

SHE is a winsome wee thing,
She is a handsome wee thing,
She is a bonnie wee thing,
This sweet wee wife o' mine.

I never saw a fairer,
I never lo'ed a dearer,
And neist[1] my heart I'll wear her,
For fear my jewel tine.

She is a winsome wee thing,
She is a handsome wee thing,
She is a bonnie wee thing,
This sweet wee wife o' mine.

The warld's wrack we share o't,
The warstle and the care o't;
Wi' her I'll blythely bear it,
And think my lot divine.

DUNCAN GRAY.[2]

DUNCAN GRAY came here to woo,
Ha, ha, the wooing o't,
On blythe yule[3] night when we were fou,
Ha, ha, the wooing o't.
Maggie coost[4] her head fu' high,
Look'd asklent and unco skeigh,[5]
Gart poor Duncan stand abeigh;[6]
Ha, ha, the wooing o't.

---

[1] Knocks.

[2] There is a peculiar rhythmus in many of our airs, and a necessity of adapting syllables to the emphasis, or what I would call the *feature-notes* of the tune, that cramp the poet, and lay him under almost insuperable difficulties. For instance, in the air, "My Wife's a wanton wee Thing," if a few lines, smooth and pretty, can be adapted to it, it is all you can expect. The following were made extempore to it: and though, on further study, I might give you something more profound, yet it might not suit the light-horse gallop of the air so well as this random clink.—BURNS *to Thomson.*

[1] Next.

[2] The foregoing I submit to your better judgment; acquit them or condemn them as seemeth good in your sight. "Duncan Gray" is that kind of light-horse gallop of an air which precludes sentiment. The ludicrous is its ruling feature.—BURNS *to Thomson.*

[3] Christmas. [4] Tossed. [5] Proud.

[6] At a shy distance.

Duncan fleech'd,[1] and Duncan pray'd;
Ha, ha, &c.
Meg was deaf as Ailsa Craig,
Ha, ha, &c.
Duncan sigh'd baith out and in,
Grat his een baith bleer't and blin',[2]
Spak o' lowpin o'er a linn;[3]
Ha, ha, &c.

Time and chance are but a tide,
Ha, ha, &c.
Slighted love is sair to bide,
Ha, ha, &c.
Shall I, like a fool, quoth he,
For a haughty hizzie die?
She may gae to—France for me!
Ha, ha, &c.

How it comes let doctors tell,
Ha, ha, &c.
Meg grew sick—as he grew well,
Ha, ha, &c.
Something in her bosom wrings,
For relief a sigh she brings;
And O, her een, they spak sic things!
Ha, ha, &c.

Duncan was a lad o' grace,
Ha, ha, &c.
Maggie's was a piteous case,
Ha, ha, &c.
Duncan couldna be her death,
Swelling pity smoor'd[4] his wrath;
Now they're crouse and cantie[5] baith,
Ha, ha, the wooing o't.

O POORTITH.

TUNE—"I HAD A HORSE."

O POORTITH cauld, and restless love,
Ye wreck my peace between ye;
Yet poortith a' I could forgive,
An' 'twere na for my Jeanie.
O why should fate sic pleasure have,
Life's dearest bands untwining?
Or why sae sweet a flower as love
Depend on Fortune's shining?

This warld's wealth when I think on,
Its pride, and a' the lave o't;
Fie, fie on silly coward man,
That he should be the slave o't.
O why, &c.

Her e'en sae bonnie blue betray
How she repays my passion;
But prudence is her o'erword aye,
She talks of rank and fashion.
O why, &c.

O wha can prudence think upon,
And sic a lassie by him?
O wha can prudence think upon,
And sae in love as I am?
O why, &c.

How blest the humble cotter's fate!
He woos his simple dearie;
The sillie bogles,[1] wealth and state,
Can never make them eerie.
O why should fate sic pleasure have,
Life's dearest bands untwining?
Or why sae sweet a flower as love
Depend on Fortune's shining?

GALLA WATER.

THERE'S braw, braw lads on Yarrow braes,
That wander thro' the blooming heather;
But Yarrow braes, nor Ettric shaws,
Can match the lads o' Galla Water.

But there is ane, a secret ane,
Aboon them a' I lo'e him better;
And I'll be his, and he'll be mine,
The bonnie lad o' Galla Water.

Altho' his daddie was nae laird,
And tho' I hae nae miekle tocher;[2]
Yet rich in kindest, truest love,
We'll tent our flocks by Galla Water.

It ne'er was wealth, it ne'er was wealth,
That coft[3] contentment, peace, or pleasure;
The bands and bliss o' mutual love,
O that's the chiefest warld's treasure!

---

[1] Besought. [2] Bleared and blind. [3] Precipice. [4] Smothered. [5] Cheerful and merry.

[1] Hobgoblins. [2] Marriage portion [3] Bought.

LORD GREGORY.[1]

O MIRK, mirk is this midnight hour,
And loud the tempest's roar;
A waefu' wanderer seeks thy tow'r,
Lord Gregory,—ope thy door.

An exile frae her father's ha',
And a' for loving thee;
At least some pity on me shaw,
If love it mayna be.

Lord Gregory, mind'st thou not the grove,
By bonnie Irwine side,
Where first I own'd that virgin-love,
I lang, lang had denied?

How aften didst thou pledge and vow,
Thou wad for aye be mine!
And my fond heart, itsel sae true,
It ne'er mistrusted thine.

Hard is thy heart, Lord Gregory,
And flinty is thy breast:
Thou dart of heaven that flashest by,
O wilt thou give me rest!

Ye mustering thunders from above,
Your willing victim see!
But spare, and pardon my fause love,
His wrangs to heaven and me!

OPEN THE DOOR TO ME, OH!

WITH ALTERATIONS.

OH, open the door, some pity to shew,
Oh, open the door to me, oh!
Tho' thou hast been false, I'll ever prove true,
Oh, open the door to me, oh!

Cauld is the blast upon my pale cheek,
But caulder thy love for me, oh!

[1] A friend of Burns writes—"We had the song of 'Lord Gregory,' which I asked for to have an opportunity of calling on Burns to recite his ballad to that tune. He did recite it, and such was the effect that a dead silence ensued."

The frost, that freezes the life at my heart,
Is nought to my pains fra thee, oh!

The wan moon is setting behind the white wave,
And time is setting with me, oh!
False friends, false love, farewell! for mair
I'll ne'er trouble them, nor thee, oh!

She has open'd the door, she has open'd it wide;
She sees his pale corse on the plain, oh!
My true love! she cried, and sank down by his side,
Never to rise again, oh!

MEG O' THE MILL.

AIR—"HEY, BONNIE LASS, WILL YOU LIE IN A BARRACK."

O KEN ye what Meg o' the Mill has gotten?
An' ken ye what Meg o' the Mill has gotten?
She has gotten a coof[1] wi' a claut[2] o' siller,
And broken the heart o' the barley Miller.

The Miller was strappin, the Miller was ruddy;
A heart like a lord, and a hue like a lady;
The Laird was a widdiefu', bleerit[3] knurl;
She's left the guid fellow and ta'en the churl.

The Miller he hecht her a heart leal and loving;
The Laird did address her wi' matter mair moving,
A fine pacing horse wi' a clear chained bridle,
A whip by her side, and a bonnie side-saddle.

[1] Blockhead. [2] A scraping. [3] Crooked, bleared.

O wae on the siller, it is sae prevailing;
And wae on the love that is fixed on a mailen![1]
A tocher's nae word in a true lover's parle,[2]
But, gie me my love, and a fig for the warl!

JESSIE.

TUNE—"BONNIE DUNDEE."

TRUE hearted was he, the sad swain o' the Yarrow,
And fair are the maids on the banks o' the Ayr,
But by the sweet side o' the Nith's winding river,
Are lovers as faithful, and maidens as fair:
To equal young Jessie seek Scotland all over;
To equal young Jessie you seek it in vain;
Grace, beauty, and elegance fetter her lover,
And maidenly modesty fixes the chain.

O, fresh is the rose in the gay, dewy morning,
And sweet is the lily at evening close;
But in the fair presence o' lovely young Jessie,
Unseen is the lily, unheeded the rose.
Love sits in her smile, a wizard ensnaring;
Enthron'd in her een he delivers his la'.
And still to her charms she alone is a stranger,—
Her modest demeanour's the jewel of a'.

WANDERING WILLIE.

HERE awa, there awa, wandering Willie;
Now tired with wandering, haud awa hame;
Come to my bosom, my ain only dearie,
Tell me thou bring'st me my Willie the same.

Winter winds blew loud and cauld at our parting,
Fears for my Willie brought the tear in my e'e;
Now welcome the simmer, and welcome my Willie,
The simmer to nature, my Willie to me!

Rest, ye wild storms, in the cave o' your slumbers;
How your dread howling a lover alarms!
Wauken, ye breezes, row gently, ye billows,
And waft my dear laddie ance mair to my arms.

But oh, if he's faithless, and minds na his Nannie,
O still flow between us, thou wide-roaring main;
May I never see it, may I never trow it,
But, dying, believe that my Willie's my ain.

LOGAN BRAES.

TUNE—"LOGAN WATER."

O LOGAN, sweetly didst thou glide
That day I was my Willie's bride;
And years sinsyne hae o'er us run,
Like Logan to the simmer sun;
But now thy flow'ry banks appear
Like drumlie winter, dark and drear,
While my dear lad maun face his faes,
Far, far frae me and Logan Braes.

Again the merry month o' May
Has made our hills and valleys gay;
The birds rejoice in leafy bowers,
The bees hum round the breathing flowers;

---

[1] Farm. [2] Speech.

[1] The song was the fruit of "three-quarters of an hour's meditation" by the poet in his elbow-chair, on the wickedness of ambition.

Blithe morning lifts his rosy eye,
And evening's tears are tears of joy:
My soul, delightless, a' surveys,
While Willie's far frae Logan Braes.

Within yon milk-white hawthorn bush,
Amang her nestlings, sits the thrush:
Her faithfu' mate will share her toil,
Or wi' his song her cares beguile:
But I wi' my sweet nurslings here,
Nae mate to help, nae mate to cheer,
Pass widow'd nights and joyless days,
While Willie's far frae Logan Braes.

O wae upon you, men o' state,
That brethren rouse to deadly hate!
As ye mak monie a fond heart mourn,
Sae may it on your heads return!
How can your flinty hearts enjoy
The widow's tears, the orphan's cry?
But soon may peace bring happy days,
And Willie hame to Logan Braes!

THERE WAS A LASS.[1]

TUNE—"BONNIE JEAN."

THERE was a lass, and she was fair,
At kirk and market to be seen;
When a' the fairest maids were met,
The fairest maid was bonnie Jean.

And aye she wrought her mammie's wark,
And aye she sang sae merrily;
The blithest bird upon the bush
Had ne'er a lighter heart than she.

But hawks will rob the tender joys
That bless the little lintwhite's nest;
And frost will blight the fairest flowers;
And love will break the soundest rest.

Young Robie was the brawest lad,
The flower and pride of a' the glen;
And he had owsen, sheep, and kye,
And wanton naigies nine or ten.

He gaed wi' Jeanie to the tryste,
He danc'd wi' Jeanie on the down;
And lang ere witless Jeanie wist,
Her heart was tint, her peace was stown.

As in the bosom o' the stream
The moon-beam dwells at dewy e'en,
So trembling, pure, was tender love
Within the breast o' bonnie Jean.

And now she works her mammie's wark,
And aye she sighs wi' care and pain;
Yet wistna what her ail might be,
Or what wad mak her weel again.

But didna Jeanie's heart loup light,
And didna joy blink in her e'e,
As Robie tauld a tale o' love,
Ae e'enin on the lily lea?

The sun was sinking in the west,
The birds sang sweet in ilka grove;
His cheek to hers he fondly prest,
And whisper'd thus his tale o' love:

"O Jeanie fair, I lo'e thee dear;
O canst thou think to fancy me?
Or wilt thou leave thy mammie's cot,
And learn to tent the farms wi' me?

"At barn or byre thou shaltna drudge,
Or naething else to trouble thee;
But stray amang the heather-bells,
And tent the waving corn wi' me."

Now what could artless Jeanie do?
She had na will to say him na:
At length she blush'd a sweet consent,
And love was aye between them twa.

[1] Miss Jean M'Murdo, of Drumlanrig.

PHILLIS THE FAIR.[1]

TUNE—"ROBIN ADAIR."

WHILE larks with little wing
Fann'd the pure air,
Tasting the breathing spring,
Forth I did fare:
Gay the sun's golden eye
Peep'd o'er the mountains high;
Such thy morn! did I cry,
Phillis the fair.

In each bird's careless song
Glad did I share;
While yon wild flowers among,
Chance led me there:
Sweet to the opening day,
Rosebuds bent the dewy spray;

[1] Said to be the sister of Jean M'Murdo.

Such thy bloom! did I say,
Phillis the fair.

Down in a shady walk,
Doves cooing were,
I mark'd the cruel hawk
Caught in a snare:
So kind may Fortune be,
Such make his destiny,
He who would injure thee
Phillis the fair.

BY ALLAN STREAM.[1]

TUNE—"ALLAN WATER."

By Allan stream I chanc'd to rove
While Phœbus sank beyond Ben-leddi;[2]
The winds were whispering thro' the grove,
The yellow corn was waving ready:
I listen'd to a lover's sang,
And thought on youthfu' pleasures manie!
And aye the wild-wood echoes rang—
O dearly do I love thee, Annie![1]

O, happy be the woodbine bower,
Nae nightly bogle mak it eerie;
Nor ever sorrow stain the hour,
The place and time I met my dearie!
Her head upon my throbbing breast,
She, sinking, said "I am thine for ever!"
While monie a kiss the seal imprest,
The sacred vow, we ne'er should sever.

The haunt o' spring's the primrose brae;
The simmer joys the flocks to follow;
How cheery, thro' her shortening day,
Is autumn, in her weeds o' yellow!
But can they melt the glowing heart,
Or chain the soul in speechless pleasure,
Or, thro' each nerve the rapture dart,
Like meeting her, our bosom's treasure!

[1] I walked out yesterday evening, with a volume of the "Museum" in my hand; when turning up "Allan Water," "What numbers shall the Muse repeat," &c., as the words appeared to me rather unworthy of so fine an air, and recollecting that it is on your list, I sat, and raved, under the shade of an old thorn, till I wrote out one to suit the measure. I may be wrong, but I think it not in my worst style. You must know, that in Ramsay's "Tea-table," where the modern song first appeared, the ancient name of the tune, Allan says, is "Allan Water," or "My love Annie's very bonnie." This last has certainly been a line of the original song; so I took up the idea, and, as you will see, have introduced the line in its place, which I presume it formerly occupied; though I likewise give you a *choosing line*, if it should not hit the cut of your fancy. "Bravo," say I: "it is a good song."—Burns *to Thomson.*

[2] A mountain west of Strathallan, 3000 feet high.—R. B

[1] Or, "O my love Annie's very bonnie."—R. B.

WHISTLE, AND I'LL COME TO YOU, MY LAD.

O whistle, and I'll come to you, my lad;
O whistle, and I'll come to you, my lad:
Tho' father and mither and a' should gae mad,
O whistle, and I'll come to you, my lad.

But warily tent, when ye come to court me,
And comena unless the back-yett be a-jee;
Syne up the back-stile, and let naebody see,
And come as ye werena coming to me.
And come, &c.

At Kirk, or at market, whene'er ye meet me,
Gang by me as tho' that ye car'dna a flie:

But steal me a blink o'your bonnie black e'e,
Yet look as ye werena lookin at me.
Yet look, &c.
O whistle, &c.

Aye vow and protest that ye carena for me,
And whiles ye may lightly my beauty a wee;
But courtna anither, tho' jokin ye be,
For fear that she wyle your fancy frae me.
For fear, &c.

O whistle, and I'll come to you, my lad;
O whistle, and I'll come to you, my lad:
Tho' father and mither and a' should gae mad,
O whistle, and I'll come to you, my lad.

HUSBAND, HUSBAND, CEASE YOUR STRIFE.

TUNE—"JO JANET."

"Husband, husband, cease your strife,
Nor longer idly rave, sir;
Tho' I am your wedded wife,
Yet I am not your slave, sir."

"One of two must still obey,
Nancy, Nancy;
Is it man, or woman, say,
My spouse, Nancy?"

"If 'tis still the lordly word,
Service and obedience;
I'll desert my sov'reign lord,
And so, good-bye, allegiance!"

"Sad will I be, so bereft,
Nancy, Nancy!
Yet I'll try to make a shift,
My spouse, Nancy."

"My poor heart then break it must,
My last hour I'm near it:
When you lay me in the dust,
Think, think how you will bear it."

"I will hope and trust in Heaven,
Nancy, Nancy;
Strength to bear it will be given,
My spouse, Nancy."

"Well, sir, from the silent dead
Still I'll try to daunt you;
Ever round your midnight bed
Horrid sprites shall haunt you."

"I'll wed another, like my dear
Nancy, Nancy;
Then all hell will fly for fear,
My spouse, Nancy."

HAD I A CAVE.

TUNE—"ROBIN ADAIR."

Had I a cave on some wild, distant shore,
Where the winds howl to the waves' dashing roar;
There would I weep my woes,
There seek my lost repose,
Till grief my eyes should close,
Ne'er to wake more.

Falsest of womankind, canst thou declare
All thy fond plighted vows—fleeting as air?
To thy new lover hie,
Laugh o'er thy perjury,
Then in thy bosom try,
What peace is there!

DELUDED SWAIN.

TUNE—"THE COLLIER'S DOCHTER."

Deluded swain, the pleasure,
The fickle Fair can give thee,
Is but a fairy treasure,
Thy hopes will soon deceive thee

The billows on the ocean,
The breezes idly roamin',
The clouds' uncertain motion,—
They are but types of woman.

O! art thou not ashamed
To doat upon a feature?
If man thou wouldst be named,
Despise the silly creature.

Go, find an honest fellow;
  Good claret set before thee:
Hold on till thou art mellow,
  And then to bed in glory.

SONG.

TUNE—"THE QUAKER'S WIFE."

Thine am I, my faithful fair,
  Thine, my lovely Nancy;
Ev'ry pulse along my veins,
  Ev'ry roving fancy.

To thy bosom lay my heart,
  There to throb and languish:
Tho' despair had wrung its core,
  That would heal its anguish.

Take away these rosy lips,
  Rich with balmy treasure!
Turn away thine eyes of love,
  Lest I die with pleasure!

What is life when wanting love?
  Night without a morning!
Love's the cloudless summer sun,
  Nature gay adorning.

WILT THOU BE MY DEARIE?[1]

A NEW SCOTS SONG.

TUNE—"THE SUTOR'S DOCHTER."

Wilt thou be my dearie?
When sorrow wrings thy gentle heart,
Wilt thou let me cheer thee?
By the treasure of my soul,
That's the love I bear thee!
I swear and vow that only thou
Shalt ever be my dearie—
Only thou, I swear and vow,
Shalt ever be my dearie.

Lassie, say thou lo'es me;
Or if thou wilt na be my ain,
Say na thou'lt refuse me:
If it winna, canna be,
Thou for thine may choose me,

Let me, lassie, quickly die,
Trusting that thou lo'es me—
Lassie, let me quickly die,
Trusting that thou lo'es me.

HERE IS THE GLEN.[1]

TUNE—"BANKS OF CREE."

Here is the glen, and here the bower,
  All underneath the birchen shade;
The village bell has toll'd the hour,
  O what can stay my lovely maid?

'Tis not Maria's whispering call;
  'Tis but the balmy breathing gale,
Mixt with some warbler's dying fall,
  The dewy star of eve to hail.

It is Maria's voice I hear!
  So calls the woodlark in the grove
His little faithful mate to cheer,
  At once 'tis music—and 'tis love.

And art thou come? and art thou true?
  O welcome, dear to love and me!
And let us all our vows renew,
  Along the flow'ry banks of Cree.

ON THE SEAS AND FAR AWAY.[2]

TUNE—"O'ER THE HILLS AND FAR AWAY."

How can my poor heart be glad,
When absent from my Sailor lad?
How can I the thought forego,
He's on the seas to meet the foe?

---

[1] Burns considered this to be one of his best songs.

[1] I got an air, pretty enough, composed by Lady Elizabeth Heron, of Heron, which she calls "The Banks of the Cree." Cree is a beautiful romantic stream; and as her ladyship is a particular friend of mine, I have written this song to it.—R. B.

[2] Burns was at first pleased with these verses, but he afterwards thought them unequal and "flimsy." And his second thoughts were the best.

Let me wander, let me rove,
Still my heart is with my love;
Nightly dreams and thoughts by day
Are with him that's far away.
On the seas and far away,
On stormy seas and far away;
Nightly dreams and thoughts by day
Are aye with him that's far away.

When in summer's noon I faint,
As weary flocks around me pant,
Haply in this scorching sun
My Sailor's thund'ring at his gun:
Bullets, spare my only joy!
Bullets, spare my darling boy!
Fate, do with me what you may,
Spare but him that's far away!

At the starless midnight hour,
When winter rules with boundless power;
As the storms the forest tear,
And thunders rend the howling air,
Listening to the doubling roar,
Surging on the rocky shore,
All I can—I weep and pray,
For his weal that's far away.

Peace, thy olive wand extend,
And bid wild War his ravage end,
Man with brother man to meet,
And as a brother kindly greet:
Then may Heaven with prosp'rous gales
Fill my Sailor's welcome sails,
To my arms their charge convey,
My dear lad that's far away.
On the seas and far away
On stormy seas and far away;
Nightly dreams and thoughts by day
Are aye with him that's far away.

HARK! THE MAVIS.

TUNE—"CA' THE YOWES TO THE KNOWES."

CHORUS.

Ca' the yowes to the knowes,
Ca' them where the heather grows,
Ca' them where the burnie rows,[1]
My bonnie dearie.

[1] Rolls.

Hark! the mavis' evening sang
Sounding Clouden's woods amang!
Then a faulding let us gang,
My bonnie dearie.
Ca' the, &c.

We'll gae down by Clouden side,
Thro' the hazels spreading wide,
O'er the waves that sweetly glide
To the moon sae clearly.
Ca' the, &c.

Yonder Clouden's silent towers,
Where at moonshine midnight hours,
O'er the dewy-bending flowers,
Fairies dance sae cheery.
Ca' the, &c.

Ghaist nor bogle shalt thou fear;
Thou'rt to love and Heaven sae dear,
Nocht of ill may come thee near,
My bonnie dearie.
Ca' the, &c.

Fair and lovely as thou art,
Thou hast stown[1] my very heart;
I can die—but canna part,
My bonnie dearie.

Ca' the yowes to the knowes,
Ca' them where the heather grows,
Ca' them where the burnie rows,
My bonnie dearie.

SHE SAYS SHE LO'ES ME BEST OF A'.[2]

TUNE—"ONAGH'S WATER-FALL."

Sae flaxen were her ringlets,
Her eyebrows of a darker hue,
Bewitchingly o'erarching
Twa laughing een o' bonnie blue.
Her smiling, sae wyling,
Wad make a wretch forget his woe
What pleasure, what treasure,
Unto these rosy lips to grow!

[1] Stolen.
[2] The lady in whose honour Burns composed this song was Miss Lorimer of Craigieburn.

Such was my Chloris' bonnie face,
  When first her bonnie face I saw,
And aye my Chloris' dearest charm,
  She says she lo'es me best of a'.

Like harmony her motion;
  Her pretty ancle is a spy
Betraying fair proportion,
  Wad make a saint forget the sky;
Sae warming, sae charming,
  Her faultless form and gracefu' air;
Ilk feature—auld Nature
  Declar'd that she could do nae mair:
Hers are the willing chains o' love,
  By conquering Beauty's sovereign law;
And aye my Chloris' dearest charm,
  She says she lo'es me best of a'.

Let others love the city,
  And gaudy show at sunny noon;
Gie me the lonely valley,
  The dewy eve, and rising moon
Fair beaming, and streaming,
  Her silver light the boughs amang;
While falling, recalling,
  The amorous thrush concludes his sang;
There, dearest Chloris, wilt thou rove
  By wimpling burn and leafy shaw,
And hear my vows o' truth and love,
  And say thou lo'es me best of a'?

MY HANDSOME NELL.[1]

TUNE—"I AM A MAN UNMARRIED."

Oh, once I lov'd a bonny lass,
  Ay, and I love her still;
And while that virtue warms my breast
  I'll love my handsome Nell.
    Fal, lal de ral, &c.

As bonny lasses I hae seen,
  And mony full as braw;[1]
But for a modest, gracefu' mien
  The like I never saw.

A bonny lass, I will confess,
  Is pleasant to the e'e,
But without some better qualities
  She's no a lass for me.

But Nelly's looks are blithe and sweet;
  And, what is best of a',
Her reputation is complete,
  And fair without a flaw.

She dresses aye sae clean and neat,
  Baith decent and genteel;
And then there's something in her gait
  Gars[2] ony dress look weel.

A gaudy dress and gentle air
  May slightly touch the heart;
But it's innocence and modesty
  That polishes the dart.

'Tis this in Nelly pleases me,
  'Tis this enchants my soul!
For absolutely in my breast
  She reigns without control.

[1] This was Nelly Fitzpatrick, the daughter of the village blacksmith. "This song," says Burns, "was the first of my performances, and done at an early period of my life, when my heart glowed with honest, warm simplicity—unacquainted and uncorrupted with the ways of a wicked world. It has many faults; but I remember I composed it in a wild enthusiasm of passion; and to this hour I never recollect it but my heart melts—my blood sallies at the remembrance."

HOW LANG AND DREARY.

TUNE—"CAULD KAIL IN ABERDEEN."

How lang and dreary is the night,
  When I am frae my dearie;
I restless lie frae e'en to morn,
  Tho' I were ne'er sae weary.

CHORUS.

For oh! her lanely nights are lang;
  And oh! her dreams are eerie;
And oh! her widow'd heart is sair,
  That's absent frae her dearie.

When I think on the lightsome days
  I spent wi' thee, my dearie?
And now that seas between us roar,—
  How can I be but eerie?
    For oh, &c.

[1] Well-dressed. [2] Makes.

How slow ye move, ye heavy hours ;
The joyless day how drearie !
It wasna sae ye glinted by,
When I was wi' my dearie.
For oh, &c.

LASSIE WI' THE LINT-WHITE LOCKS.

TUNE—"ROTHIEMURCHIE'S RANT."

CHORUS.

Lassie wi' the lint-white locks
Bonnie lassie, artless lassie,
Wilt thou wi' me tent the flocks ?
Wilt thou be my dearie, O ?

Now nature cleeds the flowery lea,
And a' is young and sweet like thee,
O wilt thou share its joys wi' me,
And say thou'lt be my dearie, O ?
Lassie wi', &c.

And when the welcome simmer-shower
Has cheer'd ilk drooping little flower,
We'll to the breathing woodbine bower
At sultry noon, my dearie, O.
Lassie wi', &c.

When Cynthia lights, wi' silver ray,
The weary shearer's hameward way,
Thro' yellow waving fields we'll stray,
And talk o' love, my dearie, O.
Lassie wi', &c.

And when the howling wintry blast
Disturbs my lassie's midnight rest ;
Enclasped to my faithfu' breast,
I'll comfort thee, my dearie, O.
Lassie wi' the lint-white locks,
Bonnie lassie, artless lassie,
Wilt thou wi' me tent the flocks ?
Wilt thou be my dearie, O ?[1]

[1] This piece has at least the merit of being a regular pastoral: the vernal moon, the summer noon, the autumnal evening, and the winter night, are regularly rounded.—R. B.

THE AULD MAN.

TUNE—"GIL MORICE."

But lately seen in gladsome green,
The woods rejoic'd the day,
Thro' gentle showers the laughing flowers
In double pride were gay :
But now our joys are fled,
On winter blasts awa !
Yet maiden May, in rich array
Again shall bring them a'.

But my white pow, nae kindly thowe[1]
Shall melt the snaws of age ;
My trunk of eild, but buss or bield,[2]
Sinks in time's wintry rage.
Oh, age has weary days,
And nights o' sleepless pain !
Thou golden time o' youthfu' prime,
Why com'st thou not again ?

THE LOVER'S MORNING SALUTE TO HIS MISTRESS.[3]

TUNE—"DEIL TAK THE WARS."

Sleep'st thou, or wak'st thou, fairest creature ?
Rosy morn now lifts his eye,
Numbering ilka bud which Nature
Waters wi' the tears o' joy :
Now thro' the leafy woods,
And by the reeking floods
Wild Nature's tenants freely, gladly stray ;
The lint white in his bower
Chants o'er the breathing flower ;
The lav'rock to the sky
Ascends wi' sangs o' joy,
While the sun and thou arise to bless the day.

Phœbus, gilding the brow o' morning,
Banishes ilk darksome shade,
Nature gladdening and adorning ;
Such to me my lovely maid.

[1] Thaw. [2] Without shelter.
[3] Miss Lorimer is reported to have inspired these verses.

When absent frae my fair,
The murky shades o' care
With starless gloom o'ercast my sullen sky:
But when in beauty's light,
She meets my ravish'd sight,
When thro' my very heart
Her beaming glories dart,
'Tis then I wake to life, to light, and joy.

CONTENTED WI' LITTLE.

TUNE—"LUMPS O' PUDDING."

CONTENTED wi' little, and cantie[1] wi' mair,
Whene'er I forgather wi' sorrow and care,
I gie them a skelp[2] as they're creepin' alang,
Wi' a cog o' guid swats,[3] and an auld Scottish sang.

I whyles claw the elbow o' troublesome thought;
But man is a sodger, and life is a faught:[4]
My mirth and guid humour are coin in my pouch,
And my Freedom's my lairdship nae monarch dare touch.

A towmond o' trouble, should that be my fa',
A night o' guid fellowship sowthers[5] it a;
When at the blythe end of our journey at last,
Wha the deil ever thinks o' the road he has past?

Blind Chance, let her snapper and stoyte[6] on her way,
Be't to me, be't frae me, e'en let the jad gae:
Come ease, or come travail; come pleasure or pain;
My warst word is—"Welcome, and welcome again!"

---

[1] Cheerful. [2] Slap.
[3] Jug of good ale. [4] Fight.
[5] Solders. [6] Mistake and stumble.

FAREWELL, THOU STREAM.

TUNE—"NANCY'S TO THE GREENWOOD GANE."

FAREWELL, thou stream that winding flows
Around Eliza's dwelling!
O Mem'ry! spare the cruel throes
Within my bosom swelling:
Condemn'd to drag a hopeless chain,
And yet in secret languish,
To feel a fire in ev'ry vein,
Nor dare disclose my anguish.

Love's veriest wretch, unseen, unknown,
I fain my griefs would cover:
The bursting sigh, th' unweeting groan,
Betray the hapless lover.
I know thou doom'st me to despair,
Nor wilt, nor canst, relieve me;
But oh, Eliza, hear one prayer,
For pity's sake forgive me!

The music of thy voice I heard,
Nor wist while it enslav'd me;
I saw thine eyes, yet nothing fear'd,
Till fears no more had sav'd me:
Th' unwary sailor thus aghast,
The wheeling torrent viewing,
'Mid circling horrors sinks at last
In overwhelming ruin.

MY NANNIE'S AWA.

TUNE—"THERE'LL NEVER BE PEACE TILL JAMIE COMES HAME."

Now in her green mantle blythe Nature arrays,
And listens the lambkins that bleat o'er the braes,
While birds warble welcome in ilka green shaw;
But to me it's delightless—my Nannie's awa.

The snaw-drap and primrose our woodlands adorn,
And violets bathe in the weet o' the morn:

They pain my sad bosom, sae sweetly they blaw,
They mind me o' Nannie—my Nannie's awa.

Thou lav'rock that springs frae the dews o' the lawn,
The shepherd to warn o' the grey-breaking dawn,
And thou mellow mavis that hails the night-fa',
Gie over for pity—my Nannie's awa.

Come Autumn sae pensive, in yellow and gray,
And soothe me wi' tidings o' nature's decay;
The dark, dreary Winter, and wild-driving snaw,
Alane can delight me—now Nannie's awa.

SWEET FA'S THE EVE.[1]

TUNE—"CRAIGIEBURN-WOOD."

Sweet fa's the eve on Craigieburn,
And blythe awakes the morrow,
But a' the pride o' spring's return
Can yield me nocht but sorrow.

I see the flowers and spreading trees,
I hear the wild birds singing;
But what a weary wight can please,
And care his bosom wringing?

Fain, fain would I my griefs impart,
Yet dare na for your anger;
But secret love will break my heart,
If I conceal it langer.

If thou refuse to pity me,
If thou shalt love anither,
When yon green leaves fa' frae the tree,
Around my grave they'll wither.

[1] Burns again celebrates Miss Lorimer. Craigieburn-wood is situate on the banks of the river Moffat. The woods of Craigieburn and of Duncrief were, at one time, favourite haunts of our poet. (Currie.)

O LASSIE, ART, THOU SLEEPING YET?

TUNE—"LET ME IN THIS AE NIGHT."

O lassie, art thou sleeping yet?
Or art thou wakin', I would wit?
For love has bound me, hand and foot,
And I would fain be in, jo.

CHORUS.

O let me in this ae night
This ae, ae, ae night;
For pity's sake this ae night,
O rise and let me in, jo.

Thou hear'st the winter wind and weet,
Nae star blinks thro' the driving sleet;
Tak pity on my weary feet,
And shield me frae the rain, jo.
O let me in, &c.

The bitter blast that round me blaws,
Unheeded howls, unheeded fa's:
The cauldness o' thy heart's the cause
Of a' my grief and pain, jo.
O let me in, &c.

HER ANSWER.

O tell na me o' wind and rain,
Upbraid na me wi' cauld disdain!
Gae back the gait ye cam again,
I winna let you in, jo.

CHORUS.

I tell you now this ae night,
This ae, ae, ae night,
And ance for a' this ae night,
I winna let you in, jo.

The snellest[1] blast, at mirkest[2] hours,
That round the pathless wand'rer pours,
Is nocht to what poor she endures,
That's trusted faithless man, jo.
I tell you now, &c.

The sweetest flower that deck'd the mead,
Now trodden like the vilest weed;
Let simple maid the lesson read,
The weird[3] may be her ain, jo.
I tell you now, &c.

[1] Bitterest. [2] Darkest. [3] Fate

The bird that charm'd his summer-day,
Is now the cruel fowler's prey:
Let witless, trusting woman say
How aft her fate's the same, jo.
I tell you now, &c.

'TWAS NA HER BONNIE BLUE E'E.

TUNE—"LADDIE, LIE NEAR ME."

'Twas na her bonnie blue e'e was my ruin;
Fair tho' she be, that was ne'er my undoin';
'Twas the dear smile when naebody did mind us,
'Twas the bewitching, sweet, stown[1] glance o' kindness.

Sair do I fear that to hope is denied me,
Sair do I fear that despair maun abide me;
But tho' fell fortune should fate us to sever,
Queen shall she be in my bosom for ever.

Chloris, I'm thine wi' a passion sincerest,
And thou hast plighted me love o' the dearest!
And thou'rt the angel that never can alter,
Sooner the sun in his motion would falter.

SONG.

TUNE—"HUMOURS OF GLEN."

Their groves o' sweet myrtles let foreign lands reckon,
Where bright-beaming summers exalt their perfume;
Far dearer to me yon lone glen o' green breckan,[2]
Wi' the burn stealing under the lang yellow broom.

[1] Stolen. [2] Fern.

Far dearer to me are yon humble broom bowers,
Where the blue-bell and gowan lurk lowly unseen:
For there lightly tripping amang the wild flowers,
A listening the linnet, aft wanders my Jean.

Tho' rich is the breeze in their gay sunny valleys,
And cauld Caledonia's blast on the wave;
Their sweet-scented woodlands that skirt the proud palace,
What are they? The haunt of the tyrant and slave!

The slave's spicy forests, and gold-bubbling fountains,
The brave Caledonian views wi' disdain;
He wanders as free as the winds of his mountains,
Save love's willing fetters, the chains o' his Jean.

ADDRESS TO THE WOODLARK.

TUNE—"WHERE'LL BONNIE ANN LIE."

O stay, sweet warbling wood-lark, stay,
Nor quit for me the trembling spray;
A hapless lover courts thy lay,
Thy soothing fond complaining.

Again, again that tender part,
That I may catch thy melting art;
For surely that wad touch her heart,
Wha kills me wi' disdaining.

Say, was thy little mate unkind,
And heard thee as the careless wind?
Oh, nocht but love and sorrow join'd
Sic notes o' wae could wauken.

Thou tells o' never-ending care;
O' speechless grief, and dark despair:
For pity's sake, sweet bird, nae mair!
Or my poor heart is broken!

HOW CRUEL ARE THE PARENTS.

TUNE—"JOHN ANDERSON, MY JO."

How cruel are the parents
Who riches only prize,
And to the wealthy booby
Poor woman sacrifice.
Meanwhile the hapless daughter
Has but a choice of strife;
To shun a tyrant father's hate,
Becomes a wretched wife.

The ravening hawk pursuing,
The trembling dove thus flies,
To shun impelling ruin
Awhile her pinion tries;
Till of escape despairing,
No shelter or retreat,
She trusts the ruthless falconer,
And drops beneath his feet.

MARK YONDER POMP.

TUNE—"DEIL TAK THE WARS."

Mark yonder pomp of costly fashion,
Round the wealthy, titled bride;
But when compar'd with real passion,
Poor is all that princely pride.
What are the showy treasures?
What are the noisy pleasures?
The gay, gaudy glare of vanity and art:
The polish'd jewel's blaze
May draw the wond'ring gaze,
And courtly grandeur bright
The fancy may delight,
But never, never can come near the heart.
But did you see my dearest Chloris,
In simplicity's array;
Lovely as yonder sweet opening flower is,
Shrinking from the gaze of day!
O then, the heart alarming,
And all resistless charming,
In Love's delightful fetters she chains the willing soul!
Ambition would disown
The world's imperial crown;
Even Avarice would deny
His worshipp'd deity,
And feel thro' every vein Love's raptures roll.

I SEE A FORM, I SEE A FACE.

TUNE—"THIS IS NO MY AIN HOUSE."

O this is no my ain lassie,
Fair tho' the lassie be;
O weel ken I my ain lassie,
Kind love is in her e'e.

I see a form, I see a face,
Ye weel may wi' the fairest place:
It wants, to me, the witching grace,
The kind love that's in her e'e.
O this is no, &c.

She's bonnie, blooming, straight, and tall,
And lang has had my heart in thrall;
And aye it charms my very saul,
The kind love that's in her e'e.
O this is no, &c.

A thief sae pawkie is my Jean,
To steal a blink, by a' unseen;
But gleg[1] as light are lovers' een,
When kind love is in the e'e.
O this is no, &c.

It may escape the courtly sparks,
It may escape the learned clerks;
But weel the watching lover marks
The kind love that's in her e'e.
O this is no, &c.

O BONNIE WAS YON ROSY BRIER.

TUNE—"I WISH MY LOVE WAS IN A MIRE."

O bonnie was yon rosy brier,
That blooms sae far frae haunt o man;
And bonnie she, and ah, how dear!
It shaded frae the e'enin[2] sun.

[1] Quick. [2] Evening.

Yon rosebuds in the morning dew,
  How pure amang the leaves sae green—
But purer was the lovers' vow
  They witness'd in their shade yestreen.

All in its rude and prickly bower,
  That crimson rose, how sweet and fair!
But love is far a sweeter flower
  Amid life's thorny path o' care.

The pathless wild and wimpling burn,
  Wi' Chloris in my arms, be mine;
And I the world nor wish, nor scorn,
  Its joys and griefs alike resign.

FORLORN, MY LOVE.

TUNE—"LET ME IN THIS AE NIGHT."

Forlorn, my love, no comfort near,
Far, far from thee, I wander here;
Far, far from thee, the fate severe
  At which I most repine, love.

CHORUS.

O wert thou, love, but near me,
But near, near, near me;
How kindly thou wouldst cheer me,
  And mingle sighs with mine, love.

Around me scowls a wintry sky,
That blasts each bud of hope and joy;
And shelter, shade, nor home have I,
  Save in those arms of thine, love.
    O wert, &c.

Cold, alter'd friendship's cruel part,
To poison fortune's ruthless dart—
Let me not break thy faithful heart,
  And say that fate is mine, love.
    O wert, &c.

But dreary tho' the moments fleet,
O let me think we yet shall meet!
That only ray of solace sweet
  Can on thy Chloris shine, love.
    O wert, &c.

LAST MAY A BRAW WOOER.

TUNE—"THE LOTHIAN LASSIE."

Last May a braw wooer cam down the lang glen,
  And sair wi' his love he did deave me;
I said there was naething I hated like men,
  The deuce gae wi'm to believe me, believe me,
  The deuce gae wi'm to believe me.

He spak o' the darts in my bonnie black een,
  And vow'd for my love he was dying;
I said he might die when he liked for Jean:
  The Lord forgie me for lying, for lying,
  The Lord forgie me for lying!

A weel-stocked mailen, himsel for the laird,
  And marriage aff-hand, were his proffers:
I never loot on that I kenn'd it, or car'd;
  But thought I might hae waur offers, waur offers,
  But thought I might hae waur offers.

But what wad ye think? in a fortnight or less,
  The deil tak his taste to gae near her!
He up the lang loan to my black cousin Bess,
  Guess ye how, the jad! I could bear her, could bear her,
  Guess ye how, the jad! I could bear her.

But a' the niest week as I fretted wi' care,
  I gaed to the tryste o' Dalgarnock,[1]
And wha but my fine fickle lover was there!
  I glowr'd as I'd seen a warlock, a warlock,
  I glowr'd as I'd seen a warlock.

---

[1] Dalgarnock is the name of a romantic spot near the Nith, where are still a ruined church and a burial-ground.—R. B.

But owre my left shouther I gae him a blink,
Lest neebors might say I was saucy;
My wooer he caper'd as he'd been in drink,
And vow'd I was his dear lassie, dear lassie,
And vow'd I was his dear lassie.

I spier'd for my cousin fu' couthy and sweet,
Gin she had recover'd her hearin,
And how her new shoon fit her auld shachl't[1] feet—
But Heavens! how he fell a swearin, a swearin,
But Heavens! how he fell a swearin.

He begged, for Gudesake, I wad be his wife,
Or else I wad kill him wi' sorrow:
So e'en to preserve the poor body in life,
I think I maun wed him to-morrow, to-morrow;
I think I maun wed him to-morrow.

[1] Twisted.

HEY FOR A LASS WI' A TOCHER.

TUNE—"BALINAMONA ORA."

Awa wi' your witchcraft o' beauty's alarms,
The slender bit beauty you grasp in your arms:
O, gie me the lass that has acres o' charms,
O, gie me the lass wi' the weel-stockit farms.

CHORUS.

Then hey, for a lass wi' a tocher, then hey, for a lass wi' a tocher,
Then hey, for a lass wi' a tocher; the nice yellow guineas for me.

Your beauty's a flower in the morning that blows,
And withers the faster, the faster it grows;
But the rapturous charm o' the bonnie green knowes,
Ilk spring they're new deckit wi' bonnie white yowes.
Then hey, &c.

And e'en when this beauty your bosom has blest,
The brightest o' beauty may cloy, when possest:
But the sweet yellow darlings wi' Geordie imprest,
The langer ye hae them—the mair they're carest.
Then hey, &c.

ALTHO' THOU MAUN NEVER BE MINE.

TUNE—"HERE'S A HEALTH TO THEM THAT'S AWA."

CHORUS.

Here's a health to ane I lo'e dear,
Here's a health to ane I lo'e dear;
Thou art as sweet as the smile when fond lovers meet,
And soft as their parting tear—Jessy![1]

Altho' thou maun never be mine,
Altho' even hope is denied;
'Tis sweeter for thee despairing,
Than aught in the world beside—Jessy!
Here's a health, &c.

I mourn thro' the gay, gaudy day,
As, hopeless, I muse on thy charms:
But welcome the dream o' sweet slumber,
For then I am lockt in thy arms—Jessy!
Here's a health, &c.

I guess by the dear angel smile,
I guess by the love-rolling e'e;
But why urge the tender confession
'Gainst fortune's fell cruel decree—Jessy!
Here's a health, &c.

[1] Miss Jessy Lewars.

THE BIRKS[1] OF ABERFELDY.

Bonnie lassie, will ye go,
Bonnie lassie, will ye go,
To the Birks of Aberfeldy?

Now simmer blinks on flowery braes,
And o'er the crystal streamlet plays,
Come let us spend the lightsome days
In the Birks of Aberfeldy.

While o'er their heads the hazels hing,
The little birdies blithely sing,
Or lightly flit on wanton wing
In the Birks of Aberfeldy.

The braes ascend like lofty wa's,
The foaming stream deep roaring fa's,
O'er-hung wi' fragrant spreading shaws,
The Birks of Aberfeldy.

The hoary cliffs are crown'd wi' flowers,
White o'er the linns the burnie pours,
And, rising, weets wi' misty showers
The Birks of Aberfeldy.

Let fortune's gifts at random flee,
They ne'er shall draw a wish frae me,
Supremely blest wi' love and thee,
In the Birks of Aberfeldy.
Bonnie lassie, will ye go,
Bonnie lassie, will ye go,
To the Birks of Aberfeldy?

[1] Near Moness, in Perthshire. The birch-trees were there very abundant.

THE YOUNG HIGHLAND ROVER.

TUNE—"MORAG."

Loud blaw the frosty breezes,
The snaws the mountains cover;
Like winter on me seizes,
Since my young Highland Rover
Far wanders nations over.
Where'er he go, where'er he stray,
May heaven be his warden;
Return him safe to fair Strathspey,
And bonnie Castle-Gordon!

The trees now naked groaning,
Shall soon wi' leaves be hinging;
The birdies dowie moaning,
Shall a' be blithely singing,
And every flower be springing.
Sae I'll rejoice the lee-lang day,
When by his mighty warden
My youth's return'd to fair Strathspey,
And bonnie Castle-Gordon.

STAY, MY CHARMER.

TUNE—"AN GILLE DUBH CIAR DHUBH."

Stay, my charmer, can you leave me?
Cruel, cruel to deceive me!
Well you know how much you grieve me;
Cruel charmer, can you go?
Cruel charmer, can you go?

By my love so ill requited;
By the faith you fondly plighted;
By the pangs of lovers slighted;
Do not, do not leave me so!
Do not, do not leave me so!

FULL WELL THOU KNOW'ST.[1]

TUNE—"ROTHIEMURCHE'S RANT."

CHORUS.

Fairest maid on Devon banks,
Crystal Devon, winding Devon,
Wilt thou lay that frown aside,
And smile as thou were wont to do?

Full well thou know'st I love thee dear;
Couldst thou to malice lend an ear?
O, did not Love exclaim, "Forbear,
Nor use a faithful lover so?"
Fairest maid, &c.

Then come, thou fairest of the fair,
Those wonted smiles, O, let me share;
And by thy beauteous self I swear,
No love but thine my heart shall know.
Fairest maid, &c.

[1] This is supposed to be the last song written by Burns. "I tried my hand on 'Rothiemurche' this morning. The measure is so difficult, that it is impossible to infuse much genius into the lines."—R. B.

STRATHALLAN'S LAMENT.[1]

THICKEST night, o'erhang my dwelling!
Howling tempests, o'er me rave!
Turbid torrents, wintry swelling,
Still surround my lonely cave!

Crystal streamlets gently flowing,
Busy haunts of base mankind,
Western breezes softly blowing,
Suit not my distracted mind.

In the cause of right engaged,
Wrongs injurious to redress,
Honour's war we strongly waged,
But the Heavens denied success.

Ruin's wheel has driven o'er us,
Not a hope that dare attend;
The wide world is all before us—
But a world without a friend!

RAVING WINDS AROUND HER BLOWING.[2]

TUNE—" M'GREGOR OF RUARA'S LAMENT."

RAVING winds around her blowing,
Yellow leaves the woodlands strowing,
By a river hoarsely roaring,
Isabella stray'd deploring:
" Farewell, hours, that late did measure
Sunshine days of joy and pleasure;
Hail, thou gloomy night of sorrow,
Cheerless night that knows no morrow!

" O'er the past too fondly wandering,
On the hopeless future pondering;
Chilly grief my life-blood freezes,
Fell despair my fancy seizes.
Life, thou soul of every blessing,
Load to misery most distressing,
O, how gladly I'd resign thee,
And to dark oblivion join thee!"

[1] Lord Strathallan, bewailing his forlorn state after the defeat of Culloden.
[2] Miss Isabella M'Leod, who had lost a sister and a brother-in-law.

MUSING ON THE ROARING OCEAN.

TUNE—" DRUIMION DUBH."

MUSING on the roaring ocean
Which divides my love and me;
Wearying Heaven in warm devotion,
For his weal where'er he be.

Hope and fear's alternate billow
Yielding late to nature's law,
Whisp'ring spirits round my pillow
Talk of him that's far awa.

Ye whom sorrow never wounded,
Ye who never shed a tear,
Care-untroubl'd, joy-surrounded,
Gaudy day to you is dear.

Gentle night, do thou befriend me;
Downy sleep, the curtain draw;
Spirits kind, again attend me,
Talk of him that's far awa!

BLITHE WAS SHE.

TUNE—" ANDREW AND HIS CUTTY GUN."

CHORUS.

Blithe, blithe and merry was she,
Blithe was she but and ben:
Blithe by the banks of Ern,
And blithe in Glenturit glen.

BY Ochtertyre grows the aik,
On Yarrow banks the birken shaw;
But Phemie[1] was a bonnier lass
Than braes o' Yarrow ever saw.
Blithe, &c.

Her looks were like a flower in May,
Her smile was like a simmer morn;
She tripped by the banks of Ern,
As light 's a bird upon a thorn.
Blithe, &c.

Her bonnie face it was as meek
As onie lamb's upon a lea;
The evening sun was ne'er sae sweet
As was the blink o' Phemie's e'e.
Blithe, &c.

[1] Miss Euphemia Murray.

The Highland hills I've wander'd wide,
  And o'er the Lowlands I hae been;
But Phemie was the blithest lass
  That ever trod the dewy green.
      Blithe, &c.

PEGGY'S CHARMS.[1]

TUNE—"NEIL GOW'S LAMENTATION FOR ABERCAIRNY."

Where, braving angry winter's storms,
  The lofty Ochils rise,
Far in their shade my Peggy's charms
  First blest my wondering eyes.
As one who, by some savage stream,
  A lonely gem surveys,
Astonish'd, doubly marks its beam
  With art's most polish'd blaze.

Blest be the wild sequester'd shade,
  And blest the day and hour,
Where Peggy's charms I first survey'd,
  When first I felt their pow'r!
The tyrant Death with grim control
  May seize my fleeting breath;
But tearing Peggy from my soul
  Must be a stronger death.

THE LAZY MIST.

IRISH AIR—"COOLUN."

The lazy mist hangs from the brow of the hill,
Concealing the course of the dark-winding rill;
How languid the scenes, late so sprightly, appear,
As Autumn to Winter resigns the pale year!
The forests are leafless, the meadows are brown,
And all the gay foppery of Summer is flown:
Apart let me wander, apart let me muse,
How quick Time is flying, how keen Fate pursues;

[1] Miss Margaret Chalmers.

How long I have lived, but how much lived in vain:
How little of life's scanty span may remain:
What aspects old Time, in his progress, has worn;
What ties cruel Fate in my bosom has torn.
How foolish, or worse, till our summit is gain'd!
And downward, how weaken'd, how darken'd, how pain'd!
This life's not worth having with all it can give,
For something beyond it poor man sure must live.

A ROSE-BUD BY MY EARLY WALK.

TUNE—"THE SHEPHERD'S WIFE."

A rose-bud by my early walk,
Adown a corn-enclosed bawk,[1]
Sae gently bent its thorny stalk,
  All on a dewy morning.

Ere twice the shades o' dawn are fled,
In a' its crimson glory spread,
And drooping rich the dewy head,
  It scents the early morning.

Within the bush, her covert nest
A little linnet fondly prest,
The dew sat chilly on her breast
  Sae early in the morning.

She soon shall see her tender brood,
The pride, the pleasure o' the wood,
Amang the fresh green leaves bedew'd,
  Awake the early morning.

So thou, dear bird, young Jeany[2] fair,
On trembling string, or vocal air,
Shall sweetly pay the tender care
  That tents thy early morning.

So thou, sweet rose-bud, young and gay
Shalt beauteous blaze upon the day,
And bless the parent's evening ray
  That watch'd thy early morning.

[1] Bank.
[2] Miss Jenny Cruikshanks.

TIBBIE, I HAE SEEN THE DAY.[1]

TUNE—"INVERCAULD'S REEL."

CHORUS.

O Tibbie, I hae seen the day,
Ye would na been sae shy;
For laik o' gear ye lightly[2] me,
But trowth, I care na by.

Yestreen I met you on the moor,
Ye spak na, but gaed by like stoure:
Ye geck at me because I'm poor,
But fient a hair care I.
O Tibbie, I hae, &c.

I doubt na, lass, but ye may think,
Because ye hae the name o' clink,
That ye can please me at a wink,
Whene'er ye like to try.
O Tibbie, I hae, &c.

But sorrow tak him that's sae mean,
Altho' his pouch o' coin were clean,
Wha follows onie saucy quean
That looks sae proud and high.
O Tibbie, I hae, &c.

Altho' a lad were e'er sae smart,
If that he want the yellow dirt,
Ye'll cast your head anither airt,
And answer him fu' dry.
O Tibbie, I hae, &c.

But if he hae the name o' gear,
Ye'll fasten to him like a brier,
Tho' hardly he for sense or lear
Be better than the kye.
O Tibbie, I hae, &c.

But, Tibbie, lass, tak my advice,
Your daddy's gear maks you sae nice;
The deil a ane wad spier your price
Were ye as poor as I.
O Tibbie, I hae, &c.

There lives a lass in yonder park,
I would na gie her in her sark,
For thee wi' a' thy thousand mark;
Ye need na look sae high.
O Tibbie, I hae, &c.

---

[1] Burns was about seventeen years old when he composed these rhymes.
[2] Despise.

I LOVE MY JEAN.[1]

TUNE—"MISS ADMIRAL GORDON'S STRATHSPEY."

Of a' the airts[2] the wind can blaw,
I dearly like the west,
For there the bonnie lassie lives,
The lassie I lo'e best;
There wild woods grow, and rivers row,
And monie a hill between;
By day and night my fancy's flight
Is ever wi' my Jean.

I see her in the dewy flowers,
I see her sweet and fair;
I hear her in the tunefu' birds,
I hear her charm the air:
There's not a bonnie flower that springs
By fountain, shaw, or green;
There's not a bonnie bird that sings,
But minds me o' my Jean.

O, WERE I ON PARNASSUS' HILL.

TUNE—"MY LOVE IS LOST TO ME."

O, were I on Parnassus' hill,
Or had of Helicon my fill,
That I might catch poetic skill,
To sing how dear I love thee!
But Nith maun be my Muse's well,
My Muse maun be thy bonnie sel;
On Corsincon[3] I'll glow'r and spell,
And write how dear I love thee.

Then come, sweet Muse, inspire my lay!
For a' the lee-lang simmer's day,
I coud na sing, I coud na say,
How much, how dear I love thee.
I see thee dancing o'er the green,
Thy waist sae jimp,[4] thy limbs sae clean,
Thy tempting looks, thy roguish een—
By Heaven and earth I love thee!

---

[1] Written "out of compliment to Mrs. Burns."
[2] Points of the compass.
[3] A hill near Ellisland. [4] Slender.

Paterson Sc

By night, by day, a-field, at hame,
The thoughts o' thee my breast inflame;
And aye I muse and sing thy name,
I only live to love thee.
Tho' I were doom'd to wander on,
Beyond the sea, beyond the sun,
Till my last weary sand was run;
Till then—and then I'd love thee.

THE BLISSFUL DAY.[1]

TUNE—"SEVENTH OF NOVEMBER."

The day returns, my bosom burns,
The blissful day we twa did meet,
Tho' winter wild in tempest toil'd,
Ne'er summer-sun was half sae sweet.
Than a' the pride that loads the tide,
And crosses o'er the sultry line;
Than kingly robes, than crowns and globes;—
Heaven gave me more, it made thee mine.

While day and night can bring delight,
Or nature aught of pleasure give;
While joys above my mind can move,—
For thee, and thee alone, I live!
When that grim foe of life below
Comes in between to make us part;
The iron hand that breaks our band,
It breaks my bliss—it breaks my heart.

THE BRAES O' BALLOCHMYLE.

TUNE—"MISS FORBES'S FAREWELL TO BANFF."

The Catrine woods were yellow seen,
The flowers decay'd on Catrine lea,
Nae lav'rock sang on hillock green,
But nature sicken'd on the e'e.

[1] The Poet declared Robert Riddel and his wife to be "one of the happiest and worthiest married couples in the world." These stanzas were composed for the anniversary of their wedding-day.

Thro' faded groves Maria sang,
Hersel in beauty's bloom the whyle,
And aye the wild wood echoes rang,
Fareweel the braes o' Ballochmyle.

Low in your wintry beds, ye flowers,
Again ye'll flourish fresh and fair;
Ye birdies dumb, in with'ring bowers,
Again ye'll charm the vocal air.
But here, alas! for me nae mair
Shall birdie charm, or flow'ret smile;
Fareweel the bonnie banks of Ayr,
Fareweel, fareweel! sweet Ballochmyle.

THE HAPPY TRIO.[1]

TUNE—"WILLIE BREW'D A PECK O' MAUT."

O, Willie brew'd a peck o' maut,
And Rob and Allan came to see;
Three blither hearts, that lee-lang[2] night,
Ye wad na find in Christendie.

CHORUS.

We are na fou, we're no that fou,
But just a drappie in our e'e;
The cock may craw, the day may daw,
And aye we'll taste the barley bree.

Here are we met, three merry boys,
Three merry boys, I trow, are we;
And monie a night we've merry been,
And monie mae we hope to be!
We are na fou, &c.

It is the moon, I ken her horn,
That's blinkin in the lift sae hie:

[1] This air is Masterson's; the song mine. The occasion of it was this. Mr. William Nicol, of the High School of Edinburgh, during the Autumn vacation, being at Moffat, honest Allan, who was at that time on a visit to Dalswinton, and I, went to pay Nicol a visit. We had such a joyous meeting, that Mr. Masterson and I agreed, each in our own way, that we should celebrate the business.—R. B.

[2] Live-long.

She shines sae bright to wyle us hame,
But, by my sooth, she'll wait a wee!
We are na fou, &c.

Wha first shall rise to gang awa,
A cuckold, coward loun is he!
Wha last beside his chair shall fa',
He is the king amang us three!
We are na fou, &c.

THE BLUE-EYED LASSIE.[1]

I GAED a' waefu' gate yestreen,
A gate, I fear, I'll dearly rue;
I gat my death frae twa sweet een,
Twa lovely een o' bonnie blue.

'Twas not her golden ringlets bright,
Her lips like roses wet wi' dew,
Her heaving bosom, lily-white;—
It was her een sae bonnie blue.

She talk'd, she smil'd, my heart she wyl'd,
She charm'd my soul I wist na how;
And aye the stound,[2] the deadly wound,
Cam frae her een sae bonnie blue.

But spare to speak, and spare to speed;
She'll aiblins listen to my vow:
Should she refuse, I'll lay my dead
To her twa een sae bonnie blue.

JOHN ANDERSON, MY JO.

JOHN ANDERSON, my jo, John,
When we were first acquent,
Your locks were like the raven,
Your bonnie brow was brent;[3]
But now your brow is beld, John,
Your locks are like the snaw;
But blessings on your frosty pow,
John Anderson, my jo.

John Anderson, my jo, John,
We clamb the hill thegither;
And monie a canty day, John,
We've had wi' ane anither:
Now we maun totter down, John,
But hand in hand we'll go,
And sleep thegither at the foot,
John Anderson, my jo.

[1] Jean Jeffry, daughter of the minister of Lochmaben.
[2] Pang. [3] High and smooth.

TAM GLEN.

TUNE—"THE MUCKING O' GEORDIE'S BYRE."

MY heart is a breaking, dear Tittie,
Some counsel unto me come len',
To anger them a' is a pity;
But what will I do wi' Tam Glen?

I'm thinking, wi' sic a braw fellow,
In poortith[1] I might mak a fen';[2]
What care I in riches to wallow,
If I maunna marry Tam Glen?

There's Lowrie the laird o' Dumeller,
"Guid-day to you, brute!" he comes ben:
He brags and he blaws o' his siller;
But when will he dance like Tam Glen?

My minnie does constantly deave[3] me,
And bids me beware o' young men;
They flatter, she says, to deceive me;
But wha can think sae o' Tam Glen?

My daddie says, gin I'll forsake him,
He'll gie me guid hunder marks ten:
But, if it's ordain'd I maun take him,
O wha will I get but Tam Glen?

Yestreen at the Valentines' dealing,
My heart to my mou gied a sten:[4]
For thrice I drew ane without failing,
And thrice it was written, Tam Glen.

The last Halloween I was waukin[5]
My droukit[6] sark-sleeve, as ye ken;
His likeness cam up the house staukin—
And the very grey breeks o' Tam Glen!

[1] Poverty. [2] Make a shift. [3] Deafen.
[4] Leap. [5] Watching. [6] Wet.

Come counsel, dear Tittie, don't tarry;
I'il gie you my bonnie black hen,
Gif you will advise me to marry
The lad I lo'e dearly, Tam Glen.

GANE IS THE DAY.

TUNE—"GUIDWIFE COUNT THE LAWIN."

GANE is the day, and mirk's the night,
But we'll ne'er stray for faute[1] o' light,
For ale and brandy's stars and moon,
And bluid-red wine's the risin sun.

CHORUS.

Then guidwife count the lawin,[2] the lawin, the lawin,
Then guidwife count the lawin, and bring a coggie mair.

There's wealth and ease for gentlemen,
And semple-folk maun fecht and fen',
But here we're a' in ae accord,
For ilka man that's drunk's a lord.
Then guidwife count, &c.

My coggie is a haly pool,[3]
That heals the wounds o' care and dool;
And pleasure is a wanton trout,
An' ye drink it a' ye'll find him out.
Then guidwife count, &c.

WHAT CAN A YOUNG LASSIE DO WI' AN AULD MAN?

TUNE—"WHAT CAN A LASSIE DO."

WHAT can a young lassie, what shall a young lassie,
What can a young lassie do wi' an auld man?
Bad luck on the penny that tempted my minnie
To sell her poor Jenny for siller an' lan'!
Bad luck on the penny, &c.

[1] Fault. [2] Reckoning. [3] Holy well.

He's always compleenin frae mornin to e'enin,
He hosts and he hirples[1] the weary day lang:
He's doylt[2] and he's dozin, his bluid it is frozen,
O, dreary's the night wi' a crazy auld man!

He hums and he hankers, he frets and he cankers,
I never can please him do a' that I can;
He's peevish, and jealous of a' the young fellows:
O, dool[3] on the day I met wi' an auld man!

My auld auntie Katie upon me takes pity,
I'll do my endeavour to follow her plan;
I'll cross him, and rack him, until I heart-break him,
And then his auld brass will buy me a new pan.

O, FOR ANE-AND-TWENTY, TAM!

TUNE—"THE MOUDIEWORT."

CHORUS.

An' O for ane-and-twenty, Tam!
An' hey, sweet ane-and-twenty, Tam!
I'll learn my kin a rattlin sang,
An' I saw ane-and-twenty, Tam.

THEY snool[4] me sair, and haud me down,
And gar me look like bluntie,[5] Tam!
But three short years will soon wheel roun',
And then comes ane-and-twenty, Tam.
And O for ane, &c.

[1] Coughs and hobbles. [2] Stupid. [3] Sorrow. [4] Oppress. [5] Snivelling.

A gleib o' lan',[1] a claut o' gear,
Was left me by my auntie, Tam;
At kith or kin I need na spier,
An' I saw ane-and-twenty, Tam.
An' O for ane, &c.

They'll hae me wed a wealthy coof,[2]
Tho' I mysel' hae plenty, Tam;
But hear'st thou, laddie, there's my loof,[3]—
I'm thine at ane-and-twenty, Tam!
An' O for ane, &c.

THE BONNIE WEE THING.

TUNE—"THE LADS OF SALTCOATS."

BONNIE wee thing, cannie wee thing,
Lovely wee thing, wast thou mine,
I wad wear thee in my bosom,
Lest my jewel I should tine.

Wistfully I look and languish
In that bonnie face of thine;
And my heart it stounds[4] wi' anguish,
Lest my wee thing be na mine.

Wit, and grace, and love, and beauty,
In ae constellation shine;
To adore thee is my duty,
Goddess o' this soul o' mine!
Bonnie wee, &c.

THE BANKS OF NITH.

TUNE—"ROBIE DONNA GORACH."

THE Thames flows proudly to the sea,
Where royal cities stately stand;
But sweeter flows the Nith to me,
Where Cummins ance had high command:
When shall I see that honour'd land,
That winding stream I loved so dear?
Must wayward fortune's adverse hand
For ever, ever keep me here?

[1] A portion of ground. [2] Blockhead. [3] Hand. [4] Throbs.

How lovely, Nith, thy fruitful vales,
Where spreading hawthorns gaily bloom;
How sweetly wind thy sloping dales,
Where lambkins wanton thro' the broom!
Tho' wandering, now, must be my doom,
Far from thy bonnie banks and braes,
May there my latest hour consume,
Amang the friends of early days!

BESSY AND HER SPINNIN WHEEL.

O LEEZE[1] me on my spinnin wheel,
O leeze me on my rock and reel;
Frae tap to tae that cleeds me bien,[2]
And haps[3] me fiel[4] and warm at e'en!
I'll set me down and sing and spin,
While laigh[5] descends the simmer sun,
Blest wi' content, and milk, and meal—
O leeze me on my spinnin wheel.

On ilka hand the burnies trot,
And meet below my theekit[6] cot;
The scented birk and hawthorn white
Across the pool their arms unite,
Alike to screen the birdie's nest,
And little fishes caller[7] rest:
The sun blinks kindly in the biel',[8]
Where blithe I turn my spinnin wheel.

On lofty aiks[9] the cushats wail,
And echo cons the doolfu' tale;
The lintwhites in the hazel braes,
Delighted, rival ither's lays:
The craik[10] amang the claver hay,
The paitrick[11] whirrin o'er the ley,
The swallow jinkin[12] round my shiel,[13]
Amuse me at my spinnin wheel.

[1] A phrase of endearment: "I am proud of thee."
[2] That abundantly clothes me.
[3] Wraps. [4] Soft. [5] Low.
[6] Thatched. [7] Sound. [8] Nook.
[9] Oaks. [10] The corn-rail.
[11] Partridge. [12] Dodging. [13] Shed.

Wi' sma' to sell, and less to buy,
Aboon distress, below envy,
O wha wad leave this humble state,
For a' the pride of a' the great?
Amid their flarin, idle toys,
Amid their cumbrous, dinsome joys,
Can they the peace and pleasure feel
Of Bessy at her spinnin wheel?

COUNTRY LASSIE.

TUNE—"JOHN, COME KISS ME NOW."

In simmer, when the hay was mawn,
And corn wav'd green in ilka field,
While claver blooms white o'er the lea,
And roses blaw in ilka bield;[1]
Blithe Bessie in the milking shiel,
Says, "I'll be wed, come o't what will;"
Out spak a dame in wrinkled eild,—
"O' guid advisement comes nae ill:

"It's ye hae wooers monie ane,
And, lassie, ye're but young, ye ken;
Then wait a wee, and cannie wale[2]
A routhie but, a routhie ben:[3]
There's Johnie o' the Buskie-glen,
Fu' is his barn, fu' is his byre;[4]
Tak this frae me, my bonnie hen,
It's plenty beets the luver's fire."[5]

"For Johnie o' the Buskie-glen
I dinna care a single flie;
He lo'es sae weel his craps and kye,[6]
He has nae luve to spare for me;
But blithe's the blink o' Robie's e'e,
And weel I wat he lo'es me dear:
Ae blink o' him I wad na gie
For Buskie-glen and a' his gear."

"O thoughtless lassie, life's a faught;[7]
The canniest gate, the strife is sair;
But aye fu' han't is fechtin[8] best,
An hungry care's an unco care:

[1] Sunny nook of a wood.
[2] Choose.
[3] A plentiful kitchen and parlour.
[4] Sheep-pen. [5] Adds fuel to fire.
[6] Crops and cows.
[7] Fight. [8] Fighting.

But some will spend, and some will spare,
An' wilfu' folk maun hae their will;
Syne as ye brew, my maiden fair,
Keep mind that ye maun drink the yill."[1]

"O, gear will buy me rigs o' land,
And gear will buy me sheep and kye;
But the tender heart o' leesome[2] luve
The gowd and siller canna buy:
We may be poor—Robie and I,—
Light is the burden luve lays on;
Content and luve brings peace and joy,
What mair hae queens upon a throne?"

FAIR ELIZA.

TUNE—"THE BONNIE BRUCKET LASSIE."

Turn again, thou fair Eliza,
Ae kind blink before we part,
Rew[3] on thy despairing lover!
Canst thou break his faithfu' heart?
Turn again, thou fair Eliza,
If to love thy heart denies,
For pity hide the cruel sentence
Under friendship's kind disguise!

Thee, dear maid, hae I offended?
The offence is loving thee;
Canst thou wreck his peace for ever,
Wha for thine wad gladly die?
While the life beats in my bosom,
Thou shalt mix in ilka throe:
Turn again, thou lovely maiden,
Ae sweet smile on me bestow.

Not the bee upon the blossom,
In the pride o' sunny noon;
Not the little sporting fairy,
All beneath the simmer moon;
Not the poet in the moment
Fancy lightens in his e'e,
Kens the pleasure, feels the rapture,
That thy presence gies to me.

[1] Ale. [2] Gladsome.
[3] Look tenderly.

SHE'S FAIR AND FAUSE.

SHE'S fair and fause that causes my smart,
I lo'ed her meikle and lang:
She's broken her vow, she's broken my heart,
And I may e'en gae hang.
A coof came in wi' rowth o' gear,[1]
And I hae tint[2] my dearest dear,
But woman is but warld's gear,
Sae let the bonnie lass gang.

Whae'er ye be that woman love,
To this be never blind,
Nae ferlie[3] 'tis tho' fickle she prove,
A woman has't by kind:
O Woman lovely, Woman fair!
An Angel form's fa'n to thy share,
'Twad been o'er meikle to've gien thee mair,
I mean an Angel mind.

[1] A blockhead came with plenty of wealth.
[2] Lost. [3] No wonder.

THE POSIE.

O LUVE will venture in, where it daur na weel be seen,
O luve will venture in, where wisdom ance has been;
But I will down yon river rove, amang the wood sae green,—
And a' to pu' a Posie to my ain dear May.

The primrose I will pu', the firstling o' the year,
And I will pu' the pink, the emblem o' my dear,
For she's the pink o' womankind, and blooms without a peer;—
And a' to be a Posie to my ain dear May.

I'll pu' the budding rose, when Phœbus peeps in view,
For it's like a baumy kiss o' her sweet bonnie mou;
The hyacinth's for constancy, wi' its unchanging blue,
And a' to be a Posie to my ain dear May.

The lily it is pure, and the lily it is fair,
And in her lovely bosom I'll place the lily there;
The daisy's for simplicity and unaffected air,
And a' to be a Posie to my ain dear May.

The hawthorn I will pu', wi' its locks o' siller gray,
Where, like an aged man, it stands at break o' day,
But the songster's nest within the bush I winna tak away;—
And a' to be a Posie to my ain dear May.

The woodbine I will pu' when the e'ening star is near,
And the diamond drops o' dew shall be her een sae clear:
The violet's for modesty which weel she fa's to wear,—
And a' to be a Posie to my ain dear May.

I'll tie the Posie round wi' the silken band o' luve,
And I'll place it in her breast, and I'll swear by a' above,
That to my latest draught o' life, the band shall ne'er remuve,—
And this will be a Posie to my ain dear May.

THE BANKS O' DOON.[1]

TUNE—"THE CALEDONIAN HUNT'S DELIGHT."

YE banks and braes o' bonnie Doon,
How can ye bloom sae fresh and fair!

[1] We have this song in an earlier and simpler form, as the writer sent it to Mr. Ballantine: Mr. Cunningham, on the authority of an Ayrshire legend, discovers the heroine of the song in

How can ye chant, ye little birds,
An' I sae weary, fu' o' care!

Thou'lt break my heart, thou warbling bird,
That wantons thro' the flowering thorn:
Thou minds me o' departed joys,
Departed—never to return.

Thou'lt break my heart, thou bonnie bird,
That sings beside thy mate;
For sae I sat, and sae I sang,
And wist na o' my fate.

Aft hae I rov'd by bonnie Doon,
To see the rose and woodbine twine;
And ilka bird sang o' its luve,
And fondly sae did I o' mine.

Wi' lightsome heart I pu'd a rose,
Fu' sweet upon its thorny tree;
And my fause luver stole my rose,
But ah! he left the thorn wi' me.

Miss Kennedy, of Dalgarrock, who broke her heart for one M'Dougall, of Logan:

Ye flowery banks o' bonnie Doon,
How can ye blume sae fair!
How can ye chant, ye little birds,
And I sae fu' o' care.

Thou'll break my heart, thou bonnie bird,
That sings upon the bough;
Thou minds me o' the happy days,
When my fause luve was true.

Thou'll break my heart, thou bonnie bird,
That sings beside thy mate;
For sae I sat, and sae I sang,
And wist na o' my fate.

Aft hae I rov'd by bonnie Doon,
To see the woodbine twine,
And ilka bird sang o' its love,
And sae did I o' mine.

Wi' lightsome heart I pu'd a rose
Frae off its thorny tree;
And my fause luver staw the rose,
But left the thorn wi' me.

GLOOMY DECEMBER.[1]

TUNE—"WANDERING WILLIE."

Ance mair I hail thee, thou gloomy December!
Ance mair I hail thee wi' sorrow and care;
Sad was the parting thou makes me remember,
Parting wi' Nancy, oh! ne'er to meet mair.
Fond lovers' parting is sweet painful pleasure,
Hope beaming mild on the soft parting hour;
But the dire feeling, O farewell for ever!
Is anguish unmingl'd and agony pure.
Wild as the winter now tearing the forest,
Till the last leaf o' the summer is flown,
Such is the tempest has taken my bosom,
Since my last hope and comfort is gone.
Still as I hail thee, thou gloomy December,
Still shall I hail thee wi' sorrow and care.
For sad was the parting thou makes me remember,
Parting wi' Nancy, oh! ne'er to meet mair.

BEHOLD THE HOUR.

TUNE—"ORAN-GAOIL."

Behold the hour, the boat arrive!
Thou go'st, thou darling of my heart:
Sever'd from thee can I survive?
But fate has will'd, and we must part!
I'll often greet this surging swell;
Yon distant isle will often hail:
"E'en here I took the last farewell;
There latest mark'd her vanish'd sail."
Along the solitary shore,
While flitting sea-fowls round me cry,

[1] On parting from Clarinda.

Across the rolling, dashing roar,
  I'll westward turn my wistful eye:
"Happy, thou Indian grove," I'll say,
  "Where now my Nancy's path may be!
While thro' thy sweets she loves to stray,
  O, tell me, does she muse on me?"

WILLIE'S WIFE.[1]

TUNE—"TIBBIE FOWLER IN THE GLEN."

WILLIE WASTLE dwalt on Tweed,
  The spot they ca'd it Linkum-doddie,
Willie was a wabster[2] guid,
  Cou'd stown a clue wi' onie bodie;
He had a wife was dour and din,[3]
  Oh, Tinkler Madgie was her mither;
  Sic a wife as Willie had,
  I wad na gie a button for her.

She has an e'e, she has but ane,
  The cat has twa the very colour;
Five rusty teeth, forbye a stump,
  A clapper tongue wad deave[4] a miller;
A whiskin beard about her mou,
  Her nose and chin they threaten ither;
  Sic a wife as Willie had,
  I wad na gie a button for her.

She's bow-hough'd,[5] she's hein-shinn'd,
  Ae limpin leg, a hand-breed[6] shorter;
She's twisted right, she's twisted left,
  To balance fair in ilka quarter:
She has a hump upon her breast,
  The twin o' that upon her shouther;
  Sic a wife as Willie had,
  I wad na gie a button for her.

Auld baudrons[7] by the ingle sits,
  An' wi' her loof her face a-washin;
But Willie's wife is nae sae trig,[8]
  She dights[9] her grunzie[10] wi' a hushion;[11]
Her walie nieves[1] like midden-creels,[2]
  Her face wad fyle[3] the Logan-water;
  Sic a wife as Willie had,
  I wad na gie a button for her

[1] Willie's wife is said to have been the wife of a farmer near Ellisland.
[2] Weaver. [3] Sullen and sallow.
[4] Deafen.
[5] Out-kneed. [6] Hand's-breadth.
[7] Cat. [8] Neat. [9] Wipes.
[10] Mouth. [11] Cushion.

AFTON WATER.[4]

FLOW gently, sweet Afton, among thy green braes,
Flow gently, I'll sing thee a song in thy praise;
My Mary's asleep by thy murmuring stream,
Flow gently, sweet Afton, disturb not her dream.

Thou stock-dove whose echo resounds thro' the glen,
Ye wild whistling blackbirds in yon thorny den,
Thou green-crested lapwing, thy screaming forbear,
I charge you disturb not my slumbering fair.

How lofty, sweet Afton, thy neighbouring hills,
Far mark'd with the courses of clear, winding rills,
There daily I wander as noon rises high,
My flocks and my Mary's sweet cot in my eye.

How pleasant thy banks and green valleys below,
Where wild in the woodlands the primroses blow;
There oft as mild ev'ning weeps over the lea,
The sweet-scented birk shades my Mary and me.

Thy crystal stream, Afton, how lovely it glides,
And winds by the cot where my Mary resides:
How wanton thy waters her snowy feet lave,
As gathering sweet flow'rets she stems thy clear wave.

[1] Big fists. [2] Dung-baskets. [3] Soil.
[4] Afton, a stream in Ayrshire.

Flow gently, sweet Afton, among thy green braes,
Flow gently, sweet river, the theme of my lays;
My Mary's asleep by thy murmuring stream,
Flow gently, sweet Afton, disturb not her dream.

LOUIS, WHAT RECK I BY THEE.

TUNE—"MY MOTHER'S AYE GLOWRING O'ER ME."

Louis, what reck I by thee,
Or Geordie on his ocean?
Dyvor, beggar loons to me,
I reign in Jeanie's[1] bosom.

Let her crown my love her law,
And in her breast enthrone me:
Kings and nations, swith awa![2]
Reif randies,[3] I disown ye!

BONNIE BELL.

The smiling Spring comes in rejoicing,
And surly Winter grimly flies:
Now crystal clear are the falling waters,
And bonnie blue are the sunny skies;
Fresh o'er the mountains breaks forth the morning,
The ev'ning gilds the ocean's swell;
All creatures joy in the sun's returning,
And I rejoice in my bonnie Bell.

The flowery Spring leads sunny Summer,
And yellow Autumn presses near,
Then in his turn comes gloomy Winter,
Till smiling Spring again appear.
Thus seasons dancing, life advancing,
Old Time and Nature their changes tell;
But never ranging, still unchanging,
I adore my bonnie Bell.

[1] Mrs. Burns. [2] Get away. [3] Sturdy beggars.

FOR THE SAKE OF SOMEBODY.

TUNE—"THE HIGHLAND WATCH'S FAREWELL."

My heart is sair, I dare na tell,
My heart is sair for somebody;
I could wake a winter night,
For the sake o' somebody.
Oh-hon! for somebody!
Oh-hey! for somebody!
I could range the world around,
For the sake o' somebody.

Ye powers that smile on virtuous love,
O sweetly smile on somebody!
Frae ilka danger keep him free,
And send me safe my somebody!
Oh-hon! for somebody!
Oh-hey! for somebody!
I wad do—what wad I not?
For the sake o' somebody!

O MAY, THY MORN.

O May, thy morn was ne'er sae sweet
As the mirk night o' December,
For sparkling was the rosy wine,
And private was the chamber:
And dear was she I dare na name,
But I will aye remember.
And dear, &c.

And here's to them that, like oursel,
Can push about the jorum;
And here's to them that wish us weel;—
May a' that's guid watch o'er them;
And here's to them we dare na tell,
The dearest o' the quorum.
And here's to, &c.

THE LOVELY LASS OF INVERNESS.

The lovely lass o' Inverness,
Nae joy nor pleasure can she see;
For e'en and morn she cries, alas!
And aye the saut tear blins her e'e:

Drumossie Moor, Drumossie day,[1]
  A waefu' day it was to me;
For there I lost my father dear,
  My father dear, and brethren three.

Their winding-sheet the bluidy clay,
  Their graves are growing green to see;
And by them lies the dearest lad
  That ever blest a woman's e'e!
Now wae to thee, thou cruel lord,
  A bluidy man I trow thou be;
For monie a heart thou hast made sair,
  That ne'er did wrang to thine or thee.

A RED, RED ROSE.

TUNE—"WISHAW'S FAVOURITE."

O, MY luve's like a red, red rose
  That's newly sprung in June:
O, my luve's like the melodie
  That's sweetly play'd in tune.

As fair art thou, my bonnie lass,
  So deep in luve am I:
And I will luve thee still, my dear,
  Till a' the seas gang dry.

Till a' the seas gang dry, my dear,
  And the rocks melt wi' the sun:
I will luve thee still, my dear,
  While the sands o' life shall run.

And fare thee weel, my only luve!
  And fare thee weel awhile!
And I will come again, my luve,
  Tho' it were ten thousand mile.

O, WAT YE WHA'S IN YON TOWN?

TUNE—"THE BONNIE LASS IN YON TOWN."

O, WAT ye wha's in yon town,
  Ye see the e'enin sun upon?
The fairest dame's[1] in yon town,
  That e'enin sun is shining on.

Now haply down yon gay green shaw,
  She wanders by yon spreading tree;
How blest, ye flow'rs that round her blaw,
  Ye catch the glances o' her e'e!

How blest, ye birds that round her sing,
  And welcome in the blooming year;
And doubly welcome be the spring,
  The season to my Lucy dear!

The sun blinks blithe on yon town,
  And on yon bonnie braes of Ayr;
But my delight in yon town,
  And dearest bliss, is Lucy fair.

Without my love, not a' the charms
  O' Paradise could yield me joy;
But gie me Lucy in my arms,
  And welcome Lapland's dreary sky.

My cave wad be a lover's bower,
  Tho' raging winter rent the air;
And she a lovely little flower,
  That I wad tent and shelter there.

O, sweet is she in yon town,
  Yon sinkin sun's gane down upon;
A fairer than's in yon town,
  His setting beam ne'er shone upon.

If angry fate is sworn my foe,
  And suffering I am doom'd to bear;
I careless quit aught else below,
  But spare me, spare me, Lucy dear.

For while life's dearest blood is warm,
  Ae thought frae her shall ne'er depart,
And she—as fairest is her form,—
  She has the truest, kindest heart.[2]

---

[1] The battle of Culloden, on Drumossie Moor.

[1] Mrs. Oswald, of Auchincruive, whose beauty and accomplishments so dazzled Burns, that he resolved to "say nothing at all" about her, "in despair of saying anything adequate."

[2] These lines are in the form of an address from the husband to his wife.

A VISION.

TUNE—"CUMNOCK PSALMS."

As I stood by yon roofless tower,[1]
Where the wa'-flower scents the dewy air,
Where the howlet mourns in her ivy bower,
And tells the midnight moon her care ;

The winds were laid, the air was still,
The stars they shot alang the sky ;
The fox was howling on the hill,
And the distant-echoing glens reply.

The stream, adown its haz'lly path,
Was rushing by the ruin'd wa',
Hasting to join the sweeping Nith,
Whase distant roarings swell and fa'.

The cauld blue north was streaming forth
Her lights, wi' hissing, eerie din ;
Athort the lift they start and shift,
Like fortune's favours, tint as win.

By heedless chance I turn'd mine eyes,
And, by the moonbeam, shook to see
A stern and stalwart ghaist arise,
Attir'd as minstrels wont to be.

Had I a statue been o' stane,
His darin look had daunted me ;
And on his bonnet grav'd was plain
The sacred posy—Libertie !

And frae his harp sic strains did flow,
Might rouse the slumbering dead to hear ;
But oh, it was a tale of woe,
As ever met a Briton's ear !

He sang wi' joy his former day,
He weeping wail'd his latter times ;
But what he said it was nae play ;
I winna venture 't in my rhymes.

[1] The tower belonged to the ruins of Lincluden Abbey, near Dumfries, a most poetical scene, and often visited by Burns.

O WERT THOU IN THE CAULD BLAST.

TUNE—"THE LASS OF LIVINGSTONE."

O, WERT thou in the cauld blast,
On yonder lea, on yonder lea ;
My plaidie to the angry airt,[1]
I'd shelter thee, I'd shelter thee.
Or did misfortune's bitter storms
Around thee blaw, around thee blaw,
Thy bield should be my bosom,
To share it a', to share it a'.

Or were I in the wildest waste,
Of earth and air, of earth and air,
The desert were a paradise,
If thou wert there, if thou wert there.
Or were I monarch o' the globe,
Wi' thee to reign, wi' thee to reign,
The only jewel in my crown,
Wad be my queen, wad be my queen.

THE HIGHLAND LASSIE.[2]

TUNE—"THE DEUKS DANG O'ER MY DADDY."

NAE gentle dames, tho' e'er sae fair,
Shall ever be my Muse's care ;
Their titles a' are empty show ;
Gie me my Highland lassie, O.

CHORUS.

Within the glen sae bushy, O,
Aboon the plain sae rushy, O,
I set me down wi' right good will,
To sing my Highland lassie, O.

Oh, were yon hills and valleys mine,
Yon palace and yon gardens fine !
The world then the love should know
I bear my Highland lassie, O.
Within the glen, &c.

[1] Quarter of the sky.
[2] Mary Campbell, my Highland lassie, was a warm-hearted, charming young creature as ever blessed a man with generous love.—R. B.

But fickle fortune frowns on me,
And I maun cross the raging sea;
But while my crimson currents flow
I'll love my Highland lassie, O.
Within the glen, &c.

Altho' thro' foreign climes I range,
I know her heart will never change,
For her bosom burns with honour's glow,
My faithful Highland lassie, O.
Within the glen, &c.

For her I'll dare the billow's roar,
For her I'll dare the distant shore,
That Indian wealth may lustre throw
Around my Highland lassie, O.
Within thy glen, &c.

She has my heart, she has my hand,
By sacred truth and honour's band!
Till the mortal stroke shall lay me low,
I'm thine, my Highland lassie, O.

Fareweel the glen sae bushy, O!
Fareweel the plain sae rushy, O!
To other lands I now must go,
To sing my Highland lassie, O!

JOCKEY'S TA'EN THE PARTING KISS.

Jockey's ta'en the parting kiss,
O'er the mountains he is gane;
And with him is a' my bliss,
Nought but griefs with me remain.

Spare my luve, ye winds that blaw,
Plashy sleets and beating rain!
Spare my luve, thou feathery snaw,
Drifting o'er the frozen plain!

When the shades of evening creep
O'er the day's fair, gladsome e'e,
Sound and safely may he sleep,
Sweetly blithe his waukening be!

He will think on her he loves,
Fondly he'll repeat her name;
For where'er he distant roves,
Jockey's heart is still at hame.

PEGGY'S CHARMS.[1]

My Peggy's face, my Peggy's form,
The frost of hermit age might warm;
My Peggy's worth, my Peggy's mind,
Might charm the first of human kind.
I love my Peggy's angel air,
Her face so truly heavenly fair,
Her native grace so void of art:
But I adore my Peggy's heart.
The lily's hue, the rose's dye,
The kindling lustre of an eye;
Who but owns their magic sway,
Who but knows they all decay!
The tender thrill, the pitying tear,
The generous purpose, nobly dear,
The gentle look that rage disarms,—
These are all immortal charms.

UP IN THE MORNING EARLY.

CHORUS.

Up in the morning's no for me,
Up in the morning early;
When a' the hills are cover'd wi' snaw,
I'm sure it's winter fairly.

Cauld blaws the wind frae east to west,
The drift is driving sairly;
Sae loud and shrill I hear the blast,
I'm sure it's winter fairly.

The birds sit chittering[2] in the thorn
A' day they fare but sparely;
And lang's the night frae e'en to morn
I'm sure it's winter fairly.
Up in the morning, &c.

THO' CRUEL FATE.

Tho' cruel fate should bid us part,
As far's the pole and line;
Her dear idea round my heart
Should tenderly entwine.

[1] Peggy was Miss Margaret Chalmers.
[2] Shivering.

Tho' mountains frown and deserts howl,
And oceans roar between;
Yet, dearer than my deathless soul,
I still would love my Jean.

*   *   *   *   *

I DREAM'D I LAY WHERE FLOWERS WERE SPRINGING.[1]

I DREAM'D I lay where flowers were springing
Gaily in the sunny beam;
List'ning to the wild birds singing,
By a falling, crystal stream:
Straight the sky grew black and daring:
Thro' the woods the whirlwinds rave;
Trees with aged arms were warring,
O'er the swelling, drumlie[2] wave.

Such was my life's deceitful morning,
Such the pleasures I enjoy'd;
But lang or noon, loud tempests, storming,
A' my flowery bliss destroy'd.
Tho' fickle fortune has deceived me,
She promis'd fair, and perform'd but ill,
Of monie a joy and hope bereav'd me,
I bear a heart shall support me still.

BONNIE ANN.[3]

YE gallants bright, I rede[4] you right,
Beware o' bonnie Ann;
Her comely face sae fu' o' grace,
Your heart she will trepan.
Her een sae bright, like stars by night,
Her skin is like the swan;
Sae jimply[5] lac'd her genty[6] waist,
That sweetly ye might span.

Youth, grace, and love, attendant move,
And pleasure leads the van;

[1] Written in the poet's eighteenth year.
[2] Muddy.
[3] Ann Masterton, the daughter of a friend of Burns.
[4] Counsel.
[5] Slenderly.
[6] Elegant.

In a' their charms, and conquering arms,
They wait on bonnie Ann.
The captive bands may chain the hands,
But love enslaves the man:
Ye gallants braw, I rede you a',
Beware o' bonnie Ann.

MY BONNIE MARY.

Go fetch to me a pint o' wine,
An' fill it in a silver tassie;[1]
That I may drink, before I go,
A service to my bonnie lassie.
The boat rocks at the pier o' Leith;
Fu' loud the wind blaws frae the ferry;
The ship rides by the Berwick-law,
And I maun leave my bonnie Mary.

The trumpets sound, the banners fly,
The glittering spears are ranked ready;
The shouts o' war are heard afar,
The battle closes thick and bloody;
But it's no the roar o' sea or shore
Wad mak me langer wish to tarry;
Nor shout o' war that's heard afar,—
It's leaving thee, my bonnie Mary.

MY HEART'S IN THE HIGHLANDS.[2]

MY heart's in the Highlands, my heart is not here;
My heart's in the Highlands a-chasing the deer;
Chasing the wild deer, and following the roe,—
My heart's in the Highlands wherever I go.
Farewell to the Highlands, farewell to the North,
The birth-place of valour, the country of worth;
Wherever I wander, wherever I rove,
The hills of the Highlands for ever I love.

[1] Measure.
[2] The first half stanza of this song is old, the rest is mine.—R. B.

Farewell to the mountains high cover'd with snow;
Farewell to the straths and green valleys below;
Farewell to the forests and wild-hanging woods;
Farewell to the torrents and loud-pouring floods.
My heart's in the Highlands, my heart is not here,
My heart's in the Highlands a-chasing the deer;
Chasing the wild deer, and following the roe,—
My heart's in the Highlands, wherever I go.

THERE'S A YOUTH IN THIS CITY.

TUNE—"NEIL GOW'S LAMENT."

THERE'S a youth in this city, it were a great pity,
That he from our lasses should wander awa;
For he's bonnie and braw, weel-favour'd witha',
And his hair has a natural buckle and a'.
His coat is the hue of his bonnet sae blue;
His fecket[1] is white as the new-driven snaw;
His hose they are blae, and his shoon like the slae,
And his clear siller buckles they dazzle us a'.
His coat is the hue, &c.

For beauty and fortune the laddie's been courtin;
Weel-featur'd, weel-tocher'd, weel-mounted and braw;
But chiefly the siller, that gars him gang till her,
The pennie's the jewel that beautifies a'.

[1] An under waistcoat having sleeves.

There's Meg wi' the mailin, that fain wad a haen him,
And Susy whase daddy was Laird o' the ha';
There's lang-tocher'd Nancy maist fetters his fancy,
—But the laddie's dear sel he lo'es dearest of a'.

THE RANTIN DOG THE DADDIE O'T.[1]

TUNE—"EAST NOOK O' FIFE."

O WHA my babie-clouts will buy?
Wha will tent me when I cry?
Wha will kiss me whare I lie?
The rantin dog the daddie o't.

Wha will own he did the faut?
Wha will buy my groanin maut?
Wha will tell me how to ca't?
The rantin dog the daddie o't.

When I mount the creepie-chair,
Wha will sit beside me there?
Gie me Rob, I seek nae mair,
The rantin dog the daddie o't.

Wha will crack to me my lane?
Wha will mak me fidgin fain?[2]
Wha will kiss me o'er again?
The rantin dog the daddie o't.

I DO CONFESS THOU ART SAE FAIR.

I DO confess thou art sae fair,
I wad been o'er the lugs[3] in luve;
Had I not found the slightest prayer,
That lips could speak, thy heart could muve.

[1] I composed this song pretty early in life, and sent it to a young girl, a very particular acquaintance of mine, who was at the time under a cloud.—R. B. The "young girl" was Elizabeth Paton.

[2] Tickled with pleasure.

[3] Ears.

I do confess thee sweet, but find
 Thou art sae thriftless o' thy sweets,
Thy favours are the silly wind
 That kisses ilka thing it meets.

See yonder rose-bud rich in dew,
 Amang its native briers sae coy,
How soon it tines its scent and hue,
 When pu'd and worn a common toy!

Sic fate ere lang shall thee betide;
 Though thou may gaily bloom awhile,
Yet soon thou shalt be thrown aside,
 Like ony common weed and vile.

YON WILD MOSSY MOUNTAINS.

Yon wild mossy mountains, sae lofty and wide,
That nurse in their bosom the youth o' the Clyde,
Where the grouse lead their coveys thro' the heather to feed,
And the shepherd tents his flock, as he pipes on his reed:
 Where the grouse, &c.

Not Gowrie's rich valley, nor Forth's sunny shores,
To me hae the charms o' yon wild mossy moors;
For there, by a lanely, sequester'd, clear stream,
Resides a sweet lassie, my thought and my dream.

Amang the wild mountains shall still be my path,
Ilk stream foaming down its ain green narrow strath;
For there, wi' my lassie, the day lang I rove,
While o'er us, unheeded, fly the swift hours o' love.

She is not the fairest, altho' she is fair;
O' nice education but sma' is her share;
Her parentage humble as humble can be;
But I lo'e the dear lassie, because she lo'es me.

To beauty what man but maun yield him a prize,
In her armour of glances, and blushes, and sighs?
And when wit and refinement hae polish'd her darts,
They dazzle our een, as they fly to our hearts.

But kindness, sweet kindness, in the fond sparkling e'e,
Has lustre out-shining the diamond to me;
And the heart beating love, as I'm clasp'd in her arms,—
O, these are my lassie's all-conquering charms!

WHA IS THAT AT MY BOWER DOOR?

Wha is that at my bower door?
 O wha is it but Findlay;
Then gae your gate, ye'se nae be here!
 Indeed maun I, quo' Findlay.
What mak ye sae like a thief?
 O come and see, quo' Findlay;
Before the morn ye'll work mischief;
 Indeed will I, quo' Findlay.

Gif I rise and let you in;
 Let me in, quo' Findlay;
Ye'll keep me waukin' wi' your din;
 Indeed will I, quo' Findlay.
In my bower if ye should stay;
 Let me stay, quo' Findlay;
I fear ye'll bide till break o' day;
 Indeed will I, quo' Findlay.

Here this night if ye remain;
 I'll remain, quo' Findlay;
I dread ye'll learn the gate again;
 Indeed will I, quo' Findlay.
What may pass within this bower—
 Let it pass, quo' Findlay;
Ye maun conceal till your last hour;
 Indeed will I, quo' Findlay.

THE BONNIE BLINK O' MARY'S E'E.

Now bank an' brae are claith'd in green,
 An' scatter'd cowslips sweetly spring;

By Girvan's fairy-haunted stream
  The birdies flit on wanton wing.
To Cassillis' banks when e'ening fa's,
  There wi' my Mary let me flee,
There catch her ilka glance o' love,
  The bonnie blink o' Mary's e'e !

The chield wha boasts o' warld's wealth,
  Is often laird o' meikle care ;
But Mary she is a' my ain,—
  Ah, fortune canna gie me mair !
Then let me range by Cassillis' banks
  Wi' her the lassie dear to me,
And catch her ilka glance o' love,
  The bonnie blink o' Mary's e'e !

FAREWELL TO NANCY.[1]

Ae fond kiss, and then we sever !
Ae fareweel, alas, for ever !
Deep in heart-wrung tears I'll pledge
  thee !
Warring sighs and groans I'll wage
  thee.
Who shall say that fortune grieves him,
While the star of hope she leaves him ?
Me, nae cheerfu' twinkle lights me ;
Dark despair around benights me.

I'll ne'er blame my partial fancy,
Naething could resist my Nancy ;
But to see her, was to love her ;
Love but her, and love for ever.
Had we never lov'd sae kindly,
Had we never lov'd sae blindly,
Never met—or never parted,
We had ne'er been broken-hearted !

Fare thee weel, thou first and fairest !
Fare thee weel, thou best and dearest !
Thine be ilka joy and treasure,
Peace, enjoyment, love, and pleasure.
Ae fond kiss, and then we sever ;
Ae fareweel, alas, for ever !
Deep in heart-wrung tears I'll pledge
  thee,
Warring sighs and groans I'll wage
  thee.

[1] Supposed to have been addressed to Clarinda.

THE BONNIE LAD THAT'S FAR AWA.

TUNE—"OWRE THE HILLS AND FAR AWA."

O how can I be blithe and glad,
  Or how can I gang brisk and braw,
When the bonnie lad that I lo'e best
  Is o'er the hills and far awa ?

It's no the frosty winter wind,
  It's no the driving drift and snaw ;
But ay the tear comes in my e'e,
  To think on him that's far awa.

My father pat me frae his door,
  My friends they hae disown'd me a' :
But I hae ane will take my part,
  The bonnie lad that's far awa.

A pair o' gloves he gae to me,
  And silken snoods[1] he gae me twa ;
And I will wear them for his sake,
  The bonnie lad that's far awa.

The weary winter soon will pass,
  And spring will cleed[2] the birken-
    shaw ;
And my sweet babie will be born,
  And he'll come hame that's far awa.

THE GOWDEN LOCKS OF ANNA.

TUNE—"BANKS OF BANNA."

Yestreen I had a pint o' wine,
  A place where body saw na' ;
Yestreen lay on this breast o' mine
  The gowden locks of Anna.
The hungry Jew in wilderness,
  Rejoicing o'er his manna,
Was naething to my hinny bliss
  Upon the lips of Anna.

Ye monarchs, tak the east and west,
  Frae Indus to Savannah !
Gie me within my straining grasp
  The melting form of Anna.

[1] Ribands for binding the hair.
[2] Clothe.

There I'll despise imperial charms,
An Empress, or Sultana,
While dying raptures in her arms,
I give and take with Anna!

Awa, thou flaunting god o' day!
Awa, thou pale Diana!
Ilk star gae hide thy twinkling ray,
When I'm to meet my Anna.
Come, in thy raven plumage, night,
Sun, moon, and stars withdrawn a';
And bring an angel pen to write
My transports wi' my Anna!

POSTSCRIPT.

Anna of the gowden locks was a maiden of Dumfries; and Burns thought so much of this piece that he recommended it to Thomson for publication; but irritated, perhaps, at his refusal, "wrote this additional postscript," says Cunningham, "in defiance of his colder-blooded critic."

The kirk and state may join, and tell
To do such things I maunna;
The kirk and state may gae to hell,
And I'll gae to my Anna.
She is the sunshine o' my ee,—
To live bot her I canna;
Had I on earth but wishes three,
The first should be my Anna.

OUT OVER THE FORTH.

Out over the Forth I look to the north,
But what is the north and its Highlands to me?
The south nor the east gie ease to my breast,
The far foreign land, or the wild rolling sea.

But look to the west when I gae to rest,
That happy my dreams and my slumbers may be;
For far in the west, lives he I lo'e best,
The lad that is dear to my babie and me.

BANKS OF DEVON.[1]

How pleasant the banks of the clear-winding Devon,
With green-spreading bushes, and flowers blooming fair!
But the bonniest flower on the banks of the Devon,
Was once a sweet bud on the braes of the Ayr.

Mild be the sun on this sweet blushing flower,
In the gay rosy morn as it bathes in the dew!
And gentle the fall of the soft vernal shower,
That steals on the evening each leaf to renew.

O, spare the dear blossom, ye orient breezes,
With chill hoary wing as ye usher the dawn!
And far be thou distant, thou reptile that seizes
The verdure and pride of the garden and lawn!

Let Bourbon exult in his gay gilded lilies,
And England triumphant display her proud rose;
A fairer than either adorns the green valleys
Where Devon, sweet Devon, meandering flows.

ADOWN WINDING NITH.

TUNE—"THE MUCKIN O' GEORDIE'S BYRE."

Adown winding Nith I did wander,
To mark the sweet flowers as they spring;
Adown winding Nith I did wander,
Of Phillis[2] to muse and to sing.

---

[1] Composed on Charlotte, a sister of the poet's friend Gavin Hamilton.
[2] Miss Phillis M'Murdo.

CHORUS.

Awa wi' your belles and your beauties,
They never wi' her can compare ;
Whaever has met wi' my Phillis,
Has met wi' the queen o' the fair.

The daisy amus'd my fond fancy,
So artless, so simple, so wild ;
Thou emblem, said I, o' my Phillis,
For she is simplicity's child.
Awa, &c.

The rosebud's the blush o' my charmer,
Her sweet balmy lip when 'tis prest :
How fair and how pure is the lily,
But fairer and purer her breast.
Awa, &c.

Yon knot of gay flowers in the arbour,
They ne'er wi' my Phillis can vie :
Her breath is the breath o' the woodbine,
Its dew-drop o' diamond, her eye.
Awa, &c.

Her voice is the song of the morning
That wakes through the green-spreading grove,
When Phœbus peeps over the mountains,
On music, and pleasure, and love.
Awa, &c.

But beauty how frail and how fleeting,
The bloom of a fine summer's day !
While worth in the mind o' my Phillis
Will flourish without a decay.
Awa, &c.

THE DEIL'S AWA WI' THE EXCISEMAN.[1]

THE Deil cam fiddling thro' the town,
And danc'd awa wi' the Exciseman ;
And ilka wife cry'd, "Auld Mahoun,
We wish you luck o' your prize, man.

"We'll mak our maut, and brew our drink,
We'll dance, and sing, and rejoice, man ;
And monie thanks to the muckle black Deil
That danc'd awa wi' the Exciseman.

"There's threesome reels, and foursome reels,
There's hornpipes and strathspeys, man ;
But the ae best dance e'er cam to our lan',
Was—The Deil's awa wi' the Exciseman.
We'll mak our maut," &c.

[1] At a meeting of his brother Excisemen in Dumfries, Burns, being called upon for a song, handed these verses to the president, written on the back of a letter.—*Cromek.*

BLITHE HAE I BEEN ON YON HILL.

TUNE—"LIGGERAM COSH."

BLITHE hae I been on yon hill,
As the lambs before me ;
Careless ilka thought and free,
As the breeze flew o'er me :
Now nae langer sport and play,
Mirth or sang can please me ?
Leslie is sae fair and coy,
Care and anguish seize me.

Heavy, heavy is the task,
Hopeless love declaring :
Trembling, I do nocht but glowr,
Sighing, dumb, despairing !
If she winna ease the thraws
In my bosom swelling ;
Underneath the grass-green sod
Soon maun be my dwelling.

O WERE MY LOVE YON LILAC FAIR.

TUNE—"HUGHIE GRAHAM."

O WERE my love yon lilac fair,
Wi' purple blossoms to the spring ;
And I a bird to shelter there,
When wearied on my little wing :

How I wad mourn, when it was torn
  By autumn wild, and winter rude!
But I wad sing on wanton wing,
  When youthfu' May its bloom renew'd.

O gin my love were yon red rose
  That grows upon the castle wa',
And I mysel' a drap o' dew,
  Into her bonnie breast to fa'!

Oh! there beyond expression blest,
  I'd feast on beauty a' the night;
Seal'd on her silk-saft faulds to rest,
  Till fley'd awa' by Phœbus' light.[1]

COME, LET ME TAKE THEE.

TUNE—"CAULD KAIL."

Come, let me take thee to my breast,
  And pledge we ne'er shall sunder:
And I shall spurn as vilest dust
  The world's wealth and grandeur:
And do I hear my Jeanie own
  That equal transports move her?
I ask for dearest life alone
  That I may live to love her.

Thus in my arms, wi' all thy charms,
  I clasp my countless treasure;
I'll seek nae mair o' heaven to share,
  Than sic a moment's pleasure:
And by thy een, sae bonnie blue,
  I swear I'm thine for ever!
And on thy lips I seal my vow,
  And break it shall I never.

WHERE ARE THE JOYS.

TUNE—"SAW YE MY FATHER?"

Where are the joys I have met in the morning,
  That danc'd to the lark's early song?
Where is the peace that awaited my wand'ring,
  At evening the wild woods among?

No more a-winding the course of yon river,
  And marking sweet flow'rets so fair:
No more I trace the light footsteps of pleasure,
  But sorrow and sad sighing care.

Is it that summer's forsaken our valleys,
  And grim, surly winter is near?
No, no! the bees humming round the gay roses
  Proclaim it the pride of the year.

Fain would I hide what I fear to discover,
  Yet long, long too well have I known:
All that has caus'd this wreck in my bosom,
  Is Jenny, fair Jenny alone.

Time cannot aid me, my griefs are immortal,
  Not hope dare a comfort bestow:
Come, then, enamour'd and fond of my anguish,
  Enjoyment I'll seek in my woe.

O SAW YE MY DEAR.

TUNE—"WHEN SHE CAM BEN SHE BOBBIT."

O saw ye my dear, my Phely?
O saw ye my dear, my Phely?
She's down i' the grove, she's wi' a new love,
  She winna come hame to her Willy.

What says she, my dearest, my Phely?
What says she, my dearest, my Phely?
She lets thee to wit that she has thee forgot,
  And for ever disowns thee, her Willy.

O had I ne'er seen thee, my Phely!
O had I ne'er seen thee, my Phely!
As light as the air, and fause as thou's fair,
  Thou'st broken the heart o' thy Willy.

[1] The third and fourth verses are copied from Witherspoon's "Collection of Scotch Songs."

THOU HAST LEFT ME EVER, JAMIE.[1]

TUNE—"FEE HIM, FATHER."

Thou hast left me ever, Jamie,
 Thou hast left me ever;
Thou hast left me ever, Jamie,
 Thou hast left me ever.
Aften hast thou vow'd that death
 Only should us sever;
Now thou'st left thy lass for aye—
 I maun see thee never, Jamie,
 I'll see thee never!

Thou hast me forsaken, Jamie,
 Thou hast me forsaken;
Thou hast me forsaken, Jamie,
 Thou hast me forsaken.
Thou canst love anither jo,
 While my heart is breaking;
Soon my weary een I'll close—
 Never mair to waken, Jamie,
 Ne'er mair to waken!

MY CHLORIS.

TUNE—"MY LODGING IS ON THE COLD GROUND."

My Chloris, mark how green the groves,[2]
 The primrose banks how fair:
The balmy gales awake the flowers,
 And wave thy flaxen hair.

The lav'rock shuns the palace gay,
 And o'er the cottage sings:
For nature smiles as sweet, I ween,
 To shepherds, as to kings.

Let minstrels sweep the skilfu' string
 In lordly lighted ha';
The shepherd stops his simple reed,
 Blithe in the birken shaw.

The princely revel may survey
 Our rustic dance wi' scorn;
But are their hearts as light as ours
 Beneath the milk-white thorn?

The shepherd, in the flowery glen,
 In shepherd's phrase will woo:
The courtier tells a finer tale;—
 But is his heart as true?

These wild-wood flowers I've pu'd, to deck
 That spotless breast of thine:
The courtiers' gems may witness love—
 But 'tis na love like mine.

CHARMING MONTH OF MAY.[1]

TUNE—"DAINTY DAVIE."

It was the charming month of May,
When all the flowers were fresh and gay,
One morning, by the break of day,
 The youthful, charming Chloe;

From peaceful slumber she arose,
Girt on her mantle and her hose,
And o'er the flowery mead she goes,
 The youthful, charming Chloe.

CHORUS.

Lovely was she by the dawn,
 Youthful Chloe, charming Chloe,
Tripping o'er the pearly lawn,
 The youthful, charming Chloe.

The feather'd people you might see
Perch'd all around on every tree,
In notes of sweetest melody
 They hail the charming Chloe:

[1] This song was written, as the author tells us, "by the lee-side of a bowl of punch," which had already conquered every other guest.

[2] On my visit the other day to my fair Chloris (that is the poetic name of the lovely goddess of my inspiration) she suggested an idea, which I, on my return from the visit, wrought into the following song.—*To Mr. Thomson*, Nov. 1794.

[1] "Cut down," to adopt the phrase of Burns, from a song in Ramsay's "Tea-Table Miscellany."

Till, painting gay the eastern skies,
The glorious sun began to rise,
Out-rivall'd by the radiant eyes
Of youthful, charming Chloe.
Lovely was she, &c.

LET NOT WOMAN E'ER COMPLAIN.

TUNE—"DUNCAN GRAY."

Let not woman e'er complain
Of inconstancy in love;
Let not woman e'er complain,
Fickle man is apt to rove:
Look abroad through Nature's range,
Nature's mighty law is change;
Ladies, would it not be strange,
Man should then a monster prove?

Mark the winds, and mark the skies;
Ocean's ebb, and ocean's flow:
Sun and moon but set to rise;
Round and round the seasons go.
Why then ask of silly man,
To oppose great Nature's plan?
We'll be constant while we can—
You can be no more, you know.

O PHILLY.[1]

TUNE—"THE SOW'S TAIL."

HE.

O Philly, happy be that day
When, roving through the gather'd hay,
My youthfu' heart was stown away,
And by thy charms, my Philly.

SHE.

O Willy, aye I bless the grove
Where first I own'd my maiden love,
Whilst thou didst pledge the Powers above
To be my ain dear Willy.

HE.

As songsters of the early year
Are ilka day mair sweet to hear,
So ilka day to me mair dear
And charming is my Philly.

SHE.

As on the brier the budding rose
Still richer breathes and fairer blows,
So in my tender bosom grows
The love I bear my Willy.

HE.

The milder sun and bluer sky,
That crown my harvest cares wi' joy,
Were ne'er sae welcome to my eye
As is a sight o' Philly.

SHE.

The little swallow's wanton wing,
Tho' wafting o'er the flowery spring,
Did ne'er to me sic tidings bring
As meeting o' my Willy.

HE.

The bee that thro' the sunny hour
Sips nectar in the opening flower,
Compar'd wi' my delight is poor,
Upon the lips o' Philly.

SHE.

The woodbine in the dewy weet,
When evening shades in silence meet,
Is nocht sae fragrant or sae sweet
As is a kiss o' Willy.

HE.

Let fortune's wheel at random rin,
And fools may tyne, and knaves may win;
My thoughts are a' bound up in ane,
And that's my ain dear Philly.

SHE.

What's a' the joys that gowd can gie
I care na wealth a single flie;
The lad I love's the lad for me,
And that's my ain dear Willy.

JOHN BARLEYCORN.

A BALLAD.

There were three Kings into the east,
Three Kings both great and high;

[1] These verses were composed in a morning walk, "through a keen-blowing frost."

An' they hae sworn a solemn oath
John Barleycorn should die.

They took a plough and plough'd him down,
Put clods upon his head;
An' they hae sworn a solemn oath
John Barleycorn was dead.

But the cheerful Spring came kindly on,
And showers began to fall;
John Barleycorn got up again,
And sore surpris'd them all.

The sultry suns of Summer came,
And he grew thick and strong,
His head weel arm'd wi' pointed spears,
That no one should him wrong.

The sober Autumn enter'd mild,
When he grew wan and pale;
His bending joints and drooping head
Show'd he began to fail.

His colour sicken'd more and more,
He faded into age;
And then his enemies began
To show their deadly rage.

They've ta'en a weapon, long and sharp,
And cut him by the knee;
Then tied him fast upon a cart,
Like a rogue for forgerie.

They laid him down upon his back,
And cudgel'd him full sore;
They hung him up before the storm,
And turn'd him o'er and o'er.

They filled up a darksome pit
With water to the brim,
They heaved in John Barleycorn,
There let him sink or swim.

They laid him out upon the floor,
To work him farther woe;
And still, as signs of life appear'd,
They toss'd him to and fro.

They wasted, o'er a scorching flame,
The marrow of his bones;
But a miller us'd him worst of all,
For he crush'd him 'tween two stones.

And they hae ta'en his very heart's blood,
And drank it round and round;
And still the more and more they drank,
Their joy did more abound.

John Barleycorn was a hero bold,
Of noble enterprise;
For if you do but taste his blood,
'Twill make your courage rise;

'Twill make a man forget his woe;
'Twill heighten all his joy:
'Twill make the widow's heart to sing,
Tho' the tear were in her eye.

Then let us toast John Barleycorn,
Each man a glass in hand;
And may his great posterity
Ne'er fail in old Scotland!

CANST THOU LEAVE ME THUS.

TUNE—"ROY'S WIFE."

CHORUS.

Canst thou leave me thus, my Katy?
Canst thou leave me thus, my Katy?
Well thou know'st my aching heart,—
And canst thou leave me thus for pity?

Is this thy plighted, fond regard,
Thus cruelly to part, my Katy?
Is this thy faithful swain's reward—
An aching, broken heart, my Katy?
Canst thou, &c.

Farewell! and ne'er such sorrows tear
That fickle heart of thine, my Katy!
Thou may'st find those will love thee dear—
But not a love like mine, my Katy.
Canst thou, &c.

ON CHLORIS BEING ILL.

TUNE—"AY WAUKIN O."

CHORUS.

Long, long the night,
Heavy comes the morrow,
While my soul's delight
Is on her bed of sorrow.

CAN I cease to care?
Can I cease to languish,
While my darling fair
Is on the couch of anguish?
Long, &c.

Every hope is fled,
  Every fear is terror;
Slumber even I dread,
  Every dream is horror.
    Long, &c.

Hear me, Pow'rs divine!
  Oh! in pity hear me!
Take aught else of mine,
  But my Chloris spare me!
    Long, &c.

THE RIGS O' BARLEY.

TUNE—"CORN RIGS ARE BONNIE."

It was upon a Lammas night,
  When corn rigs are bonnie,
Beneath the moon's unclouded light,
  I held awa to Annie:
The time flew by, wi' tentless heed,
  Till 'tween the late and early,
Wi' sma' persuasion she agreed
  To see me thro' the barley.

The sky was blue, the wind was still,
  The moon was shining clearly;
I set her down, wi' right good will,
  Amang the rigs o' barley:
I ken't her heart was a' my ain;
  I lov'd her most sincerely;
I kiss'd her owre and owre again
  Amang the rigs o' barley.

I lock'd her in my fond embrace;
  Her heart was beating rarely;
My blessing on that happy place,
  Amang the rigs o' barley!
But by the moon and stars so bright,
  That shone that hour so clearly!
She aye shall bless that happy night
  Amang the rigs o' barley.

I hae been blythe wi' comrades dear;
  I hae been merry drinkin;
I hae been joyfu' gath'rin gear;
  I hae been happy thinking:
But a' the pleasures e'er I saw,
  Tho' three times doubl'd fairly,
That happy night was worth them a',
  Amang the rigs o' barley.

CHORUS.

Corn rigs, an' barley rigs,
  An' corn rigs are bonnie:
I'll ne'er forget that happy night
  Amang the rigs wi' Annie.

FAREWELL TO ELIZA.[1]

TUNE—"GILDEROY."

From thee, Eliza, I must go,
  And from my native shore;
The cruel fates between us throw
  A boundless ocean's roar;
But boundless oceans, roaring wide,
  Between my Love and me,
They never, never can divide
  My heart and soul from thee.

Farewell, farewell, Eliza dear,
  The maid that I adore!
A boding voice is in mine ear,
  We part to meet no more!
But the last throb that leaves my heart,
  While death stands victor by,
That throb, Eliza, is thy part,
  And thine that latest sigh!

MY NANNIE, O.

Behind yon hills where Lugar flows,
  'Mang moors an' mosses many, O,
The wintry sun the day has clos'd,
  And I'll awa to Nannie, O.

The westlin wind blaws loud an' shrill:
  The night's baith mirk and rainy, O!
But I'll get my plaid, an' out I'll steal,
  An' owre the hill to Nannie, O.

My Nannie's charming, sweet, an' young;
  Nae artfu' wiles to win ye, O:
May ill befa' the flattering tongue
  That wad beguile my Nannie, O.

---

[1] The editors of Burns have discovered two Elizas—and perhaps a future inquirer may enlarge the number.

Her face is fair, her heart is true,
As spotless as she's bonnie, O:
The op'ning gowan, wat wi' dew,
Nae purer is than Nannie, O.

A country lad is my degree,
An' few there be that ken me, O;
But what care I how few they be?
I'm welcome aye to Nannie, O.

My riches a's my penny-fee,
An' I maun guide it cannie, O;
But warl's gear ne'er troubles me,
My thoughts are a', my Nannie, O.

Our auld Guidman delights to view
His sheep an' kye thrive bonnie, O;
But I'm as blythe that hauds his pleugh,
An' has nae care but Nannie, O.

Come weal, come woe, I care na by,
I'll tak what Heaven will sen' me, O;
Nae ither care in life have I,
But live, an' love my Nannie, O.

GREEN GROW THE RASHES.[1]

A FRAGMENT.

CHORUS.

Green grow the rashes, O;
Green grow the rashes, O;
The sweetest hours that e'er I spent,
Were spent amang the lasses, O!

THERE's nought but care on ev'ry han',
In ev'ry hour that passes, O;
What signifies the life o' man,
An' 'twere na for the lasses, O.
Green grow, &c.

The warly race may riches chase,
An' riches still may fly them, O;
An' tho' at last they catch them fast,
Their hearts can ne'er enjoy them, O.
Green grow, &c.

But gie me a canny hour at e'en,
My arms about my dearie, O;
An' warly cares, an' warly men,
May a' gae tapsalteerie, O!
Green grow, &c.

For you sae douse, ye sneer at this,
Ye're nought but senseless asses, O;
The wisest man the warl' e'er saw,
He dearly lov'd the lasses, O.
Green grow, &c.

Auld Nature swears, the lovely dears
Her noblest work she classes, O;
Her 'prentice han' she tried on man,
An' then she made the lasses, O.
Green grow, &c.

[1] On this song Burns indites the following note:—"I do not see that the turn of mind and pursuits of such a one as the above verses describe—one who spends the hours and thoughts which the vocations of the day can spare — with Ossian, Shakespeare, Thomson, Shenstone, Sterne, &c., are in the least more inimical to the sacred interests of piety and virtue, than the, even lawful, bustling and straining after the world's riches and honours."

NOW WESTLIN WINDS.

TUNE—"I HAD A HORSE, I HAD NAE MAIR."

Now westlin winds and slaught'ring guns
Bring autumn's pleasant weather;
The moorcock springs, on whirring wings,
Amang the blooming heather:
Now waving grain, wide o'er the plain,
Delights the weary farmer;
And the moon shines bright, when I rove at night
To muse upon my charmer.

The partridge loves the fruitful fells;
The plover loves the mountains;
The woodcock haunts the lonely dells;
The soaring hern the fountains:
Thro' lofty groves the cushat roves,
The path of man to shun it;
The hazel bush o'erhangs the thrush,
The spreading thorn the linnet.

Thus ev'ry kind their pleasure find,
The savage and the tender;
Some social join, and leagues combine;
Some solitary wander;

Avaunt, away! the cruel sway,
  Tyrannic man's dominion;
The sportsman's joy, the murd'ring cry,
  The flutt'ring gory pinion!

But, Peggy dear, the ev'ning's clear,
  Thick flies the skimming swallow;
The sky is blue, the fields in view,
  All fading-green and yellow:
Come, let us stray our gladsome way,
  And view the charms of nature;
The rustling corn, the fruited thorn,
  And ev'ry happy creature.

We'll gently walk, and sweetly talk,
  Till the silent moon shine clearly;
I'll grasp thy waist, and, fondly prest,
  Swear how I love thee dearly:
Not vernal show'rs to budding flow'rs,
  Not autumn to the farmer,
So dear can be, as thou to me,
  My fair, my lovely charmer!

THE BIG-BELLIED BOTTLE.

TUNE—"PREPARE, MY DEAR BRETHREN, TO THE TAVERN LET'S FLY."

No churchman am I for to rail and to write,
No statesman nor soldier to plot or to fight,
No sly man of business contriving a snare,
For a big-bellied bottle's the whole of my care.

The peer I don't envy, I give him his bow;
I scorn not the peasant, tho' ever so low;
But a club of good fellows, like those that are here,
And a bottle like this, are my glory and care.

Here passes the squire on his brother—his horse;
There centum per centum, the cit with his purse;
But see you the Crown how it waves in the air?
There a big-bellied bottle still eases my care.

The wife of my bosom, alas! she did die;
For sweet consolation to church I did fly;
I found that old Solomon proved it fair,
That the big-bellied bottle's a cure for all care.

I once was persuaded a venture to make;
A letter inform'd me that all was to wreck;
But the pursy old landlord just waddled up-stairs
With a glorious bottle that ended my cares.

"Life's cares they are comforts,"[1] a maxim laid down
By the bard, what d'ye call him, that wore the black gown;
And, faith, I agree with th' old prig to a hair,
For a big-bellied bottle's a heav'n of care.

A STANZA ADDED IN A MASON LODGE.

Then fill up a bumper, and make it o'erflow,
And honours masonic prepare for to throw;
May ev'ry true brother of the compass and square
Have a big-bellied bottle when harass'd with care.

THE AUTHOR'S FAREWELL TO HIS NATIVE COUNTRY.[2]

TUNE—"ROSLIN CASTLE."

The gloomy night is gath'ring fast,
Loud roars the wild inconstant blast,

---

[1] Young's "Night Thoughts."

[2] Burns had been visiting the minister of Loudon, and his homeward path led him over solitary moors in a dark and windy evening of autumn. For some days, in his own words, he had been "skulking from covert to covert under all the terrors of a jail;" and expecting almost immediately to em-

Yon murky cloud is foul with rain,
I see it driving o'er the plain;
The hunter now has left the moor,
The scatter'd coveys meet secure,
While here I wander, prest with care,
Along the lonely banks of Ayr.

The Autumn mourns her rip'ning corn
By early Winter's ravage torn:
Across her placid, azure sky,
She sees the scowling tempest fly:
Chill runs my blood to hear it rave,
I think upon the stormy wave,
Where many a danger I must dare,
Far from the bonnie banks of Ayr.

'Tis not the surging billow's roar,
'Tis not that fatal, deadly shore;
Tho' death in ev'ry shape appear,
The wretched have no more to fear:
But round my heart the ties are bound,
That heart transpierc'd with many a wound;
These bleed afresh, those ties I tear,
To leave the bonnie banks of Ayr.

Farewell, old Coila's hills and dales,
Her heathy moors and winding vales;
The scenes where wretched fancy roves,
Pursuing past, unhappy loves!
Farewell, my friends! Farewell, my foes!
My peace with these, my love with those—
The bursting tears my heart declare;
Farewell, the bonnie banks of Ayr!

THE FAREWELL.

TO THE BRETHREN OF ST. JAMES'S LODGE, TARBOLTON.

TUNE—"GUID NIGHT, AND JOY BE WI' YOU A'!"

ADIEU! a heart-warm, fond adieu!
Dear brothers of the mystic tie!
Ye favour'd, ye enlighten'd few,
Companions of my social joy!
Tho' I to foreign lands must hie,
Pursuing Fortune's slidd'ry ba',
With melting heart, and brimful eye,
I'll mind you still, tho' far awa'.

Oft have I met your social band,
And spent the cheerful, festive night;
Oft, honour'd with supreme command,
Presided o'er the sons of light:
And by that hieroglyphic bright,
Which none but craftsmen ever saw!
Strong mem'ry on my heart shall write
Those happy scenes when far awa'!

May freedom, harmony, and love,
Unite you in the grand design,
Beneath the Omniscient eye above,
The glorious Architect Divine!
That you may keep th' unerring line,
Still rising by the plummet's law,
Till Order bright completely shine,
Shall be my pray'r when far awa'.

And You,[1] farewell! whose merits claim,
Justly, that highest badge to wear!
Heav'n bless your honour'd, noble name,
To Masonry and Scotia dear!
A last request permit me here,
When yearly ye assemble a',
One round—I ask it with a tear,
To him, the Bard that's far awa'.

AND MAUN I STILL ON MENIE[2] DOAT.

TUNE—"JOCKEY'S GREY BREEKS."

AGAIN rejoicing Nature sees
Her robe assume its vernal hues,
Her leafy locks wave in the breeze,
All freshly steep'd in morning dews.

CHORUS.[3]

And maun I still on Menie doat,
And bear the scorn that's in her e'e?

---

bark for Jamaica, he designed these lines as a "farewell dirge to his native land."

[1] Sir John Whiteford, the Grand Master.

[2] Menie is the common abbreviation of Marianne.—R. B.

[3] This chorus is part of a song composed by a gentleman in Edinburgh, a particular friend of the author.—R. B.

For its jet, jet black, an' its like a hawk,
An' it winna let a body be !

In vain to me the cowslips blaw,
In vain to me the vi'lets spring;
In vain to me, in glen or shaw,
The mavis and the lintwhite sing.
And maun I still, &c.

The merry ploughboy cheers his team,
Wi' joy the tentie seedsman stalks,
But life to me's a weary dream,
A dream of ane that never wauks.
And maun I still, &c.

The wanton coot[1] the water skims,
Amang the reeds the ducklings cry,
The stately swan majestic swims,
And everything is blest but I.
And maun I still, &c.

The sheep-herd steeks his faulding slap,[2]
And owre the moorland whistles shrill;
Wi' wild, unequal, wand'ring step
I meet him on the dewy hill.
And maun I still, &c.

And when the lark, 'tween light and dark,
Blythe waukens by the daisy's side,
And mounts and sings on flittering[3] wings,
A woe-worn ghaist I hameward glide.
And maun I still, &c.

Come Winter, with thine angry howl,
And raging bend the naked tree;
Thy gloom will soothe my cheerless soul,
When Nature all is sad like me!

And maun I still on Menie doat,
And bear the scorn that's in her e'e?
For its jet, jet black, an' it's like a hawk,
An' it winna let a body be.

---

[1] Water-fowl.
[2] Shuts the gate of the fold.
[3] Trembling.

HIGHLAND MARY.[1]

TUNE—"KATHARINE OGIE."

Ye banks, and braes, and streams around
The castle o' Montgomery,
Green be your woods, and fair your flowers,
Your waters never drumlie![2]
There simmer first unfald her robes,
And there the langest tarry;
For there I took the last fareweel
O' my sweet Highland Mary.

How sweetly bloom'd the gay green birk,
How rich the hawthorn's blossom,
As underneath their fragrant shade,
I clasp'd her to my bosom!
The golden hours, on angel wings,
Flew o'er me and my dearie;
For dear to me, as light and life,
Was my sweet Highland Mary.

Wi' monie a vow, and lock'd embrace,
Our parting was fu' tender;
And, pledging aft to meet again,
We tore oursels asunder;
But oh! fell death's untimely frost,
That nipt my flower sae early!
Now green's the sod, and cauld's the clay,
That wraps my Highland Mary!

O pale, pale now, those rosy lips,
I aft hae kiss'd sae fondly!
And closed for aye the sparkling glance,
That dwelt on me sae kindly!

---

[1] The foregoing song pleases myself; I think it is in my happiest manner. You will see at first glance that it suits the air. The subject of the song is one of the most interesting passages of my youthful days; and I own that I should be much flattered to see the verses set to an air which would ensure celebrity. Perhaps, after all, 'tis the still growing prejudice of my heart that throws a borrowed lustre over the merits of the composition.—R. B.
[2] Muddy.

And mould'ring now in silent dust,
That heart that lo'ed me dearly !
But still within my bosom's core
Shall live my Highland Mary.

AULD LANG SYNE.[1]

SHOULD auld acquaintance be forgot,
And never brought to min' ?
Should auld acquaintance be forgot,
And days o' lang syne?

CHORUS.

For auld lang syne, my dear,
For auld lang syne,
We'll tak a cup o' kindness yet,
For auld lang syne.

We twa hae run about the braes,
And pu'd the gowans fine ;
But we've wander'd mony a weary foot
Sin auld lang syne.
For auld, &c.

We twa hae paidl't i' the burn,
From mornin sun till dine ;
But seas between us braid hae roar'd
Sin auld lang syne.
For auld, &c.

And here's a hand, my trusty fiere,[2]
And gie's a hand o' thine ;
And we'll tak a right guid willie-waught,[3]
For auld lang syne.
For auld, &c.

And surely ye'll be your pint-stowp,
And surely I'll be mine ;
And we'll tak a cup o' kindness yet
For auld lang syne.
For auld, &c.[4]

---

[1] An old song into which Burns threw some of his own fire.

[2] Friend. [3] Draught.

[4] Your meeting, which you so well describe, with your old schoolfellow and friend, was truly interesting. Out upon the ways of the world ! They spoil these "social offsprings of the heart." Two veterans of the "men of the world" would have met with little more heart-workings than two old hacks worn out on the road. Apropos, is not the Scotch phrase, "Auld lang syne," exceedingly expressive? There is an old song and tune which has often thrilled through my soul; I shall give you the verses in the other sheet. Light be the turf on the breast of the heaven-inspired poet who composed this glorious fragment !—*To Mrs. Dunlop, Dec.* 17, 1788; and to *Mr. Thomson, September,* 1793 :—The air is but *mediocre ;* but the following song, the old song of the olden times, and which has never been in print, nor even in manuscript, until I took it down from an old man's singing, is enough to recommend any air.

BANNOCKBURN.[1]

ROBERT BRUCE'S ADDRESS TO HIS ARMY.

TUNE—"HEY TUTTIE, TAITIE."

SCOTS, wha hae wi' Wallace bled,
Scots, wham Bruce has aften led ;
Welcome to your gory bed,
Or to glorious victorie.

Now's the day, and now's the hour
See the front o' battle lour :
See approach proud Edward's pow'r—
Edward ! chains and slaverie !

---

[1] A friend had got a "grey Highland shelty" for Burns, and he made a little excursion on it into Galloway. He was particularly struck with the scenery round Kenmore. From that place he and his companion took the Moor-road to Gatehouse, the dreary country being lighted up by frequent gleams of a thunderstorm, which soon poured down a flood of rain. Burns spoke not a word. "What do you think he was about ?" asked his fellow-traveller, relating the adventure. "He was charging the English army alone with Bruce at Bannockburn. He was engaged in the same manner on our ride home from St. Mary's Isle. I did not disturb him. Next day he produced the following address of Bruce to his troops."—Mr. SYME, *quoted by Currie*, i. 211.

Wha will be a traitor knave?
Wha can fill a coward's grave?
Wha sae base as be a slave?
  Traitor! coward! turn and flee?

Wha for Scotland's King and law
Freedom's sword will strongly draw,
Free-man stand, or free-man fa'?
  Caledonian! on wi' me!

By Oppression's woes and pains!
By your sons in servile chains,
We will drain our dearest veins,
  But they shall—they shall be free!

Lay the proud usurpers low!
Tyrants fall in every foe!
Liberty's in every blow!
  Forward! let us do, or die![1]

THE GALLANT WEAVER.

TUNE—"THE AULD WIFE AYONT THE FIRE."

Where Cart rins rowin[2] to the sea,
By monie a flow'r and spreading tree,
There lives a lad, the lad for me,
  He is a gallant weaver.

Oh, I had wooers aught or nine,
They gied me rings and ribbons fine;
And I was fear'd my heart would tine,
  And I gied it to the weaver.

My daddie sign'd my tocher-band,[3]
To gie the lad that has the land,
But to my heart I'll add my hand,
  And gie it to the weaver.

While birds rejoice in leafy bowers:
While bees rejoice in opening flowers;
While corn grows green in simmer showers,
  I'll love my gallant weaver.

[1] Independent of my enthusiasm as a Scotchman, I have rarely met with anything in history which interests my feelings as a man equal with the story of Bannockburn. On the one hand, a cruel but able usurper leading on the finest army in Europe to extinguish the last spark of freedom among a greatly-daring and greatly-injured people; on the other hand, the desperate relics of a gallant nation, devoting themselves to rescue their bleeding country, or to perish with her.—Burns *to Earl of Buchan*, Jan. 12, 1794.

[2] Rolling. [3] Marriage bond.

SONG.

Anna, thy charms my bosom fire,
  And waste my soul with care;
But ah! how bootless to admire,
  When fated to despair!

Yet in thy presence, lovely fair,
  To hope may be forgiven;
For, sure, 'twere impious to despair
  So much in sight of heaven.

FOR A' THAT AND A' THAT.

Is there, for honest poverty,
  That hangs his head, and a' that?
The coward-slave, we pass him by,
  We dare be poor for a' that!
    For a' that, and a' that,
      Our toils obscure, and a' that;
    The rank is but the guinea stamp;
      The man's the gowd for a' that.

What tho' on hamely fare we dine,
  Wear hodden-grey,[1] and a' that;
Gie fools their silks, and knaves their wine,
  A man's a man, for a' that.
    For a' that, and a' that,
      Their tinsel show, and a' that:
    The honest man, tho' e'er sae poor,
      Is King o' men for a' that.

Ye see yon birkie,[2] ca'd a lord,
  Wha struts, and stares, and a' that;
Tho' hundreds worship at his word,
  He's but a coof[3] for a' that:
    For a' that, and a' that,
      His riband, star, and a' that,
    The man of independent mind,
      He looks and laughs at a' that.

[1] Coarse woollen cloth.

[2] Conceited fellow. [3] Blockhead.

A prince can mak a belted knight,
A marquis, duke, and a' that;
But an honest man's aboon his might,
Guid faith, he mauna fa'[1] that!
For a' that, and a' that,
Their dignities, and a' that,
The pith o' sense, and pride o' worth,
Are higher ranks than a' that.

Then let us pray that come it may,
As come it will for a' that;
That sense and worth, o'er a' the earth,
May bear the gree,[2] and a' that;
For a' that, and a' that,
It's coming yet, for a' that;
That man to man, the warld o'er,
Shall brothers be for a' that.

TO MR. CUNNINGHAM.

TUNE—"THE HOPELESS LOVER."

Now spring has clad the groves in green,
And strew'd the lea wi' flowers;
The furrow'd, waving corn is seen
Rejoice in fostering showers;
While ilka thing in nature join
Their sorrows to forego,
O why thus all alone are mine
The weary steps of woe!

The trout within yon wimpling burn
Glides swift, a silver dart,
And safe beneath the shady thorn
Defies the angler's art:
My life was once that careless stream
That wanton trout was I;
But love, wi' unrelenting beam,
Has scorch'd my fountain dry.

The little flow'ret's peaceful lot,
In yonder cliff that grows,
Which, save the linnet's flight, I wot,
Nae ruder visit knows,
Was mine: till love has o'er me past,
And blighted a' my bloom,
And now beneath the withering blast,
My youth and joy consume.

The waken'd lav'rock warbling springs,
And climbs the early sky,
Winnowing blithe her dewy wings
In morning's rosy eye;
As little reckt I sorrow's power,
Until the flowery snare
O' witching love, in luckless hour,
Made me the thrall o' care.

O had my fate been Greenland snows,
Or Afric's burning zone,
Wi' man and nature leagu'd my foes,
So Peggy ne'er I'd known!
The wretch whase doom is, "Hope nae mair!"
What tongue his woes can tell?
Within whose bosom, save despair,
Nae kinder spirits dwell.

[1] Try. [2] May be conquerors.

WHY, WHY TELL THY LOVER.

TUNE—"THE CALEDONIAN HUNT'S DELIGHT."

Why, why tell thy lover,
Bliss he never must enjoy?
Why, why undeceive him,
And give all his hopes the lie?

O why, while fancy, raptur'd, slumbers,
Chloris, Chloris, all the theme!
Why, why wouldst thou, cruel,
Wake thy lover from his dream?

CALEDONIA.

TUNE—"THE CALEDONIAN HUNT'S DELIGHT."

There was once a day, but old Time then was young,
That brave Caledonia, the chief of her line,
From some of your northern deities sprung:
(Who knows not that brave Caledonia's divine?)
From Tweed to the Orcades was her domain,
To hunt, or to pasture, or do what she would:
Her heavenly relations there fixed her reign,
And pledg'd her their godheads to warrant it good.

A lambkin in peace, but a lion in war,
  The pride of her kindred the heroine grew;
Her grandsire, old Odin, triumphantly swore,
  "Whoe'er shall provoke thee, th' encounter shall rue!"
With tillage, or pasture, at times she would sport,
  To feed her fair flocks by her green rustling corn;
But chiefly the woods were her fav'rite resort,
  Her darling amusement, the hounds and the horn.

Long quiet she reign'd; till thitherward steers
  A flight of bold eagles from Adria's[1] strand;
Repeated, successive, for many long years,
  They darken'd the air, and they plunder'd the land:
Their pounces were murder, and terror their cry,
  They'd conquer'd and ruin'd a world beside;
She took to her hills, and her arrows let fly—
  The daring invaders they fled or they died.

The fell Harpy-raven took wing from the north,
  The scourge of the seas and the dread of the shore;
The wild Scandinavian boar issu'd forth
  To wanton in carnage and wallow in gore:[2]
O'er countries and kingdoms their fury prevail'd,
  No arts could appease them, no arms could repel;
But brave Caledonia in vain they assail'd,
  As Largs well can witness, and Loncartie tell.[3]

The Cameleon-savage disturb'd her repose,
  With tumult, disquiet, rebellion, and strife;
Provok'd beyond bearing, at last she arose,
  And robb'd him at once of his hopes and his life:
The Anglian lion, the terror of France,
  Oft prowling, ensanguin'd the Tweed's silver flood;
But, taught by the bright Caledonian lance,
  He learned to fear in his own native wood.

Thus bold, independent, unconquer'd, and free,
  Her bright course of glory for ever shall run:
For brave Caledonia immortal must be;
  I'll prove it from Euclid as clear as the sun:
Rectangle-triangle, the figure we'll choose,
  The upright is Chance, and old Time is the base;
But brave Caledonia's the hypothenuse;
  Then, ergo, she'll match them, and match them always.[1]

ON THE BATTLE OF SHERIFF-MUIR, BETWEEN THE DUKE OF ARGYLE AND THE EARL OF MAR.[2]

TUNE—"THE CAMERONIAN RANT."

"O CAM ye here the fight to shun?
  Or herd the sheep wi' me, man?

---

[1] The Romans.

[2] The Saxons and Danes.

[3] Two famous battles in which the Danes or Norwegians were defeated.—*Currie.*

[1] This singular figure of poetry refers to the 47th proposition of Euclid. In a right-angled triangle, the square of the hypothenuse is always equal to the square of the two other sides.—*Currie.*

[2] This poem, I am pretty well con-

Or were you at the Sherra-muir,
And did the battle see, man?"
I saw the battle sair and tough,
And reeking-red ran monie a sheugh,[1]
My heart, for fear, gae sough for sough,
To hear the thuds,[2] and see the cluds,[3]
O' clans frae woods, in tartan duds,[4]
Wha glaum'd[5] at Kingdoms three, man.

The red-coat lads, wi' black cockades,
To meet them were na slaw, man;
They rush'd and push'd, and blude out-gush'd,
And monie a bouk[6] did fa', man;
The great Argyle led on his files,
I wat they glanced twenty miles:
They hack'd and hash'd, while broad-swords clash'd,
And thro' they dash'd, and hew'd and smash'd,
Till *fey*[7] men died awa, man.

But had you seen the philibegs,
And skyrin tartan trews,[8] man,
When in the teeth they dar'd our Whigs,
And covenant true blues, man;
In lines extended lang and large,
When bayonets oppose the targe,
And thousands hasten'd to the charge,
Wi' Highland wrath they frae the sheath,
Drew blades o' death, till, out o' breath,
They fled like frighted doos,[9] man.

"O how deil, Tam, can that be true?
The chase gaed frae the north, man:
I saw mysel, they did pursue
The horsemen back to Forth, man;
And at Dumblane, in my ain sight,
They took the brig[10] wi' a' their might,
And straught to Stirling wing'd their flight;
But, cursed lot! the gates were shut,
And monie a huntit, poor red-coat,
For fear amaist did swarf,[11] man."

vinced, is not my brother's, but more ancient than his birth.—G. B.

[1] Ditch. [2] Noises. [3] Clouds.
[4] Clothes. [5] Snatched at. [6] Body.
[7] Marked for death.
[8] Trousers. [9] Doves.
[10] Bridge. [11] Swoon.

My sister Kate cam up the gate
Wi' crowdie unto me, man;
She swore she saw some rebels run
Frae Perth unto Dundee, man:
Their left-hand general had nae skill,
The Angus lads had nae guid-will
That day their neebors' blood to spill;
For fear, by foes, that they should lose
Their cogs o' brose, they scar'd at blows,
And so it goes, you see, man.

They've lost some gallant gentlemen
Amang the Highland clans, man;
I fear my Lord Panmure is slain,
Or fallen in en'mies hands, man:
Now wad ye sing this double fight,
Some fell for wrang, and some for right;
But monie bade the world guid-night;
Then ye may tell, how pell and mell,
By red claymores, and muskets' knell,
Wi' dying yell, the Tories fell,
And Whigs to hell did flee, man.

THE DUMFRIES VOLUNTEERS.

TUNE—"PUSH ABOUT THE JORUM."

April, 1795.

Does haughty Gaul invasion threat?
Then let the louns beware, Sir.
There's wooden walls upon our seas,
And volunteers on shore, Sir.
The Nith shall run to Corsincon,[1]
And Criffel[2] sink to Solway,
Ere we permit a foreign foe
On British ground to rally!
Fal de ral, &c.

O let us not like snarling tykes[3]
In wrangling be divided;
Till slap come in an unco loon[4]
And with a rung[5] decide it.

[1] A high hill at the source of the Nith.
[2] A mountain at the mouth of the same river.
[3] Dogs. [4] Ragamuffin. [5] Cudgel.

Be Britain still to Britain true,
  Amang oursels united;
For never but by British hands
  Maun British wrangs be righted!
    Fal de ral, &c.

The kettle o' the kirk and state,
  Perhaps a claut may fail in't;
But deil a foreign tinkler loon
  Shall ever ca'[1] a nail in't;
Our fathers' bluid the kettle bought,
  And wha wad dare to spoil it;—
By heaven, the sacrilegious dog
  Shall fuel be to boil it.
    Fal de ral, &c.

The wretch that wad a tyrant own,
  And the wretch, his true-born brother,
Who would set the mob aboon the throne,
  May they be d—d together!
Who will not sing, "God save the King,"
  Shall hang as high's the steeple;
But while we sing, "God save the King,"
  We'll ne'er forget the People.

O, WHA IS SHE THAT LO'ES ME.

TUNE—"MORAG."

O WHA is she that lo'es me,
  And has my heart a-keeping?
O sweet is she that lo'es me,
  As dews o' simmer weeping,
  In tears the rose-buds steeping.

CHORUS.

  O that's the lassie o' my heart,
    My lassie, ever dearer;
  O that's the queen o' womankind,
    And ne'er a ane to peer her.

If thou shalt meet a lassie,
  In grace and beauty charming,
That e'en thy chosen lassie,
  Erewhile thy breast sae warming,
  Had ne'er sic powers alarming;
    O that's, &c.

[1] Drive.

If thou hadst heard her talking,
  And thy attentions plighted,
That ilka body talking,
  But her, by thee is slighted,
  And thou art all delighted;
    O that's, &c.

If thou hast met this fair one;
  When frae her thou hast parted,
If every other fair one,
  But her, thou hast deserted,
  And thou art broken-hearted;
    O that's the lassie o' my heart,
      My lassie ever dearer;
    O that's the queen o' womankind,
      And ne'er a ane to peer her.

CAPTAIN GROSE.

TUNE—"SIR JOHN MALCOLM."

KEN ye ought o' Captain Grose?
    Igo and ago,
If he's amang his friends or foes?
    Iram, coram, dago.

Is he South, or is he North?
    Igo and ago,
Or drowned in the river Forth?
    Iram, coram, dago.

Is he slain by Highland bodies?
    Igo and ago,
And eaten like a wether-haggis?
    Iram, coram, dago.

Is he to Abram's bosom gane?
    Igo and ago,
Or haudin Sarah by the wame?
    Iram, coram, dago.

Where'er he be, the Lord be near him!
    Igo and ago;
As for the deil, he daur na steer[1] him.
    Iram, coram, dago.

But please transmit th' enclosed letter,
    Igo and ago,
Which will oblige your humble debtor,
    Iram, coram, dago.

So may ye hae auld stanes in store,
    Igo and ago,

[1] Molest.

The very stanes that Adam bore,
Iram, coram, dago.

So may ye get in glad possession,
Igo and ago,
The coins o' Satan's coronation!
Iram, coram, dago.

WHISTLE OWRE THE LAVE O'T.

First when Maggy was my care,
Heaven, I thought, was in her air;
Now we're married—spier nae mair[1]—
Whistle owre the lave o't.
Meg was meek, and Meg was mild,
Bonnie Mag was nature's child—
Wiser men than me's beguil'd;—
Whistle owre the lave o't.[2]

How we live, my Meg and me,
How we love and how we 'gree,
I care na by how few may see—
Whistle owre the lave o't.
Wha I wish were maggots' meat,
Dish'd up in her winding-sheet,
I could write—but Meg maun see't—
Whistle owre the lave o't.

YOUNG JOCKEY.

Young Jockey was the blithest lad
In a' our town or here awa;
Fu' blithe he whistled at the gaud,[3]
Fu' lightly danc'd he in the ha'!
He roos'd[4] my een sae bonnie blue,
He roos'd my waist sae genty sma';
An' aye my heart came to my mou,
When ne'er a body heard or saw.

My Jockey toils upon the plain,
Thro' wind and weet, thro' frost and snaw;
And o'er the lea I look fu' fain
When Jockey's owsen[5] hameward ca'.

[1] Inquire no more.
[2] The rest of it.
[3] The plough.
[4] Praised.
[5] Oxen.

An' aye the night comes round again,
When in his arms he taks me a';
An' aye he vows he'll be my ain
As lang's he has a breath to draw.

M'PHERSON'S[1] FAREWELL.

Farewell, ye dungeons dark and strong,
The wretch's destinie:
M'Pherson's time will not be long
On yonder gallows tree.

CHORUS.

Sae rantingly, sae wantonly,
Sae dauntingly gaed he;
He play'd a spring and danc'd it round,
Below the gallows tree.

Oh, what is death but parting breath?—
On monie a bloody plain
I've dar'd his face, and in this place
I scorn him yet again!
Sae rantingly, &c.

Untie these bands from off my hands,
And bring to me my sword!
And there's no a man in all Scotland,
But I'll brave him at a word.
Sae rantingly, &c.

I've liv'd a life of sturt[2] and strife;
I die by treachery:
It burns my heart I must depart
And not avenged be.
Sae rantingly, &c.

Now farewell, light, thou sunshine bright,
And all beneath the sky!
May coward shame distain his name,
The wretch that dares not die!
Sae rantingly, &c.

[1] A noted Highland robber, whose daring is portrayed in the verses. He broke his violin at the foot of the gallows.
[2] Trouble.

LAWSON

THE DEAN OF FACULTY.

A NEW BALLAD.

TUNE—"THE DRAGON OF WANTLEY."

DIRE was the hate at old Harlaw
  That Scot to Scot did carry;
And dire the discord Langside saw
  For beauteous, hapless Mary:
But Scot with Scot ne'er met so hot,
  Or were more in fury seen, Sir,
Than 'twixt Hal and Bob[1] for the famous job—
  Who should be Faculty's Dean, Sir.

This Hal, for genius, wit, and lore,
  Among the first was number'd;
But pious Bob, 'mid learning's store,
  Commandment tenth remember'd.
Yet simple Bob the victory got,
  And won his heart's desire;
Which shows that heaven can boil the pot,
  Though the devil — in the fire.

Squire Hal, besides, had, in this case,
  Pretensions rather brassy,
For talents to deserve a place
  Are qualifications saucy;
So their worships of the Faculty,
  Quite sick of merit's rudeness,
Chose one who should owe it all, d'ye see,
  To their gratis grace and goodness.

As once on Pisgah purg'd was the sight
  Of a son of Circumcision,
So may be, on this Pisgah height,
  Bob's purblind, mental vision;
Nay, Bobby's mouth may be open'd yet,
  Till for eloquence you hail him,
And swear he has the Angel met
  That met the ass of Balaam.

In your heretic sins may ye live and die,
  Ye heretic eight and thirty!
But accept, ye sublime Majority,
  My congratulations hearty.

[1] Henry Erskine and Robert Dundas.

With your Honours and a certain King,
  In your servants this is striking—
The more incapacity they bring,
  The more they're to your liking.

I'LL AYE CA' IN BY YON TOWN.

I'LL aye ca' in by yon town,
  And by yon garden green again;
I'll aye ca' in by yon town,
  And see my bonnie Jean again.

There's nane sall ken, there's nane sall guess,
  What brings me back the gate again,
But she, my fairest faithfu' lass,
  And stownlins[1] we sall meet again.

She'll wander by the aiken tree,
  When trystin-time draws near again;
And when her lovely form I see,
  O haith, she's doubly dear again!

A BOTTLE AND FRIEND.

There's nane that's blest of human kind,
  But the cheerful and the gay, man.
    Fal, lal, &c.

HERE's a bottle and an honest friend!
  What wad ye wish for mair, man?
Wha kens, before his life may end,
  What his share may be o' care, man?
Then catch the moments as they fly,
  And use them as ye ought, man:—
Believe me, happiness is shy,
  And comes not aye when sought, man.

I'LL KISS THEE YET.

TUNE—"THE BRAES O' BALQUIDDER."

CHORUS.

I'll kiss thee yet, yet,
  And I'll kiss thee o'er again,
An' I'll kiss thee yet, yet,
  My bonnie Peggy Alison!

[1] By stealth.

Ilk care and fear, when thou art near,
  I ever mair defy them, O;
Young Kings upon their hansel[1] throne
  Are no sae blest as I am, O!
        I'll kiss thee, &c.

When in my arms, wi' a' thy charms,
  I clasp my countless treasure, O;
I seek nae mair o' Heaven to share,
  Than sic a moment's pleasure, O!
        I'll kiss thee, &c.

And by thy een sae bonnie blue,
  I swear I'm thine for ever, O;—
And on thy lips I seal my vow,
  And break it shall I never, O!
        I'll kiss thee, &c.

ON CESSNOCK BANKS.[2]

TUNE—"IF HE BE A BUTCHER NEAT AND TRIM."

On Cessnock banks a lassie[3] dwells;
  Could I describe her shape and mien;
Our lasses a' she far excels,
  An' she's twa sparkling, roguish een.

She's sweeter than the morning dawn,
  When rising Phœbus first is seen,
And dew-drops twinkle o'er the lawn;
  An' she's twa sparkling, roguish een.

She's stately like yon youthful ash
  That grows the cowslip braes between,
And drinks the stream with vigour fresh;
  An' she's twa sparkling, roguish een.

She's spotless like the flow'ring thorn,
  With flow'rs so white, and leaves so green,
When purest in the dewy morn;
  An' she's twa sparkling, roguish een.

Her looks are like the vernal May,
  When ev'ning Phœbus shines serene,
While birds rejoice on every spray;
  An' she's twa sparkling, roguish een.

Her hair is like the curling mist
  That climbs the mountain-sides at e'en,
When flow'r-reviving rains are past;
  An' she's twa sparkling, roguish een.

Her forehead's like the show'ry bow,
  When gleaming sunbeams intervene,
And gild the distant mountain's brow;
  An' she's twa sparkling, roguish een.

Her cheeks are like yon crimson gem,
  The pride of all the flowery scene,
Just opening on its thorny stem;
  An' she's twa sparkling, roguish een.

Her teeth are like the nightly snow
  When pale the morning rises keen,
While hid the murmuring streamlets flow;
  An' she's twa sparkling, roguish een.

Her lips are like yon cherries ripe,
  That sunny walls from Boreas screen,
They tempt the taste and charm the sight;
  An' she's twa sparkling, roguish een.

Her breath is like the fragrant breeze,
  That gently stirs the blossom'd bean,
When Phœbus sinks behind the seas;
  An' she's twa sparkling, roguish een.

Her voice is like the ev'ning thrush
  That sings on Cessnock banks unseen,
While his mate sits nestling in the bush;
  An' she's twa sparkling, roguish een.

But it's not her air, her form, her face,
  Tho' matching beauty's fabled queen,
'Tis the mind that shines in ev'ry grace,
  An' chiefly in her roguish een.

PRAYER FOR MARY.[1]

TUNE—"BLUE BONNETS."

Powers celestial, whose protection
  Ever guards the virtuous fair,

---

[1] Throne first occupied.

[2] This song was an early production. It was recovered by the editor from the oral communication of a lady residing at Glasgow, whom the bard in early life affectionately admired.—*Cromek.*

[3] The "lassie" was Ellison Begbie, a farmer's daughter, but then the servant of a family living about two miles from Burns.

[1] Probably written on Highland

While in distant climes I wander,
Let my Mary be your care:
Let her form sae fair and faultless,
Fair and faultless as your own,—
Let my Mary's kindred spirit
Draw your choicest influence down.

Make the gales you waft around her
Soft and peaceful as her breast;
Breathing in the breeze that fans her,
Soothe her bosom into rest;
Guardian angels, O protect her,
When in distant lands I roam;
To realms unknown while fate exiles me,
Make her bosom still my home.

YOUNG PEGGY.[1]

TUNE—"LAST TIME I CAM O'ER THE MUIR."

YOUNG Peggy blooms our bonniest lass,
Her blush is like the morning,
The rosy dawn, the springing grass,
With early gems adorning:
Her eyes outshine the radiant beams
That gild the passing shower,
And glitter o'er the crystal streams,
And cheer each fresh'ning flower.

Her lips more than the cherries bright,
A richer dye has grac'd them,
They charm th' admiring gazer's sight,
And sweetly tempt to taste them:
Her smile is as the ev'ning mild,
When feather'd pairs are courting,
And little lambkins wanton wild,
In playful bands disporting.

Were Fortune lovely Peggy's foe,
Such sweetness would relent her,
As blooming Spring unbends the brow
Of surly savage Winter.
Detraction's eye no aim can gain
Her winning powers to lessen;

Mary, on the eve of the Poet's departure to the West Indies.—*Cromek*.

[1] This was one of the poet's earliest compositions.—*Cromek*.

And fretful envy grins in vain,
The poison'd tooth to fasten.

Ye Pow'rs of Honour, Love, and Truth,
From ev'ry ill defend her:
Inspire the highly favour'd youth
The destinies intend her:
Still fan the sweet connubial flame
Responsive in each bosom;
And bless the dear parental name
With many a filial blossom.

THERE'LL NEVER BE PEACE TILL JAMIE COMES HAME.

A SONG.

BY yon castle wa' at the close of the day,
I heard a man sing, tho' his head it was grey?
And as he was singing, the tears fast down came—
There'll never be peace till Jamie comes hame.

The church is in ruins, the state is in jars,
Delusions, oppressions, and murderous wars;
We dare na weel say't, but we ken wha's to blame—
There'll never be peace till Jamie comes hame.

My seven braw sons for Jamie drew sword,
And now I greet round their green beds in the yerd;
It brak the sweet heart o' my faithfu' auld dame—
There'll never be peace till Jamie comes hame.

Now life is a burden that bows me down,
Sin' I tint my bairns, and he tint his crown;
But till my last moment my words are the same—
There'll never be peace till Jamie comes hame.

THERE WAS A LAD.

TUNE—"DAINTIE DAVIE."

THERE was a lad was born at Kyle,[1]
But what'n a day o' what'n a style
I doubt it's hardly worth the while
To be sae nice wi' Robin.

Robin was a rovin' Boy,
Rantin' rovin', rantin' rovin';
Robin was a rovin' Boy,
Rantin' rovin' Robin.

Our monarch's hindmost year but ane
Was five-and-twenty years begun,
'Twas then a blast o' Janwar win'
Blew hansel in on Robin.

The gossip keekit in his loof,
Quo' she, wha lives will see the proof,
This waly boy will be nae coof,—
I think we'll ca' him Robin.

He'll hae misfortunes great and sma',
But aye a heart aboon them a',
He'll be a credit till us a',
We'll a' be proud o' Robin.

But, sure as three times three mak nine,
I see, by ilka score and line,
This chap will dearly like our kin',
So leeze me on thee, Robin.

Guid faith, quo' she, I doubt ye, gar,
Ye gar the lasses lie aspar,
But twenty fauts ye may hae waur,
So blessins on thee, Robin!

Robin was a rovin' Boy,
Rantin' rovin', rantin' rovin';
Robin was a rovin' Boy,
Rantin' rovin' Robin.

TO MARY.[2]

TUNE—"EWE-BUGHTS, MARION."

WILL ye go to the Indies, my Mary,
And leave auld Scotia's shore?
Will ye go to the Indies, my Mary,
Across the Atlantic's roar?

O sweet grows the lime and the orange,
And the apple on the pine:
But a' the charms o' the Indies
Can never equal thine.

I hae sworn by the Heavens to my Mary,
I hae sworn by the Heavens to be true;
And sae may the Heavens forget me,
When I forget my vow!

O plight me your faith, my Mary,
And plight me your lily-white hand;
O plight me your faith, my Mary,
Before I leave Scotia's strand.

We hae plighted our troth, my Mary,
In mutual affection to join,
And curst be the cause that shall part us!
The hour and the moment o' time.

MARY MORISON.

TUNE—"BIDE YE YET."

O MARY, at thy window be,
It is the wish'd, the trysted hour!
Those smiles and glances let me see,
That make the miser's treasure poor;
How blithely wad I bide the stoure,[1]
A weary slave frae sun to sun;
Could I the rich reward secure,
The lovely Mary Morison.

Yestreen, when to the trembling string
The dance gaed thro' the lighted ha',
To thee my fancy took its wing,
I sat, but neither heard nor saw:
Tho' this was fair, and that was braw,
And yon the toast of a' the town,
I sigh'd, and said amang them a',
"Ye are na Mary Morison."

---

[1] Kyle, a district of Ayrshire.

[2] Mary Campbell. In my very early years, when I was thinking of going to the West Indies, I took the following farewell of a dear girl.—R. B.

[1] Dust.

O Mary, canst thou wreck his peace,
Wha for thy sake wad gladly die?
Or canst thou break that heart of his,
Whase only faut is loving thee?
If love for love thou wilt na gie,
At least be pity to me shown!
A thought ungentle canna be
The thought o' Mary Morison.

THE SODGER'S RETURN.[1]

AIR—"THE MILL, MILL, O."

When wild war's deadly blast was blawn,
And gentle peace returning,
Wi' mony a sweet babe fatherless,
And mony a widow mourning:
I left the lines and tented field,
Where lang I'd been a lodger,
My humble knapsack a' my wealth,
A poor and honest sodger.

A leal, light heart was in my breast,
My hand unstain'd wi' plunder;
And for fair Scotia, hame again,
I cheery on did wander.
I thought upon the banks o' Coil,
I thought upon my Nancy,
I thought upon the witching smile
That caught my youthful fancy.

At length I reach'd the bonnie glen,
Where early life I sported;
I pass'd the mill, and trysting thorn,
Where Nancy aft I courted:
Wha spied I but my ain dear maid,
Down by her mother's dwelling!
And turn'd me round to hide the flood
That in my een was swelling.

Wi' alter'd voice, quoth I, "Sweet lass,
Sweet as yon hawthorn blossom,
O! happy, happy may he be,
That's dearest to thy bosom!
My purse is light, I've far to gang,
And fain wad be thy lodger;
I've serv'd my King and Country lang—
Take pity on a sodger!"

Sae wistfully she gaz'd on me,
And lovelier was than ever:
Quo' she, "A sodger ance I lo'ed,
Forget him shall I never:
Our humble cot, and hamely fare,
Ye freely shall partake it,
That gallant badge, the dear cockade,
Ye're welcome for the sake o't."

She gaz'd—she redden'd like a rose—
Syne[1] pale like onie lily;
She sank within my arms and cried,
"Art thou my ain dear Willie?"
"By Him who made yon sun and sky,
By whom true love's regarded,
I am the man; and thus may still
True lovers be rewarded!

"The wars are o'er, and I'm come hame
And find thee still true-hearted;
Tho' poor in gear, we're rich in love,
And mair we'se ne'er be parted."
Quo' she, "My grandsire left me gowd,
A mailen[2] plenish'd fairly;
And come, my faithful sodger lad,
Thou'rt welcome to it dearly!"

For gold the merchant ploughs the main,
The farmer ploughs the manor;
But glory is the sodger's prize;
The sodger's wealth is honour:
The brave poor sodger ne'er despise,
Nor count him as a stranger,
Remember he's his country's stay
In day and hour o' danger.

A MOTHER'S LAMENT FOR THE DEATH OF HER SON.

TUNE—"FINLAYSTON HOUSE."

Fate gave the word, the arrow sped,
And pierc'd my darling's heart;

---

[1] A soldier, passing by the window of an inn, suggested these touching lines. The Poet called him in, and asked him to relate his adventures.

[1] Then. [2] Farm.

And with him all the joys are fled
  Life can to me impart!
By cruel hands the sapling drops,
  In dust dishonour'd laid:
So fell the pride of all my hopes,
  My age's future shade.

The mother-linnet in the brake
  Bewails her ravish'd young;
So I, for my lost darling's sake,
  Lament the live-day long.
Death, oft I've fear'd thy fatal blow,
  Now, fond, I bare my breast;
O, do thou kindly lay me low
  With him I love, at rest!

MY FATHER WAS A FARMER.[1]

TUNE—"THE WEAVER AND HIS SHUTTLE, O."

My Father was a Farmer, upon the Carrick border, O,
And carefully he bred me in decency and order, O;
He bade me act a manly part, though I had ne'er a farthing, O—
For without an honest manly heart, no man was worth regarding, O.

Then out into the world my course I did determine, O;
Tho' to be rich was not my wish, yet to be great was charming, O:
My talents they were not the worst; nor yet my education, O;
Resolv'd was I at least to try to mend my situation, O.

In many a way, and vain essay, I courted Fortune's favour, O;
Some cause unseen still stept between, to frustrate each endeavour, O:
Sometimes by foes I was o'erpower'd; sometimes by friends forsaken, O;
And when my hope was at the top, I still was worst mistaken, O.

Then, sore harass'd, and tir'd at last, with Fortune's vain delusion, O;
I dropt my schemes, like idle dreams, and came to this conclusion, O:
The past was bad, and the future hid; its good or ill untried, O;
But the present hour was in my pow'r, and so I would enjoy it, O.

No help, nor hope, nor view had I; nor person to befriend me, O;
So I must toil, and sweat and broil, and labour to sustain me, O.
To plough and sow, to reap and mow, my father bred me early, O;
For one, he said, to labour bred, was a match for Fortune fairly, O.

Thus all obscure, unknown, and poor, thro' life I'm doom'd to wander, O;
Till down my weary bones I lay in everlasting slumber, O;
No view nor care, but shun whate'er might breed me pain or sorrow, O;
I live to-day as well's I may, regardless of to-morrow, O.

But cheerful still, I am as well as a monarch in a palace, O;
Tho' Fortune's frown still hunts me down, with all her wonted malice, O;
I make indeed my daily bread, but ne'er can make it further, O;
But, as daily bread is all I need, I do not much regard her, O.

When sometimes by my labour, I earn a little money, O,
Some unforeseen misfortune comes gen'rally upon me, O;
Mischance, mistake, or by neglect, or my good-natur'd folly, O;
But come what will, I've sworn it, still, I'll ne'er be melancholy, O.

All you who follow wealth and power, with unremitting ardour, O,
The more in this you look for bliss, you leave your view the farther, O:
Had you the wealth Potosi boasts, or nations to adore you, O,
A cheerful honest-hearted clown I will prefer before you, O.

---

[1] The following song is a wild rhapsody, miserably deficient in versification; but as the sentiments are the genuine feelings of my heart, for that reason I have a particular pleasure in conning it over.—R. B. Mr. Cunningham found traces of the Poet's early history in these lines.

BONNIE LESLEY.[1]

TUNE—"THE COLLIER'S BONNIE DOCHTER."

O SAW ye bonnie Lesley,
As she gae'd o'er the border?
She's gane, like Alexander,
To spread her conquests farther.

To see her is to love her,
And love but her for ever;
For Nature made her what she is,
And ne'er made sic anither!

Thou art a queen, Fair Lesley,
Thy subjects we, before thee:
Thou art divine, Fair Lesley,
The hearts o' men adore thee.

The Deil he could na scaith thee,
Or aught that wad belang thee;
He'd look into thy bonnie face,
And say, "I canna wrang thee."

The Powers aboon will tent thee:
Misfortune sha'na steer[2] thee;
Thou'rt like themselves, sae lovely,
That ill they'll ne'er let near thee.

Return again, Fair Lesley,
Return to Caledonie!
That we may brag, we hae a lass
There's nane again sae bonnie.

AMANG THE TREES.

TUNE—"THE KING OF FRANCE, HE HAD A RACE."

AMANG the trees, where humming bees
At buds and flowers were hinging, O,
Auld Caledon drew out her drone,
And to her pipe was singing, O:
'Twas Pibroch,[3] Sang, Strathspey, or Reels,
She dirl'd them aff fu' clearly, O,
When there cam a yell o' foreign squeels,
That dang her tapsalteerie, O.—

Their capon craws and queer ha, ha's,
They made our lugs grow eerie, O;
The hungry bike did scrape and pike
Till we were woe and weary, O:
But a royal ghaist wha ance was cas'd
A prisoner aughteen year awa,
He fir'd a fiddler in the north
That dang them tapsalteerie, O.

* * * * * *

WHEN FIRST I CAME TO STEWART KYLE.

TUNE—"I HAD A HORSE AND I HAD NAE MAIR."

WHEN first I came to Stewart Kyle,
My mind it was na steady,
Where'er I gaed, where'er I rade,
A mistress still I had aye:

But when I came roun' by Mauchline town,
Not dreadin' onie body,
My heart was caught before I thought,
And by a Mauchline lady.

* * * * * *

ON SENSIBILITY.

TO MY DEAR AND MUCH-HONOURED FRIEND, MRS. DUNLOP, OF DUNLOP.

AIR—"SENSIBILITY."

SENSIBILITY, how charming,
Thou, my friend, canst truly tell;
But distress, with horrors arming,
Thou hast also known too well.

Fairest flower, behold the lily,
Blooming in the sunny ray:
Let the blast sweep o'er the valley,
See it prostrate on the clay.

Hear the wood-lark charm the forest,
Telling o'er his little joys;
Hapless bird! a prey the surest
To each pirate of the skies.

[1] Miss Lesley Baillie. The ballad was composed by Burns after spending a day with the lady's family, then on their way to England.
[2] Hurt.
[3] A Highland war-song adapted to the bagpipe.

Dearly bought, the hidden treasure
  Finer feelings can bestow;
Chords, that vibrate sweetest pleasure,
  Thrill the deepest notes of woe.

MONTGOMERIE'S PEGGY.[1]

TUNE—"GALLA WATER."

ALTHO' my bed were in yon muir,
  Amang the heather, in my plaidie,
Yet happy, happy would I be,
  Had I my dear Montgomerie's Peggy.

When o'er the hill beat surly storms,
  And winter nights were dark and rainy;
I'd seek some dell, and in my arms
  I'd shelter dear Montgomerie's Peggy.

Were I a Baron proud and high,
  And horse and servants waiting ready,
Then a' 'twad gie o' joy to me,
  The sharin't wi' Montgomerie's Peggy.

* * * * * *

ON A BANK OF FLOWERS.

ON a bank of flowers, in a summer day,
  For summer lightly drest,
The youthful blooming Nelly lay,
  With love and sleep opprest;

When Willie, wand'ring thro' the wood,
  Who for her favour oft had sued,
He gaz'd, he wish'd, he fear'd, he blush'd,
  And trembled where he stood.

Her closed eyes, like weapons sheath'd,
  Were seal'd in soft repose;
Her lips, still as she fragrant breath'd,
  It richer dy'd the rose.

The springing lilies sweetly prest,
  Wild, wanton kiss'd her rival breast;
He gazed, he wish'd, he fear'd, he blush'd,
  His bosom ill at rest.

Her robes, light waving in the breeze,
  Her tender limbs embrace!
Her lovely form, her native ease,
  All harmony and grace!

Tumultuous tides his pulses roll,
  A faltering ardent kiss he stole;
He gaz'd, he wish'd, he fear'd, he blush'd,
  And sigh'd his very soul.

As flies the partridge from the brake,
  On fear-inspired wings;
So Nelly, starting, half awake,
  Away affrighted springs:

But Willie follow'd—as he should,
  He overtook her in the wood:
He vow'd, he pray'd, he found the maid
  Forgiving all, and good.

O RAGING FORTUNE'S WITHERING BLAST.

O RAGING Fortune's withering blast
  Has laid my leaf full low, O!
O raging Fortune's withering blast
  Has laid my leaf full low, O!

My stem was fair, my bud was green,
  My blossom sweet did blow, O!
The dew fell fresh, the sun rose mild,
  And made my branches grow, O.

But luckless Fortune's northern storms
  Laid a' my blossoms low, O!
But luckless Fortune's northern storms
  Laid a' my blossoms low, O!

EVAN BANKS.

TUNE—"SAVOURNA DELISH."

SLOW spreads the gloom my soul desires,
The sun from India's shore retires:

---

[1] My Montgomerie's Peggy was my deity for six or eight months. I have tried to imitate, in this extempore thing, that irregularity in the rhyme which, when judiciously done, has such a fine effect on the ear.—R. B.

To Evan Banks with temp'rate ray,
Home of my youth, he leads the day.

Oh! Banks to me for ever dear!
Oh! stream, whose murmurs still I hear!
All, all my hopes of bliss reside
Where Evan mingles with the Clyde.

And she, in simple beauty drest,
Whose image lives within thy breast;
Who trembling heard my parting sigh,
And long pursued me with her eye:

Does she, with heart unchang'd as mine,
Oft in the vocal bowers recline?
Or, where yon grot o'erhangs the tide,
Muse while the Evan seeks the Clyde?

Ye lofty banks that Evan bound,
Ye lavish woods that wave around,
And o'er the stream your shadows throw,
Which sweetly winds so far below;

What secret charm to mem'ry brings,
All that on Evan's border springs!
Sweet Banks! ye bloom by Mary's side:
Blest stream! she views thee haste to Clyde.

Can all the wealth of India's coast
Atone for years in absence lost!
Return, ye moments of delight,
With richer treasures bless my sight!

Swift from this desert let me part,
And fly to meet a kindred heart!
Nor more may aught my steps divide
From that dear stream which flows to Clyde!

WOMEN'S MINDS.

TUNE—"FOR A' THAT."

THO' women's minds, like winter winds,
May shift and turn, and a' that,
The noblest breast adores them maist,
A consequence I draw that.

For a' that, and a' that,
And twice as meikle's a' that,
The bonnie lass that I lo'e best
She'll be my ain for a' that.

But there is ane aboon the lave,
Has wit, and sense, and a' that;
A bonnie lass, I like her best,
And wha a crime dare ca' that?
For a' that, &c.

TO MARY IN HEAVEN.[1]

TUNE—"MISS FORBES' FAREWELL TO BANFF."

THOU ling'ring star, with less'ning ray,
That lov'st to greet the early morn,
Again thou usher'st in the day
My Mary from my soul was torn.
O Mary! dear departed shade!
Where is thy place of blissful rest?
Seest thou thy lover lowly laid?
Hear'st thou the groans that rend his breast?

That sacred hour can I forget?
Can I forget the hallow'd grove,
Where by the winding Ayr we met,
To live one day of parting love?
Eternity will not efface
Those records dear of transports past;
Thy image at our last embrace;
Ah! little thought we 'twas our last!

Ayr gurgling kiss'd his pebbled shore,
O'erhung with wild woods, thick'ning green;
The fragrant birch, and hawthorn hoar,
Twin'd am'rous round the raptur'd scene.
The flowers sprang wanton to be prest,
The birds sang love on ev'ry spray,—
Till too, too soon, the glowing west
Proclaim'd the speed of winged day.

Still o'er these scenes my mem'ry wakes,
And fondly broods with miser care!
Time but th' impression deeper makes,
As streams their channels deeper wear.

---

[1] The Mary Campbell already mentioned. The stanzas were composed while Burns lay on some sheaves in the harvest-field, with his eyes fixed on a star of exceeding brightness.

My Mary, dear departed shade!
Where is thy blissful place of rest?
Seest thou thy lover lowly laid?
Hear'st thou the groans that rend his breast?

TO MARY.

Could aught of song declare my pains,
Could artful numbers move thee,
The Muse should tell, in labour'd strains,
O Mary, how I love thee!

They who but feign a wounded heart
May teach the lyre to languish;
But what avails the pride of art,
When wastes the soul with anguish?

Then let the sudden bursting sigh
The heart-felt pang discover;
And in the keen, yet tender eye,
O read the imploring lover.

For well I know thy gentle mind
Disdains art's gay disguising;
Beyond what fancy e'er refin'd,
The voice of nature prizing.

O LEAVE NOVELS.

O leave novels, ye Mauchline belles,
Ye're safer at your spinning-wheel;
Such witching books are baited hooks
For rakish rooks, like Rob Mossgiel.

Your fine Tom Jones and Grandisons,
They make your youthful fancies reel,
They heat your brains, and fire your veins,
And then you're prey for Rob Mossgiel.

Beware a tongue that's smoothly hung;
A heart that warmly seems to feel;
That feeling heart but acts a part,—
'Tis rakish art in Rob Mossgiel.

The frank address, the soft caress,
Are worse than poison'd darts of steel;
The frank address, and politesse,
Are all finesse in Rob Mossgiel.

ADDRESS TO GENERAL DUMOURIER.

A PARODY ON ROBIN ADAIR.[1]

You're welcome to despots, Dumourier;
You're welcome to despots, Dumourier;
How does Dampiere do?
Aye, and Bournonville too?
Why did they not come along with you, Dumourier?

I will fight France with you, Dumourier;
I will fight France with you, Dumourier;
I will fight France with you;
I will take my chance with you;
By my soul I'll dance a dance with you, Dumourier.

Then let us fight about, Dumourier;
Then let us fight about, Dumourier;
Then let us fight about,
Till freedom's spark is out,
Then we'll be d—d, no doubt, Dumourier.

SWEETEST MAY.

Sweetest May, let love inspire thee;
Take a heart which he designs thee;
As thy constant slave regard it;
For its faith and truth reward it.
Proof o' shot to birth or money,
Not the wealthy, but the bonnie;
Not high-born, but noble-minded,
In love's silken band can bind it!

ONE NIGHT AS I DID WANDER.

TUNE—"JOHN ANDERSON, MY JO."

One night as I did wander,
When corn begins to shoot,
I sat me down to ponder,
Upon an auld tree-root:

[1] "Robin Adair" begins, "You're welcome to Paxton, Robin Adair."

Auld Ayre ran by before me,
And bicker'd to the seas;
A cushat crowded o'er me,
That echoed thro' the braes.

* * * *

THE WINTER IT IS PAST.[1]

A FRAGMENT.

THE winter it is past, and the simmer's come at last,
And the little birds sing on every tree;
Now everything is glad, while I am very sad,
Since my true love is parted from me.
The rose upon the brier, by the waters running clear,
May have charms for the linnet or the bee;
Their little loves are blest, and their little hearts at rest,
But my true love is parted from me.

FRAGMENT.

HER flowing locks, the raven's wing,
Adown her neck and bosom hing;
How sweet unto that breast to cling,
And round that neck entwine her!

Her lips are roses wet wi' dew!
O, what a feast her bonnie mou!
Her cheeks a mair celestial hue,
A crimson still diviner!

THE CHEVALIER'S LAMENT.[2]

TUNE—"CAPTAIN O'KEAN."

THE small birds rejoice in the green leaves returning,
The murmuring streamlet winds clear thro' the vale;
The hawthorn trees blow in the dews of the morning,
And wild scatter'd cowslips bedeck the green dale:

But what can give pleasure, or what can seem fair,
While the lingering moments are number'd by care?
No flowers gaily springing, nor birds sweetly singing,
Can soothe the sad bosom of joyless despair.

The deed that I dar'd could it merit their malice,
A King, or a Father, to place on his throne?
His right are these hills, and his right are these valleys,
Where the wild beasts find shelter, but I can find none.

But 'tis not my sufferings thus wretched, forlorn;
My brave gallant friends, 'tis your ruin I mourn:
Your deeds prov'd so loyal in hot bloody trial,
Alas! can I make you no sweeter return?

THE BELLES OF MAUCHLINE.

TUNE—"BONNIE DUNDEE."

IN Mauchline there dwells six proper young Belles,
The pride of the place and its neighbourhood a',
Their carriage and dress, a stranger would guess,
In Lon'on or Paris they'd gotten it a':
Miss Miller is fine, Miss Markland's divine,
Miss Smith she has wit, and Miss Betty is braw:

[1] Gilbert Burns denied his brother's authorship of this fragment, which, in early boyhood, he had heard their mother sing.

[2] These admirable stanzas are supposed to be spoken by the young Prince Charles Edward, when wandering in the Highlands of Scotland, after his fatal defeat at Culloden.—*Thomson.*

There's beauty and fortune to get wi'
Miss Morton,
But Armour's the jewel for me o'
them a'.

YE HAE LIEN A' WRANG, LASSIE.

CHORUS.

Ye hae lien a' wrang, lassie,
Ye've lien a' wrang,
Ye've lien in an unco[1] bed,
And wi' a fremit[2] man.

Your rosy cheeks are turn'd sae wan,
Ye're greener than the grass, lassie;
Your coatie's shorter by a span,
Yet ne'er an inch the less, lassie.

O lassie, ye hae play'd the fool,
And ye will feel the scorn, lassie;
For aye the brose ye sup at e'en,
Ye bock[3] them ere the morn, lassie.

Oh, ance ye danc'd upon the knowes,[4]
And through the wood ye sang, lassie;
But in the herrying o' a bee byke,[5]
I fear ye've gat a stang, lassie.

HERE'S A HEALTH TO THEM THAT'S AWA.

Here's a health to them that's awa,
Here's a health to them that's awa;
And wha winna wish guid luck to our
cause,
May never guid luck be their fa'!
It's guid to be merry and wise,
It's guid to be honest and true,
It's guid to support Caledonia's cause,
And bide by the buff and the blue.

Here's a health to them that's awa,
Here's a health to them that's awa;
Here's a health to Charlie[6] the chief
o' the clan,
Altho' that his band be sma'.

[1] Strange. [2] Stranger. [3] Vomit. [4] Hills. [5] Bee-hive. [6] Charles Fox.

May liberty meet wi' success!
May prudence protect her frae evil!
May tyrants and tyranny tine in the
mist,
And wander their way to the Devil!

Here's a health to them that's awa,
Here's a health to them that's awa;
Here's health to Tammie,[1] the Nor-
land laddie,
That lives at the lug o' the law!
Here's freedom to him that wad read,
Here's freedom to him that wad write!
There's nane ever fear'd that the truth
should be heard
But they wham the truth wad indite.
Here's a health to them that's awa,
Here's a health to them that's awa;
Here's Chieftain M'Leod,[2] a chieftain
worth gowd,
Tho' bred amang mountains o' snaw!

DAMON AND SYLVIA.

TUNE—"THE TITHER MORN, AS I FORLORN."

Yon wan'd'ring rill, that marks the hill,
And glances o'er the brae, Sir,
Slides by a bower where monie a flower
Sheds fragrance on the day, Sir.

There Damon lay, with Sylvia gay:
To love they thought nae crime, Sir;
The wild-birds sang, the echoes rang,
While Damon's heart beat time, Sir.

MY LADY'S GOWN THERE'S GAIRS UPON'T.

CHORUS.

My lady's gown there's gairs upon't,
And gowden flowers sae rare upon't;
But Jenny's jimps and jirkinet,
My lord thinks muckle mair upon't.

[1] Thomas Erskine.
[2] M'Leod, chief of that clan.

My lord a-hunting he is gane,
But hounds or hawks wi' him are nane,
By Colin's cottage lies his game,
If Colin's Jenny be at hame.
My lady's gown, &c.

My lady's white, my lady's red,
And kith and kin o' Cassillis' blude,
But her ten-pund lands o' tocher guid
Were a' the charms his lordship lo'ed.
My lady's gown, &c.

Out o'er yon muir, out o'er yon moss,
Whare gor-cocks thro' the heather pass,
There wons auld Colin's bonnie lass,
A lily in the wilderness.
My lady's gown, &c.

Sae sweetly move her genty limbs,
Like music notes o' lover's hymns:
The diamond dew in her een sae blue,
Where laughing love sae wanton swims.
My lady's gown, &c.

My lady's dink,[1] my lady's drest,
The flower and fancy o' the west;
But the lassie that a man lo'es best,
O that's the lass to make him blest.
My lady's gown, &c.

O AYE MY WIFE SHE DANG ME.

CHORUS.

O aye my wife she dang me,
An' aft my wife she bang'd me;
If ye gie a woman a' her will,
Guid faith, she'll soon o'ergang ye.

On peace and rest my mind was bent,
And fool I was I marry'd;
But never honest man's intent
As cursedly miscarry'd.

Some sairie[2] comfort still at last,
When a' their days are done, man,
My pains o hell on earth is past,
I'm sure o' bliss aboon, man,
O aye my wife, &c.

[1] Neat. [2] Sorrowful.

THE BANKS OF NITH.

A BALLAD.

To thee, lov'd Nith, thy gladsome plains,
Where late wi' careless thought I rang'd,
Though prest wi' care and sunk in woe,
To thee I bring a heart unchang'd.

I love thee, Nith, thy banks and braes,
Tho' mem'ry there my bosom tear;
For there he rov'd that brake my heart,
Yet to that heart, ah, still how dear!

BONNIE PEG.

As I came in by our gate end,
As day was waxin' weary,
O wha came tripping down the street,
But bonnie Peg, my dearie!

Her air sae sweet, and shape complete,
Wi' nae proportion wanting,
The Queen of Love did never move
Wi' motion mair enchanting.

Wi' linked hands, we took the sands
A-down yon winding river;
And, oh! that hour and broomy bower,
Can I forget it ever?

O LAY THY LOOF IN MINE, LASS.

CHORUS.

O lay thy loof[1] in mine, lass,
In mine, lass, in mine, lass;
And swear in thy white hand, lass,
That thou wilt be my ain.

A slave to Love's unbounded sway,
He aft has wrought me meikle wae;
But now he is my deadly fae,
Unless thou be my ain.
O lay thy loof, &c.

There's monie a lass has broke my rest,
That for a blink I hae lo'ed best;

[1] Palm of the hand.

But thou art Queen within my breast,
For ever to remain.
O lay thy loof, &c.

O GUID ALE COMES.

CHORUS.

O guid ale comes, and guid ale goes,
Guid ale gars me sell my hose—
Sell my hose, and pawn my shoon,
Guid ale keeps my heart aboon.

I HAD sax owsen in a pleugh,
They drew a' weel eneugh,
I sell'd them a' just ane by ane;
Guid ale keeps my heart aboon.

Guid ale hauds me bare and busy,
Gars me moop wi' the servant hizzie,
Stand i' the stool when I hae done,
Guid ale keeps my heart aboon.
O guid ale comes, &c.

O WHY THE DEUCE.

EXTEMPORE. APRIL, 1782.

O WHY the deuce should I repine,
And be an ill foreboder?
I'm twenty-three, and five feet nine—
I'll go and be a sodger.

I gat some gear wi' meikle care,
I held it weel thegither;
But now it's gane and something mair,
I'll go and be a sodger.

POLLY STEWART.

TUNE—"YE'RE WELCOME, CHARLIE STEWART."

CHORUS.

O lovely Polly Stewart,
O charming Polly Stewart,
There's ne'er a flower that blooms in May,
That's half so fair as thou art.

THE flower it blaws, it fades, it fa's,
And art can ne'er renew it;
But worth and truth eternal youth
Will gie to Polly Stewart.

May he, whase arms shall fauld thy charms,
Possess a leal and true heart;
To him be given to ken the heaven
He grasps in Polly Stewart!
O lovely, &c.

ROBIN SHURE IN HAIRST.

CHORUS.

Robin shure in hairst,
I shure wi' him,
Fient a heuk had I,
Yet I stack by him.

I GAED up to Dunse,
To warp a wab o' plaiden,
At his daddie's yett,
Wha met me but Robin.

Was na Robin bauld,
Tho' I was a cotter,
Play'd me sic a trick,
And me the eller's dochter?
Robin shure, &c.

Robin promis'd me
A' my winter vittle;
Fient haet he had but three
Goose feathers and a whittle.
Robin shure, &c.

THE FIVE CARLINS.[1]—AN ELECTION BALLAD.

TUNE—"CHEVY CHASE."

THERE were five Carlins in the south,
They fell upon a scheme,
To send a lad to Lun'on town
To bring us tidings hame.

[1] The five boroughs of Dumfriesshire and Kirkcudbright.

Not only bring us tidings hame,
  But do our errands there,
And aiblins gowd and honour baith
  Might be that laddie's share.

There was Maggie[1] by the banks o' Nith,
  A dame wi' pride enough;
And Marjorie[2] o' the monie Lochs,
  A Carlin auld an' teugh.

And blinkin Bess[3] o' Annandale,
  That dwells near Solway side,
And whisky Jean[4] that took her gill
  In Galloway so wide.

And auld black Joan[5] fra Creighton peel,
  O' gipsy kith an' kin,
Five weightier Carlins were na found
  The south countrie within.

To send a lad to Lon'on town[6]
  They met upon a day,
And monie a knight, and monie a Laird,
  That errand fain would gae.

O! monie a Knight, and monie a Laird,
  This errand fain would gae;
But nae ane could their fancy please,
  O! ne'er a ane but twae.

The first ane was a belted Knight,[7]
  Bred o' a border clan;
An' he wad gae to Lon'on town,
  Might nae man him withstan';

And he wad doe their errands weel,
  And meikle he wad say,
And ilka ane at Lon'on court
  Wad bid to him guid day.

Then neist came in a sodger youth,[8]
  And spak wi' modest grace,
An' he wad gae to Lon'on town,
  If sae their pleasure was.

He wad nae hecht[9] them courtly gift,
  Nor meikle speech pretend;
But he wad hecht an honest heart
  Wad ne'er desert his friend.

Now, whom to choose, and whom refuse,
  To strife thae Carlins fell;
For some had gentle folk to please,
  And some wad please themsel.

Then out spak mim-mou'd Meg o' Nith,
  An' she spak out wi' pride,
An' she wad send the sodger youth
  Whatever might betide.

For the auld guidman o' Lon'on court
  She dinna care a pin,
But she wad send the sodger youth
  To greet his eldest son.

Then up sprang Bess o' Annandale:
  A deadly aith she's ta'en,
That she wad vote the border Knight,
  Tho' she should vote her lane.

For far-aff fowls hae feathers fair,
  An' fools o' change are fain:
But I hae tried this border Knight,
  An' I'll trie him yet again.

Says auld black Joan frae Creighton peel,
  A Carlin stout and grim,
The auld guidman, or young guidman,
  For me may sink or swim!

For fools may prate o' right and wrang,
  While knaves laugh them to scorn:
But the sodger's friends hae blawn the best,
  Sae he shall bear the horn.

Then whiskey Jean spak owre her drink,
  "Ye weel ken, kimmers a',
The auld guidman o' Lon'on court,
  His back's been at the wa'.

An' monie a friend that kiss'd his caup,
  Is now a fremit wight;
But it's ne'er sae wi' whiskey Jean,—
  We'll send the border Knight."

Then slow raise Marjorie o' the Lochs,
  And wrinkled was her brow;
Her ancient weed was russet gray,
  Her auld Scots heart was true.

"There's some great folks set light by me,
  I set as light by them;
But I will send to Lon'on town,
  Wha I lo'e best at hame."

---

[1] Dumfries. [2] Lochmaben.
[3] Annan. [4] Kirkcudbright.
[5] Sanquhar.
[6] The five boroughs returned one member.
[7] Sir James Johnstone
[8] Captain Miller. [9] Offer.

So how this mighty plea will end,
Nae mortal wight can tell;
God grant the King, and ilka man,
May look weel to himsel'![1]

THE DEUKS DANG O'ER MY DADDIE.

THE bairns gat out wi' an unco shout,
The deuks dang o'er my daddie, O!
The fient ma care, quo' the feirie auld wife,
He was but a paidlin body, O!
He paidles out, and he paidles in,
An' he paidles late and early, O;
Thae seven lang years I hae lien by his side,
An' he is but a fusionless carlie, O.

O haud your tongue, my feirie auld wife,
O haud your tongue now, Nansie, O:
I've seen the day, and sae hae ye,
Ye wadna been sae donsie, O:
I've seen the day ye butter'd my brose,
And cuddl'd me late and earlie, O;
But downa do's come o'er me now,
And, oh, I feel it sairly, O!

THE LASS THAT MADE THE BED TO ME.

WHEN Januar' wind was blawing cauld,
As to the north I took my way,
The mirksome night did me enfauld,
I knew na where to lodge till day.

By my good luck a maid I met,
Just in the middle o' my care;
And kindly she did me invite
To walk into a chamber fair.

I bow'd fu' low unto this maid,
And thank'd her for her courtesie;
I bow'd fu' low unto this maid,
And bade her mak a bed to me.

She made the bed baith large and wide,
Wi' twa white hands she spread it down;

[1] Miller was elected.

She put the cup to her rosy lips,
And drank, "Young man, now sleep ye soun."

She snatch'd the candle in her hand,
And frae my chamber went wi' speed;
But I call'd her quickly back again
To lay some mair below my head.

A cod[1] she laid below my head,
And served me wi' due respect;
And to salute her wi' a kiss,
I put my arms about her neck.

"Haud aff your hands, young man," she says,
"And dinna sae uncivil be;
If ye hae onie love for me,
O wrang na my virginite!"

Her hair was like the links o' gowd,
Her teeth were like the ivorie;
Her cheeks like lilies dipt in wine,
The lass that made the bed to me.

Her bosom was the driven snaw,
Twa drifted heaps sae fair to see;
Her limbs the polish'd marble stane,
The lass that made the bed to me.

I kissed her owre and owre again,
And aye she wist na what to say;
I laid her 'ween me and the wa',
The lassie thought na lang till day.

Upon the morrow when we rose,
I thank'd her for her courtesie;
But aye she blush'd, and aye she sigh'd,
And said, "Alas! ye've ruin'd me."

I clasp'd her waist, and kiss'd her syne,
While the tear stood twinklin in her e'e;
I said, "My lassie, dinna cry,
For ye aye shall mak the bed to me."

She took her mither's Holland sheets,
And made them a' in sarks to me:
Blythe and merry may she be,
The lass that made the bed to me.

The bonnie lass made the bed to me,
The braw lass made the bed to me:
I'll ne'er forget till the day I die,
The lass that made the bed to me!

[1] A pillow.

THE UNION.

TUNE—"SUCH A PARCEL OF ROGUES IN A NATION."

Farewrel to a' Scottish fame,
  Fareweel our ancient glory!
Fareweel even to the Scottish name,
  Sae fam'd in martial story!
Now Sark rins o'er the Solway sands,
  And Tweed rins to the ocean,
To mark where England's province stands;
  Such a parcel of rogues in a nation!

What guile or force could not subdue,
  Through many warlike ages,
Is wrought now by a coward few,
  For hireling traitors' wages.
The English steel we could disdain,
  Secure in valour's station,
But English gold has been our bane;—
  Such a parcel of rogues in a nation!

O would, or had I seen the day
  That treason thus could sell us,
My auld grey head had lien in clay,
  Wi' Bruce and loyal Wallace!
But pith and power, till my last hour
  I'll mak this declaration,
We're bought and sold for English gold:—
  Such a parcel of rogues in a nation!

THERE WAS A BONNIE LASS.

There was a bonnie lass, and a bonnie, bonnie lass,
  And she lo'ed her bonnie laddie, dear;
Till war's loud alarms tore her laddie frae her arms,
  Wi' monie a sigh and tear.

Over sea, over shore, where the cannons loudly roar,
  He still was a stranger to fear:
And nocht could him quell, or his bosom assail,
  But the bonnie lass he lo'ed sae dear.

MY HARRY WAS A GALLANT GAY.

TUNE—"HIGHLANDER'S LAMENT."

My Harry was a gallant gay,
  Fu' stately strode he on the plain!
But now he's banish'd far away,
  I'll never see him back again.

CHORUS.

  O for him back again,
  O for him back again,
I wad gie a' Knockhaspie's land,
  For Highland Harry back again.

When a' the lave gae to their bed,
  I wander dowie up the glen;
I sit me down and greet my fill,
  And aye I wish him back again.
    O for him, &c.

O were some villains hangit high,
  And ilka body had their ain,
Then I might see the joyfu' sight,
  My Highland Harry back again!
    O for him, &c.

THE HERMIT.[1]

Whoe'er thou art, these lines now reading,
Think not, though from the world receding,
I joy my lonely days to read in
    This desert drear,—
That fell remorse, a conscience bleeding,
    Hath led me here.

No thought of guilt my bosom sours—
Free-will'd I fled from courtly bow'rs;
For well I saw in halls and tow'rs,
    That lust and pride,
The arch-fiend's dearest, darkest pow'rs,
    In state preside.

---

[1] Written on a marble sideboard, in the Hermitage belonging to the Duke of Athole, in the wood of Aberfeldy.

I saw mankind with vice encrusted;
I saw that honour's sword was rusted;
That few for aught but folly lusted;
That he was still deceiv'd, who trusted
To love, or friend;—
And hither came, with men disgusted,
My life to end.

In this lone cave, in garments lowly,
Alike a foe to noisy folly,
And brow-brent gloomy melancholy,
I wear away
My life, and in my office holy
Consume the day.

This rock my shield, when storms are blowing,
The limpid streamlet yonder flowing,
Supplying drink, the earth bestowing
My simple food;
But few enjoy the calm I know in
This desert wood.

Content and comfort bless me more in
This grot, than e'er I felt before in
A palace,—and with thoughts still soaring
To God on high,
Each night and morn with voice imploring,
This wish I sigh:—

Let me, O Lord, from life retire,
Unknown each guilty, worldly fire,
Remorse's throb, or loose desire;—
And when I die,
Let me in this belief expire—
To God I fly!

Stranger! if full of youth and riot,
And yet no grief has marr'd thy quiet,
Thou haply throw'st a scornful eye at
The Hermit's prayer;
But if thou hast good cause to sigh at
Thy fault or care,—

If thou hast known false love's vexation,
Or hast been exiled from thy nation,
Or guilt affrights thy contemplation,
And makes thee pine—
Oh! how must thou lament thy station,
And envy mine!

TIBBIE DUNBAR.

TUNE—"JOHNNY M'GILL."

O WILT thou go wi' me, sweet Tibbie Dunbar?
O wilt thou go wi' me, sweet Tibbie Dunbar?
Wilt thou ride on a horse, or be drawn in a car,
Or walk by my side, O sweet Tibbie Dunbar?
I care na thy daddie, his lands and his money,
I care na thy kin, sae high and sae lordly:
But say thou wilt hae me for better, for waur,
And come in thy coatie, sweet Tibbie Dunbar?

WEE WILLIE.

WEE Willie Gray, and his leather wallet;
Peel a willow-wand to be him boots and jacket:
The rose upon the brier will be him trouse and doublet,
The rose upon the brier will be him trouse and doublet!
Wee Willie Gray, and his leather wallet;
Twice a lily flower will be him sark and cravat;
Feathers of a flee wad feather up his bonnet,
Feathers of a flee wad feather up his bonnet.

CRAIGIE-BURN WOOD.

Beyond thee, dearie, beyond thee, dearie,
And O to be lying beyond thee;
O sweetly, soundly, weel may he sleep,
That's laid in the bed beyond thee.

SWEET closes the evening on Craigie-
burn Wood,
And blithely awakens the morrow;
But the pride of the spring in the
Craigie-burn Wood
Can yield to me nothing but sorrow.
Beyond thee, &c.

I see the spreading leaves and flowers,
I hear the wild birds singing;
But pleasure they hae nane for me,
While care my heart is wringing.
Beyond thee, &c.

I canna tell, I maun na tell,
I dare na for your anger;
But secret love will break my heart,
If I conceal it langer.
Beyond thee, &c.

I see thee gracefu', straight and tall,
I see thee sweet and bonnie,
But oh, what will my torments be,
If thou refuse my Johnnie!
Beyond thee, &c.

To see thee in anither's arms,
In love to lie and languish,
'Twad be my dead, that will be seen,
My heart wad burst wi' anguish.
Beyond thee, &c.

But, Jeanie, say thou wilt be mine—
Say, thou lo'es nane before me;
An' a' my days o' life to come,
I'll gratefully adore thee.
Beyond thee, &c,

HERE'S HIS HEALTH IN WATER..

TUNE—"THE JOB OF JOURNEY-WORK."

ALTHO' my back be at the wa',
And tho' he be the fautor;
Altho' my back be at the wa',
Yet, here's his health in water!
O! wae gae by his wanton sides,
Sae brawlie he could flatter;
Till for his sake I'm slighted sair,
And dree the kintra clatter.
But tho' my back be at the wa',
And tho' he be the fautor;
But tho' my back be at the wa',
Yet, here's his health in water!

AS DOWN THE BURN THEY TOOK THEIR WAY.

As down the burn they took their way,
And thro' the flowery dale;
His cheek to hers he aft did lay,
And love was aye the tale.

With "Mary, when shall we return,
Sic pleasure to renew?"
Quoth Mary, "Love, I like the burn,
And aye shall follow you."

LADY ONLIE.

TUNE—"RUFFIAN'S RANT."

A' THE lads o' Thornie-bank,
When they gae to the shore o' Bucky,
They'll step in an' tak' a pint
Wi' Lady Onlie, honest Lucky!
Lady Onlie, honest Lucky,
Brews guid ale at shore o' Bucky;
I wish her sale for her guid ale,
The best on a' the shore o' Bucky.

Her house sae bien, her curch sae clean,
I wat she is a dainty chucky;
And cheerlie blinks the ingle-gleed
Of Lady Onlie, honest Lucky!
Lady Onlie, honest Lucky,
Brews guid ale at shore o' Bucky;
I wish her sale for her guid ale,
The best on a' the shore o' Bucky.

AS I WAS A WANDERING.

TUNE—"RINN MEUDIAL MO MHEAL-LADH."

As I was a wand'ring ae midsummer
e'enin',
The pipers and youngsters were ma-
kin' their game;
Amang them I spied my faithless fause
lover,
Which bled a' the wounds o' my
dolour again.

Weel, since he has left me, my pleasure gae wi' him;
I may be distress'd, but I winna complain;
I flatter my fancy I may get anither,
My heart it shall never be broken for ane.

I could na get sleeping till dawin for greetin',[1]
The tears trickled down like the hail and the rain:
Had I na got greetin', my heart wad a broken,
For, oh! love forsaken's a tormenting pain.

Although he has left me for greed o' the siller,
I dinna envy him the gains he can win;
I rather wad bear a' the lade o' my sorrow
Than ever hae acted sae faithless to him.

Weel, since he has left me, may pleasure gae wi' him,
I may be distress'd, but I winna complain;
I flatter my fancy I may get anither,
My heart it shall never be broken for ane.

BANNOCKS O' BARLEY.

TUNE—"THE KILLOGIE."

Bannocks o' bear[2] meal,
Bannocks o' barley;
Here's to the Highlandman's
Bannocks o' barley.
Wha in a brulzie
Will first cry a parley?
Never the lads wi'
The bannocks o' barley.

Bannocks o' bear meal,
Bannocks o' barley;
Here's to the lads wi'
The bannocks o' barley.
Wha in his wae-days
Were loyal to Charlie?
Wha' but the lads wi'
The bannocks o' barley.

[1] Till dawn for weeping. [2] Barley.

OUR THRISSLES[1] FLOURISHED FRESH AND FAIR.

TUNE—"AWA, WHIGS, AWA."

CHORUS.

Awa, Whigs, awa!
Awa, Whigs, awa!
Ye're but a pack o' traitor louns,
Ye'll do nae good at a'.

Our thrissles flourish'd fresh and fair
And bonnie bloom'd our roses;
But Whigs came in like frost in June,
And wither'd a' our posies.

Our ancient crown's fa'en in the dust—
Deil blin' them wi' the stoure o't;
And write their names in his black beuk,
Wha gae the Whigs the power o't.

Our sad decay in Church and State
Surpasses my descriving;
The Whigs came o'er us for a curse,
And we hae done wi' thriving.

Grim vengeance lang has ta'en a nap,
But we may see him wauken;
Gude help the day when royal heads
Are hunted like a maukin.

Awa, Whigs, awa!
Awa, Whigs, awa!
Ye're but a pack o' traitor louns,
Ye'll do nae gude at a'.

PEG-A-RAMSEY.

TUNE—"CAULD IS THE E'ENIN' BLAST."

Cauld is the e'enin' blast
O' Boreas o'er the pool,
And dawin' it is dreary,
When birks are bare at Yule.

[1] Thistles.

O bitter blaws the e'enin' blast
  When bitter bites the frost,
And in the mirk and dreary drift
  The hills and glens are lost.

Ne'er sae murky blew the night
  That drifted o'er the hill,
But a bonnie Peg-a-Ramsey
  Gat grist to her mill.

COME BOAT ME O'ER TO CHARLIE.[1]

TUNE—"O'ER THE WATER TO CHARLIE."

COME boat me o'er, come row me o'er,
  Come boat me o'er to Charlie;
I'll gie John Ross another bawbee,
  To boat me o'er to Charlie.
    We'll o'er the water and o'er the sea,
      We'll o'er the water to Charlie;
    Come weal, come woe, we'll gather and go,
      And live or die wi' Charlie.

I lo'e weel my Charlie's name,
  Tho' some there be abhor him:
But O, to see auld Nick gaun hame,
  And Charlie's faes before him!
I swear and vow by moon and stars,
  And sun that shines so early,
If I had twenty thousand lives,
  I'd die as aft for Charlie.
    We'll o'er the water and o'er the sea,
      We'll o'er the water to Charlie;
    Come weal, come woe, we'll gather and go!
      And live or die wi' Charlie!

[1] An old song, restored by Burns.

BRAW LADS OF GALLA WATER.

TUNE—"GALLA WATER."

CHORUS.

Braw, braw lads of Galla Water;
  O braw lads of Galla Water:
I'll kilt my coats aboon my knee,
  And follow my love through the water.

SAE fair her hair, sae brent[1] her brow,
  Sae bonny blue her een, my dearie;
Sae white her teeth, sae sweet her mou',
  The mair I kiss she's aye my dearie.

O'er yon bank and o'er yon brae,
  O'er yon moss amang the heather;
I'll kilt my coats aboon my knee,
  And follow my love through the water.

Down amang the broom, the broom,
  Down amang the broom, my dearie,
The lassie lost a silken snood,
  That cost her mony a blirt and bleary.[2]
    Braw, braw lads of Galla Water;
      O braw lads of Galla Water:
    I'll kilt my coats aboon my knee,
      And follow my love through the water.

COMING THROUGH THE RYE.

TUNE—"COMING THROUGH THE RYE."

COMING through the rye, poor body,
  Coming through the rye,
She draiglet a' her petticoatie,
  Coming through the rye.
Jenny's a' wat, poor body,
  Jenny's seldom dry;
She draiglet a' her petticoatie,
  Coming through the rye.

Gin a body meet a body
  Coming through the rye;
Gin a body kiss a body—
  Need a body cry?
Gin a body meet a body
  Coming through the glen,
Gin a body kiss a body—
  Need the world ken?
Jenny's a' wat, poor body;
  Jenny's seldom dry;
She draiglet a' her petticoatie,
  Coming through the rye.

[1] High and smooth.
[2] Outburst of grief.

THE LASS OF ECCLEFECHAN.

TUNE—"JACKY LATIN."

GAT ye me, O gat ye me,
  O gat ye me wi' naething?
Rock and reel, and spinnin' wheel,
  A mickle quarter basin.
Bye attour,[1] my gutcher[2] has
  A hich house and a laigh ane,
A' forbye, my bonnie sel',
  The toss[3] of Ecclefechan.

O haud your tongue now, Luckie Laing,
  O haud your tongue and jauner;[4]
I held the gate till you I met,
  Syne I began to wander:
I tint my whistle and my sang,
  I tint my peace and pleasure;
But your green graff, now, Luckie Laing,
  Wad airt me to my treasure.

HAD I THE WYTE.

TUNE—"HAD I THE WYTE SHE BADE ME."

HAD I the wyte,[5] had I the wyte,
  Had I the wyte she bade me;
She watch'd me by the hie-gate side,
  And up the loan[6] she shaw'd me;
And when I wadna venture in,
  A coward loon she ca'd me;
Had kirk and state been in the gate,
  I lighted when she bade me.

Sae craftilie she took me ben,
  And bade me make nae clatter;
"For our ramgunshoch, glum guidman
  Is out and ower the water:"
Whae'er shall say I wanted grace,
  When I did kiss and dawte[7] her,
Let him be planted in my place,
  Syne say I was the fautor.

Could I for shame, could I for shame,
  Could I for shame refuse her?
And wadna manhood been to blame,
  Had I unkindly used her?
He clawed her wi' the ripplin-kame,[1]
  And blue and bluidy bruised her;
When sic a husband was frae hame,
  What wife but had excused her?

I dighted ay her een sae blue,
  And bann'd the cruel randy;
And weel I wat her willing mou'
  Was e'en like sugar-candy.
A gloamin-shot it was I trow,
  I lighted on the Monday;
But I came through the Tysday's dew,
  To wanton Willie's brandy.

[1] Moreover. [2] Grandsire. [3] Toast. [4] Talking. [5] Blame. [6] Milking-place. [7] Fondle.

HEE BALOU.[2]

TUNE—"THE HIGHLAND BALOU."

HEE balou! my sweet wee Donald,
Picture o' the great Clanronald;
Brawlie kens our wanton chief
Wha got my young Highland thief.

Leeze me on thy bonnie craigie,[3]
An' thou live, thou'll steal a naigie:[4]
Travel the country thro' and thro',
And bring hame a Carlisle cow.

Thro' the Lawlands, o'er the border,
Weel, my babie, may thou furder:[5]
Herry[6] the louns o' the laigh countree,
Syne[7] to the Highlands hame to me.

HER DADDIE FORBAD.

TUNE—"JUMPIN' JOHN."

HER daddie forbad, her minnie forbad;
  Forbidden she wadna be:
She wadna trow't[8] the browst she brew'd
  Wad taste sae bitterlie.
    The lang lad they ca' Jumpin' John
      Beguiled the bonnie lassie;
    The lang lad they ca' Jumpin' John
      Beguiled the bonnie lassie.

[1] Instrument for dressing flax. [2] A child's lullaby. [3] Neck. [4] Horse. [5] Succeed. [6] Plunder [7] Then. [8] Believe it.

A cow and a cauf, a yowe and a hauf,
And thretty gude shillins and three;
A vera gude tocher, a cotter-man's dochter,
The lass with the bonnie black e'e.
The lang lad they ca' Jumpin' John
Beguiled the bonnie lassie;
The lang lad they ca' Jumpin' John
Beguiled the bonnie lassie.

HERE'S TO THY HEALTH, MY BONNIE LASS.

TUNE—"LAGGAN BURN."

Here's to thy health, my bonnie lass,
Gude night, and joy be wi' thee;
I'll come nae mair to thy bower door,
To tell thee that I lo'e thee.
O dinna think, my pretty pink,
But I can live without thee:
I vow and swear I dinna care
How lang ye look about ye.

Thou'rt aye sae free informing me
Thou hast nae mind to marry;
I'll be as free informing thee
Nae time hae I to tarry.
I ken thy friends try ilka means,
Frae wedlock to delay thee;
Depending on some higher chance—
But fortune may betray thee.

I ken they scorn my low estate,
But that does never grieve me;
But I'm as free as any he,
Sma' siller will relieve me.
I count my health my greatest wealth,
Sae lang as I'll enjoy it:
I'll fear nae scant, I'll bode nae want,
As lang's I get employment.

But far-aff fowls hae feathers fair,
And aye until ye try them:
Tho' they seem fair, still have a care,
They may prove waur than I am.
But at twal at night, when the moon shines bright,
My dear, I'll come and see thee;
For the man that lo'es his mistress weel,
Nae travel makes him weary.

HEY, THE DUSTY MILLER.

TUNE—"THE DUSTY MILLER."

Hey, the dusty miller,
And his dusty coat;
He will win a shilling,
Or he spend a groat.
Dusty was the coat,
Dusty was the colour,
Dusty was the kiss
That I got frae the miller.

Hey, the dusty miller,
And his dusty sack;
Leeze me on the calling
Fills the dusty peck.
Fills the dusty peck,
Brings the dusty siller;
I wad gie my coatie
For the dusty miller.

THE CARDIN' O'T.[1]

TUNE—"SALT FISH AND DUMPLINGS."

I coft a stane o' haslock woo',
To make a wat[2] to Johnny o't;
For Johnny is my only jo,
I lo'e him best of ony yet.
The cardin' o't, the spinnin' o't,
The warpin' o't, the winnin' o't;
When ilka ell cost me a groat,
The tailor staw the lynin o't.

For though his locks be lyart gray,[3]
And tho' his brow be beld aboon;
Yet I hae seen him on a day,
The pride of a' the parishen.

---

[1] "The little of this song to which antiquity lays claim, is so trifling that the whole may be said to be the work of Burns. The tenderness of Johnnie's wife can only be fully felt by those who know that hause-lock wool is the softest and finest of the fleece, and is shorn from the throats of sheep in the summer heat."—*A. Cunningham.*
[2] An outer garment.
[3] Mingled with gray.

The cardin' o't, the spinnin' o't,
The warpin' o't, the winnin' o't;
When ilka ell cost me a groat,
The tailor staw the lynin o't.

THE JOYFUL WIDOWER.

TUNE—"MAGGY LAUDER."

I MARRIED with a scolding wife
The fourteenth of November;
She made me weary of my life,
By one unruly member.
Long did I bear the heavy yoke,
And many griefs attended;
But, to my comfort be it spoke,
Now, now her life is ended.

We lived full one-and-twenty years,
A man and wife together;
At length from me her course she steer'd,
And gone I know not whither:
Would I could guess, I do profess,
I speak, and do not flatter,
Of all the women in the world,
I never could come at her.

Her body is bestowed well,
A handsome grave does hide her;
But sure her soul is not in hell,
The deil would ne'er abide her.
I rather think she is aloft,
And imitating thunder;
For why,—methinks I hear her voice
Tearing the clouds asunder.

THENIEL MENZIE'S BONNIE MARY.

TUNE—"THE RUFFIAN'S RANT."

IN coming by the brig[1] o' Dye,
At Darlet we a blink did tarry;
As day was dawin in the sky,
We drank a health to bonnie Mary.
Theniel Menzie's bonnie Mary,
Theniel Menzie's bonnie Mary;
Charlie Gregor tint his plaidie,
Kissin' Theniel's bonnie Mary.

[1] Bridge.

Her een sae bright, her brow sae white,
Her haffet[1] locks as brown's a berry,
An' aye they dimpled wi' a smile
The rosy cheeks o' bonnie Mary.
Theniel Menzie's bonnie Mary,
Theniel Menzie's bonnie Mary;
Charlie Gregor tint his plaidie
Kissin' Theniel's bonnie Mary.

We lap an' danced the lee-lang day,
Till piper lads were wae an' weary,
But Charlie gat the spring to pay
For kissin' Theniel's bonnie Mary.
Theniel Menzie's bonnie Mary,
Theniel Menzie's bonnie Mary;
Charlie Gregor tint his plaidie
Kissin' Theniel's bonnie Mary.

THE FAREWELL.

TUNE—"IT WAS A' FOR OUR RIGHTFU' KING."

IT was a' for our rightfu' King,
We left fair Scotland's strand;
It was a' for our rightfu' King,
We e'er saw Irish land,
My dear,—
We e'er saw Irish land.

Now a' is done that men can do,
And a' is done in vain;
My love and native land farewell,
For I maun cross the main,
My dear,—
For I maun cross the main.

He turn'd him right, and round about,
Upon the Irish shore:
And gae his bridle-reins a shake,
With adieu for evermore,
My dear,—
With adieu for evermore.

The sodger from the wars returns,
The sailor frae the main;
But I hae parted frae my love,
Never to meet again,
My dear,—
Never to meet again.

[1] By the side of the head.

When day is gane, and night is come,
And a' folk bound to sleep;
I think on him that's far awa,
The lee-lang night, and weep,
My dear,—
The lee-lang night, and weep.

IT IS NA, JEAN, THY BONNIE FACE.

TUNE—"THE MAID'S COMPLAINT."

It is na, Jean, thy bonnie face
Nor shape that I admire,
Although thy beauty and thy grace
Might weel awake desire.
Something, in ilka part o' thee,
To praise, to love, I find;
But dear as is thy form to me,
Still dearer is thy mind.

Nae mair ungen'rous wish I hae,
Nor stronger in my breast,
Than if I canna mak thee sae,
At least to see thee blest.
Content am I, if Heaven shall give
But happiness to thee:
And as wi' thee I'd wish to live,
For thee I'd bear to die.

JAMIE, COME TRY ME.

TUNE—"JAMIE, COME TRY ME."

CHORUS.

Jamie, come try me;
Jamie, come try me;
If thou would win my love,
Jamie, come try me.

If thou should ask my love,
Could I deny thee?
If thou would win my love,
Jamie, come try me.

If thou should kiss me, love,
Wha could espy thee?
If thou wad be my love,
Jamie, come try me.

Jamie, come try me,
Jamie, come try me;
If thou would win my love
Jamie, come try me.

LANDLADY, COUNT THE LAWIN.

TUNE—"HEY TUTTI, TAITI."

Landlady, count the lawin,[1]
The day is near the dawin;
Ye're a' blind drunk, boys,
And I'm but jolly fou.
Hey tutti, taiti,
How tutti, taiti—
Wha's fou now?

Cog an' ye were aye fou,
Cog an' ye were aye fou,
I wad sit and sing to you,
If ye were aye fou.

Weel may ye a' be!
Ill may we never see!
God bless the King, boys,
And the companie!
Hey tutti, taiti,
How tutti, taiti—
Wha's fou now?

MY LOVE SHE'S BUT A LASSIE YET.[2]

TUNE—"LADY BADINGSCOTH'S REEL."

My love she's but a lassie yet;
My love she's but a lassie yet;
We'll let her stand a year or twa,
She'll no be half sae saucy yet.
I rue the day I sought her, O;
I rue the day I sought her, O;
Wha gets her needs na say she's woo'd,
But he may say he's bought her, O!

---

[1] Reckoning.
[2] This song and the following one were only partly written by Burns.

Come, draw a drap o' the best o't yet;
  Come, draw a drap o' the best o't yet;
Gae seek for pleasure where ye will,
  But here I never miss'd it yet.
We're a' dry wi' drinking o't;
  We're a' dry wi' drinking o't;
The minister kiss'd the fiddler's wife,
  An' could na preach for thinkin' o't.

MY HEART WAS ANCE.

TUNE—"TO THE WEAVERS GIN YE GO."

My heart was ance as blythe and free
  As simmer days were lang,
But a bonnie, westlin weaver lad
  Has gart[1] me change my sang.
    To the weavers gin ye go, fair maids,
      To the weavers gin ye go;
    I rede you right, gang ne'er at night,
      To the weavers gin ye go.

My mither sent me to the town,
  To warp a plaiden wab;
But the weary, weary warpin o't
  Has gart me sigh and sab.

A bonnie westlin weaver lad
  Sat working at his loom;
He took my heart as wi' a net,
  In every knot and thrum.[2]

I sat beside my warpin wheel,
  And aye I ca'd it roun';
But ever shot and every knock,
  My heart it gae a stoun.

The moon was sinking in the west,
  Wi' visage pale and wan,
As my bonnie westlin weaver lad
  Convoy'd me thro' the glen.

But what was said, or what was done,
  Shame fa' me gin I tell;
But, oh! I fear the kintra soon
  Will ken as weel's mysel.

[1] Made.
[2] Thread remaining at the end of a web.

To the weavers gin ye go, fair maids,
  To the weavers gin ye go;
I rede[1] you right, gang ne'er at night,
  To the weavers gin ye go.

LOVELY DAVIES.[2]

TUNE—"MISS MUIR."

O how shall I, unskilfu', try
  The poet's occupation,
The tunefu' powers, in happy hours,
  That whisper inspiration?
Even they maun dare an effort mair
  Than aught they ever gave us,
Or they rehearse, in equal verse,
  The charms o' lovely Davies.
Each eye it cheers, when she appears,
  Like Phœbus in the morning,
When past the shower, and ev'ry flower
  The garden is adorning.
As the wretch looks o'er Siberia's shore,
  When winter-bound the wave is;
Sae drops our heart when we maun part
  Frae charming, lovely Davies.

Her smile's a gift, frae 'boon the lift,
  That maks us mair than princes;
A sceptr'd hand, a King's command,
  Is in her darting glances:
The man in arms, 'gainst female charms,
  Even he her willing slave is;
He hugs his chain, and owns the reign
  Of conquering, lovely Davies.
My muse to dream of such a theme,
  Her feeble powers surrenders;
The eagle's gaze alone surveys
  The sun's meridian splendours:

[1] Advise.
[2] Deborah Davies, the youngest daughter of Dr. Davies, of Tenby, South Wales. She was the victim of an unrequited attachment for an officer who died abroad. In a letter to this lady, Burns calls woman "the blood-royal of life."

I wad in vain essay the strain,
  The deed too daring brave is;
I'll drap the lyre, and mute admire
  The charms o' lovely Davies.

KENMURE'S ON AND AWA.

TUNE—"O, KENMURE'S ON AND AWA, WILLIE."

O, KENMURE's on and awa, Willie!
  O, Kenmure's on and awa!
And Kenmure's lord's the bravest lord
  That ever Galloway saw.

Success to Kenmure's band, Willie!
  Success to Kenmure's band;
There's no a heart that fears a Whig,
  That rides by Kenmure's hand.

Here's Kenmure's health in wine, Willie!
  Here's Kenmure's health in wine;
There ne'er was a coward o' Kenmure's blude,
  Nor yet o' Gordon's line.

O, Kenmure's lads are men, Willie!
  O, Kenmure's lads are men;
Their hearts and swords are metal true—
  And that their faes shall ken.

They'll live or die wi' fame, Willie!
  They'll live or die wi' fame;
But soon wi' sounding victorie,
  May Kenmure's lord come hame.

Here's him that's far awa, Willie!
  Here's him that's far awa;
And here's the flower that I lo'e best—
  The rose that's like the snaw.

THE CAPTAIN'S LADY.

TUNE—"O MOUNT AND GO."

CHORUS.

O, mount and go
  Mount and make you ready;
O, mount and go,
  And be the Captain's Lady.

WHEN the drums do beat,
  And the cannons rattle,
Thou shalt sit in state,
  And see thy love in battle.

When the vanquish'd foe
  Sues for peace and quiet,
To the shades we'll go,
  And in love enjoy it.
    O, mount and go,
    Mount and make you ready;
    O, mount and go,
    And be the Captain's Lady.

LADY MARY-ANN.

TUNE—"CRAIGTOWN'S GROWING."

O, LADY Mary-Ann
  Looks o'er the castle wa',
She saw three bonnie boys
  Playing at the ba';
The youngest he was
  The flower amang them a';
My bonnie laddie's young,
  But he's growing yet.

O father! O father!
  An' ye think it fit,
We'll send him a year
  To the college yet:
We'll sew a green ribbon
  Round about his hat,
And that will let them ken
  He's to marry yet.

Lady Mary-Ann
  Was a flower i' the dew,
Sweet was its smell,
  And bonnie was its hue!
And the langer it blossom'd
  The sweeter it grew;
For the lily in the bud
  Will be bonnier yet.

Young Charlie Cochran
  Was the sprout of an aik;
Bonnie and bloomin'
  And straught was its make:
The sun took delight
  To shine for its sake,
And it will be the brag
  O' the forest yet.

The simmer is gane
  When the leaves they were green,
And the days are awa
  That we hae seen;
But far better days
  I trust will come again,
For my bonnie laddie's young,
  But he's growin' yet.

THE HIGHLAND WIDOW'S LAMENT.[1]

OH! I am come to the low countrie,
  Och-on, och-on, och-rie!
Without a penny in my purse,
  To buy a meal to me.

It was na sae in the Highland hills,
  Och-on, och-on, och-rie!
Nae woman in the country wide
  Sae happy was as me.

For then I had a score o' kye,
  Och-on, och-on, och-rie!
Feeding on yon hills so high,
  And giving milk to me.

And there I had threescore o' yowes,
  Och-on, och-on, och-rie!
Skipping on yon bonnie knowes,
  And casting woo' to me.

I was the happiest of a' the clan,
  Sair, sair may I repine;
For Donald was the brawest lad,
  And Donald he was mine.

Till Charlie Stewart cam' at last,
  Sae far to set us free;
My Donald's arm was wanted then,
  For Scotland and for me.

Their waefu' fate what need I tell?—
  Right to the wrang did yield:
My Donald and his country fell
  Upon Culloden's field.

Oh! I am come to the low countrie,
  Och-on, och-on, och-rie!
Nae woman in the warld wide
  Sae wretched now as me.

[1] I do not know on what authority Mr. Cunningham assigns this Jacobite song to Burns; for I have heard old ladies sing it who remember its existence anterior to the poet's time.—*Motherwell.*

MERRY HAE I BEEN TEETHIN' A HECKLE.

TUNE—"LORD BREADALBANE'S MARCH."

O MERRY hae I been teethin' a heckle,[1]
  And merry hae I been shapin' a spoon;
O merry hae I been cloutin[2] a kettle,
  And kissin' my Katie when a' was done.
O a' the lang day I ca' at my hammer,
  An' a' the lang day I whistle and sing,
An' a' the lang night I cuddle my kimmer,[3]
  An' a' the lang night am as happy's a king.

Bitter in dool I lickit my winnins,
  O' marrying Bess, to gie her a slave:
Blest be the hour she cool'd in her linnens,
  And blythe be the bird that sings on her grave.
Come to my arms, my Katie, my Katie;
  An' come to my arms, and kiss me again!
Drunken or sober, here's to thee, Katie!
  An' blest be the day I did it again.

RATTLIN', ROARIN' WILLIE.

TUNE—"RATTLIN', ROARIN' WILLIE."

O RATTLIN,' roarin' Willie,
  O, he held to the fair,
An' for to sell his fiddle,
  An' buy some other ware;
But parting wi' his fiddle,
  The saut tear blin't his e'e;
And rattlin', roarin' Willie,
  Ye're welcome hame to me!

[1] A board with sharp steel prongs for dressing hemp.
[2] Repairing. [3] Young girl.

O Willie, come sell your fiddle,
  O sell your fiddle sae fine;
O Willie, come sell your fiddle,
  And buy a pint o' wine!
If I should sell my fiddle,
  The warl' would think I was mad,
For mony a rantin' day
  My fiddle and I hae had.

As I cam by Crochallan,
  I cannily keekit ben—
Rattlin', roarin' Willie
  Was sitting at yon board en';
Sitting at yon board en',[1]
  And amang guid companie;
Rattlin', roarin' Willie,
  Ye're welcome hame to me!

O MALLY'S MEEK, MALLY'S SWEET.

As I was walking up the street,
  A barefit maid I chanced to meet;
But O the road was very hard
  For that fair maiden's tender feet.
    O Mally's meek, Mally's sweet,
      Mally's modest and discreet,
    Mally's rare, Mally's fair,
      Mally's every way complete.

It were more meet that those fine feet
  Were weel laced up in silken shoon,
And 'twere more fit that she should sit
  Within yon chariot gilt aboon.

Her yellow hair, beyond compare,
  Comes trinkling[2] down her swan-white neck,
And her two eyes, like stars in skies,
  Would keep a sinking ship frae wreck.
    O Mally's meek, Mally's sweet,
      Mally's modest and discreet,
    Mally's rare, Mally's fair,
      Mally's every way complete.

SAE FAR AWA.

TUNE—"DALKEITH MAIDEN BRIDGE."

O, SAD and heavy should I part,
  But for her sake sae far awa;
Unknowing what my way may thwart,
  My native land sae far awa.
Thou that of a' things Maker art,
  That form'd this Fair sae far awa,
Gie body strength, then I'll ne'er start
  At this my way sae far awa.

How true is love to pure desert,
  So love to her, sae far awa:
And nocht can heal my bosom's smart,
  While, oh! she is sae far awa.
Nane other love, nane other dart,
  I feel but hers, sae far awa;
But fairer never touch'd a heart
  Than hers, the Fair sae far awa.

[1] End. [2] Trickling.

O STEER HER UP.

TUNE—"O STEER HER UP, AND HAUD HER GAUN."

O, STEER[1] her up, and haud her gaun—
  Her mother's at the mill, jo;
And gin she winna take a man,
  E'en let her take her will, jo:
First shore her wi' a kindly kiss,
  And ca' another gill, jo,
And gin she take the thing amiss,
  E'en let her flyte her fill, jo.

O steer her up, and be na blate,
  An' gin she take it ill, jo,
Then lea'e the lassie till her fate,
  And time nae longer spill, jo:
Ne'er break your heart for ae rebute,
  But think upon it still, jo;
Then gin the lassie winna do't,
  Ye'll fin' anither will, jo.

O, WHARE DID YE GET.

TUNE—"BONNIE DUNDEE."

O, WHARE did ye get that hauver-meal[2] bannock?
  O silly blind body, O dinna ye see?
I gat it frae a brisk young sodger laddie,
  Between Saint Johnston and bonnie Dundee.

[1] Stir. [2] Oatmeal.

O gin I saw the laddie that gae me't!
Aft has he doodled me up on his knee;
May Heaven protect my bonnie Scots laddie,
And send him safe hame to his babie and me!

My blessin's upon thy sweet wee lippie,
My blessin's upon thy bonnie e'e brie!
Thy smiles are sae like my blythe sodger laddie,
Thou's ay be dearer and dearer to me!
But I'll big a bower on yon bonnie banks,
Where Tay rins wimplin' by sae clear;
And I'll cleed[1] thee in the tartan sae fine,
And mak thee a man like thy daddie dear.

THE FÊTE CHAMPÊTRE.[2]

TUNE—"KILLIECRANKIE."

O WHA will to Saint Stephen's house,
To do our errands there, man?
O wha will to Saint Stephen's house,
O' th' merry lads of Ayr, man?
Or will we send a man-o'-law?
Or will we send a sodger?
Or him[3] wha led o'er Scotland a'
The meikle Ursa-Major?

Come, will ye court a noble lord,
Or buy a score o' lairds, man?
For worth and honour pawn their word,
Their vote shall be Glencaird's, man?
And gies them coin, ane gies them wine,
Anither gies them clatter;
Anbank,[4] wha guess'd the ladies' taste,
He gies a Fête Champêtre.

When Love and Beauty heard the news
The gay green-woods amang, man;
Where gathering flowers and busking bowers,
They heard the blackbird's sang, man;
A vow, they seal'd it with a kiss,
Sir Politics to fetter
As theirs alone, the patent-bliss,
To hold a Fête Champêtre.

Then mounted Mirth, on gleesome wing
O'er hill and dale she flew, man;
Ilk wimpling burn, ilk crystal spring,
Ilk glen and shaw she knew, man:
She summon'd every social sprite,
That sports by wood or water,
On th' bonny banks of Ayr to meet,
And keep this Fête Champêtre.

Cauld Boreas, wi' his boisterous crew,
Were bound to stakes like kye, man;
And Cynthia's car, o' silver fu',
Clamb up the starry sky, man:
Reflected beams dwell in the streams,
Or down the current shatter;
The western breeze steals through the trees,
To view this Fête Champêtre.

How many a robe sae gaily floats!
What sparkling jewels glance, man!
To Harmony's enchanting notes,
As moves the mazy dance, man.
The echoing wood, the winding flood,
Like Paradise did glitter,
When angels met, at Adam's yett,[1]
To hold their Fête Champêtre.

When Politics came there, to mix
And make his ether-stane,[2] man!
He circled round the magic ground,
But entrance found he nane, man:
He blush'd for shame, he quat[3] his name,
Forswore it, every letter,
Wi' humble prayer to join and share
This festive Fête Champêtre.

SIMMER'S A PLEASANT TIME.

TUNE—"AY WAUKIN O."

SIMMER'S a pleasant time,
Flow'rs of ev'ry colour;

[1] Clothe.
[2] Given by Mr. Cunningham, of Enterkin. [3] Boswell.
[4] A place belonging to Mr. Cunningham, and which, after the Scottish custom, bestows a name on the Laird.

[1] Gate. [2] Adder-stone. [3] Quit.

The water rins o'er the heugh,[1]
And I long for my true lover.
Ay waukin O,
Waukin still and wearie:
Sleep I can get nane
For thinking on my dearie.

When I sleep I dream,
When I wauk I'm eerie;
Sleep I can get nane
For thinking on my dearie.

Lanely night comes on,
A' the lave are sleeping;
I think on my bonnie lad,
And I bleer my een with greetin'.
Ay waukin O,
Waukin still and wearie;
Sleep I can get nane
For thinking on my dearie.

THE BLUDE-RED ROSE AT YULE MAY BLAW.

TUNE—"TO DAUNTON ME."

The blude red rose at Yule may blaw,
The Simmer lilies bloom in snaw,
The frost may freeze the deepest sea;
But an auld man shall never daunton me.

To daunton me, and me sae young,
Wi' his fause heart and flatt'ring tongue,
That is the thing you ne'er shall see;
For an auld man shall never daunton me.

For a' his meal and a' his maut,
For a' his fresh beef and his saut,
For a' his gold and white monie,
An auld man shall never daunton me.

His gear may buy him kye and yowes,
His gear may buy him glens and knowes;
But me he shall not buy nor fee,
For an auld man shall never daunton me.

[1] Crag.

He hirples twa-fauld as he dow,
Wi' his teethless gab and his auld beld pow,
And the rain rains down frae his red bleer'd e'e—
That auld man shall never daunton me.

To daunton me, and me sae young,
Wi' his fause heart and flatt'ring tongue,
That is the thing you ne'er shall see;
For an auld man shall never daunton me.

THE HIGHLAND LADDIE.

TUNE—"IF THOU'LT PLAY ME FAIR PLAY."

The bonniest lad that e'er I saw,
Bonnie laddie, Highland laddie,
Wore a plaid and was fu' braw,
Bonnie Highland laddie.
On his head a bonnet blue,
Bonnie laddie, Highland laddie,
His loyal heart was firm and true,
Bonnie Highland laddie.

Trumpets sound and cannons roar,
Bonnie lassie, Lawland lassie,
And a' the hills wi' echoes roar,
Bonnie Lawland lassie.
Glory, Honour, now invite,
Bonnie lassie, Lawland lassie,
For freedom and my King to fight,
Bonnie Lawland lassie.

The sun a backward course shall take,
Bonnie laddie, Highland laddie,
Ere aught thy manly courage shake;
Bonnie Highland laddie.
Go, for yoursel procure renown,
Bonnie laddie, Highland laddie,
And for your lawful King his crown;
Bonnie Highland laddie!

THE COOPER O' CUDDIE.

TUNE—"BOB AT THE BOWSTER."

The cooper o' Cuddie cam' here awa,
And ca'd the girrs out owre us a'—

And our gude-wife has gotten a ca'
  That anger'd the silly guid-man, O.
We'll hide the cooper behind the door,
Behind the door, behind the door;
We'll hide the cooper behind the door,
  And cover him under a mawn,[1] O.

He sought them out, he sought them in,
Wi', Deil hae her! and, Deil hae him!
But the body was sae doited and blin',[2]
  He wist na where he was gaun, O.

They cooper'd at e'en, they cooper'd at morn,
Till our guid-man has gotten the scorn;
On ilka brow she's planted a horn,
  And swears that they shall stan', O,
We'll hide the cooper behind the door,
Behind the door, behind the door,
We'll hide the cooper behind the door,
  And cover him under a mawn, O.

[1] Basket. [2] Stupified and blind.

THE TAILOR.

TUNE—"THE TAILOR FELL THRO' THE BED, THIMBLES AN' A'."

The Tailor fell thro' the bed, thimbles an' a',
The Tailor fell thro' the bed, thimbles an a',
The blankets were thin, and the sheets they were sma',
The Tailor fell thro' the bed, thimbles an' a'.
The sleepy bit lassie, she dreaded nae ill,
The sleepy bit lassie, she dreaded nae ill;
The weather was cauld, and the lassie lay still,
She thought that a tailor could do her nae ill.
Gie me the groat again, canny young man;
Gie me the groat again, canny young man;
The day it is short, and the night it is lang,
The dearest siller that ever I wan!
There's somebody weary wi' lying her lane;
There's somebody weary wi' lying her lane;
There's some that are dowie,[1] I trow wad be fain
To see the bit tailor come skippin' again.

NITHSDALE'S WELCOME HAME.

The noble Maxwells and their powers
  Are coming o'er the border,
And they'll gae bigg[2] Terreagle's towers,
  An' set them a' in order.
And they declare Terreagle's fair,
  For their abode they choose it;
There's no a heart in a' the land,
  But's lighter at the news o't.

Tho' stars in skies may disappear,
  And angry tempests gather;
The happy hour may soon be near
  That brings us pleasant weather:
The weary night o' care and grief
  May hae a joyful morrow;
So dawning day has brought relief—
  Fareweel our night o' sorrow!

THE TITHER MORN.

  The tither morn,
  When I forlorn,
Aneath an aik sat moaning,
  I did na trow,
  I'd see my jo,
Beside me, 'gain the gloaming.
  But he sae trig
  Lap o'er the rig,
And dawtingly did cheer me,
  When I, what reck,
  Did least expec'
To see my lad so near me.

  His bonnet he,
  A thought ajee,

[1] Worn with grief. [2] Build.

Cock'd sprush when first he clasp'd me:
And I, I wat,
Wi' fainness grat,
While in his grips he press'd me.
Deil tak' the war!
I, late and air,
Hae wish'd since Jock departed;
But now as glad
I'm wi' my lad,
As short syne broken-hearted.

Fu' aft at e'en
Wi' dancing keen,
When a' were blythe and merry,
I car'd na by,
Sae sad was I
In absence o' my dearie.
But, praise be blest,
My mind's at rest,
I'm happy wi' my Johnny:
At kirk and fair,
I'se ay be there,
And be as canty's ony.

THE CARLE OF KELLYBURN BRAES.

TUNE—"KELLYBURN BRAES."

There lived a carle on Kellyburn braes,
(Hey, and the rue grows bonnie wi' thyme),
And he had a wife was the plague o' his days;
And the thyme it is wither'd, and rue is in prime.

Ae day as the carle gaed up the lang glen,
(Hey, and the rue grows bonnie wi' thyme),
He met wi' the Devil; says, "How do you fen?"
And the thyme it is wither'd, and rue is in prime.

"I've got a bad wife, sir; that's a' my complaint,
(Hey, and the rue grows bonnie wi' thyme),
For, saving your presence, to her ye're a saint;"
And the thyme it is wither'd, and rue is in prime.

"It's neither your stot[1] nor your staig[2] I shall crave,
(Hey, and the rue grows bonnie wi' thyme),
But gie me your wife, man, for her I must have;"
And the thyme it is wither'd, and rue is in prime.

"O welcome, most kindly," the blythe carle said,
(Hey, and the rue grows bonnie wi' thyme),
"But if ye can match her, ye're waur nor ye're ca'd;"
And the thyme it is wither'd, and rue is in prime.

The Devil has got the auld wife on his back,
(Hey, and the rue grows bonnie wi' thyme),
And, like a poor pedler, he's carried his pack;
And the thyme it is wither'd, and rue is in prime.

He's carried her hame to his ain hallan-door,
(Hey, and the rue grows bonnie wi' thyme),
Syne bade her gae in, for a b— and a w—;
And the thyme it is wither'd, and rue is in prime.

Then straight he makes fifty, the pick o' his band,
(Hey, and the rue grows bonnie wi' thyme),
Turn out on her guard in the clap of a hand;
And the thyme it is wither'd, and rue is in prime.

The carlin gaed thro' them like ony wud[3] bear,
(Hey, and the rue grows bonnie wi' thyme),
Whae'er she gat hands on came near her nae mair;
And the thyme it is wither'd, and rue is in prime.

---

[1] Ox. [2] Two-year old horse. [3] Wild.

A reekit[1] wee Devil looks over the wa',
(Hey, and the rue grows bonnie wi' thyme),
"O, help, master, help, or she'll ruin us a';"
And the thyme it is wither'd, and rue is in prime.

The Devil he swore by the edge o' his knife,
(Hey, and the rue grows bonnie wi' thyme),
He pitied the man that was tied to a wife;
And the thyme it is wither'd, and rue is in prime.

The Devil he swore by the kirk and the bell,
(Hey, and the rue grows bonnie wi' thyme),
He was not in wedlock, thank heav'n, but in hell;
And the thyme it is wither'd, and rue is in prime.

Then Satan has travell'd again wi' his pack,
(Hey, and the rue grows bonnie wi' thyme),
And to her auld husband he's carried her back;
And the thyme it is wither'd, and rue is in prime.

"I hae been a Devil the feck o' my life,
(Hey, and the rue grows bonnie wi' thyme),
But ne'er was in hell, till I met wi' a wife;"
And the thyme it is wither'd, and rue is in prime.

THERE WAS A LASS.

TUNE—"DUNCAN DAVISON."

THERE was a lass, they ca'd her Meg,
And she held o'er the moors to spin;
There was a lad that follow'd her,
They ca'd him Duncan Davison.

[1] Smoking.

The moor was dreigh,[1] and Meg was skeigh,[2]
Her favour Duncan could na win;
For wi' the roke she wad him knock,
And ay she shook the temper-pin.

As o'er the moor they lightly foor,
A burn was clear, a glen was green,
Upon the banks they eased their shanks,
And ay she set the wheel between:
But Duncan swore a haly aith,
That Meg should be a bride the morn;
Then Meg took up her spinnin' graith,[3]
And flung them a' out o'er the burn.

We'll big a house—a wee, wee house,
And we will live like King and Queen,
Sae blythe and merry we will be
When ye set by the wheel at e'en.
A man may drink and no be drunk;
A man may fight and no be slain;
A man may kiss a bonnie lass,
And ay be welcome back again.

THE PLOUGHMAN.

TUNE—"UP WI' THE PLOUGHMAN."

THE ploughman he's a bonnie lad,
His mind is ever true, jo,
His garters knit below his knee,
His bonnet it is blue, jo.

CHORUS.

Then up wi't a', my ploughman lad,
And hey, my merry ploughman;
Of a' the trades that I do ken,
Commend me to the ploughman.

My ploughman he comes hame at e'en,
He's aften wat and weary;
Cast off the wat, put on the dry,
And gae to bed, my Dearie!
Up wi't a', &c.

I will wash my ploughman's hose,
And I will dress his o'erlay;[4]
I will mak my ploughman's bed,
And cheer him late and early.
Up wi't a', &c.

[1] Tedious. [2] Proud.
[3] Gear. [4] Cravat.

I hae been east, I hae been west,
  I hae been at Saint Johnston,
The bonniest sight that e'er I saw
  Was th' ploughman laddie dancin'.
    Up wi't a', &c.

Snaw-white stockins on his legs,
  And siller buckles glancin';
A guid blue bannet on his head,
  And O, but he was handsome!
    Up wi't a', &c.

Commend me to the barn yard,
  And the corn-mou, man;
I never gat my coggie fou
  Till I met wi' the ploughman.
    Up wi't a', &c.

THE CARLES OF DYSART.

TUNE—"HEY CA' THRO'."

Up wi' the carles o' Dysart,
  And the lads o' Buckhaven,
And the kimmers[1] o' Largo,
  And the lasses o' Leven.
    Hey, ca' thro', ca' thro',
      For we hae mickle ado;
    Hey, ca' thro', ca' thro',
      For we hae mickle ado.

We hae tales to tell,
  And we hae sangs to sing;
We hae pennies to spend,
  And we hae pints to bring.
We'll live a' our days,
  And them that come behin',
Let them do the like,
  And spend the gear they win.
    Hey, ca' thro', ca' thro',
      For we hae mickle ado;
    Hey, ca' thro', ca' thro',
      For we hae mickle ado.

WEARY FA' YOU, DUNCAN GRAY.

TUNE—"DUNCAN GRAY."

Weary fa' you, Duncan Gray—
  Ha, ha, the girdin o't!

[1] Gossips.

Wae gae by you, Duncan Gray—
  Ha, ha, the girdin o't!
When a' the lave gae to their play,
Then I maun sit the lee-lang day,
And jog the cradle wi' my tae,
  And a' for the girdin o't.

Bonnie was the Lammas moon—
  Ha, ha, the girdin o't!
Glowrin' a' the hills aboon—
  Ha, ha, the girdin o't!
The girdin brak, the beast cam down,
I tint my curch,[1] and baith my shoon;
Ah! Duncan, ye're an unco loon—
  Wae on the bad girdin o't!

But, Duncan, gin ye'll keep your aith—
  Ha, ha, the girdin o't!
Ise bless you wi' my hindmost breath—
  Ha, ha, the girdin o't!
Duncan, gin ye'll keep your aith,
The beast again can bear us baith,
And auld Mess John will mend the skaith,[2]
  And clout the bad girdin o't.

MY HOGGIE.[3]

TUNE—"WHAT WILL I DO GIN MY HOGGIE DIE."

What will I do gin my Hoggie die?
  My joy, my pride, my Hoggie!
My only beast, I had nae mae,
  And vow but I was vogie![4]
The lee-lang night we watch'd the fauld,
  Me and my faithfu' doggie;
We heard nought but the roaring linn,
  Amang the braes sae scroggie;[5]
But the houlet cry'd frae the castle wa',
  The blitter frae the boggie,
The tod[6] reply'd upon the hill,
  I trembled for my Hoggie.

[1] Lost the covering for the head.
[2] Damage.
[3] The *hoggie*, alias pet ewe, was Margaret Brodie, of Coxton, in Banffshire. The song was taken down by Burns from the singing of an old woman in Liddesdale.—*Buchan.*
[4] Vain. [5] Bushy. [6] Fox.

When day did daw, and cocks did craw,
  The morning it was foggie;
An unco tyke [1] lap o'er the dyke,
  And maist has kill'd my Hoggie.

WHERE HAE YE BEEN.

TUNE—"KILLIECRANKIE."

WHARE hae ye been sae braw, lad?
  Where hae ye been sae brankie, [2] O?
O, whare hae ye been sae braw, lad?
  Cam ye by Killiecrankie, O?
An' ye had been whare I hae been,
  Ye wad na been so cantie, O;
An' ye had seen what I hae seen,
  On the braes o' Killiecrankie, O.

I fought at land, I fought at sea:
  At hame I fought my auntie, O;
But I met the Devil an' Dundee,
  On the braes o' Killiecrankie, O.
The bauld Pitcur fell in a furr, [3]
  An' Clavers got a clankie, O;
Or I had fed an Athole gled, [4]
  On the braes o' Killiecrankie, O.

COCK UP YOUR BEAVER.

TUNE—"COCK UP YOUR BEAVER."

WHEN first my brave Johnnie lad
  Came to this town,
He had a blue bonnet
  That wanted the crown;
But now he has gotten
  A hat and a feather,—
Hey, brave Johnnie lad,
  Cock up your beaver!

Cock up your beaver,
  And cock it fu' sprush,
We'll over the border
  And gie them a brush;
There's somebody there
  We'll teach better behaviour—
Hey, brave Johnnie lad,
  Cock up your beaver!

[1] Dog. [2] Gaudy.
[3] Furrow. [4] Hawk.

THE HERON BALLADS. [1]

FIRST BALLAD.

WHOM will you send to London town
  To Parliament and a' that?
Or wha in a' the country round
  The best deserves to fa' that?
    For a' that, an' a' that,
    Thro' Galloway and a' that,
    Where is the laird, or belted knight,
    That best deserves to fa' that?

Wha sees Kerroughtree's open yett,
  And wha is't never saw that?
Wha ever wi' Kerroughtree met,
  And has a doubt of a' that;
    For a' that, an' a' that,
    Here's Heron yet for a' that;
    The independent patriot,
    The honest man, an' a' that.

Tho' wit and worth in either sex,
  St. Mary's Isle can shaw that;
Wi' dukes an' lords let Selkirk mix,
  And weel does Selkirk fa' that.
    For a' that, an' a' that,
    Here's Heron yet for a' that!
    The independent commoner
    Shall be the man for a' that.

But why should we to nobles jouk?
  And it's against the law that;
For why, a lord may be a gouk,
  Wi' ribbon, star, an' a' that.
    For a' that, an' a' that,
    Here's Heron yet for a' that!
    A lord may be a lousy loun,
    Wi' ribbon, star, an' a' that.

A beardless boy comes o'er the hills,
  Wi' uncle's purse an' a' that;
But we'll hae ane frae 'mang oursels,
  A man we ken, an' a' that.
    For a' that, an' a' that!
    Here's Heron yet for a' that!
    For we're not to be bought an' sold
    Like naigs, an' nowt, an' a' that.

[1] This is the first of several ballads which Burns wrote to serve Patrick Heron, of Kerroughtree, in two elections, in which he was opposed, first by Gordon, of Balmaghie, and secondly by the Hon. Montgomery Stewart.—*Allan Cunningham.*

Then let us drink the Stewartry,
  Kerroughtree's laird, an' a' that,
Our representative to be,
  For weel he's worthy a' that.
    For a' that, an' a' that,
    Here's Heron yet for a' that!
    A House of Commons such as he,
    They would be blest that saw that.

THE ELECTION.

SECOND BALLAD.

Fy, let us a' to Kirkcudbright,
  For there will be bickerin' there;
For Murray's light-horse are to muster,
  And O, how the heroes will swear!
An' there will be Murray commander,
  And Gordon the battle to win;
Like brothers they'll stand by each other,
  Sae knit in alliance an' kin.

An' there will be black-lippit Johnnie,
  The tongue o' the trump to them a';
An' he get na hell for his haddin',
  The Deil gets na justice ava';
An' there will be Kempleton's birkie,
  A boy no sae black at the bane,
But, as for his fine nabob fortune,
  We'll e'en let the subject alane.

An' there will be Wigton's new sheriff,
  Dame Justice fu' brawlie has sped,
She's gotten the heart of a Bushby,
  But, Lord, what's become o' the head?
An' there will be Cardoness, Esquire,
  Sae mighty in Cardoness' eyes;
A wight that will weather damnation,—
  For the Devil the prey will despise.

An' there will be Douglasses doughty,
  New christ'ning towns far and near!
Abjuring their democrat doings,
  By kissing the —— o' a peer;
An' there will be Kenmure sae gen'rous,
  Whose honour is proof to the storm;—
To save them from stark reprobation,
  He lent them his name to the firm.

But we winna mention Redcastle,
  The body, e'en let him escape!
He'd venture the gallows for siller,
  An' 'twere na the cost o' the rape.

An' where is our King's lord-lieutenant,
  Sae fam'd for his grateful' return?
The billie is gettin' his questions,
  To say in St. Stephen's the morn.

An' there will be lads o' the gospel,
  Muirhead, wha's as gude as he's true;
An' there will be Buittle's apostle,
  Wha's more o' the black than the blue;
An' there will be folk from St. Mary's,
  A house o' great merit and note,
The Deil ane but honours them highly,—
  The Deil ane will gie them his vote!

An' there will be wealthy young Richard,
  Dame Fortune should hing by the neck;
For prodigal, thriftless, bestowing,
  His merit had won him respec':
An' there will be rich brother nabobs,
  Though nabobs, yet men of the first,
An' there will be Collieston's whiskers,
  An' Quintin, o' lads not the worst.

An' there will be stamp-office Johnnie,
  Tak tent how ye purchase a dram;
An' there will be gay Cassencarrie,
  An' there will be gleg Colonel Tam;
An' there will be trusty Kerroughtree,
  Whose honour was ever his law;
If the virtues were pack'd in a parcel,
  His worth might be sample for a'.

An' can we forget the auld major,
  Wha'll ne'er be forgot in the Greys;
Our flatt'ry we'll keep for some other,
  Him only 'tis justice to praise.
An' there will be maiden Kilkerran,
  And also Barskimming's gude knight,
An' there will be roarin' Birtwhistle,
  Wha, luckily, roars in the right.

An' there, frae the Niddesdale's border,
  Will mingle the Maxwells in droves;
Teugh Johnnie, staunch Geordie, an' Walie,
  That griens[1] for the fishes an' loaves;
An' there will be Logan Mac Douall,
  Sculdudd'ry an' he will be there,
An' also the wild Scot o' Galloway,
  Sodgerin', gunpowder Blair.

[1] Longs.

Then hey the chaste interest o' Broughton,
An' hey for the blessings 'twill bring!
It may send Balmaghie to the Commons,
In Sodom 'twould make him a King;
An' hey for the sanctified Murray,
Our land who wi' chapels has stor'd;
He founder'd his horse among harlots,
But gied the auld naig to the Lord.

AN EXCELLENT NEW SONG.

THIRD BALLAD.

WHA will buy my troggin,[1]
Fine election ware:
Broken trade o' Broughton,
A' in high repair?
Buy braw troggin,
Frae the banks o' Dee;
Wha wants troggin
Let him come to me.

There's a noble Earl's
Fame and high renown,
For an auld sang—
It's thought the gudes were stown.
Buy braw troggin, &c.

Here's the worth o' Broughton
In a needle's e'e;
Here's a reputation
Tint by Balmaghie.
Buy braw troggin, &c.

Here's an honest conscience
Might a prince adorn;
Frae the downs o' Tinwald—
Sae was never worn.
Buy braw troggin, &c.

Here's the stuff and lining,
O' Cardoness' head;
Fine for a sodger,
A' the wale o' lead.
Buy braw troggin, &c.

Here's a little wadset,
Buittle's scrap o' truth,
Pawn'd in a gin-shop,
Quenching holy drouth.
Buy braw troggin, &c.

Here's armorial bearings
Frae the manse o' Urr;
The crest, an auld crab-apple
Rotten at the core.[1]
Buy braw troggin, &c.

Here is Satan's picture,
Like a bizzard gled,[2]
Pouncing poor Redcastle
Sprawlin' as a taed.
Buy braw troggin, &c.

Here's the worth and wisdom
Collieston can boast;
By a thievish midge
They had been nearly lost.
Buy braw troggin, &c.

Here is Murray's fragments
O' the ten commands;
Gifted by black Jock
To get them aff his hands.
Buy braw troggin, &c.

Saw ye e'er sic troggin?
If to buy ye're slack,
Hornie's turnin' chapman,—
He'll buy a' the pack.
Buy braw troggin, &c

YE SONS OF OLD KILLIE.

TUNE—"SHAWNBOY."

YE sons of old Killie, assembled by Willie,
To follow the noble vocation;
Your thrifty old mother has scarce such another
To sit in that honoured station.
I've little to say, but only to pray,
As praying's the ton of your fashion;
A prayer from the Muse you may well excuse,
'Tis seldom her favourite passion.

---

[1] *Troggin* is the merchandise of a travelling hawker.

[1] The allusion is to Dr. Muirhead, Minister of Urr.

[2] Hawk.

Ye powers who preside o'er the wind and the tide,
  Who marked each element's border;
Who formed this frame with beneficent aim,
  Whose sovereign statute is order;
Within this dear mansion may wayward contention
  Or withered envy ne'er enter;
May secrecy round be the mystical bound,
  And brotherly love be the centre!

YE JACOBITES BY NAME.[1]

TUNE—"YE JACOBITES BY NAME."

Ye Jacobites by name, give an ear, give an ear;
  Ye Jacobites by name, give an ear;
    Ye Jacobites by name,
      Your fautes I will proclaim,
        Your doctrines I maun blame—
          You shall hear.

What is right and what is wrang, by the law, by the law?
  What is right and what is wrang by the law?
    What is right and what is wrang?
      A short sword and a lang,
        A weak arm, and a strang
          For to draw.

What makes heroic strife, fam'd afar, fam'd afar?
  What makes heroic strife fam'd afar?
    What makes heroic strife?
      To whet th' assassin's knife,
        Or hunt a parent's life
          Wi' bluidie war.

Then let your schemes alone, in the state, in the state;
  Then let your schemes alone in the state;
    Then let your schemes alone,
      Adore the rising sun,
        And leave a man undone
          To his fate.

[1] Burns founded this song on some old verses, in which it was intimated that the extinction of the House of Stuart was sought for by other weapons than the sword. It cannot be denied that if the House of Hanover had the affection of the people and the law of the land on their side, the exiled princes had the best poetry. This may be accounted for. The romantic adventures and daring exploits and deep sufferings of Prince Charles enlisted sympathy on his side; and the minstrels, regarding his fate and that of his brave companions as furnishing matter for poetry only, sung with a pathos and force which will likely be long remembered. —A. C.

SONG—AH, CHLORIS.

TUNE—"MAJOR GRAHAM."

Ah, Chloris, since it may na be,
  That thou of love wilt hear;
If from the lover thou maun flee,
  Yet let the friend be dear.

Altho' I love my Chloris mair
  Than ever tongue could tell;
My passion I will ne'er declare,
  I'll say I'll wish thee well:

Tho' a' my daily care thou art,
  And a' my nightly dream,
I'll hide the struggle in my heart,
  And say it is esteem.

EXTEMPORE ANSWER TO AN INVITATION.

The King's most humble servant I,
  Can scarcely spare a minute;
But I'll be wi' ye by an' bye;
  Or else the Deil's be in it.

My bottle is my holy pool,
That heals the wounds o' care an' dool;
And pleasure is a wanton trout,
An' ye drink it, ye'll find him out.

KATHARINE JAFFRAY.

There liv'd a lass in yonder dale,
And down in yonder glen, O,
And Katharine Jaffray was her name,
Weel known to many men, O.

Out came the Lord of Lauderdale,
Out frae the south countrie, O,
All for to court this pretty maid,
Her bridegroom for to be, O.

He's tell'd her father and mother baith,
As I hear sindry say, O,
But he has na tell'd the lass hersel,
Till on her wedding day, O.

Then cam the Laird o' Lochinton,
Out frae the English border,
All for to court this pretty maid,
All mounted in good order.

THE COLLIER LADDIE.

O whare live ye, my bonnie lass,
And tell me how they ca' ye?
My name, she says, is Mistress Jean,
And I follow my Collier laddie.

O see ye not yon hills and dales,
The sun shines on sae brawlie:
They a' are mine, and they shall be thine,
Gin ye'll leave your Collier laddie.

And ye shall gang in rich attire,
Weel buskit up fu' gaudy;
And ane to wait at every hand,
Gin ye'll leave your Collier laddie.

Tho' ye had a' the sun shines on,
And the earth conceals sae lowly;
I would turn my back on you and it a',
And embrace my Collier laddie.

I can win my five pennies in a day,
And spend it at night fu' brawlie;
I can mak my bed in the Collier's neuk,
And lie down wi' my Collier laddie.

Luve for luve is the bargain for me,
Tho' the wee cot-house should haud me;
And the warld before me to win my bread,
And fare fa' my Collier laddie.

WHEN I THINK ON THOSE HAPPY DAYS.

When I think on the happy days
I spent wi' you, my dearie;
And now what lands between us lie,
How can I be but eerie!

How slow ye move, ye heavy hours,
As ye were wae and weary!
It was na sae ye glinted by,
When I was wi' my dearie.

EPPIE M'NAB.

O saw ye my dearie, my Eppie M'Nab?
O saw ye my dearie, my Eppie M'Nab?
She's down in the yard, she's kissin' the laird:
She winna come hame to her ain Jock Rab.
O come thy ways to me, my Eppie M'Nab!
O come thy ways to me, my Eppie M'Nab!
Whate'er thou has done, be it late, be it soon,
Thou's welcome again to thy ain Jock Rab.

What says she, my dearie, my Eppie M'Nab?
What says she, my dearie, my Eppie M'Nab?
She lets thee to wit, that she has thee forgot,
And for ever disowns thee, her ain Jock Rab.
O had I ne'er seen thee, my Eppie M'Nab!
O had I ne'er seen thee, my Eppie M'Nab!
As light as the air, and fause as thou's fair,
Thou's broken the heart o' thy ain Jock Rab.

TO CHLORIS.[1]

BEHOLD, my love, how green the groves,
The primrose banks how fair;
The balmy gales awake the flow'rs,
And wave thy flaxen hair.
The lav'rock shuns the palace gay,
And o'er the cottage sings;
For Nature smiles as sweet, I ween,
To shepherds as to Kings.

Let minstrels sweep the skilfu' string,
In lordly lighted ha';
The shepherd stops his simple reed
Blythe in the birken shaw.
The princely revel may survey
Our rustic dance wi' scorn;
But are their hearts as light as ours,
Beneath the milk-white thorn?

The shepherd, in the flowery glen,
In shepherd's phrase will woo;
The courtier tells a finer tale,
But is his heart as true?
These wild wood flow'rs I've pu'd to deck
That spotless breast o' thine;
The courtier's gems may witness love,
But 'tis na love like mine.

AN' O! MY EPPIE.

AN' O! my Eppie,
My jewel, my Eppie!
Wha wadna be happy
Wi' Eppie Adair?
By love, and by beauty,
By law, and by duty,
I swear to be true to
My Eppie Adair!

An' O! my Eppie,
My jewel, my Eppie!
Wha wadna be happy
Wi' Eppie Adair?
A' pleasure exile me,
Dishonour defile me,
If e'er I beguile thee,
My Eppie Adair!

[1] On my visit the other day to my fair Chloris, she suggested an idea, which I, on my return from my visit, wrought into the following song. How do you like the simplicity and tenderness of this pastoral?—R. B., *Nov.*, 1794.

GUDEE'N TO YOU, KIMMER.

GUDEE'N to you, Kimmer,
And how d'ye do?
Hiccup, quo' Kimmer,
The better that I am fou.
We're a' noddin, nid, nid, noddin,
We're a' noddin at our house at hame.

Kate sits i' the neuk,
Suppin hen broo;[1]
Deil tak Kate
An' she be na noddin too!
We're a' noddin, &c.

How's a' wi' you, Kimmer,
And how do ye fare?
A pint o' the best o't,
And twa pints mair.
We're a' noddin, &c.

How's a' wi' you, Kimmer,
And how do ye thrive;
How mony bairns hae ye?
Quo' Kimmer, I hae five.
We're a' noddin, &c.

Are they a' Johnny's?
Eh! atweel na:
Twa o' them were gotten
When Johnny was awa.
We're a' noddin, &c.

Cats like milk,
And dogs like broo;
Lads like lasses weel,
And lasses lads too.
We're a' noddin, &c.

O WAT YE WHA THAT LO'ES ME.

TUNE—"MORAG."

O WAT ye wha that lo'es me,
And has my heart a-keeping?

[1] Broth.

O sweet is she that lo'es me,
As dews o' summer weeping,
In tears the rose-buds steeping:
O that's the lassie o' my heart,
My lassie, ever dearer;
O that's the queen o' woman-kind,
And ne'er a ane to peer her.

If thou shalt meet a lassie,
In grace and beauty charming;
That e'en thy chosen lassie,
Erewhile thy breast sae warming,
Had ne'er sic powers alarming:
O that's the lassie, &c.

If thou hast heard her talking,
And thy attention's plighted,
That ilka body talking,
But her, by thee is slighted,
And thou art all delighted:
O that's the lassie, &c.

If thou hast met this fair one,—
When frae her thou hast parted,
If every other fair one,
But her, thou hast deserted,
And thou art broken-hearted:
O that's the lassie, &c.

THERE'S NEWS, LASSES.

THERE'S news, lasses, news,
Gude news I have to tell,
There's a boat fu' o' lads
Come to our town to sell.
The wean wants a cradle,
And the cradle wants a cod,[1]
And I'll no gang to my bed
Until I get a nod.

Father, quo' she, Mither, quo' she,
Do what you can,
I'll nae gang to my bed
Till I get a man.
The wean, &c.

I hae as gude a craft rig
As made o' yird and stane;
And waly fa' the ley-crap,
For I maun till't again.
The wean, &c.

[1] Pillow.

O THAT I HAD NE'ER BEEN MARRIED.

O THAT I had ne'er been married,
I wad never had nae care;
Now I've gotten wife and bairns,
An' they cry crowdie[1] ever mair.
Ance crowdie, twice crowdie,
Three times crowdie in a day;
Gin ye crowdie ony mair,
Ye'll crowdie a' my meal away.

Waefu' want and hunger fley[2] me,
Glowerin by the hallan en';
Sair I fecht[3] them at the door,
But ay I'm eerie they come ben.
Ance crowdie, &c.

FRAE THE FRIENDS AND LAND I LOVE.[4]

FRAE the friends and land I love,
Driven by Fortune's felly[5] spite,
Frae my best belov'd I rove,
Never mair to taste delight;
Never mair maun hope to find
Ease frae toil, relief frae care;
When remembrance wracks the mind,
Pleasures but unveil despair.

Brightest climes shall mirk appear,
Desert ilka blooming shore,
Till the Fates, nae mair severe,
Friendship, love, and peace restore;
Till Revenge wi' laurel'd head
Bring our banished hame again;
And ilk loyal, bonnie lad
Cross the seas and win his ain.

[1] Oatmeal, water, and butter.
[2] Scare. [3] Fought.
[4] Burns, in his notes on the "Musical Museum," says of this song, "I added the last four lines by way of giving a turn to the theme of the poem such as it is." It has been suggested by his editors, that Burns mended his song as the Highlander mended his gun, by giving to it a new stock, a new lock, and a new barrel.
[5] Relentless.

SCROGGAM.

THERE was a wife wonn'd in Cockpen,
Scroggam ;
She brew'd guid ale for gentlemen,
Sing auld Cowl, lay you down by me,
Scroggam, my dearie, ruffum.

The gudewife's dochter fell in a fever,
Scroggam ;
The priest o' the parish fell in anither;
Sing auld Cowl, lay you down by me.
Scroggam, my dearie, ruffum.

They laid the twa i' the bed thegither,
Scroggam ;
That the heat o' the tane might cool the tither;
Sing auld Cowl, lay you down by me,
Scroggam, my dearie, ruffum.

THE TEARS I SHED.[1]

THE tears I shed must ever fall ;
I mourn not for an absent swain,
For thought may past delights recall,
And parted lovers meet again.
I weep not for the silent dead,
Their toils are past, their sorrows o'er,
And those they lov'd their steps shall tread,
And death shall join to part no more.

Tho' boundless oceans roll'd between,
If certain that his heart is near,
A conscious transport glads each scene,
Soft is the sigh, and sweet the tear.
E'en when by Death's cold hand remov'd,
We mourn the tenant of the tomb,
To think that even in death he lov'd,
Can gild the horrors of the gloom.

But bitter, bitter are the tears
Of her who slighted love bewails ;
No hope her dreary prospect cheers,
No pleasing melancholy hails.
Hers are the pangs of wounded pride,
Of blasted hope, of wither'd joy :
The prop, she lean'd on, pierc'd her side ;
The flame, she fed, burns to destroy.

In vain does memory renew,
The hours once ting'd in transport's dye ;
The sad reverse soon starts to view,
And turns the thought to agony.
Even conscious virtue cannot cure
The pangs to every feeling due :
Ungenerous youth ! thy boast how poor,
To steal a heart, and break it too !

No cold approach, no alter'd mien,
Just what would make suspicion start ;
No pause the dire extremes between,
He made me blest—and broke my heart !
From hope, the wretched's anchor, torn,
Neglected, and neglecting all,
Friendless, forsaken, and forlorn,
The tears I shed must ever fall.

[1] The first four lines of the last stanza were added by Burns ; the song being the composition of Miss Cranstoun, afterwards the wife of Dugald Stewart.

THE TWA HERDS.[1]

Blockheads with reason wicked wits abhor,
But Fool with Fool is barbarous civil war.—POPE.

O A' ye pious godly flocks,
Weel fed in pastures orthodox,
Wha now will keep you frae the fox,
Or worrying tykes?[2]

[1] The Twa "Herds" were the minister of Riccarton, and the assistant-minister of Kilmarnock, whose controversial animosity burst out in blows during a walk home after a "Sacrament" sermon. Burns recorded the feat of arms in a "burlesque lamentation," which, as he informs us, with a certain description of the clergy, as well as laity, met with a roar of applause. Burns gave a copy to a friend, and professed ignorance of the writer.

[2] Dogs.

Or wha will tent the waifs and crocks,[1]
About the dykes?

The twa best herds in a' the wast,
That e'er gae gospel horn a blast,
These five and twenty simmers past,
O, dool to tell!
Hae had a bitter black out-cast
Atween themsel.

O, Moodie, man, and wordy Russell,
How could you raise so vile a bustle,
Ye'll see how New-light herds will whistle,
And think it fine!
The Lord's cause ne'er gat sic a twistle,
Sin' I ha'e min'.

O, Sirs! whae'er wad hae expeckit
Your duty ye wad sae negleckit,
Ye wha were ne'er by lairds respeckit,
To wear the plaid,
But by the brutes themselves eleckit
To be their guide.

What flock wi' Moodie's flock could rank,
Sae hale and hearty every shank,
Nae poison'd sour Arminian stank
He let them taste;
Frae Calvin's well, aye clear, they drank,—
O' sic a feast!

The thummart,[2] wil'-cat, brock, and tod,[3]
Weel kend his voice thro' a' the wood,
He smell'd their ilka hole and road,
Baith out and in,
And weel he lik'd to shed their bluid,
And sell their skin.

What herd like Russell tell'd his tale,
His voice was heard thro' muir and dale,
He kend the Lord's sheep, ilka tail,
O'er a' the height,
And saw gin they were sick or hale,
At the first sight.

He fine a mangy sheep could scrub,
Or nobly fling the gospel club,

[1] Stray sheep and old ewes.
[2] Pole-cat. [3] Badger and fox.

And New-light herds could nicely drub,
Or pay their skin;
Could shake them owre the burning dub,[1]
Or heave them in.

Sic twa—O! do I live to see't,
Sic famous twa should disagreet,
An' names, like "villain," "hypocrite,"
Ilk ither gi'en,
While New-light herds wi' laughin' spite,
Say "neither's lien"!

A' ye wha tent the gospel fauld,
There's Duncan deep, and Peebles shaul,[2]
But chiefly thou, apostle Auld,
We trust in thee,
That thou wilt work them, het and cauld,
Till they agree.

Consider, Sirs, how we're beset;
There's scarce a new herd that we get,
But comes frae 'mang that cursed set
I winna name;
I hope frae Heaven to see them yet
In fiery flame.

Dalrymple has been lang our fae,
M'Gill has wrought us meikle wae,
And that curs'd rascal ca'd M'Quhae,
And baith the Shaws,
That aft hae made us black and blae,
Wi' vengefu' paws.

Auld Wodrow lang has hatch'd mischief,
We thought aye death wad bring relief,
But he has gotten, to our grief,
Ane to succeed him,
A chiel wha'll soundly buff our beef;[3]
I meikle dread him.

And monie a ane that I could tell,
Wha fain would openly rebel,
Forbye turn-coats amang oursel,
There's Smith for ane,
I doubt he's but a grey-nick quill,[4]
And that ye'll fin'.

[1] Pond. [2] Shallow.
[3] Give us a severe beating.
[4] Unfit for a pen.

O ! a' ye flocks, owre a' the hills,
By mosses, meadows, moors, and fells,
Come join your counsels and your skills,
To cowe the lairds,
And get the brutes the power themsels
To choose their herds.

Then Orthodoxy yet may prance,
And Learning in a woody dance,
And that fell cur ca'd Common Sense,
That bites sae sair,
Be banish'd owre the seas to France ;
Let him bark there.

Then Shaw's and D'rymple's eloquence,
M'Gill's close nervous excellence,
M'Quhae's pathetic manly sense,
And guid M'Math,
Wi' Smith, wha thro' the heart can glance,
May a' pack aff.

HOLY WILLIE'S PRAYER.[1]

O Thou, wha in the Heavens dost dwell,
Wha, as it pleases best thysel',
Sends ane to Heaven, and ten to Hell,
A' for thy glory,
And no for onie guid or ill
They've done afore thee !

I bless and praise thy matchless might,
Whan thousands thou hast left in night,
That I am here afore thy sight,
For gifts an' grace,
A burning an' a shining light,
To a' this place.

What was I, or my generation,
That I should get such exaltation ?
I, wha deserve such just damnation,
For broken laws,
Five thousand years 'fore my creation,
Thro' Adam's cause.

When frae my mither's womb I fell,
Thou might hae plung'd me into Hell,
To gnash my gums, to weep and wail,
In burnin' lake,
Where damned Devils roar and yell,
Chain'd to a stake.

Yet I am here a chosen sample,
To show thy grace is great and ample ;
I'm here a pillar in thy temple,
Strong as a rock,
A guide, a buckler, an example
To a' thy flock.

O L—d, thou kens what zeal I bear,
When drinkers drink, and swearers swear,
And singin there, and dancing here,
Wi' great an' sma' :
For I am keepit by thy fear,
Free frae them a'.

But yet, O L—d ! confess I must,
At times I'm fash'd wi' fleshly lust,
An' sometimes, too, wi' warldly trust,—
Vile self gets in ;
But thou remembers we are dust,
Defil'd in sin.

O L—d ! yestreen, thou kens, wi' Meg—
Thy pardon I sincerely beg,
O ! may 't ne'er be a livin' plague
To my dishonour,
An' I'll ne'er lift a lawless leg
Again upon her.

Besides I farther maun allow,
Wi' Lizzie's lass, three times I trow ;
But, L—d, that Friday I was fou,
When I came near her,
Or else thou kens thy servant true
Wad ne'er hae steer'd her

---

[1] Sir Walter Scott regarded Holy Willie's Prayer as "a piece of satire more exquisitely severe than any which Burns afterwards wrote." The Poet assures us that it alarmed "the Kirk-Sessions so much, that they had several meetings to look over their spiritual artillery." The hero of the poem was a farmer, William Fisher, near Mauchline, said to be very pharisaic and hypocritical ; one of that class of professors whom Sterne described as making every stride look like a check on their desires. Fisher was an elder in the kirk, and had offended Burns by his persecution of Mr. Hamilton, who thoughtlessly set a beggar to work in his garden on a Sunday morning, and was excommunicated in consequence.

May be thou lets this fleshly thorn
Beset thy servant e'en and morn,
Lest he owre high and proud should turn,
'Cause he's sae gifted;
If sae, thy hand maun e'en be borne,
Until thou lift it.

L—d, bless thy chosen in this place,
For here thou hast a chosen race;
But G—d confound their stubborn face,
And blast their name,
Wha bring thy elders to disgrace,
An' public shame.

L—d, mind Gawn Hamilton's deserts,
He drinks, an' swears, an' plays at cartes,
Yet has sae monie takin arts,
Wi' great an' sma',
Frae God's ain priests the people's hearts
He steals awa'.

An' when we chasten'd him therefore,
Thou kens how he bred sic a splore,[1]
As set the warld in a roar
O' laughin' at us;—
Curse thou his basket and his store,
Kail and potatoes.

L—d, hear my earnest cry an' pray'r,
Against that presbyt'ry o' Ayr;
Thy strong right hand, L—d, make it bare,
Upo' their heads;
L—d, weigh it down, and dinna spare,
For their misdeeds.

O L—d my G—d, that glib-tongu'd Aiken,
My very heart and saul are quakin,
To think how we stood sweatin, shakin,
An' swat wi' dread,
While he wi' hinging lips gaed snakin,
And hid his head.

L—d, in the day of vengeance try him:
L—d, visit them wha did employ him,
And pass not in thy mercy by 'em,
Nor hear their pray'r:
But, for thy people's sake, destroy 'em,
And dinna spare.

[1] Riot.

But, L—d, remember me and mine
Wi' mercies temp'ral and divine,
That I for gear and grace may shine,
Excell'd by nane,
An' a' the glory shall be thine,
Amen, Amen.[1]

EPITAPH ON HOLY WILLIE.

Here Holy Willie's sair worn clay
Taks up its last abode;
His saul has taen some other way,
I fear the left-hand road.

Stop! there he is, as sure's a gun,
Poor silly body, see him;
Nae wonder he's as black's the grun
Observe wha's standing wi' him.

Your brunstane devilship, I see,
Has got him there before ye;
But haud your nine-tail cat a-wee,
Till ance you've heard my story.

Your pity I will not implore,
For pity ye hae nane;
Justice, alas! has gien him o'er,
And mercy's day is gane.

But hear me, Sir, deil as ye are,
Look something to your credit;
A coof like him wad stain your name,
If it were kent ye did it.

[1] Against some passages it has been objected that they breathe a spirit of irreligion. But if we consider the ignorance and fanaticism of the lower class of people when these poems were written, a fanaticism of that pernicious sort which sets *faith* in opposition to *good works*, the fallacy and danger of which a mind so enlightened as our poet's could not but perceive, we shall not look upon his lighter Muse as the enemy of religion, though she has sometimes been a little unguarded in her ridicule of hypocrisy.—*H. Mackenzie.* —(The "Lounger," No. 97.)

LINES WRITTEN EXTEMPORE IN A LADY'S POCKET-BOOK.

GRANT me, indulgent Heav'n, that I may live,
To see the miscreants feel the pains they give ;
Deal Freedom's sacred treasures free as air,
Till slave and despot be but things which were.

VERSES ADDRESSED TO J. RANKINE.

I AM a keeper of the law
In some sma' points, although not a',
Some people tell me gin I fa',
Ae way or ither,
The breaking of ae point, tho' sma',
Breaks a' thegither.

I hae been in for't ance or twice,
And winna say owre far for thrice,
Yet never met with that surprise
That broke my rest,
But now a rumour's like to rise,
A whaup's i' the nest.

ON SCARING SOME WATER FOWL IN LOCH-TURIT, A WILD SCENE AMONG THE HILLS OF OCHTERTYRE.

WHY, ye tenants of the lake,
For me your wat'ry haunt forsake?
Tell me, fellow-creatures, why
At my presence thus you fly ?
Why disturb your social joys,
Parent, filial, kindred ties ?—
Common friend to you and me,
Nature's gifts to all are free :
Peaceful keep your dimpling wave,
Busy feed, or wanton lave ;
Or, beneath the sheltering rock,
Bide the surging billow's shock.
Conscious, blushing for our race,
Soon, too soon, your fears I trace ;
Man, your proud, usurping foe,
Would be lord of all below ;
Plumes himself in Freedom's pride,
Tyrant stern to all beside.
The eagle, from the cliffy brow,
Marking you his prey below,
In his breast no pity dwells,
Strong Necessity compels.
But Man, to whom alone is giv'n
A ray direct from pitying Heav'n,
Glories in his heart humane—
And creatures for his pleasure slain.
In these savage, liquid plains,
Only known to wandering swains,
Where the mossy riv'let strays,
Far from human haunts and ways,
All on Nature you depend,
And life's poor season peaceful spend.
Or, if man's superior might
Dare invade your native right,
On the lofty ether borne,
Man with all his pow'rs you scorn ;
Swiftly seek, on clanging wings,
Other lakes and other springs ;
And the foe you cannot brave,
Scorn at least to be his slave.

A TOAST.[1]

INSTEAD of a Song, boys, I'll give you a Toast,—
Here's the memory of those on the twelfth that we lost :
That we lost, did I say? nay, by Heav'n, that we found ;
For their fame it shall last while the world goes round.
The next in succession, I'll give you the King,
Whoe'er would betray him, on high may he swing !
And here's the grand fabric, our free Constitution,
As built on the base of the great Revolution.

---

[1] Given on occasion of the celebration of the naval victory, April 12, 1782.

And, longer with Politics not to be cramm'd,
Be Anarchy curs'd, and be Tyranny d—'d;
And who would to Liberty e'er prove disloyal,
May his son be a hangman, and he his first trial!

EPIGRAM.

One Queen Artemisia, as old stories tell,
When depriv'd of her husband she loved so well,
In respect for the love and affection he'd shown her,
She reduc'd him to dust, and she drank up the powder.

But Queen Netherplace, of a diff'rent complexion,
When call'd on to order the fun'ral direction,
Would have eat her dear lord, on a slender pretence,
Not to show her respect, but—to save the expense.

ANOTHER.[1]

Whoe'er he be that sojourns here,
I pity much his case,
Unless he come to wait upon
The Lord their God, his Grace.[2]

There's naething here but Highland pride,
And Highland scab and hunger;
If Providence has sent me here,
'Twas surely in an anger.

[1] Written at Inverary.
[2] The Duke of Argyll.

ON SEEING THE BEAUTIFUL SEAT OF LORD GALLOWAY.

What dost thou in that mansion fair?
Flit, Galloway, and find
Some narrow, dirty, dungeon cave,
The picture of thy mind!

ON THE SAME.

No Stewart art thou, Galloway,
The Stewarts all were brave;
Besides, the Stewarts were but fools,
Not one of them a knave.

ON THE SAME.[1]

Bright ran thy line, O Galloway,
Thro' many a far-fam'd sire!
So ran the far-fam'd Roman way,
So ended in a mire!

TO THE SAME,

ON THE AUTHOR BEING THREATENED WITH HIS RESENTMENT.

Spare me thy vengeance, Galloway,
In quiet let me live:
I ask no kindness at thy hand,
For thou hast none to give.

VERSES TO J. RANKINE.

Ae day, as Death, that grusome carl,
Was driving to the tither warl'
A mixtie-maxtie[2] motley squad,
And monie a guilt-bespotted lad;
Black gowns of each denomination,
And thieves of every rank and station,
From him that wears the star and garter,
To him that wintles[3] in a halter;
Asham'd himsel to see the wretches,
He mutters, glowrin at the b——s,

[1] These were some of the satirical fruits of the Heron contest.
[2] Confusedly mixed. [3] Staggers.

"By G— I'll not be seen behint them,
Nor 'mang the sp'ritual core present them,
Without, at least, ae honest man,
To grace this d--d infernal clan."
By Adamhill a glance he threw,
"L— G—!" quoth he, "I have it now,
There's just the man I want, i' faith,"
And quickly stoppit Rankine's breath.

EXTEMPORANEOUS EFFUSION, ON BEING APPOINTED TO THE EXCISE.

SEARCHING auld wives' barrels,
Och, hon! the day!
That clartie[1] barm should stain my laurels;
But—what'll ye say?
These movin' things, ca'd wives and weans,
Wad move the very hearts o' stanes!

ON HEARING THAT THERE WAS FALSEHOOD IN THE REV. DR. B——'S VERY LOOKS.

THAT there is falsehood in his looks
I must and will deny:
They say their master is a knave—
And sure they do not lie.

POVERTY.

IN politics if thou wouldst mix,
And mean thy fortunes be;
Bear this in mind,—be deaf and blind,
Let great folks hear and see.

---

[1] Dirty.

ON A SCHOOLMASTER IN CLEISH PARISH, FIFESHIRE.

HERE lie Willie Michie's banes;
O Satan, when ye tak him,
Gie him the schoolin' o' your weans,
For clever Deils he'll mak them!

LINES

WRITTEN AND PRESENTED TO MRS. KEMBLE, ON SEEING HER IN THE CHARACTER OF YARICO.

Dumfries Theatre, 1794.

KEMBLE, thou cur'st my unbelief
Of Moses and his rod;
At Yarico's sweet notes of grief
The rock with tears had flow'd.

I MURDER hate by field or flood,
Tho' glory's name may screen us;
In wars at hame I'll spend my blood,
Life-giving war to Venus.

The deities that I adore
Are social Peace and Plenty;
I'm better pleased to make one more,
Than be the death of twenty.

LINES

WRITTEN ON A WINDOW, AT THE KING'S ARMS TAVERN, DUMFRIES.

YE men of wit and wealth, why all this sneering
'Gainst poor Excisemen? give the cause a hearing;
What are your landlords' rent-rolls? taxing ledgers:
What premiers, what? even Monarch's mighty gaugers:
Nay, what are priests, those seeming godly wise men?
What are they, pray, but spiritual Excisemen?

LINES

WRITTEN ON THE WINDOW OF THE GLOBE TAVERN, DUMFRIES.

THE greybeard, Old Wisdom, may boast of his treasures,
Give me with gay Folly to live;
I grant him his calm-blooded, time-settled pleasures,
But Folly has raptures to give.

LINES

WRITTEN UNDER THE PICTURE OF THE CELEBRATED MISS BURNS.

CEASE, ye prudes, your envious railing,
Lovely Burns has charms—confess:
True it is, she had one failing,
Had a woman ever less?

EPIGRAM

ON ELPHINSTONE'S TRANSLATION OF MARTIAL'S EPIGRAMS.

O THOU, whom Poetry abhors,
Whom Prose had turned out of doors,
Heard'st thou that groan?—proceed no further,
'Twas laurel'd Martial roaring murder.

EPITAPH

ON A COUNTRY LAIRD, NOT QUITE SO WISE AS SOLOMON.

BLESS the Redeemer, O Cardoness,
With grateful lifted eyes,
Who said that not the soul alone,
But body, too, must rise:

For had He said, "The soul alone
From death I will deliver,"
Alas! alas! O Cardoness,
Then thou hadst slept for ever!

EPITAPH

ON WEE JOHNNY.[1]

Hic jacet wee Johnny.

WHOE'ER thou art, O reader, know
That death has murder'd Johnny!
An' here his body lies fu' low——
For saul he ne'er had ony.

EPITAPH

ON A CELEBRATED RULING ELDER.

HERE sowter[2] Hood in Death does sleep;
To h—l, if he's gane thither,
Satan, gie him thy gear to keep,
He'll haud it weel thegither.

EPITAPH

FOR ROBERT AIKEN, ESQ.

KNOW thou, O stranger to the fame
Of this much lov'd, much honour'd name!
(For none that knew him need be told)
A warmer heart death ne'er made cold.

EPITAPH

FOR GAVIN HAMILTON, ESQ.

THE poor man weeps—here Gavin sleeps,
Whom canting wretches blam'd:
But with such as he, where'er he be,
May I be sav'd, or d—'d!

EPITAPH ON MY FATHER.

O YE, whose cheek the tear of pity stains,
Draw near with pious rev'rence and attend!

[1] John Wilson, who printed an edition of Burns's Poems. [2] Shoemaker.

Here lie the loving husband's dear remains,
The tender father, and the gen'rous friend;

The pitying heart that felt for human woe;
The dauntless heart that fear'd no human pride;
The friend of man, to vice alone a foe,
"For ev'n his failings lean'd to virtue's side."

EPITAPH

ON JOHN DOVE, INNKEEPER, MAUCHLINE.

HERE lies Johnny Pidgeon;
What was his religion?
Wha e'er desires to ken,
To some other warl'
Maun follow the carl,
For here Johnny Pidgeon had nane!

Strong ale was ablution,
Small beer persecution,
A dram was memento mori;
But a full flowing bowl
Was the saving his soul,
And port was celestial glory.

EPITAPH

ON JOHN BUSHBY,[1] WRITER, IN DUMFRIES.

HERE lies John Bushby, honest man,
Cheat him, Devil, if you can.

[1] "Went to the churchyard where Burns is buried. A bookseller accompanied us. Went on to visit the grave. 'There,' said the bookseller to us, pointing to a pompous monument a few yards off, 'there lies Mr. John Bushby, a remarkably clever man; he was an attorney, and hardly ever lost a cause he undertook. Burns made many a lampoon upon him, and there they rest, as you see.'"—*Memoirs of Wordsworth*, i. 214.

A BARD'S EPITAPH.

Is there a whim-inspired fool,
Owre fast for thought, owre hot for rule,
Owre blate[1] to seek, owre proud to snool,[2]
Let him draw near;
And owre this grassy heap sing dool,
And drap a tear.

Is there a Bard of rustic song,
Who, noteless, steals the crowds among,
That weekly this area throng,
O, pass not by!
But, with a frater-feeling strong,
Here, heave a sigh.

Is there a man whose judgment clear,[3]
Can others teach the course to steer,
Yet runs, himself, life's mad career
Wild as the wave;
Here pause—and, thro' the starting tear,
Survey this grave.

The poor Inhabitant below
Was quick to learn, and wise to know,
And keenly felt the friendly glow,
And softer flame;
But thoughtless follies laid him low,
And stain'd his name!

Reader, attend—whether thy soul
Soars fancy's flights beyond the pole,
Or darkling grubs this earthly hole,
In low pursuit;
Know, prudent, cautious *self-control*
Is wisdom's root.

[1] Bashful. [2] Submit tamely.

[3] Burns might have remembered Goldsmith's picture of an author:—A *child* of the public he is in all respects; for while he is so able to direct others, how incapable is he frequently found of guiding himself! His simplicity exposes him to all the insidious approaches of cunning; his sensibility to the slightest invasions of contempt. Though possessed of fortitude to stand unmoved the expected bursts of an earthquake, yet of feelings so exquisitely poignant, as to agonize under the slightest disappointment.—*The Present State of Polite Learning, chapter* X.

GLOSSARY.

THE *ch* and *gh* have always the guttural sound. The sound of the English diphthong *oo*, is commonly spelled *ou*. The French *u*, a sound which often occurs in the Scottish language, is marked *oo*, or *ui*. The *a* in genuine Scottish words, except when forming a diphthong, or followed by an *e* mute after a single consonant, sounds generally like the broad English *a* in *wall*. The Scottish diphthong *ae* always, and *ea* very often, sound like the French *e* masculine. The Scottish diphthong *ey* sounds like the Latin *ei*.

A', All
Aback, away, aloof
Abeigh, at a shy distance
Aboon, above, up
Abread, abroad, in sight
Abreed, in breadth
Addle, putrid water, &c.
Ae, one
Aff, off; Aff loof, unpremeditated
Afore, before
Aft, oft
Aften, often
Agley, off the right line ; wrong
Aiblins, perhaps
Ain, own
Airle-penny, Airles, earnest money
Airn, iron
Aith, an oath
Aits, oats
Aiver, an old horse
Aizle, a hot cinder
Alake, alas
Alane, alone
Akwart, awkward
Amaist, almost
Amang, among
An', and ; if
Ance, once
Ane, one ; and
Anent, over against
Anither, another
Ase, ashes
Asklent, asquint ; aslant
Asteer, abroad ; stirring
Athart, athwart
Aught, possession ; as, In a' my aught, in all my possession
Auld lang syne, olden time, days of other years
Auld, old
Auldfarran, or, auld farrant, sagacious, cunning, prudent
Ava, at all
Awa', away
Awfu' awful
Awn, the beard of barley, oats, &c.

Awnie, bearded
Ayont, beyond

BA', Ball
Backets, ash boards
Backlins, coming; coming back, returning
Back, returning
Bad, did bid
Baide, endured, did stay
Baggie, the belly
Bainie, having large bones, stout
Bairn, a child
Bairntime, a family of children, a brood
Baith, both
Ban, to swear
Bane, bone
Bang, to beat; to strive
Bardie, diminutive of bard
Barefit, barefooted
Barmie, of or like barm
Batch, a crew, a gang
Batts, bots
Baudrons, a cat
Bauld, bold
Bawk, bank
Baws'nt, having a white stripe down the face
Be, to let be; to give over; to cease
Bear, barley
Beastie, diminutive of beast
Beet, to add fuel to fire
Beld, bald
Belyve, by and by
Ben, into the spence or parlour; a spence
Benlomond, a noted mountain in Dumbartonshire
Bethankit, grace after meat
Beuk, a book
Bicker, a kind of wooden dish; a short race
Bie, or Bield, shelter
Bien, wealthy, plentiful
Big, to build
Biggin, building; a house
Biggit, built
Bill, a bull
Billie, a brother; a young fellow
Bing, a heap of grain, potatoes, &c.
Birk, birch
Birken-shaw, Birchen-wood-shaw, a small wood
Birkie, a clever fellow
Birring, the noise of partridges, &c., when they spring
Bit, crisis, nick of time
Bizz, a bustle, to buzz
Blastie, a shrivelled dwarf; a term of contempt
Blastit, blasted
Blate, bashful, sheepish
Blather, bladder
Bladd, a flat piece of anything; to slap
Blaw, to blow, to boast
Bleerit, bleared, sore with rheum
Bleert and blin', bleared and blind
Bleezing, blazing
Blellum, an idle talking fellow
Blether, to talk idly; nonsense
Bleth'rin', talking idly
Blink, a little while; a smiling look; to look kindly; to shine by fits
Blinker, a term of contempt
Blinkin, smirking
Blue-gown, one of those beggars who get annually, on the King's birth-day, a blue cloak or gown, with a badge
Bluid, blood

Bluntie, a sniveller, a stupid person
Blype, a shred, a large piece
Bock, to vomit, to gush intermittently
Bocked, gushed, vomited
Bodle, a small gold coin
Bogles, spirits, hobgoblins
Bonnie, or bonny, handsome, beautiful
Bonnock, a kind of thick cake of bread, a small jannock, or loaf made of oatmeal
Boord, a board
Boortree, the shrub elder; planted much of old in hedges of barn-yards, &c.
Boost, behaved, must needs
Bore, a hole in the wall
Botch, an angry tumour
Bousing, drinking
Bow-kail, cabbage
Bowt, bended, crooked
Brackens, fern
Brae, a declivity; a precipice; the slope of a hill
Braid, broad
Braindg't, reeled forward
Braik, a kind of harrow
Braindge, to run rashly forward
Brak, broke, made insolvent
Branks, a kind of wooden curb for horses
Brash, a sudden illness
Brats, coarse clothes, rags, &c.
Brattle, a short race; hurry; fury
Braw, fine, handsome
Brawly, or brawlie, very well; finely; heartily
Braxie, a morbid sheep
Breastie, diminutive of breast
Breastit, did spring up or forward
Breckan, fern
Breef, an invulnerable or irresistible spell
Breeks, breeches
Brent, smooth
Brewin', brewing
Brie, juice, liquid
Brig, a bridge
Brisket, the breast, the bosom
Brither, a brother
Brock, a badger
Brogue, a hum; a trick
Broo, broth; a trick
Broose, broth; a race at country weddings, who shall first reach the bridegroom's house on returning from church
Browster-wives, ale-house wives
Brugh, a burgh
Bruilzie, a broil, a combustion
Brunstane, brimstone
Brunt, did burn, burnt
Brust, to burst; burst
Buchan-bullers, the boiling of the sea among the rocks of Buchan
Buckskin, an inhabitant of Virginia
Bught, a pen
Bughtin-time, the time of collecting the sheep in the pens to be milked
Buirdly, stout made; broad made
Bum-clock, a humming beetle that flies in the summer evenings
Bumming, humming as bees
Bummle, to blunder
Bummler, a blunderer
Bunker, a window-seat
Burdies, diminutive of birds
Bure, did bear
Burn, water, a rivulet
Burnewin, *i.e.*, burn the wind, a blacksmith

Burnie, diminutive of burn
Buskie, bushy
Buskit, dressed
Busks, dresses
Buss, shelter
Bussle, a bustle ; to bustle
But, bot, with ; without
But an' ben, the country kitchen and parlour
By himsel, lunatic, distracted
Byke, a bee-hive
Byre, a cow-stable ; a sheep-pen

CA', to call, to name ; to drive
Ca't, or ca'd, called, driven ; calved
Cadger, a carrier
Cadie, or Caddie, a person ; a young fellow
Caff, chaff
Caird, a tinker
Cairn, a loose heap of stones
Calf-ward, a small enclosure for calves
Callan, a boy
Caller, fresh ; sound ; refreshing
Canie, or cannie, gentle, mild ; dexterous
Cannilie, dexterously ; gently
Cantie, or canty, cheerful, merry
Cantraip, a charm, a spell
Cape-stane, cope-stone ; key-stone
Careerin, cheerfully
Carl, an old man
Carlin, an old stout woman
Cartes, cards
Caudron, a cauldron
Cauld, cold
Caulk and keel, chalk and red clay
Caup, a wooden drinking-vessel
Cesses, taxes
Chanter, a part of a bagpipe
Chap, a person, a fellow ; a blow
Chaup, a stroke, a blow
Cheekit, checked
Cheep, a chirp ; to chirp
Chiel, or cheel, a young fellow
Chimla, or chimlie, a fire-grate, a fire-place
Chimla-lug, the fireside
Chittering, shivering, trembling
Chockin, choking
Chow, to chew ; Cheek for chow, side by side
Chuffie, fat-faced
Clachan, a small village about a church ; a hamlet
Claise, or claes, clothes
Claith, cloth
Claithing, clothing
Claivers, nonsense ; not speaking sense
Clap, clapper of a mill
Clarkit, wrote
Clash, an idle tale, the story of the day
Clatter, to tell idle stories ; an idle story
Claught, snatched at, laid hold of
Claut, to clean ; to scrape
Clauted, scraped
Clavers, idle stories
Claw, to scratch
Cleed, to clothe
Cleeds, clothes
Cleekit, having caught
Clinkin, jerking ; clinking
Clinkumbell, he who rings the church-bell
Clips, shears
Clishmaclaver, idle conversation
Clock, to hatch ; a beetle
Clockin, hatching
Cloot, the hoof of a cow, sheep, &c.

Clootie, an old name for the Devil
Clour, a bump or swelling after a blow
Cluds, clouds
Coaxin, wheedling
Coble, a fishing boat
Cockernony, a lock of hair tied upon a girl's head; a cap
Coft, bought
Cog, a wooden dish
Coggie, diminutive of cog
Coila, from Kyle, a district of Ayrshire; so called, saith tradition, from Coil, or Coilus, a Pictish monarch
Collie, a general and sometimes a particular name for country curs
Collieshangie, quarrelling, an uproar
Commaun, command
Cood, the cud
Coof, a blockhead, a ninny
Cookit, appeared and disappeared by fits
Coost, did cast
Coot, the ancle or foot
Cootie, a wooden kitchen dish:—also, those fowls whose legs are clad with feathers are said to be cootie
Corbies, a species of the crow
Core, corps; party; clan
Corn't, fed with oats
Cotter, the inhabitant of a cot-house, or cottager
Couthie, kind, loving
Cove, a cave
Cowe, to terrify; to keep under, to lop; fright; a branch of furze, broom, &c.
Cowp, to barter; to tumble over; a gang
Cowpit, tumbled
Cowrin, cowering
Cowt, a colt
Cozie, snug
Cozily, snugly
Crabbit, crabbed, fretful
Crack, conversation; to converse
Crackin, conversing
Craft, or croft, a field near a house (in old husbandry)
Craiks, cries or calls incessantly; a bird
Crambo-clink, or crambo-jingle, rhymes, doggrel verses
Crank, the noise of an ungreased wheel
Crankous, fretful, captious
Cranreuch, the hoar frost
Crap, a crop; to crop
Craw, a crow of a cock; a rook
Creel, a basket; to have one's wits in a creel, to be crazed; to be fascinated
Creepie-stool, the same as cutty-stool
Creeshie, greasy
Crood, or croud, to coo as a dove
Croon, a hollow and continued moan; to make a noise like the continued roar of a bull; to hum a tune
Crooning, humming
Crouchie, crook-backed
Crouse, cheerful; courageous
Crousely, cheerfully; courageously
Crowdie, a composition of oatmeal and boiled water, sometimes from the broth of beef, mutton, &c.
Crowdie-time, breakfast-time
Crowlin, crawling
Crummock, a cow with crooked horns
Crump, hard and brittle; spoken of bread
Crunt, a blow on the head with a cudgel

Cuif, a blockhead, a ninny
Cummock, a short staff with a crooked head
Curchie, a courtesy
Curler, a player at a game on the ice, practised in Scotland, called curling
Curlie, curled, whose hair falls naturally in ringlets
Curling, a well-known game on the ice
Curmurring, murmuring; a slight rumbling noise
Curpin, the crupper
Cushat, the dove, or wood-pigeon
Cutty, short; a spoon broken in the middle
Cutty-stool, the stool of repentance

DADDIE, a father
Daffin, merriment; foolishness
Daft, merry, giddy; foolish
Daimen, rare, now and then; daimen-icker, an ear of corn now and then
Dainty, pleasant, good humoured, agreeable
Daise, daez, to stupify
Dales, plains, valleys
Darklins, darkling
Daud, to thrash, to abuse
Daur, to dare
Daurg, or daurk, a day's labour
Daurt, dared
Davoc, David
Dawd, a large piece
Dawtit, or dawtet, fondled, caressed
Dearies, diminutive of dears
Dearthfu', dear
Deave, to deafen
Deil-ma-care! no matter! for all that!
Deleerit, delirious
Descrive, to describe
Dight, to wipe; to clean corn from chaff
Dight, cleaned from chaff
Ding, to worst, to push
Dink, neat, tidy, trim
Dinna, do not
Dirl, a slight tremulous stroke or pain
Dizen, or dizz'n, a dozen
Doited, stupified, hebetated
Dolt, stupified, crazed
Donsie, unlucky
Dool, sorrow; to sing dool, to lament, to mourn
Doos, doves
Dorty, saucy, nice
Douce, or douse, sober, wise, prudent
Doucely, soberly, prudently
Dought, was or were able
Doup, backside
Doup-skelper, one that strikes the tail
Dour and din, sullen and sallow
Doure, stout, durable; sullen, stubborn
Dow, am or are able, can
Dowff, pithless, wanting force
Dowie, worn with grief, fatigue, &c., half asleep
Downa, am or are not able, cannot
Doylt, stupid
Dozent, stupified, impotent
Drap, a drop; to drop
Draigle, to soil by trailing, to draggle among wet, &c.
Drapping, dropping
Draunting, drawling; of a slow enunciation
Dreep, to ooze, to drop
Dreigh, tedious, long about it
Dribble, drizzling; slaver
Drift, a drove
Droddum, the breech

Drone, part of a bagpipe
Droop-rumpl't, that drops at the crupper
Droukit, wet
Drounting, drawling
Drouth, thirst, drought
Drucken, drunken
Drumly, muddy
Drummock, meal and water mixed in a raw state
Drunt, pet, sour humour
Dub, a small pond
Duds, rags, clothes
Duddie, ragged
Dung, worsted; pushed, driven
Dunted, beaten, boxed
Dush, to push as a ram, &c.
Dusht, pushed by a ram, ox, &c.

E'E, the eye
Een, the eyes
E'ening, evening
Eerie, frighted, dreading spirits
Eild, old age
Elbuck, the elbow
Eldritch, ghastly, frightful
Eller, an elder, or church officer
En', end
Enbrugh, Edinburgh
Eneugh, enough
Especial, especially
Ettle, to try, to attempt
Eydent, diligent

FA', fall; lot; to fall
Fa's, does fall; water-falls
Faddom't, fathomed
Fae, a foe
Faem, foam
Faiket, unknown
Fairin, a fairing; a present
Fallow, fellow
Fand, did find
Farl, a cake of oaten bread, &c.
Fash, trouble, care; to trouble, to care for
Fasht, troubled
Fasteren-e'en, Fasten's Even
Fauld, a fold; to fold
Faulding, folding
Faut, fault
Faute, want, lack
Fawsont, decent, seemly
Feal, a field; smooth
Fearfu', frightful
Feart, frighted
Feat, neat, spruce
Fecht, to fight
Fechtin, fighting
Feck, many, plenty
Fecket, an under waistcoat with sleeves
Feckfu', large, brawny, stout
Feckless, puny, weak, silly
Feckly, weakly
Feg, a fig
Feide, feud, enmity
Feirrie, stout, vigorous, healthy
Fell, keen, biting; the flesh immediately under the skin; a field pretty level, on the side or top of a hill
Fen, successful struggle; fight
Fend, to live comfortably
Ferlie, or ferley, to wonder; a wonder: a term of contempt
Fetch, to pull by fits
Fetch'd, pulled intermittently
Fidge, to fidget
Fiel, soft, smooth
Fient, fiend, a petty oath
Fier, sound, healthy; a brother; a friend

Fissle, to make a rustling noise; to fidget; a bustle
Fit, a foot
Fittie-lan', the nearer horse of the hindmost pair in the plough
Fizz, to make a hissing noise, like fermentation
Flainen, flannel
Fleech, to supplicate in a flattering manner
Fleech'd, supplicated
Fleechin, supplicating
Fleesh, a fleece
Fleg, a kick, a random stroke
Flether, to decoy by fair words
Fletherin, flattering
Fley, to scare, to frighten
Flichter, to flutter, as young nestlings when their dam approaches
Flinders, shreds, broken pieces, splinters
Flinging-tree, a piece of timber hung by way of partition between two horses in a stable; a flail
Flisk, to fret at the yoke
Flisket, fretted
Flitter, to vibrate like the wings of small birds
Flittering, fluttering, vibrating
Flunkie, a servant in livery
Fodgel, squat and plump
Foord, a ford
Forbears, forefathers
Forbye, besides
Forfairn, distressed; worn out, jaded
Forfoughten, fatigued
Forgather, to meet, to encounter with
Forgie, to forgive
Forjesket, jaded with fatigue
Fother, fodder
Fou, full; drunk
Foughten, troubled, harassed
Fouth, plenty, enough, or more than enough
Fow, a bushel, &c.; also a pitch-fork
Frae, from; off
Frammit, strange, estranged from, at enmity with
Fraeth, froth
Frien', friend
Fu', full
Fud, the scut, or tail of the hare, cony, &c.
Fuff, to blow intermittently
Fuff't, did blow
Funnie, full of merriment
Fur, a furrow
Furm, a form, bench
Fyke, trifling cares; to piddle, to be in a fuss about trifles
Fyle, to soil, dirty
Fyl't, soiled, dirtied

GAB, the mouth; to speak boldly, or pertly
Gaberlunzie, an old man
Gadsman, a ploughboy, the boy that drives the horses in the plough
Gae, to go; gaed, went; gaen, or gane, gone; gaun, going
Gaet, or gate, way, manner; road
Gairs, triangular pieces of cloth sewed on the bottom of a gown, &c.
Gang, to go, to walk
Gar, to make, to force to
Gar't, forced to
Garten, a garter
Gash, wise, sagacious; talkative; to converse
Gashin, conversing

Gaucy, jolly, large
Gaud, a plough
Gear, riches; goods of any kind
Geck, to toss the head in wantonness or scorn
Ged, a pike
Gentles, great folks, gentry
Genty, elegantly formed, neat
Geordie, a guinea
Get, a child, a young one
Ghaist, a ghost
Gie, to give; gied, gave; gien, given
Giftie, diminutive of gift
Giglets, playful girls
Gillie, diminutive of gill
Gilpey, a half grown, half informed boy or girl, a romping lad, a hoiden
Gimmer, a ewe from one to two years old
Gin, if; against
Gipsy, a young girl
Girn, to grin, to twist the features in rage, agony, &c.
Girning, grinning
Gizz, a periwig
Glaiket, inattentive, foolish
Glaive, a sword
Gawky, half-witted, foolish, romping
Glaizie, glittering; smooth like glass
Glaum, to snatch greedily
Glaum'd, aimed, snatched
Gleck, sharp, ready
Gleg, sharp, ready
Gleib, glebe
Glen, a dale, a deep valley
Gley, a squint; to squint; a-gley, off at side, wrong
Glib-gabbet, smooth and ready in speech
Glint, to peep
Glinted, peeped
Glintin, peeping
Gloamin, the twilight
Glowr, to stare, to look; a stare, a look
Glowred, looked, stared
Glunsh, a frown, a sour look
Goavan, looking round with a strange, inquiring gaze; staring stupidly
Gowan, the flower of the wild daisy, hawkweed, &c.
Gowany, daisied, abounding with daisies
Gowd, gold
Gowff, the game of golf; to strike as the bat does the ball at golf
Gowff'd, struck
Gowk, a cuckoo: a term of contempt
Gowl, to howl
Grane, or grain, a groan; to groan
Grain'd and grunted, groaned and grunted
Graining, groaning
Graip, a pronged instrument for cleaning stables
Graith, accoutrements, furniture, dress, gear
Grannie, grandmother
Grape, to grope
Graipit, groped
Grat, wept, shed tears
Great, intimate, familiar
Gree, to agree; to bear the gree, to be decidedly victor
Gree't, agreed
Greet, to shed tears, to weep
Greetin, crying, weeping
Grippet, catched, seized
Groat, to get the whistle of one's groat, to play a losing game

Grousome, loathsomely grim
Grozet, a gooseberry
Grumph, a grunt; to grunt
Grumphie, a sow
Grun', ground
Grunstane, a grindstone
Gruntle, the phiz; a grunting noise
Grunzie, mouth
Grushie, thick; of thriving growth
Gude, the Supreme Being; good
Guid, good
Guid-morning, good morrow
Guid-e'en, good evening
Guidfather, guidmother, father-in-law and mother-in-law
Guidman and guidwife, the master and mistress of the house; young guidman, a man newly married
Guid-willie, liberal; cordial
Gully, or gullie, a large knife
Gumlie, muddy
Gusty, tasteful

HA', hall
Ha'-Bible, the great Bible that lies in the hall
Hae, to have
Haen, had, the participle
Haet, fient haet, a petty oath of negation; nothing
Haffet, the temple, the side of the head
Hafflins, nearly half, partly
Hag, a scar, or gulf in mosses and moors
Haggis, a kind of pudding boiled in the stomach of a cow or sheep
Hain, to spare, to save
Hain'd, spared
Hairst, harvest
Haith, a petty oath
Haivers, nonsense, speaking without thought
Hal', or hald, an abiding-place
Hale, whole, tight, healthy
Hallun, a particular partition-wall in a cottage, or more properly a seat of turf at the outside
Hallowmass, Hallow-eve, the 31st of October
Haly, holy
Hame, home
Hamely, homely, affable
Han', or haun', hand
Hap, an outer garment, mantle, plaid, &c., to wrap, to cover; to hop
Happer, a hopper
Happing, hopping
Hap step an' loup, hop skip and leap
Harkit, hearkened
Harn, very coarse linen
Hash, a fellow that neither knows how to dress nor act with propriety
Hastie, dry; chapped; barren
Hastit, hastened
Haud, to hold
Haughs, low lying, rich lands; valleys
Haurl, to drag, to peel
Haurlin, peeling
Haverel, a half-witted person; half-witted
Havins, good manners, decorum, good sense
Hawkie, a cow, properly one with a white face
Heapit, heaped
Healsome, healthful, wholesome
Hearse, hoarse
Hear't, hear it
Heather, heath

Hech! oh! strange!
Hecht, promised; to foretell something that is to be got or given; foretold; the thing foretold: offered
Heckle, a board in which are fixed a number of sharp pins, used in dressing hemp, flax, &c.
Heeze, to elevate, to raise
Helm, the rudder or helm
Herd, to tend flocks; one who tends flocks
Herrin, a herring
Herry, to plunder; most properly to plunder birds' nests
Herryment, plundering, devastation
Hersel, herself; also a herd of cattle of any sort
Het, hot
Heugh, a craig, a coalpit
Hilch, a hobble; to halt
Hilchin, halting
Himsel, himself
Hiney, honey
Hing, to hang
Hirple, to walk crazily, to creep
Hissel, so many cattle as one person can attend
Hitch, a loop, a knot
Hizzie, a hussy, a young girl
Hoddin, the motion of a sage countryman riding on a cart-horse; humble
Hog-score, a kind of distance-line, in curling, drawn across the rink
Hog-shouther, a kind of horse-play, by justling with the shoulder; to justle
Hool, outer skin or case, a nut-shell; a peascod
Hoolie, slowly, leisurely
Hoolie! take leisure! stop!
Hoord, a hoard; to hoard
Hoordit, hoarded
Horn, a spoon made of horn
Hornie, one of the many names of the Devil
Host, or hoast, to cough; a cough
Hostin, coughing
Hosts, coughs
Hotch'd, turned topsyturvy; blended, mixed
Houghmagandie, fornication
Houlet, an owl
Housie, diminutive of a house
Hove, to heave, to swell
Hoved, heaved, swelled
Howdie, a midwife
Howe, hollow; a hollow or dell
Howebackit, sunk in the back, spoken of a horse, &c.
Howff, a tippling house; a house of resort
Howk, to dig
Howkin, digging
Howkit, digged
Howlet, an owl
Hoy, to urge
Hoy't, urged
Hoyse, to pull upwards
Hoyte, to amble crazily
Hughoc, diminutive of Hugh
Hurcheon, a hedgehog
Hurdies, the loins; the crupper
Hushion, a cushion

I', in
Icker, an ear of corn
Ier-oe, a great grandchild
Ilk, or ilka, each, every
Ill-willie, ill-natured, malicious, niggardly

Ingine, genius, ingenuity
Ingle, fire; fire-place
Ise, I shall or will
Ither, other; one another

JAD, jade; also a familiar term among countryfolks for a giddy young girl
Jauk, to dally, to trifle
Jaukin, trifling, dallying
Jaup, a jerk of water; to jerk as agitated water
Jaw, coarse raillery; to pour out; to shut; to jerk as water
Jerkinet, a jerkin, or short gown
Jillet, a jilt, a giddy girl
Jimp, to jump; slender in the waist; handsome
Jimps, easy stays
Jink, to dodge, to turn a corner; a sudden turning; a corner
Jinker, that turns quickly; a gay sprightly girl; a wag
Jinkin, dodging
Jirk, a jerk
Jocteleg, a kind of knife
Jôuk, to stoop, to bow the head
Jow, to jow, a verb which includes both the swinging motion and pealing sound of a large bell
Jundie, to justle

KAE, a daw
Kail, colewort; a kind of broth
Kail-runt, the stem of colewort
Kain, fowls, &c., paid as rent by a farmer
Kebbuck, a cheese
Keckle, to giggle; to titter
Keek, a peep: to peep
Kelpies, a sort of mischievous spirits, said to haunt fords and ferries at night, especially in storms
Ken, to know; kend or kenn'd, knew
Kennin, a small matter
Kenspeckle, well known, easily known
Ket, matted, hairy; a fleece of wool
Kilt, to truss up the clothes
Kimmer, a young girl, a gossip
Kin, kindred; kin', kind, *adj.*
King's-hood, a certain part of the entrails of an ox, &c.
Kintra, country
Kintra cooser, country stallion
Kirn, the harvest-supper; a churn
Kirsen, to christen, or baptize
Kist, a chest; a shop counter
Kitchen, anything that eats with bread; to serve for soup, gravy, &c.
Kith, kindred
Kittle, to tickle; ticklish; lively, apt
Kittlin, a young cat
Kiuttle, to cuddle
Kiuttlin, cuddling
Knaggie, like knags, or points of rocks
Knap, to strike smartly; a smart blow
Knappin-hammer, a hammer for breaking stones
Knowe, a small round hillock
Knurl, a dwarf
Kye, cows
Kyle, a district in Ayrshire
Kyte, the belly
Kythe, to discover; to show one's self

LADDIE, diminutive of lad
Laggen, the angle between the side and bottom of a wooden dish
Laigh, low
Lairing, wading, and sinking in snow, mud, &c.

Laith, loath
Laithfu', bashful, sheepish
Lallans, the Scottish dialect of the English language
Lambie, diminutive of lamb
Lampit, a kind of shell-fish, a limpet
Lan', land; estate
Lane, lone; my lane, thy lane, &c., myself alone, &c.
Lanely, lonely
Lang, long; to think lang, to long, to weary
Lap, did leap
Lave, the rest, the remainder, the others
Laverock, the lark
Lawin, shot, reckoning, bill
Lawlan, lowland
Lea'e, to leave
Leal, loyal, true, faithful
Lea-rig, grassy ridge
Lear (pronounced lare), learning
Lee-lang, live-long
Leesome, pleasant
Leeze-me, a phrase of congratulatory endearment; I am happy in thee, or proud of thee
Leister, a three-pronged dart for striking fish
Leugh, did laugh
Leuk, a look; to look
Libbet, gelded
Lift, the sky
Lightly, sneeringly; to sneer at
Lilt, a ballad; a tune; to sing
Limmer, a kept mistress, a strumpet
Limp't, limped, hobbled
Link, to trip along
Linkin, tripping
Linn, a waterfall; a precipice
Lint, flax; Lint i' the bell, flax in flower
Lintwhite, a linnet
Loan, or loanin, the place of milking
Loof, the palm of the hand
Loot, did let
Looves, plural of loof
Loun, a fellow, a ragamuffin; a woman of easy virtue
Loup, jump, leap
Lowe, a flame
Lowin, flaming
Lowrie, abbreviation of Lawrence
Lowse, to loose
Lows'd, loosed
Lug, the ear; a handle
Lugget, having a handle
Luggie, a small wooden dish with a handle
Lum, the chimney
Lunch, a large piece of cheese, flesh, &c.
Lunt, a column of smoke; to smoke
Luntin, smoking
Lyart, of a mixed colour, grey

MAE, more
Mair, more
Maist, most, almost
Maistly, mostly
Mak, to make
Makin, making
Mailen, a farm
Mallie, Molly
Mang, among
Manse, the parsonage-house, where the minister lives
Manteele, a mantle
Mark, marks. (This and several other nouns which in English require an *s* to form the plural, are in Scotch,

like the words sheep, deer, the same in both numbers)
Marled, variegated; spotted
Mar's year, the year 1715
Mashlum, meslin, mixed corn
Mask, to mash, as malt, &c.
Maskin-pat, a tea-pot
Maud, maad, a plaid worn by shepherds, &c.
Maukin, a hare
Maun, must
Mavis, the thrush
Maw, to mow
Mawin, mowing
Meere, a mare
Meikle, meickle, much
Melancholious, mournful
Melder, corn, or grain of any kind, sent to the mill to be ground
Mell, to meddle. Also a mallet for pounding barley in a stone trough
Melvie, to soil with meal
Men', to mend
Mense, good manners, decorum
Menseless, ill-bred, rude, impudent
Messin, a small dog
Midden, a dunghill
Midden-hole, a gutter at the bottom of a dunghill
Mim, prim, affectedly meek
Min', mind; resemblance
Mind't, mind it; resolved, intending
Minnie, mother, dam
Mirk, mirkest, dark, darkest
Misca', to abuse, to call names
Misca'd, abused
Mislear'd, mischievous, unmannerly
Misteuk, mistook
Mither, a mother
Mixtie-maxtie, confusedly mixed
Moistify, to moisten
Mony, or monie, many
Mools, dust, earth, the earth of the grave; to rake i' the mools, to lay in the dust
Moop, to nibble as a sheep
Moorlan', of or belonging to moors
Morn, the next day, to-morrow
Mou, the mouth
Moudiwort, a mole
Mousie, diminutive of mouse
Muckle, or mickle, great, big, much
Musie, diminutive of muse
Muslin-kail, broth composed simply of water, shelled barley, and greens
Mutchkin, an English pint
Mysel, myself

NA, no, not, nor
Nae, no, not any
Naething, or naithing, nothing
Naig, a horse
Nane, none
Nappy, ale; to be tipsy
Negleckit, neglected
Neuk, a nook
Niest, next
Nieve, the fist
Nievefu', handful
Niffer, an exchange; to exchange, to barter
Niger, a negro
Nine-tailed-cat, a hangman's whip
Nit, a nut
Norland, of or belonging to the north
Notic't, noticed
Nowte, black cattle

O', of
Ochils, name of mountains

O haite, O faith! an oath
Ony, or onie, any
Or, is often used for ere, before
Ora, or orra, supernumerary, that can be spared
O't, of it
Ourie, shivering; drooping
Oursel, or oursels, ourselves
Outlers, cattle not housed
Owre, over; too
Owre-hip, a way of fetching a blow with the hammer over the arm

PACK, intimate, familiar; twelve stone of wool
Painch, paunch
Paitrick, a partridge
Pang, to cram
Parle, speech
Parritch, oatmeal pudding, a well-known Scotch dish
Pat, did put; a pot
Pattle, or pettle, a plough-staff
Paughty, proud, haughty
Pauky, or pawkie, cunning, sly
Pay't, paid; beat
Pech, to fetch the breath short, as in an asthma
Pechan, the crop, the stomach
Peelin, peeling, the rind of fruit
Pet, a domesticated sheep, &c.
Pettle, to cherish; a plough-staff
Philabegs, short petticoats worn by the Highlandmen
Phraise, fair speeches, flattery; to flatter
Phraisin, flattery
Pibroch, Highland war music adapted to the bagpipe
Pickle, a small quantity
Pine, pain, uneasiness
Pit, to put
Placad, public proclamation
Plack, an old Scotch coin, the third part of a Scotch penny, twelve of which make an English penny.
Plackless, penniless, without money
Platie, diminutive of plate
Plew, or pleugh, a plough
Pliskie, a trick
Poind, to seize cattle or goods for rent, as the laws of Scotland allow
Poortith, poverty
Pou, to pull
Pouk, to pluck
Poussie, a hare, or cat
Pout, a poult, a chick
Pou't, did pull
Pow, the head, the skull
Pownie, a little horse
Powther, or pouther, powder
Powthery, like powder
Preen, a pin
Prent, to print; print
Prie, to taste
Prie'd, tasted
Prief, proof
Prig, to cheapen; to dispute
Priggin, cheapening
Primsie, demure, precise
Propone, to lay down, to propose
Provoses, provosts
Puddock-stool, a mushroom, fungus
Pund, pound; pounds
Pyle, a pyle o' caff, a single grain of chaff

QUAT, to quit
Quak, to quake
Quey, a cow from one to two years old

RAGWEED, the herb ragwort
Raible, to rattle nonsense
Rair, to roar
Raize, to madden, to inflame
Ram-feezl'd, fatigued; overspread
Ram-stam, thoughtless, forward
Raploch, properly a coarse cloth; but used as an adnoun for coarse
Rarely, excellently, very well
Rash, a rush; rash-buss, a bush of rushes
Ratton, a rat
Raucle, rash; stout; fearless
Raught, reached
Raw, a row
Rax, to stretch
Ream, cream; to cream
Reaming, brimful, frothing
Reave, rove
Reck, to heed
Rede, counsel; to counsel
Red-wat-shod, walking in blood over the shoe-tops
Red-wud, stark mad
Ree, half drunk, fuddled
Reek, smoke
Reekin, smoking
Reekit, smoked; smoky
Remead, remedy
Requite, requited
Rest, to stand restive
Restit, stood restive; stunted; withered
Restricked, restricted
Rew, to repent, to compassionate
Rief, reef, plenty
Rief randies, sturdy beggars
Rig, a ridge
Rigwiddie, rigwoodie, the rope or chain that crosses the saddle of a horse to support the spokes of a cart; spare, withered, sapless
Rin, to run, to melt
Rinnin, running
Rink, the course of the stones, a term in curling on ice
Rip, a handful of unthreshed corn
Riskit, made a noise like the tearing of roots
Rockin, spinning on the rock, or distaff
Rood, stands likewise for the plural roods
Roon, a shred, a border or selvage
Roose, to praise, to commend
Roosty, rusty
Roun', round, in the circle of neighbourhood
Roupet, hoarse, as with a cold
Routhie, plentiful
Row, to roll, to wrap
Row't, rolled, wrapped
Rowte, to low, to bellow
Rowth, or routh, plenty
Rowtin, lowing
Rozet, rosin
Rung, a cudgel
Runkled, wrinkled
Runt, the stem of colewort or cabbage
Ruth, sorrow
Ryke, to reach

SAE, so
Saft, soft
Sair, to serve; a sore
Sairly, or sairlie, sorely
Sair't, served
Sark, a shirt; a shift
Sarkit, provided in shirts
Saugh, the willow
Saul, soul

Saumont, salmon
Saunt, a saint
Saut, salt, *adj.* salt.
Saw, to sow
Sawin, sowing
Sax, six
Scaith, to damage, to injure; injury
Scar, a cliff
Scaud, to scald
Scauld, to scold
Scaur, apt to be scared
Scawl, a scold; a termagant
Scon, a cake of bread
Sconner, a loathing; to loathe
Scraich, to scream as a hen, partridge, &c.
Screed, to tear; a rent
Scrieve, to glide swiftly along
Scrievin, gleesomely; swiftly
Scrimp, to scant
Scrimpet, did scant; scanty
See'd, did see
Seizin, seizing
Sel, self; a body's sel, one's self alone
Sell't, did sell
Sen', to send
Sen't, I, &c., sent, or did send it; send it
Servan', servant
Settlin', settling; to get a settlin', to be frighted into quietness
Sets, sets off, goes away
Shachled, distorted; shapeless
Shaird, a shred, a shard
Shangan, a stick cleft at one end to put in the tail of a dog, &c., by way of mischief, or to frighten him away
Shaver, a humorous wag; a barber
Shaw, to show; a small wood in a hollow
Sheep-shank; to think one's self nae sheep-shank, to be conceited
Sherra-muir, Sheriff-moor, the battle fought in the rebellion, A.D. 1715
Sheugh, a ditch, a trench, a sluice
Shiel, a shed
Shill, shrill
Shog, a shock; a push off at one side
Shool, shovel
Shoon, shoes
Shore, to offer, to threaten
Shor'd, offered
Shouther, the shoulder
Shure, did shear, shore
Sic, such
Sicker, sure, steady
Sidelins, sidelong, slanting
Siller, silver; money
Simmer, summer
Sin, a son
Sin', since
Skaith. *See* Scaith
Skellum, a worthless fellow
Skelp, to strike, to slap; to walk with a smart tripping step; a smart stroke
Skelpie-limmer, a reproachful term in female scolding
Skelpin, stepping, walking
Skiegh, or skeigh, proud, nice, high-mettled
Skinklin, a small portion
Skirl, to shriek, to cry shrilly
Skirling, shrieking, crying
Skirl't, shrieked
Sklent, slant; to run aslant, to deviate from truth
Sklented, ran, or hit, in an oblique direction
Skouth, freedom to converse without restraint; range, scope

Skriegh, a scream; to scream
Skyrin, shining; making a great show
Skyte, force, very forcible motion
Slae, a sloe
Slade, did slide
Slap, a gate; a breach in a fence
Slaver, saliva; to emit saliva
Slaw, slow
Slee, sly; sleest, sliest
Sleekit, sleek; sly
Sliddery, slippery
Slype, to fall over, as a wet furrow from the plough
Slypet, fell
Sma', small
Smeddum, dust, powder; mettle, sense
Smiddy, a smithy
Smoor, to smother
Smoor'd, smothered
Smoutie, smutty, obscene, ugly
Smytrie, a numerous collection of small individuals
Snapper, to stumble; a stumble
Snash, abuse, Billingsgate
Snaw, snow; to snow
Snaw-broo, melted snow
Snawie, snowy
Sneck, snick, the latch of a door
Sned, to lop, to cut off
Sneeshin, snuff
Sneeshin-mill, a snuff-box
Snell, bitter, biting
Snick-drawing, trick-contriving, crafty
Snirtle, to laugh restrainedly
Snood, a ribbon for binding the hair
Snool, one whose spirit is broken with oppressive slavery; to submit tamely, to sneak
Snoove, to go smoothly and constantly; to sneak
Snowk, to scent or snuff, as a dog, &c.
Snowkit, scented, snuffed
Sonsie, having sweet, engaging looks; lucky, jolly
Soom, to swim
Sooth, truth, a pretty oath
Sough, a heavy sigh, a sound dying on the ear
Souplè, flexible; swift
Souter, a shoemaker
Sowens, a dish made of oatmeal: the seeds of oatmeal soured, &c., flummery
Sowp, a spoonful, a small quantity of anything liquid
Sowth, to try over a tune with a low whistle
Sowther, solder; to solder, to cement
Spae, to prophesy, to divine
Spaul, a limb
Spairge, to dash, to soil, as with mire
Spaviet, having the spavin
Spean, spane, to wean
Speat, or spate, a sweeping torrent after rain or thaw
Speel, to climb
Spence, the country parlour
Spier, to ask, to inquire
Spier't, inquired
Splatter, a splutter, to splutter
Spleughan, a tobacco-pouch
Splore, a frolic; a noise, riot
Sprackle, sprachle, to clamber
Sprattle, to scramble
Spreckled, spotted, speckled
Spring, a quick air in music; a Scottish reel
Sprit, a tough-rooted plant, something like rushes
Sprittie, full of spirits

Spunk, fire, mettle; wit
Spunkie, mettlesome, fiery; will-o'-wisp, or ignis fatuus
Spurtle, a stick, used in making oatmeal pudding or porridge
Squad, a crew, a party
Squatter, to flutter in water, as a wild duck
Squattle, to sprawl
Stacher, to stagger
Stack, a rick of corn, hay, &c.
Staggie, the diminutive of stag
Stalwart, strong, stout
Stan, to stand; stan't, did stand
Stane, a stone
Stang, an acute pain; a twinge; to sting
Stank, did stink; a pool of standing water
Stap, stop
Stark, stout
Startle, to run as cattle stung by the gad-fly
Staumrel, a blockhead; half-witted
Staw, did steal; to surfeit
Stech, to cram the belly
Stechin, cramming
Steek, to shut; a stitch
Steer, to molest; to stir
Steeve, firm, compacted
Stell, a still
Sten, to rear as a horse
Sten't, reared
Stents, tribute; dues of any kind
Stey, steep; steyest, steepest
Stibble, stubble; stibble-rig, the reaper in harvest who takes the lead
Stick an' stow, totally, altogether
Stile, a crutch; to halt, to limp
Stimpart, the eighth part of a Winchester bushel
Stirk, a cow or bullock a year old
Stock, a plant or root of colewort, cabbage, &c.
Stockin, a stocking: throwing the stockin; when the bride and bridegroom are put into bed, and the candle out, the former throws a stocking at random among the company, and the person whom it strikes is the next that will be married
Stoiter, to stagger, to stammer
Stooked, made up in shocks as corn
Stoor, sounding hollow, strong, and hoarse
Stot, an ox
Stoup, or stowp, a kind of jug or dish with a handle
Stoure, dust, more particularly dust in motion
Stowlins, by stealth
Stown, stolen
Stoyte, to stumble
Strack, did strike
Strae, straw; to die a fair strae death, to die in bed
Straik, did strike
Straikit, stroked
Strappin, tall and handsome
Straught, straight; to straighten
Streek, stretched, tight; to stretch
Striddle, to straddle
Stroan, to spout, to piss
Studdie, an anvil
Stumpie, diminutive of stump
Strunt, spirituous liquor of any kind; to walk sturdily; huff, sullenness
Stuff, corn or pulse of any kind
Sturt, trouble; to molest
Sturtin, frighted
Sucker, sugar

Sud, should
Sugh, the continued rushing noise of wind or water
Southron, southern; an old name for the English nation
Swaird, sward
Swall'd, swelled
Swank, stately, jolly
Swankie, or swanker, a tight strapping young fellow or girl
Swap, an exchange; to barter
Swarf, to swoon; a swoon
Swat, did sweat
Swatch, a sample
Swats, drink; good ale
Sweaten, sweating
Sweer, lazy, averse; dead-sweer, extremely averse
Swoor, swore, did swear
Swinge, to beat; to whip
Swirl, a curve; an eddying blast, or pool; a knot in wood
Swirlie, knaggie, full of knots
Swith, get away
Swither, to hesitate in choice; an irresolute wavering in choice
Syne, since, ago; then

TACKETS, a kind of nails for driving into the heels of shoes
Tae, a toe; three-tae'd, having three prongs
Tairge, a target
Tak, to take; takin, taking
Tamtallan, the name of a mountain
Tangle, a sea-weed
Tap, the top
Tapetless, heedless, foolish
Tarrow, to murmur at one's allowance
Tarrow't, murmured
Tarry-breeks, a sailor
Tauld, or tald, told
Taupie, a foolish, thoughtless young person
Tauted, or tautie, matted together; spoken of hair or wool
Tawie, that allows itself quietly to be handled; spoken of a horse, cow, &c.
Teat, a small quantity
Tedding, spreading after the mower
Teen, to provoke; provocation
Ten-hours' bite, a slight feed to horses while in the yoke, in the forenoon
Tent, a field-pulpit; heed, caution; to take heed; to tend or herd cattle
Tentie, heedful, cautious
Tentless, heedless
Teugh, tough
Thack, thatch; thack an' rape, clothing necessaries
Thae, these
Thairms, small guts; fiddle-strings
Thankit, thanked
Theekit, thatched
Thegither, together
Themsel, themselves
Thick, intimate, familiar
Thieveless, cold, dry, spited: spoken of a person's demeanour
Thir, these
Thirl, thrill
Thirled, thrilled, vibrated
Thole, to suffer, to endure
Thowe, a thaw; to thaw
Thowless, slack, lazy
Thrang, throng, a crowd
Thrapple, throat, windpipe
Thrave, twenty-four sheaves or two shocks of corn; a considerable number

Thraw, to sprain, to twist; to contradict
Thrawin, twisting, &c.
Thrawn, sprained, twisted; contradicted
Threap, to maintain by dint of assertion
Threshin, thrashing
Threteen, thirteen
Thristle, thistle
Through, to go on with; to make out
Throuther, pell-mell, confusedly
Thud, to make a loud intermittent noise
Thumpit, thumped
Thysel, thyself
Till't, to it
Timmer, timber
Tine, to lose; tint, lost
Tinkler, a tinker
Tint the gate, lost the way
Tip, a ram
Tippence, twopence
Tirl, to make a slight noise; to uncover
Tirlin, uncovering
Tither, the other
Tittle, to whisper
Tittlin, whispering
Tocher, marriage portion
Tod, a fox
Toddle, to totter, like the walk of a child
Toddlin, tottering
Toom, empty; to empty
Toop, a ram
Toun, a hamlet; a farm-house
Tout, the blast of a horn or trumpet; to blow a horn, &c.
Tow, a rope
Towmond, a twelvemonth
Towzie, rough, shaggy
Toy, a very old fashion of female head-dress
Toyte, to totter like old age
Transmugrified, transmigrated, metamorphosed
Trashtrie, trash
Trews, trowsers
Trickie, full of tricks
Trig, spruce, neat
Trimly, excellently
Trow, to believe
Trowth, truth, a petty oath
Tryste, an appointment; a fair
Trysted, appointed; to tryste, to make an appointment
Try't, tried
Tug, raw hide, of which in old times plough-traces were frequently made
Tulzie, a quarrel; to quarrel, to fight
Twa, two
Twa-three, a few
'Twad, it would
Twal, twelve; twal-pennie worth, a small quantity, a pennyworth. N.B. One penny English is 12d. Scotch.
Twin, to part
Tyke, a dog

UNCO, strange, uncouth; very, very great, prodigious
Uncos, news
Unkenn'd, unknown
Unsicker, unsure, unsteady
Unskaith'd, undamaged, unhurt
Unweeting, unwittingly, unknowingly
Upo', upon
Urchin, a hedgehog

VAP'RIN, vapouring

Vera, very
Virl, a ring round a column, &c.
Vittle, corn of all kinds, food

WA', wall; wa's, walls
Wabster, a weaver
Wad, would; to bet; a bet, a pledge
Wadna, would not
Wae, wo, sorrowful
Waefu', woful, sorrowful, wailing
Waesucks! or waes me! alas! O the pity!
Waft, the cross thread that goes from the shuttle through the web; woof
Wair, to lay out, to expend
Wale, choice; to choose
Waled, chose, chosen
Walie, ample, large, jolly; also an interjection of distress
Wame, the belly
Wamefu', a bellyful
Wanchancie, unlucky
Wanrestfu', restless
Wark, work
Wark-lume, a tool to work with
Warl, or warld, world
Warlock, a wizard
Warly, worldly, eager on amassing wealth
Warran, a warrant; to warrant
Warst, worst
Warstl'd or warsl'd, wrestled
Wastrie, prodigality
Wat, wet; I wat, I wot, I know
Water-brose, brose made of meal and water simply, without the addition of milk, butter, &c.
Wattle, a twig, a wand
Wauble, to swing, to reel
Waught, a draught
Waukit, thickened as fullers do cloth
Waukrife, not apt to sleep
Waur, worse; to worst
Waur't, worsted
Wean, or weanie, a child
Wearie, or weary; many a weary body, many a different person
Weason, weasand
Weaving the stocking. *See* Stockin, p. 276
Wee, little; Wee things, little ones; Wee bit, a small matter
Weel, well; Weelfare, welfare
Weet, rain, wetness
Weird, fate
We'se, we shall
Wha, who
Whaizle, to wheeze
Whalpit, whelped
Whang, a leathern string; a piece of cheese, bread, &c.; to give the strappado
Whare, where; Whare'er, wherever
Whase, whose
Whatreck, nevertheless
Wheep, to fly nimbly, jerk; penny-wheep, small beer
Whid, the motion of a hare running, but not frighted; a lie
Whiddin, running as a hare or cony
Whigmeleeries, whims, fancies
Whingin, crying, complaining, fretting
Whirligigums, useless ornaments, trifling appendages
Whisht, silence; to hold one's whisht, to be silent
Whisk, to sweep, to lash
Whiskit, lashed
Whissle, a whistle; to whistle
Whitter, a hearty draught of liquor

Whun-stane, a whin-stone
Whyles, whiles, sometimes
Wi', with
Wicht, wight, powerful, strong; inventive; of a superior genius
Wick, to strike a stone in an oblique direction; a term in curling
Wicker, willow (the smaller sort)
Wiel, a small whirlpool
Wifie, a diminutive or endearing term for wife
Wilyart, bashful and reserved; avoiding society or appearing awkward in it; wild, strange, timid
Wimple, to meander
Wimpl't, meandered
Wimplin, waving, meandering
Win, to win, to winnow
Win't, winded as a bottom of yarn
Win', wind; Win's, winds
Winna, will not
Winnock, a window
Winsome, hearty, vaunted, gay
Wintle, a staggering motion; to stagger, to reel
Winze, an oath
Wiss, to wish
Withoutten, without
Wizen'd, hide-bound, dried, shrunk
Wonner, a wonder: a contemptuous appellation
Wons, dwells
Woo', wool
Woo, to court, to make love to
Woodie, a rope, more properly one made of withes or willows
Wooer bab, the garter knotted below the knee with a couple of loops
Wordy, worthy
Worset, worsted
Wow, an exclamation of pleasure or wonder
Wrack, to tease, to vex
Wraith, a spirit or ghost; an apparition exactly like a living person, whose appearance is said to forebode the person's approaching death
Wrang, wrong; to wrong
Wreeth, a drifted heap of snow
Wud, mad, distracted
Wumble, wimble
Wyle, to beguile
Wyliecoat, a flannel vest
Wyte, blame; to blame

YAD, an old mare; a worn-out horse
Ye; this pronoun is frequently used for thou
Year is used both for singular and plural, years
Yearlings, born in the same year, coevals
Yearn, earn, an eagle, an ospray
Yearns, longs much
Yell, barren, that gives no milk
Yerk, to lash, to jerk
Yerkit, jerked, lashed
Yestreen, yesternight
Yett, a gate, such as is usually at the entrance into a farm-yard or field
Yill, ale
Yird, earth
Yokin, yoking; a bout
Yont, beyond
Yoursel, yourself
Yowe, an ewe
Yowie, diminutive of yowe
Yule, Christmas

INDEX

TO THE POEMS, SONGS, &c.

C

D

J

K

L

M

INDEX

TO THE FIRST LINES.

F

G

H

O

P

R

S

T

www.ingramcontent.com/pod-product-compliance
Lightning Source LLC
LaVergne TN
LVHW020128110826
845151LV00001B/311

* 9 7 8 1 4 2 5 5 4 0 2 5 8 *